MARRIAGE, DEATH, AND ESTATE NOTICES FROM GEORGETOWN, S.C. NEWSPAPERS 1791–1861

by
Brent H. Holcomb, C.A.L.S.

Copyright © 1979 by:

The Rev. Silas Emmett Lucas, Jr.

All rights reserved. No part of this publication may be reproduced, stored in a retrieval system or transmitted in any form or by any means without the prior written permission of the publisher.

Please Direct All Correspondence and Book Orders to:

Southern Historical Press, Inc.
PO Box 1267
375 West Broad Street
Greenville, SC 29602-1267
or
southernhistoricalpress@gmail.com

----

southernhistoricalpress.com

ISBN #0-89308-150-7

INTRODUCTION

It goes without saying that any newspapers of the period concerned here are valuable. However, those of Georgetown are particularly so because of the fire which destroyed the records of Georgetown District in 1865. (These records were burned in Cheraw, South Carolina, where they had been sent for safe keeping.) Georgetown Judicial District was among the last to be broken up into counties. Marion County was formed in 1798; Horry District, in 1801; Williamsburg District in 1804 or 1806. Until these counties or districts were formed, the probates and deeds were recorded in the district seat in Georgetown. (The later Georgetown County was originally called Winyaw County.) Even after these districts were formed, their legal notices were still published in the Georgetown newspapers, their being the closest ones. For the reasons just stated marriage, death and estate noitces are included here. I have not padded this volume with information which might be of minimal genealogical value: notices of sheriff's sales, lists of letters at the post office, etc.

These newspapers are located in three main repositories: the South Caroliniana Library, the Charleston Library Society, and the Duke University Library. Most of these issues can be seen, either original or microfilm, at the South Caroliniana Library. Those not available there are so noted. My thanks to these institutions for their cooperation. My special thanks to Mr. Eldred Spell of Smoaks, S. C., and Mr. William A. Skipper, of Columbia, S. C., who assisted me in copying notices from issues located in the Charleston Library Society.

                                        Brent H. Holcomb, C. A. L. S.
                                        Columbia, South Carolina
                                        April 26, 1978

THE SOUTH CAROLINA INDEPENDENT GAZETTE AND GEORGETOWN CHRONICLE

Issue of May 21, 1791 (Volume 1, #8)

All persons having demands against the estate of Doctor Bedford Williams, deceased, are requested to render them early as possible to the subscribers.... James Shackleford
Savage Smith

By permission of Hugh Horry, Esq., Ordinary of Georgetown district....The household furniture horse and Mare and four head of cattle which are to be sold for the purpose of making a division of the estate agreeable to the last will and testament of Mary Guess....   John Rhodes, Executor
May 14.

By permission of the Ordinary of Georgetown district...to be sold at public auction, part of the personal estate of John Martin, deceased.   Abraham Cohen
                                Isaac Danford, Admors.

Issue of June 4, 1791

Married, Mr. Adam Marshall, of Greenvel, merchant to Miss Polly Gregg, daughter of James Gregg, Esq.
Died at Philadelphia, Nicholas Eveleigh, Esq. comptroller of the treasury of the United States. and Francis Hopkinson, Esq. district judge of the U. S. for Pennsylvania.
at Richmond, John Dixon, Esq., many years printer for the commonwealth of Virginia.

All persons having demands against Thomas Dias, deceased, are desired to render them as the law directs.... John Cogdell,
May 28.   Executor.

All persons having any demands against the estate of Col. William Davis, late of Pedee, deceased, are desired to send in a state of their demands....   Henry Davis, Executor.
May 28.

Issue of June 11, 1791

The creditors of the late Alex. Keith, Esq., deceased are requested to deliver a state of their demands...to the subscribers or at Messrs. A. & F. Motte in Charleston.
                            John Keith
                            Matthew Irvine
                Administrators with the will annexed.

By permission of Hugh Horry, Esq., ordinary of Georgetown district, will be sold at the plantation of Mr. Peter June, Santee, on 2d July--several Negroes belonging to the estate of Sarah Fendel, William June and Sarah June.-.for the purpose of satisfying the remaining debts due against the estate of Peter June, deceased.
June 11   Joseph Johnson, Adm'or.

By permission of the Ordinary of Georgetown district, will be sold at the Point, Georgeotwn, all the household furniture of William Allston senior deceased....   Benjamin Allston, Jun.
June 11   Administrator.

THE SOUTH CAROLINA INDEPENDENT GAZETTE AND GEORGETOWN CHRONICLE

Issue of June 25, 1791

Died in Charleston on the 19th instant, Master Benjamin Bonneau Harvey, eldest son of Mr. Jacob Wm. Harvey of this place. last Tuesday, Thomas Herbert Harvey, his youngest son.

On Wednesday in this town, Master Charles Ford, youngest son of Mr. Stephen Ford, junior, deceased, late of Black River.

Issue of November 5, 1791

Died on Thursday, the 25th of September last, in Williamsburgh township, Capt. James Witherspoon, in the 33d year of his age.

Issue of September 8, 1792

All persons indebted to the estate of Alexander M'Crea senior, Alexander M'Crea junior, or Mrs. Margaret M'Crea, deceased are desired to make immediate payment....   Joseph Scott
   Samuel Paxton(?)
   Administrators.

Joseph Raven Matthews, late of Georgetown, shopkeeper, having assigned his estate to the subscribers in trust for the benefit of his creditors....   John Shackleford
   Solomon Cohen.

Issue of September 15, 1792

Charleston, Sept. 4

Died on Sunday morning, the 2d instant, at two o'clock, Mordecai Gist, brig. general in the late army of the United States. Yesterday his remains were deposited in the St. Michael's churchyard...attached to the Society of the Cincinnati.

And on Saturday 9th inst., Mr. Isaac B. Dwight, formerly of Georgetown. And yesterday in the 65th year of her age, Mrs. Ann Timothy proprietor of the State Gazette.

Died on Tuesday last, Miss Ann Hardwick, the only daughter of Mr. John Hardwick of this place.

And yesterday morning, Mr. Michael Broaderick, whose death was occasioned by an accident that befel (sic) him the day before.

THE GEORGETOWN CHRONICLE AND SOUTH CAROLINA WEEKLY ADVERTISER

Issue of March 22, 1796

By permission of Cornelius Dupre, Esq., Ordinary, will be sold, three Negroes belonging to the estate of Josiah Cockfield, deceased.
March 15.   Ann Cockfield, Adm'x.
   William Cockfield, Admr.

To be sold--five negroes appraised as the estate of Edward Croft, deceased, being the remaining part that was left to T. Boone, dec'd.
March 15.   Thos Boone, Adm'r with the will annexed.

Issue of January 17, 1797

Agreeable to the last will and testament of Elizabeth Weaver deceased, several negroes will be sold....
January 5.   J. Shackelford) Ex'ors.
   R. Brownfield)

Several negroes advertiser for sale as the property of Francis Huger of Sampit. I do forbid the sale of sd. Negroes, they being the property of Ann Huger, my daughter.   Mary Huger
Sampit, 17th Jan 1797.

By permission of C. DuPre, Esq., Ordinary of Georgetown district, will be sold all the property belonging to the late John Norum....   John Mason
   James Zuil, Administrators.

All persons to whom the estate of Paul Villepontoux deceased is indebted, are requested to render in their demands.
Sept. 13.   Paul Michau jun.) Ex'ors.
   Benj. Allston jun.)

Notice is hereby Given that Mr. Andrew Smith, butcher, late of Georgetown, having died intestate, his creditors are called upon to administer on his effects.
December 22.   Margaret Smith.

Issue of September 23, 1797

A negro to be sold, the property of the estate of W. Thompson, deceased, late of Black-Mingo.
Sept. 5, 1797.   Thos Potts, Adm'r.

Married by the Revd. Mr. Matthews at Newton, on Thursday evening last, Captain John Harvey of this town to the amiable and accomplished Miss Charlotte Villepontoux of the former place.

All persons who have demands against the estate of Major John Waties, deceased, are requested to render them.
   Eras. Rothmahler,
   Attorney to the Admr'x.

Issue of November 1, 1797

   Philadelphia, Oct. 11[?]
Died at Germantown, of a lingering disorder, John Wilcox.
Died, Mr. David Thomas, high constable of Southwark.

THE GEORGETOWN CHRONICLE AND SOUTH CAROLINA WEEKLY ADVERTISER

All persons who have demands against the estate of Col. John Baxter, deceased, are requested to render them to Moses Myers, Esqr....
June 24.
John M'Ree and
Jane M'Ree, late
Jane Baxter, Extx.

All persons who have any demands against the estate of William Williams deceased, are requested to render in their accounts... to William Williams Jr.

GEORGETOWN GAZETTE

(The issues from 1798-1800 are found in the Charleston Library Society, Charleston, S. C. Their file begins with May 15, 1798 (Vol. I, #2). Although the issue of May 8, 1798 (Vol. I, #1) is extant and can be seen on microfilm at the South Caroliniana Library, it contains no notices of interest for this volume.)

Issue of May 29, 1798

Died on Thursday evening last, after a lingering illness, Miss Elenor Ramsay.

Issue of June 12, 1798

Died on Thursday last, Mr. John Roberts.
Died on the 20th of March, at Leith, in Scotland, James Cassels, esq. of Flask, in the 62d year of his age. He has been for many years an inhabitant of this State.

Issue of June 26, 1798

Departed this life on the 18th instant, in the 27th year of his age, Dr. Samuel Heron...discourse by Rev. Mr. Spierin. (eulogy).

Issue of July 3, 1798

All persons indebted to the estate of Capt. Charles Weston, late of Waccamaw deceased, are requested to make immediate payment...   Elizabeth Ward, admx.
Waccamaw, May 30.   or B. Allston, Admr.

Issue of July 24, 1798

All those having demands against the estate of Thomas Leigh, deceased, are requested to lodge statement of the same in the hands of Robert Heriot esq....   Sarah Snipes, adm'x.
July 24   William Snipes, adm'r.

Issue of July 31, 1798

All persons indebted to the estate of Conrad Shum, late of Georgetown, baker, deceased are desired to make payment.
July 31.   Ann Shum, administratrix.

Issue of August 21, 1798

Those persons to whom the estate of Capt. John Thompson, mariner, deceased, is in anywise indebted....
August 14   Ann Thompson, adm'x.

By permission of Cornelius Du Pre, Esq., Ordinary, will be sold...all the personal property of Dr. Samuel Heron, deceased....
August 21   Robert Brownfield, admr.

By permission of Cornelius Du Pre, Esq., Ordinary for Georgetown District, will be sold...the personal property of Alexander Stewart, late of Holly-Hill, deceased...by order of P. Donnolly, administrator.   Thomas Hutchinson, V. M.
August 21.

GEORGETOWN GAZETTE

Issue of September 18, 1798

To be sold on Waccamaw, at the Chaple (sic)...the last remains of the personal property of Capt. John Morrall, deceased...
Sept. 11   Peter Nicholson, executor.

Issue of September 18, 1798

Died on Thursday morning last, Mrs. Jane Anderson, aged 55 years. A very respectable inhabitant to this town.

Issue of September 25, 1798

Departed this life on Sunday morning last, Mrs. Jane Marshall, milliner...interred in the Protestant episcopal church...funeral sermon by Rev. Mr. Munds.
Died, yesterday morning, Mrs. Wright.

Issue of November 6, 1798

Married on the 25th ult., by the Rev. Dr. Malcomson, Mr. Joseph White, near Black-Mingo, to the amiable Miss Judith Grier, of Peedee, both of Winyaw county.

Issue of November 16, 1798

Last Tuesday morning a coroner's inquest was held on the body of William Walker, who had the preceding night shot himself....
Departed this life on Sunday night last, in the 32d year of her age, Mrs. Mary Ann Branford(?) (eulogy).

Issue of November 20, 1798

Died, yesterday morning, Mrs. Sarah Hautreux, wife of Mr. Peter Hautreux...(eulogy).
Died on Sunday evening, the 18th inst., Mr. Travis Chambers, house carpenter.

Issue of November 23, 1798

Married on Tuesday evening last, by Rev. Mr. Botsford, James Green, Esq., to Mrs. Elizabeth Henning.

Issue of November 30, 1798

By permission of Cornelius DuPre, Esq., Ordinary...will be sold at the New Mills on the Big Swamp, about four miles from Witherspoon's Ferry, on Lynch's Creek, all the personal Estate of Ralph Smith deceased....
Nov. 30.   John Smith, Andrew Smith, John
                              Smith, Administrators.

Issue of December 4, 1798

Will be sold at the Blacksmith's shop on Broad-Street, all the stock of Iron, etc., belonging to the estate of David Patterson, deceased.
Nov. 30.   Abraham Cohen, adm'r.

GEORGETOWN GAZETTE

Issue of December 7, 1798

Died, on the 19th of November, in the 29th year of his age, Alexander Cunningham, Esq., lieut. of the Kingstree 3d Company of the Upper Battalion of the 26th Regt. of this State...left a widow and numerous circle of relations....

Issue of December 11, 1798

Died on Tuesday, the 4th instant, Mrs. Mary Lessesne, aged 64 years and 2 months. On Wednesday, the 6th her remains were carried to the Episcopal Church.

Issue of December 14, 1798

All persons having legal demands against Mr. Robert Kirkpatrick, late of All Saints Parish, deceased....
December 14.   Thomas Chapman, Executor.

Issue of December 25, 1798

Died at Columbia, Capt. Boykin, and Flemming Bates, esq., members of the legislature.

Issue of January 9, 1799

All persons having demands against the estate of Henry Tait, Esq., late of this town....
January 1   James Tait, Adm'r.
                                    Hannah Tait, Adm'rx.

By permission of Cornelius DuPre, Ordinary, will be sold at the plantation of Benjamin Screven, Esq., part of the personal property of Jacob Dunnam deceased....
January 9   John P. Dunnam, Adm'r.

Issue of January 23, 1799

Died, on Friday last, in Stephens' parish, Mr. Peter Lesesne, of this place.

Issue of January 30, 1799

All persons who have accounts with the estate of Mr. John Porter, deceased...settle with Mr. James Vinson....
January 23.   Elizabeth Porter, executrix.

All persons having any demands against Edward Mitchell, late of Prince George parish, deceased....
January 30   Ann Mitchell, Executrix.
                                    Thomas Mitchell)
                                    John Elias Moore) Executors
                                    Ephraim Bowen   )

(Another notices states that Mrs. Mitchell intended to remove northward.)

GEORGETOWN GAZETTE

Issue of February 6, 1799

Tract for sale on the South side Sampit Creek, 400 acres, part of 800 acres granted to James Stewart in the year 1735, adj. John Wether's land...to make division among the heirs of Benjamin Darrell, deceased.
January 30.

By permission of Cornelius DuPre, Ordinary...to be sold before the Market House in Georgetown, part of the personal estate of Mr. Harrington Godfrey, deceased....
February 6.

All persons having legal demands against Mr. Harrington Godfrey, deceased....   Benjamin H. Godfrey) Administrators.
February 6.   John Shackelford   )

Issue of February 13, 1799

All persons having demands against Mr. Caleste Prudent Bachelier, late of Georgetown deceased...
                        John Shackelford, adm'r.

By permission of the Ordinary of Georgetown District, will be sold...estate of Benjamin Blanchard, deceased.
February 6.   Henry Blanchard, adm'r.

All persons who have demands against Mr. Peter Lesesne, Junr., deceased....
February 13.   Buleh Lesesne, adm'x.

All persons having legal Demands against John Hargate, late of Winyaw County, decd....
February 13.   Francis T. Deliesseline, admn.

Issue of February 20, 1799

All persons having legal Demands against the estate of John Orr, esq., deceased....   Alex. Pettigrew) Executors.
February 20.   Timothy Dargan)

Issue of February 27, 1799

By permission of Cornelius DuPre, Ordinary of Georgetown District, will be sold on the plantation where I now reside, personal property of Mrs. Jane Anderson deceased....
February 27.   Alex. Anderson.

All persons having any Demands against the estate of William Frazer, deceased, late of Black Mingo....
February 20.   Robert Frazer, adm'r.

Issue of March 20, 1799

Married on Saturday evening last, by the Rev. Mr. Spieren, Dr. Robert Brownfield to Miss Susanna Heriot.

Issue of March 27, 1799

To be sold, the personal estate of Isaac Danford, deceased....
March 27.   Thomas Chapman, Adm'r.

GEORGETOWN GAZETTE

Issue of April 17, 1799

Married on the 4th instant, by the Rev. Mr. Speirin(sic), Mr. George Ford, to Miss Sarah Helen, both of Black River.

Issue of April 24, 1799

All persons having Demands against James Garrell, late of Kingston county, Deceased....
April 24.   Samuel Garrell, admr.

Died last Saturday morning, Mrs. Ann Taylor, aged 40 years and 8 months...(eulogy).

Issue of May 15, 1799

Married on Thursday last, at Black-Mingo, by the Rev. Mr. Knox, Mr. John Screven, to the amiable Miss Martha Brockinton.
Died, suddenly, on Sunday night last, Mrs. Donnolly, consort of Mr. Patrick Donnolly.

Issue of June 26, 1799

Married on Tuesday evening, the 18th inst., by the Rev. G. H. Spierin, the Rev. Edmund Botsford, to Mrs. Ann Deliesseline.
And on Saturday evening last, by the Rev. Mr. Spierin, Samuel Isaac Thurston, Esq., merchant of Wilmington, N. C., to Mrs. Jane Futhey, of this town, relict of the late John Futhey, Esq.

All persons indebted to the estate of Dr. Samuel Heron...
June 26.   Robert Heriot.

Issue of July 10, 1799

From the Virginia Federalist.
On the 6th instant, departed this life, Patrick Henry, Esq., of Charlotte county. (eulogy).

Issue of July 24, 1799

Will be sold a Negro man, the property of Stephen Carr, deceased....   Thomas Hutchinson, V. M.
July 24

Issue of August 14, 1799

Died on the 9th instant, at North-Island, Mrs. Elizabeth Huger, the consort of the late general Isaac Huger, decd.

Issue of August 28, 1799

Died on Wednesday morning last, Mrs. Mary Johnson.

Issue of September 4, 1799

Elegy on the death of Miss Sarah Ann Withers. (poem, Georgetown, August 28, 1799)
Died on Thursday last, Mr. Robert Askins, carrier of the mail between this place and Charleston.

GEORGETOWN GAZETTE

Died on Saturday last, Mr. James Archibald M'Bride. (eulogy).

Issue of September 18, 1799

All persons having any demands against Elizabeth DuPre, late of Winyaw County, deceased....
September 18.   Francis G. Deliesseline, Executor.

Issue of September 25, 1799

Died on the 22d instant, aged 66 years, Mrs. Esther Rothmahler, wife of Job Rothmahler, Esq. (eulogy).
Died on Monday last, Miss Elizabeth T. Deliesseline, daughter of Francis G. Deliesseline, Esq.
Died on Waccamaw, near Georgetown, on the 15th instant, aged 62 years, Mrs. Sarah Pawley, widow of the late Col. George Pawley ....(eulogy).

Issue of October 2, 1799

Died on Saturday morning last, in the 33d year of her age, Mrs. Margaret Spierin, wife of the Rev. G. H. Spierin, of this place. (eulogy).

Issue of October 16, 1799

Married last Thursday evening, at Black River, by the Rev. Dr. Fraser, John Coachman, Esq. to Miss Hannah Green.

Issue of October 23, 1799

All persons having any Demands against the estate of Mr. Anthony Potts, late of Winyaw County...
October 6.   Patrick Connelly, Administrator.

Married in Charleston, on Tuesday evening, the 15th instant, by the Rev. Mr. Jenkins, Moses Glover, Esq., to Mrs. Hepburn, widow of James Hepburn, Esq., late of the town of Naffau, New-Providence.

Issue of October 30, 1799

Died last Wednesday evening, Mr. Kelly George, after a short indisposition.
Died last evening in the 50th year of his age, Mr. Abel Goodwin, an old inhabitant of this town.

Issue of November 20, 1799

All persons having any Demands against the late Mrs. Mary Johnson of Georgetown....
November 13   John Keith, Executor.

Issue of December 4, 1799

Died on Friday morning last, Capt. Shivers Budd.

All persons indebted to Wm Lynch of Georgetown, Blacksmith....
Dec. 4.   William Lynch.

GEORGETOWN GAZETTE

Issue of December 11, 1799

Married on Monday evening last, by the Rev. George H. Spierin, Mr. Francis Shackelford, merchant of Georgetown, to Mrs. Mary Gibbes, of Sampit.

Issue of December 18, 1799

Died in Williamsburgh, on the 28th ult., Mr. James Graham, millright.

To be sold, part of the estate of Mr. Stafford Gibbes, deceased, of Kingston County....
December 18.   John Withers, adm'r.

Issue of January 1, 1800

Died at Black-Mingo, on Sunday the 22d ult., Mrs. Mary Ann White, widow of Capt. Anthony White Sen., aged 63 years.

Issue of January 4, 1800

Death notices of Gen. George Washington...on Saturday evening about 11 o'clock. from Alexandria, Dec. 16.

Issue of January 8, 1800

Married in Charleston on Thursday last, by the Rev. Dr. Hollinshed, Mr. James Vinson, merchant, to Mrs. Eliza Porter, both late of this place.
Died on the 23d ult., in Charleston, in the 23d year of her age, Miss Patsey Goodwin, daughter of the late Abel Goodwin of this town.

Issue of January 11, 1800

Died on Wednesday morning last, in the 76th year of her age, Job Rothmahler, Esq.

Issue of January 15, 1800

To those indebted to the Estate of Mr. Christopher Taylor...
January 15.   Thomas Chapman) Executors.
                           John N. Taylor)

Issue of January 22, 1800

All persons indebted to the estate of Ebenezer Vereen...
January 22.   Benjamin Britton) Executors.
                           Jane Vereen   )

Issue of February 5, 1800

Will be sold all the personal estate of Samuel Nesmith, Esq....
February 5.   Samuel Nesmith)
                           William Snow   )
                           John Graham   ) Administrators.
                           Benj. Britton)

GEORGETOWN GAZETTE

Issue of February 8, 1800

Married at Waccamaw, on Tuesday evening last, by the Rev. Mr. Spierin, Doctor William Allston of this town, to Miss Mary Pyatt, daughter of the late John Pyatt, Esq.

Issue of February 12, 1800

All persons having demands against the estate of Mr. Abel Goodwin....   Anne Goodwin, Adm'x.

Issue of February 19, 1800

Died, last Sunday evening, Mrs. Elizabeth Roberts.

Issue of March 5, 1800

Died at Villebon, near Black-Mingo, on the night of the 28th of February last, Patrick Dollard, aged 54 years...left a disconsolate relict...(eulogy).

Issue of March 22, 1800

All persons having any demands against the estate of Stran Conyers, late of Williamsburgh District....
March 22   William Witherspoon, administrator.

Issue of April 19, 1800

Married on Tuesday evening by the Rev. George H. Spierin, Anthony Toomer, Esq., of Charleston, to Miss Charlotte Cheeseborough, daughter of the late Mr. John Cheeseborough, of this place.

Issue of April 30, 1800

Married on Thursday the 24th inst., at Springfield, Waccamaw, by the Rev. G. H. Spierin, Thomas Young, Esq., of Waccamaw, to the amiable Miss Mary Allston.

To be sold, all the personal property of Mr. John Farm, late of this place...
April 30.   Archibald Taylor, Administrator.

Issue of May 3, 1800

Married on the 1st instant, by the Rev. George H. Spierin, Dr. Oliver Hawes of Wrentham, Mass., to Miss Mary Bonneau Leigh, daughter of the late Mr. John Leigh.

Issue of May 10, 1800

Married last Thursday evening, by the Rev. Mr. Spierin, Mr. Samuel Dubois, of the city of Philadelphia, to Miss Ann B. Shackelford, of this place.

Issue of May 17, 1800

To be sold, the estate of Mrs. Elizabeth Roberts....
May 17   P. Trapier, attorney for the admr.

GEORGETOWN GAZETTE

Issue of June 21, 1800

All persons indebted to James Magill, late of Winyaw County, deceased.... John Magill acting Executor.
Waccamaw, June 19.   Ann Magill, Executrix.

Issue of July 26, 1800

Died at Boston, Mr. Thomas Park, AE 50, an active naval officer in the Revolution.

Issue of August 9, 1800

Died last Wednesday evening, in the prime of life, Mr. William Gibson, baker.

Issue of August 20, 1800

A negro, the property of James B. Read, was killed by lightning last Monday afternoon, on Waccamaw.

Issue of August 27, 1800

All persons having any Demands against Mrs. Mary Davidson, late of Williamsburgh County, deceased....
August 30(sic)   James Davidson, Administrator.

Issue of September 10, 1800

Died on Sunday morning last, Mrs. Elizabeth Blackwell, consort of Mr. Michael Blackwell.

Issue of September 13, 1800

Died on the 29th ultimo, at his plantation, on Pedee, Major John Singellton...an officer in the Revolution.
Died, last Tuesday evening, Mr. James Murray, of Fayetteville, N. C. And on Wednesday morning, Mr. Richard Ashman, joiner.

Issue of September 17, 1800

Died on his passage from Charleston to Boston, the 31st of July, Mr. James Vinson, late merchant of this town, aged 31, eldest son of Deacon Samuel Vinson, of New Port, R. I. (eulogy).

Issue of September 24, 1800

Died on Saturday the 20th instant, Master Isaac Cohen, eldest son of Mr. Solomon Cohen.

Issue of October 8, 1800

Died on the 15th inst., Mr. Thomas Barron, at his plantation on Saluda River.

Issue of October 15, 1800

All persons having any Demand against the estate of Mr. John Drennan, of Black River...
October 15.   Tabitha Drennan, Administratrix.

GEORGETOWN GAZETTE

Issue of October 18, 1800

Married last Thursday evening, by the Rev. Mr. Botsford, Mr. William Vereen sen. of Black River, to Miss Eliza P. Wilks, of Georgetown.

Issue of October 22, 1800

Died on Monday morning last, Mr. John Tamplet, taylor, of this town.

Issue of November 5, 1800

Died at his father's house in Darlington District, Capt. John Augustus Benton, eldest son of Col. Lamuel Benton, aged 25 years ...left father, mother, sisters and brothers...(eulogy).

Issue of November 19, 1800

Married at Greenville, Capt. John Smith, late of Georgetown, to Mrs. M. Wilson, widow of the late Dr. Wilson of that place.

To be sold, all personal estate of William Tomson.
November 19   Abraham Cohen, V. M.

Issue of November 22, 1800

To be sold, all personal property of Robert Day, late of All Saint's deceased....
Nov. 22   James Dellet, Administrator.

All persons having demands against Maj. John Singellton, late of Peedee...
Nov. 8   Dorothy Singellton, Executrix.

Issue of November 29, 1800

All persons having demands against the estate of William Tomson, deceased.   Jane Tomson, Administratrix.
Nov. 29   Solomon Cohen, Administrator.

To be sold...the estate of Anthony White the elder....
Nov. 29   Joseph White, executor of Anthony
                         White, who was executor of Anthony
                         White the elder.

Issue of December 3, 1800

Married last Saturday evening, by the Rev. Mr. Botsford, Mr. William Grant, attorney at law, to Miss Eleanor Davis, both of this town.

Issue of December 6, 1800

All persons having legal demands against Henry Tamplet(Late of Black River) deceased....   Charles Carr)
Dec. 6   T. Chapman) Executors.

GEORGETOWN GAZETTE

Issue of December 10, 1800

To be sold, at the late residence of Mr. Peter Guerry, deceased of Black River. Catharine Guerry, Administratrix.
Dec. 10.

Issue of December 17, 1800

Notice of Estate of John Augustus Benton, late of Darlington District, deceased. Lamuel Benton, admr.
also for the estate of Maj. John Kimbrough, deceased.
Lamuel Benton, admr. with the will annexed.
Darlington, Nov. 20.

Issue of December 24, 1800

All persons having legal Demands against the estate of Patrick Dollard, late of Black Mingo, deceased....
Black-Mingo, Dec. 9, 1800. Ann Dollard, Administratrix.

Issue of January 3, 1801

By permission of Cornelius De Pre, Esq. Ordinary for Georgetown District, will be sold, on 1 Feb next, in Georgetown, Six Negroes and some Plantation Tools, being the property of the estate of Henry Saultus, deceased. By order of David Swanson, Executor.
January 3 Lizar Joseph.

All persons indebted to the estate of Col. Thomas Evans, of Marlborough District, are requested to render in their accounts... make payment to C. H. B. Poellnitz, or Thomas Evans, Administrators.
December 27.

By permission of Cornelius Du Pre, Esq. Ordinary for Georgetown district, will be sold all the personal Estate of Lemuel Wilks, deceased.... Paul Michae, Jun. Executor.
December 20.

Issue of January 7, 1801

All those to whom Abraham Cohen, Esq. of Georgetown, deceased, is indebted, are requested to exhibit statements....Solomon Cohen, Moses Myers, Jacob Myers, Eras. Rothmahler, Executors.
January 7.

Issue of January 14, 1801

To all those who are indebted to the estate of Abel Goodwin, deceased, or Ann Goodwin, executrix, are desired to make immediate payment....Ann Goodwin.
January 14.

Issue of January 17, 1801

All persons indebted to the estate of William Britton, deceased, late of Marion district, are desired to come forward and settle their accounts...Simon Edwards, Ececutor.
January 17.

GEORGETOWN GAZETTE

Issue of January 24, 1801

By permission of Cornelius Du Pre, Esq. Ordinary for Georgetown District, will be sold 16th of February, a negro woman and child, being the property of the estate of John Britton, deceased. By order of the administrator, Salomon & Joseph.
January 24.

Issue of January 31, 1801

By permission of Cornelius Du Pre, Esq., Ordinary for Georgetown District, will be sold...part of the personal estate of Dr. Robert Vanzilver, deceased....James Dellet, Adm'r.
January 31.

All persons having Demands against the estate of Richard Groves, taylor, late of Georgetown, deceased....
January 31   William Grant,
                  Attorney for the administrator.

Issue of February 4, 1801

Those persons having demands against Mr. Richard Ashman, ship-joiner, are requested to render in statements....
February 4   Lizar Joseph, Adm'r.

Issue of February 14, 1801

All persons having demands against the estate of Mr. Thomas Blackwell, deceased, of Black River, have notice to bring in their demands....   Michael Blackwell,
February 14   Executor.

All persons having demands against Jordan Gibson, late of Peedee, deceased, are requested to furnish statements....
February 7   Nathaniel Gibson,
                  Executor.

Issue of February 18, 1801

Died, yesterday morning, Mrs. Martha Campbell, consort of Mr. Alexander Campbell.

Issue of February 25, 1801

Married, at Charleston, last Thursday evening, by the right rev. bishop Smith, Samuel Wragg, Esq. of Georgetown, to Miss Mary Ashby I'on.

All persons having any legal demands against the estate of Dr. Robert Vanzilver, deceased, are requested to send them in....
February 25   James Dellet,
                  Administrator.

All persons having demands against Captain John B. Harvey, mariner, late of Georgetown, deceased, are requested to furnish statements....
February 25   John Langton,
                  Agent for the Administratrix.

GEORGETOWN GAZETTE

All persons who have any demands against the estate of the late Mr. Lewis Pitcock, are requested to render the same to Mr. Savage Smith...   Mary Pitcock,
February 25   Administratrix.

Issue of March 4, 1801

Married, at Albany (New-York) Joseph Alston, Esq. son of Wm. Allston, Esq. of Waccamaw, to Miss Theodosia Burr, only child of Mr. Burr, vice-president of the United States.

Issue of April 1, 1801

Died, at Edinburgh, on the 27th Dec. at a very advanced age, the Rev. Hugh Blair, D. D. Professor of Rhetoric and Belles Letters in the University of Edinburgh, one of the Ministers of the High Church, and author of the Sermons which have been so greatly admired.

By permission of Cornelius Du Pre, Esq. Ordinary for Georgetown District, will be sold at the lower plantation of J. J. Pringle, Esq. on Peedee, on 16th April...estate of William Rhodes deceased.
April 1   Thomas Hutchinson, V. M.

Issue of April 4, 1801

All persons indebted to the late Samuel Murdock, deceased, are requested to make payment....
April 4   William Murdock,
                    Administrator with the will annexed.

Issue of April 8, 1801

Charleston, March 30.
Married on Thursday evening last, at Prince William's parish, John Alston, Esq., second son of William Alston, to Miss Sarah M'Pherson, daughter of Isaac M'Pherson, esq. deceased.
April 2
Yesterday departed this life, at the age of 55 years, Dr. Henry Collins Flagg, an eminent physician and inhabitant of this city, and a member of the Cincinnait--a native of Rhode-Island, but had long resided in this state.... In the late contest with Great Britain, he took an active and decided part with his countrymen and accepted the appointment of surgeon to the first S. C. continental regiment....

Issue of April 25, 1801

Died, on Tuesday morning last, in the 37th year of his age, at his plantation on Peedee, George Skinner, Esq.

Issue of April 29, 1801

Died on Friday last, capt. S. Simons, of Peedee.
Died, at his house in Slough Lane, near Windsor, (England) on Sunday the 1st of March, Dr. Herschel, the celebrated astronomer, and discoverer of the new planet Georgium Sidus.

GEORGETOWN GAZETTE

Issue of May 9, 1801

Married, at Black-Mingo, on Wednesday evening last, by the Rev. Mr. Knox, Mr. John Wilson, to Mrs. Ann Dollard.
Died, at Charleston, last Thursday morning, John M'Iver, Printer, joint proprietor of the City Gazette.

Issue of May 13, 1801

Married, on Thursday evening last, by the Rev. Mr. Holt, Mr. Samuel Hasford, to Miss Ann Huggins.

Issue of May 20, 1801

Died, on Tuesday, April 7th, in the 67th year of his age, at his plantation, on Great Pee Dee river, Frederick Charles Hans Bruno, Baron de Poellnitz.

Issue of May 23, 1801

All persons having demands against the estate of the late Archibald M'Donald, of Williamsburgh district, are requested to bring them in....   James Ballantine,
May 23   Administrator with the will annexed.

Issue of May 27, 1801

Died, yesterday morning, master William Pasiley, youngest son of Robert Paisley, Esq. aged 19 months.

Issue of May 30, 1801

Will be sold, on Monday, the 29th of June, at the plantation where the late Shadrack Simons resided, near the road leading from Britton's ferry, agreeably (sic) to his last will and testament...
May 30   Francis Green,   )Executors
                                Ben. Allston, jun.)

Notice to the Public. I have forbid the sale of the land of Joseph Wragg, since the 12th instant, having had an inditement against the said Joseph Wragg for the sum of eight thousand pounds sterling, on damage of the estate of Peter Mouzon, in the federal court, since the 6th day of August 1796, which will be on trial the next sitting of the court in this place. Charles Bedout,
May 30   Executor of said estate.

Married on Thursday evening last, by the Rev. Mr. Fraser, the Rev. George H. Spierin, to Mrs. Mary Tucker.
Married on the 7th inst. at the city of Anapolis(sic), by Bishop Carroll, the hon. Robert G. Harper, late member of Congress from South-Carolina, to Miss Carroll, daughter of the hon. Charles Carroll, of Carrollton.

Issue of June 10, 1801

Married on Satruday evening last, by the Rev. Mr. Botsford, the Rev. Joseph B. Cook, of Beaufort, to Miss Elenor S. Walker, of this town.

GEORGETOWN GAZETTE

All persons having demands against the estate of William Lester, deceased, late of Black River, are requested to bring them in....
June 10,   Robert Lester, Executor.

Issue of June 13, 1801

All persons having demands against the estate of Jonas G. Du Pre, late of Williamsburgh county, deceased, are requested to render them...   Arthur Duningham, Ex'r or
June 13.   Mary Du Pre, Executrix.

Issue of June 17, 1801

All persons who have claims upon the estate of Esther Rambert, late of Winyaw, deceased, are requested to make them known....
June 17.   C. Brown, Adm'r.

Issue of June 20, 1801

Died lately, at Cedar Hill, the residence of Allard Belin, Esq., Miss Esther Martha Belin, a remarkable promising fine child, and his only one.

Issue of June 27, 1801

Married, at Black-Mingo, by the Rev. Mr. Hiddleston, on Sunday evening last, capt. S. D. Carter, to Miss Patty Poss. And, on the same evening, by the Rev. Mr. Hiddleston, Mr. William North, to Miss Deborah White. (see below)

Married, at Westminster, Mr. Edward Lock, to Miss Rhoda Gun. What is a gun without a lock. (N. H. Pap.)

Issue of July 1, 1801

The two marriages, mentioned in last Saturday's paper, to have taken place at Black-Mingo, were premature. The person who gave the information to the printer is a Dr. Charles M'Crea, who has since thought proper to deny his having done so, but of which sufficient proof is not wanting.

Died, at Lancaster, in Pennsylvania, on the 6th inst. John Wilkes Kittera, Esq., late a member of the House of Representatives of the United States.

Issue of July 4, 1801

The Subscriber requests all those indebted to Mr. John Holmes, jun. deceased, to make immediate payment....
July 1   Maybery Holmes, Administrator.

Issue of July 8, 1801

Died, on Sunday night last, Mr. Joseph Durant.

Issue of July 14, 1801

Died, last Sunday night, Mr. Benjamin Williamson, a valuable citizen, in whose death a wife and several young children feel the severest loss.

GEORGETOWN GAZETTE

Issue of July 29, 1801

All persons who were anywise indebted to Dr. John Brown, late of All Saints parish, deceased, are requested to make immediate payment....
Long Bay, All Saints Parish,   John Green, Ex'r.
25th July, 1801

Issue of August 15, 1801

Died, yesterday morning, after a lingering illness, Miss Ann M'Pherson.

Issue of August 19, 1801

Married, in Charleston, late Thursday evening, by the Rev. Dr. Purcell, lieutenant William Smith, of the frigate John Adams, to Miss Harriet Valk.

All persons indebted to Enos Tart, late of Pee Dee, deceased, are remake (sic) immediate payment...
August 19.   John Tart, Executor.

Issue of August 22, 1801

Departed this life, on Thursday evening last, Miss Mary Hutchinson, daughter of Thomas Hutchinson, Esq.

Issue of August 26, 1801

Died, yesterday morning, after a short illness, Thomas Hutchinson, Esq. His remains were interred in the evening with military honots, attended by his friends and numerous acquaintances.

All persons having demands against the estate of Mr. Benjamin Williamson, late of Georgetown, are requested to bring them in....
August 26   Sarah Williamson, Administratrix.

Issue of September 2, 1801

Died at Boston, on the 8th ult., aged 53 years, Mrs. Mary Taylor, consort of Archibald Taylor, Esq. of this town.

Issue of September 9, 1801

All persons having demands against the estate of Mr. John Grier, of Peedee, deceased, are requested to send them in....
September 9.   Thomas W. White, Administrator
                          with the will annexed.

Issue of September 12, 1801

On Tuesday last a melanchoyl accident took place between North and South Islands. Several gentlemen were in a boat coming to Georgetown, when she was unfortunately capsized, by which accident Mr. Samuel Dubois and Mr. Nathaniel Vail, who were in the boat, were drowned in attempting to attain the shore.
Mr. Dubois (a native of Philadelphia) had resided amongst us several years...left an affectionate wife and child....
Mr. Vail, the son of Capt. Vail, arrived here a few weeks ago with his father, and had just recovered from a severe illness. His body was found on Thursday morning, and buried in the Baptist

GEORGETOWN GAZETTE

burial ground the same evening....
Died on Wednesday last, after a short illness, Mrs. Ann Botsford, the amiable consort of the Rev. Edmund Botsford--an irreparable loss to a large family.
Died at Black-Mingo, on the 3d instant, Miss Sarah Williams, aged 3 years.

Issue of September 16, 1801

Died, on Monday last, Mr. Woolf Aronson.

Issue of September 19, 1801

Died, in All Saints parish, on the 12th instant, Mrs. Mary C. Allston, wife of Benjamin Allston sen, Esq.

Issue of September 26, 1801

By permission of Cornelius Du Pre, Esq., Ordinary for Georgetown District, will be sold, before the subscriber's store, the personal estate of Caleste Prudent Bachalier, deceased....
September 26.   John Shackelford, Administrator.
By permission of Cornelius Du Pre, Esq., Ordinary for Georgetown District, will be sold about 30 miles from Georgetown, on Black river, at the residence of Mr. Joseph Alexander Glass, deceased, two Negroes...
September 26.   Mary Glass, Adm'x.
                          William Adams, Adm'r.

Issue of September 30, 1801

Married, on Tuesday th- 22d instant, Mr. Michael Blackwell, to Mrs. Mary Du Pre, of Williamsburgh township.

Issue of October 3, 1801

All persons having demands against George Skinner, Esq., deceased, late of Peedee, are requested to render them in....
October 3   Elizabeth Skinner, Administratrix.

Issue of October 7, 1801

Died, on Sunday morning, the 27th Sept near Black-Mingo, Thomas Fuller, a native of Connecticut...he resided only three months in Mingo, during which he was employed in the education of children.
All persons having demands against the late Mr. Thomas Hutchinson, deceased, of Georgetown, are desired to render the same....
October 7   Mary Hutchinson, Administratrix.

Issue of October 24, 1801

Died, yesterday morning, after a severe illness, Mr. John Burd, Proprietor and Editor of this Gazette.

Issue of November 7, 1801

Died, on the 28th ult., after a long and painful indisposition, Master Robert Heriot, son of William Heriot, Esquire.
Died, yesterday, Miss Emily Heriot, daughter of George Heriot,

GEORGETOWN GAZETTE

Esquire, aged 8 years, 2 months and 21 days.

The creditors of George Shinner, deceased, are solicited to render in a Statement to Mr. William Magell, or to the subscriber ....
November 7   Elisabeth Shinner, Administratrix.

Issue of November 11, 1801

Died on the morning of the 5th inst., Mr. John Mc'Culloch, of This Town, Merchant.

Died, at North-Santee, on Saturday morning, November 7th, Francis Huger, Esquire, third son of General Huger, deceased.

Issue of November 25, 1801

Wittown, Nov. 20
Died on the 16th instant, after a few hours illness, Captain John Brockinton, a worthy citizen of this village. (eulogy).

Issue of November 28, 1801

All persons having legal Demands against Mr. Wolf Aaronson (late of Georgetown), deceased, are required to render statements....
November 25.   T. Chapman.

Issue of December 2, 1801

Married, yesterday Evening, by the Rev. Dr. Gallaher, Mons. Daniel Remoussin, Planter of the Island of Santo-Domingo, to Mrs. Mary Snipes.

Sale, by Permission of Cornelius Du Pre, Esq., on Tuesday 22 December, will be sold the personal estate of the late Mr. Isaac Deliesseline....
December 2.   Francis G. Deliesseline,
                       Savage Smith, Administrators.

Issue of December 5, 1801

Died, on Tuesday last, Mr. Thomas Hancock, many years an Inhabitant of this Town.

Died on the 8th ult. at Silver Bluff, Edgefield district, aged 35 years, the Hon. Ephraim Ramsay, one of the Associate judges of South Carolina. (eulogy).

Will be sold at Black-Mingo, or Wilton, on Friday, the 18th inst., all the personal estate of the late Mr. John Mason....
December 5   Archibald Taylor, Administrator.

Issue of December 12, 1801

Married on Thursday evening, by the Rev. Mr. Botsford, Col. John Ervin, of Pee Dee, to Mrs. Hannah Blackwell, of this town.

Married, near Stateburg, on the evening of the 5th instant, by the Rev. I. M. Roberts, Col. Colclough, of Santee, to the amiable Mrs. Elizabeth Wright.

Died at Salem (Massachusetts), Mr. Weld Gardner, merchant, aged 56, son of the late Samuel Gardner Esq. Deceased. By his death the following legacies become due, given by Mr. George Gardner, deceased, brother of Mr. wm. Gardner, in 1773.

GEORGETOWN GAZETTE

Issue of December 16, 1801

Died, at Beaufort, Port Republica, on the night of the 4th instant, in the 80th year of her age, Mrs. Mary Barnwell, relict of the late Col. Nathaniel Barnwell. (eulogy).
Died at Wilmington (Massachusetts), Mrs. Abigail Butters, aged 90. The longevity of the family tow hich the deceased belonged is well worthy of notice. She was the last of ten children, born of Abraham and Sarah Jacquith; whose ages at their decease were as follow: Abraham, 88; John, 77; Adford, 80; Ebenezer, 86; Benjamin 85; Sarah, 84; Mary, 86; Elizabeth, 70; Abigail, 90, and Hannah, 82, amounting to 828 years!
Married on Thursday evening, the 3d instant, by the reverend Thomas D. Birden, Mr. Phineas Pierfon, of Combahee, to Mrs. Catharine Garvin, of the Horse Shoe.

Issue of December 19, 1801

All persons indebted to the late John Brockington, of Blackmingo, deceased, are requested to make immediate payment....
December 19.   Martha Brockinton, Administratrix.

Issue of December 23, 1801

Married at Wiltown, on Tuesday evening, by the Rev. Mr. Knox, Mr. Thomas Commander, to Miss Margaret Shepherd.
Charleston, December 28(sic)
Marriages.
On Thursday evening, the 10th instant, by the Rev. Dr. Kieth, Mr. Henry W. Paxton, to Miss Eliza Ann Yeadon, both of this city. On the 12th instant, by the Rev. Dr. Keith, Mr. William Butler Minott, to Miss Jane Field Smith, both of this city.
Departed this life on the 13th instant, Mrs. Mary Besselleu, second daughter of Mr. John Riley senior, and wife of Mr. Charles Besselleu, of Jacksonborough, in the 18th year of her age....

Issue of December 26, 1801

Married on Wednesday evening, by the Rev. Mr. Wayne, Mr. John Vener, to Mrs. Hester Cross, widow of the late Capt. Cross.

Issue of December 30, 1801

Died, at Charleston, on the 22d inst., in the 30th year of his age, James Horne, Esq., in the 30th year of his age(sic)....

Issue of February 15, 1804

All persons having demands against the late Richard Mansfield, of Sampit, are requested to send them in....
February 4   Francis Withers, Ex'r.

Issue of May 30, 1804

All persons indebted to the estate of the late Thomas Young, deceased, are requested to make payment....
April 25   Mary Young, administratrix,
                            John Keith, administrator.

GEORGETOWN GAZETTE

Died on Monday morning, the 28th inst., Mrs. Eliza P. Vereen, of Pee Dee. In the morning of life this dutiful and affectionate wife and tender mother is taken....

All those who have any demands against the estate of Mary Tucker (late of Georgetown) are requested to render statements....
May 23   Bethel Threadcraft, Adm'r.

Issue of February 19, 1806

Died, on Saturday last, Mr. John M'Culloch, a man whose honesty, uprightness, and suavity of manners endeared him to all those with whom he was acquainted.

All persons indebted to the estate of William Strother, late of Marlborough District, deceased, are particularly called on to make immediate payment....
January 18.   Charles Strother, Administrator.
                                 Lucy Strother, Administratrix.

Issue of February 26, 1806

Departed this life on Tuesday the 18th inst., Capt. Mathew Fleming, aged forty-nine years...left a widow and thr-e children. (eulogy).

All persons indebted to the estate of John Chisolm, merchant, of Little Pee Dee, deceased, are requested to make immediate payment....   Ignatius Flowers, Executor.
February 26   Emily Chisolm, Executrix.
All persons having legal demands against the estate of William Hoole, deceased, are requested to render statements....
February 26   Mary Hoole, Executrix.
All persons having demands against the estate of Mr. John W. Elliott, deceased, are requested to render accounts....
February 22   Thomas Ballow)
                                 John Carnes) Execut.

Issue of April 26, 1806

Married in Charleston, on Sunday evening, the 20th inst., by the Rev. Dr. Jenkins, Charles Lesesne, Esq. of this town, to Miss Eliza Ann Segeant, of that city.

All persons who are indebted to Mathew Fleming dec. are requested to make payment....   Hariot Fleming, Administratrix.
April 9   William Wayne, Administrator.
All persons who have any demands against the estate of William Henry Lide, late of Georgetown, shopkeeper, are requested to render them....
April 5   Jacob Myers, Adm'r.

Issue of June 4, 1806

All persons having any demands against the estate of John M'Cullough, late of Black River, planter, are requested to render the same....
April 16   James Lane, Adm'r.

GEORGETOWN GAZETTE

All persons having any demands against the estate of Ann Goodwin, late of Georgetown, deceased, are requested to render them....   Samuel Taylor,
May 22   Administrator with the will annexed.

All persons having any claims on the estate of Mr. John Morison, late of Georgetown, deceased, are requested to deliver the same...to the subscriber on Lynch's Creek, Kershaw District.
March 15   Keneth Morison, Administrator.

Issue of July 19, 1806

All persons having just claims against the late Mr. Francis Shackelford, are desired to render statements....
June 28   Thomas Chapman.

Issue of July 30, 1806

All persons having legal demands against the estate of William Ford, deceased, late of Black River, planter....
April 26   W. James, Acting Executor.

Died on Tuesday evening the 22d inst., Mr. Alexander Hamilton, in the 28th year of his age.

All persons having just claims against the late Mr. Andrew M'Farlan, Printer....   Mary M'Farlan, Adm'x.
July 30, 1806.

All persons who have any demands against Solomon Rhodus, late of Williamsburgh District, who are entitled to legacies under his last will and testament.... Nancy Rhodus, Executrix.
July 30, 1806.

Issue of June 20, 1807

All persons indebted to the late Mr. Walter Crawley, are requested to make payment and all those to whom he was indebted....
December 10   John Taylor, Senr., Administrator.

All persons having any demands against the estate of Samuel Mulliken, of Georgetown District, deceased, are requested to make payment....
April 4   David Prior, Administrator.

All persons having any demands against the late Charles Bedout, are requested to render them....
October 8   John Taylor, Senr., Administrator.

All persons who have demands against the Estate of Richard Singleton, late of Horry District, deceased, are requested to render statements...to the subscriber in Horry District.
June 20, 1807   John Singleton, Executor.

Issue of June 27, 1807

Married on Friday the 19th inst., by the Revd. Mr. Lilly, Mr. Childermas Croft, to Miss Dupuy Perdriau, both of this place.

All persons having demands against Gabriel Rambert, Esq., late of Black River, deceased, are requested to render them....
April 21, 1807.   Jer. Cuttino)
                D. Swanston) Adm'rs.

All persons indebted to the Estate of Mr. Alexander Chovin, late of Santee, deceased, are requested to make immediate payment .... June 27.   Hugh Frazer, A. Collins, Ex'rs.

GEORGETOWN GAZETTE

Issue of July 1, 1807

The subscriber having administered on the Estate and effects which were of Mr. Alexander Anderson of Sampit, deceased....
July 1   Alexander Collins.
All persons who are indebted to the estate of Mr. John W. Elliott, Jeweller, late of Georgetown, deceased, are requested to make payment....   Martha Elliott,
July 1   Administratrix.

Issue of February 24, 1808

Those persons indebted to the estate of William Heriot, Esq., deceased are called on...to make payment.
December 19   Robert Heriot, Executor.
All persons indebted to the late Rev. Samuel Lilley, are called upon for immediate payment.
                                Anthony Toomer, Administrator.
All persons indebted to the Estate of Josias Allston, late of Georgetown, are requested to make immediate payment....
December 23   Benjamin Allston, Sen.
                                John M. Taylor, Administrators.
All persons indebted to the Estate of Edward Thomas, late of Sampit, are requested to make payment to the executors.
January 27   Edward Gibbes Thomas
                                Samuel Thomas
                                Francis Withers
                                Thomas Waring
By permission of Samuel Smith, Esq., Ordinary for Georgetown District, will be sold all the personal estate of the late Samuel Lilly.
February 20.

Issue of March 19, 1808

All persons who are indebted to the Estate of Thomas Wilson, late of Blackriver, are requested to make immediate payment
March 5   William Thomason, Administrator.
All persons who are indebted to the estate of the late John Cogdell, Esq. are requested to make payment.
March 12   B. Allston Senr)
                                J. S. Cogdell) Executors.
                                J. Keith   )

Issue of June 15, 1808

Died, at his plantation on Horse Creek, in Scriven County, (Georgia), Mr. MIchael Dougherty, aged 135 years, and was one of the first settlers of that state...died on 29th May 1808.

Issue of August 6, 1808

Died on Monday the first inst., in the 33d year of his age, Mr. Abel Bishop, a native of West-Haven in the State of Connecticut.

GEORGETOWN GAZETTE

Issue of December 5, 1810

All persons who may have any claims against the estate of Childermas Croft, Esq., decd., of Georgetown, are hereby requested to render the same....
December 5   J. B. White, Qual. Executor.

Issue of April 10, 1813

All persons indebted to the estate of Major William Murray, are called on for payment....   Ann D. Murray, Executrix.
March 3.   A. Marvin, Executor.
Died, last evening, Mr. David Tarbox, printer. AE 21. (eulogy).

All persons having demands against Mr. Perceval Pawley, late of Waccamaw, deceased, are requested to render statements.
March 3   John Withers,
                               George Pawley, Administrators.

Issue of April 17, 1813

Married at Black Mingo, on the 8th inst., Patrick Cormack, Esq. of Kingstree, to Miss Charlotte A. Donnelly, of this town.
All persons having demands against Mrs. Martha Wilson, late of Georgetown, deceased....
April 17   Francis Withers.
All persons having any demands against James Summers Dick, late of Black River, Georgetown District, are requested to render them....   Leonard White,
                               William White, Administrators.

[The issues of July 5, 1815 through February 8, 1817, with the exception of the issue of September 21, 1816, are located in the Duke University Library.]

Issue of July 5, 1815

Married on Pee Dee, on Tuesday evening, the 27th ult., by the Rev. Mr. Green, James M. Grier, Esq. to Miss Eliza Covan, all of said place.

Issue of July 8, 1815

Died at his residence on Sampit, on Tuesday morning the 4th instant, James Walker, Esq. in the 50th year of his age. A wife and a number of children have to lament his loss.
At North Inlet, on Thursday the 6th inst., Sarah Ford, daughter of Thomas Ford, aged 3 years.
In this place, yesterday morning, Mary Charlotte Dowdney, daughter of Mr. Thomas Dowdney, aged 3 years and 8 months.

Issue of July 12, 1815

The creditors of Alexander Campbell, late of Georgetown, deceased, are required to render statements....
July 8   T. Chapman, Adm'r.

Issue of July 15, 1815

Died at Trumbull, Connecticut, on the 10th ult., Mrs. Jerusha

Fayerweather....
　　Died at Herefordshire, Eng., Miss Lucy King, aged 21. (eulogy).

Issue of July 26, 1815

　　Married on Sunday evening last, by the Rev. Mr. Bass, Mr. M. Holmes to Miss Ann Jaudon, both of this place.
　　Casualty--Drowned, on Friday evening last, at South Bay, where he had been for the purpose of bathing, Mr. John Morrison, formerly of the house of Miller, Morrison & Co. of Charleston.
Courier.

　　Married at New-Brunswick, William Oultcalt, to Miss Elizabeth Primer.
　　Also, by the Rev. Peter D. Freligh, Mr. Philip Dubois, to Miss Esther Freer, daughter of Captain Zacharias Freer, all of the town of New Paltz.

Issue of August 19, 1815

　　Death of James A. Bayard.....
　　Died at his seat near Georgetown (Col.), Philip Burton Key, Esq., in his 58th year. He served many years as a member of the Legislature of Maryland, and lately as a member of Congress.
　　At Philadelphia on the 6th instant, John Smith, Esq., Post Captain in the u. S. Navy..a native of S. C.
　　at Randon, near Cork (I.), Miss Eliza Neilson, a young lady of rare accomplishments.
　　At New York, Mr. John Bartin, aged one hundred and three years and 3 months and 8 days.
　　At Westmoreland, N. H. General George Aldrich, aged 77 years, an old and respectable revolutionary soldier.

Issue of August 26, 1815

　　Died on Wednesday evening last, Mowren Wayne, aged 3 years and 5 months, only son of Mr. Jacob Wayne, of this town.
　　Married at Washington City, on the 11th inst., Mr. Joseph F. W. Harriss, to Miss Sophia Douglass Abercrombie, both of the theatre.
　　On the 17th inst., at the same place, Mr. William Anderson, to Miss Euphemia Jefferson, daughter of Mr. Joseph Jefferson, all of the Theatre.
　　All persons having demands against the estate of Paul Jaudon, deceased, are requested to make payment....　　Samuel Peedreau, March 3d, 1815　　　　　　　　　　　　　Qualified Executor.
　　All persons having demands against the estate of Solomon Buddon, deceased....　　　　　　　　　　Samuel Peedreau, April 15, 1815　　　　　　　　　　　　　　　Administrator.

Issue of August 30, 1815

　　Died some time since, at Kingstree, S. C., in the 21st year of his age, Mr. Isabel Harvey, batter, a native of Connecticut.
　　Died on the 15th inst.,at his seat near Salisbury, N. C., General John Steele, long known as a distinguished statesman. (eulogy).
　　At Hartford, on the 17th inst., in the 57th year of his age, his honor Chauncey Goodrich, Lieutenant Governor of the State of connecticut.
　　On the 18th inst., in Union District, S. C., Mr. John Hart, aged 27 years, a native of Charleston.

GEORGETOWN GAZETTE

In Charleston, on the 22d inst., Mr. Archibald S. Ball, in the 49th year of his age.
In Naples, N. York, on the 27th ult., a fine healthy infant, aged 7 weeks, son of Dr. O. Fuller of that place....
In Woodford county, Kentucky, on the 26th ult., Francis Peart. This gentleman died without any child....

Issue of September 2, 1815

Departed this life on the 27th ult., on his way to North Carolina, the Reverend Daniel Brown, A. M., pastor of the Presbyterian Church, at Indiantown, Williamsburgh, S. C....left a wife with a family of weak children....(eulogy).

Issue of September 9, 1815

Married at Pembroke, Mr. Jonathan Black, aged 83, to the widow Betsey Robertson, aged 78.   Northern paper.

Issue of September 23, 1815

Died on Wednesday evening last, Capt. Goram Smith, aged 39 years, a native of Hollowell (Maine.).

Issue of March 27, 1816 [in this order on microfilm]

The subscribers having obtained letters of Administration upon the estate of Moses G. Crosby, earnestly request all those indebted by note, bond, etc.....   Jane Crosby   ) Admx's.
                                              Mary Broderick)
All persons having any demands against the estate of the late Mrs. Elizabeth Gilbert, deceased....   James Murdock,
                                              Qualified Administrator.

Issue of October 4, 1815

Died at North-Inlet yesterday morning, Mrs. Elizabeth Graham, in the 75th year of her age.

Issue of October 7, 1815

Died on the 4th inst., Elizabeth Ann Cuttino, aged 7 years, 7 months, and 14 days, eldest daughter of Peter Cuttino, Esq. of this town.

Issue of October 11, 1815

Died in Wake county, N. C., on the 10th inst., Mary Rowland, aged one hundred and three years.

Issue of October 18, 1815

Died on Pee Dee, on the 10th inst., Mr Samuel Cogdell Grier, in the 25th year of his age. He has left an aged mother, a fond wife, and numerous relatives....
On Pee Dee, on Saturday last, Master Samuel Anthony, AE 6 years, youngest son of Thomas W. White, Esq.
Yesterday morning, Robert AE 2 years and 7 months, son of Thomas Chapman, Esq. of this town.

Issue of October 21, 1815

William S. Hasell, Esq., the Editor of this Gazette is no more...expired on Friday last. (eulogy).

Issue of November 8, 1815

Departed this life on the 15th inst., in Laurens district, Mr. Solomon Niblet, aged one hundred and forty three years. He was born in England, where he lived until he was 19 years of age; he emigrated to this countyr, and resided in the state of Maryland until about 55 years ago. Columbia State Gazette, 31st ult.
Died on the 21st of October, in Columbia co., Ga., the Rev. Abda Christian, a preacher of the Methodist Society, aged 40 years.

Issue of November 18, 1815

Died in Baltimore, on the 7th inst., the Rev. Archibald Walker, a native of Ireland, and a Clergyman of the Episcopal Church. (eulogy).
A short time since in Cambridge, N. Y., Mr. Solomon Cronce, he married two sisters, with each of whom he lived alternately, a week at a time, during the whole period of his connubial connection....left two wives and 26 children.
lately, aged 60, in Trenaw, Cornwal (E.), a person known as the Giant Chillcott.

Issue of November 22, 1815

Married, at New-Haven, (Conn.), Mr. Rufus Siewson, to Miss Maria M'Duel.

Issue of November 25, 1815

All persons having demands against Dr. Edmund H. Tucker.... Nov. 25   G. W. Heriot, Adm'r.
Died at his seat in Columbia co., on Monday morning, 13th inst., Major John B. Barnes, aged 36 years.
In Petersbury, on the 10th inst., George Keith Taylor, the most celebrated lawyer in the state of Virginia.
In this town, on Sunday evening, the 12th inst., Mr. Paul Tarbox, in the 39th year of his age.

Issue of November 29, 1815

Married in Raleigh, N. C., on the 21st inst., by the Rev. Joseph Caldwell of Chapel Hill, Col. Edward B. Dudley of Wilmington, to Miss Eliza R. C. Haywood, of the former place.
Died in Greene co., N. C., on the 21st Oct., in the 29th year of his age, J. S. Durden, Esq.
Persons to whom the Estate of the late James Walker, Esq. is indebted are requested to render statements.... Mary Walker,
Nov. 29   Executrix.

Issue of December 9, 1815

Married, near this place, (torn) by the Rev. E. Botsford, (torn) to Miss Frances E. Breneau.
in this town, on Thursday morning, Mr. Thomas Holes, to Miss Eleanor McDonald.

GEORGETOWN GAZETTE

Died at La Fourche, on the 21st inst., Gen. Stephen A. Hopkins, of Donaldsonville.... New-Orleans paper
on Firday the 24th ult., at the plantation of Dr. Tidyman, in the parish of St. James, Santee, Mr. George Bear, at the advanced age of 80. He was born near the city of Manheim, in Germany, and resided in this state between forty and fifty years.
In Philadelphia, on the 25th ult., Joseph Tarbell, Esq. a Post Captain in the Navy of the U. S.....
in this town, on the 5th instant, Mrs. Mary Elizabeth Gilbert, aged 18 years, consort of the late Wiley Gilbert.

Issue of December 23, 1815

Married in Lynn, (Mass.) Uncle Nehemiah Bassett, aged 68, to Miss Nancy Fern, aged 25.

Issue of March 2, 1816

Estate sale at the plantation of the late Paul Michau, deceased, on Santee....　　　　Noah Michau, Adm'r.
February 10

Issue of March 6, 1816

All persons to whom the Estate of the late Robert Bostwick is indebted are requested to render in statements...
March 4.　　　　　　　　　Wm. M. Bostwick, Executor.

Issue of March 9, 1816

Married in Darlington District, a few weeks since, Capt. Sam'l Bacot, to Miss Emily Deliesseline.
In the same District, Mr. William Archer, to Miss Ann Shields.
In the same District, Mr. George Malone to Miss Mary Todd.
In the same District, on Wednesday evening last, the Rev. John Good to Mrs. Susannah Connell.
Estate sale of George Parker, deceased, part of the estate of Christopher Small, deceased.....　Francis Small, Adm'r.
March 9

Issue of March 16, 1816

Died, on the 3d instant, Mrs. Kinloch, the wife of Francis Kinloch, Esq. and eldest daughter of the Hon. John Rutledge, decd. (eulogy).　　Courier
Died in Amsterdam, aged 107, Moses Gomez Carwaldo, a Jew born in Portugal in 1706, and who emigrated from thence in 1729 an account of his religion. He was twice married, and had many children, of whom the eldest died when 78 years of age, and the youngest is only 22 years; both were the children of the first wife. His second wife was delivered of a child in 1798, who died shortly after, in 1804, he had seen his fifth generations.
in Virginia, Dr. William Hereford, aged 52....

Issue of March 20, 1816

Died in Huntingdon, (Conn.) on the 16th ult., Rev. David Ely, D. D., aged 66....
in Plainfield (Conn.) on the 13th ult., the Rev. John Benedict, D. D., aged 72 years, Pastor of the Congregational Church

GEORGETOWN GAZETTE

in that town.
    in Weare (N.H.), Jan. 29, Nancy Gove Cram, aged 40. (eulogy) on the 5th instant, at his residence in St. Mathew's parish, Capt Robert Hails, an old Revolutionary Officer.
    At Wilmington, N. C., on the 1st instant, John London, Esq., President of the Bank of Cape Fear, in the 70th year of his age....

Issue of March 23, 1816

    Married in Virginia, Mr. George West, aged 106 years, to Mrs. Mary Gardner, aged 80.
    Died on Wednesday morning last, Mr. Charles B. Course, aged 25 years and 8 months, and of the house of Isaac Course & Son, and eldest son of Isaac Course, Esq. of this town.
    lately, in Williamsburgh District, Daniel H. Gellaspie.

Issue of March 30, 1816

    Married a short time since in Charleston, Frederick Kinloch, Esq. of the U. S. Army, to Miss Mary P. Lowndes, eldest daughter of Mr. Thomas Lowndes.
    Died in Raleigh, N. C., the Rev. James W. Thompson, a minister of the Presbyterian Church. (eulogy).
    From the Belfast Commercial Chronicle Jan. 10. Died on the 14th of December at the farm of Knockfin, parish of Glenelg, and county of Inverness, at the advanced age of 102, Allan Morrison, farmer,
    At Kirkston, Glenelg, on Friday the 15th December, Mary M'Conlag, aged 105 years....
    Agnes M'Rae still lives in good health at the age of 104 within a few miles of Glenelg....

Issue of April 3, 1816

    Died at Halifax (N.S.), on the 28th December last, the Right Rev. and Hon. Charles Inglis, D. D., Bishop of that Diocese and first Protestant Bishop that was ever appointed to a British Colony--aged 82.
    In Fredericktown (Maryland), Rev. George Askins, for many years a zealous Preacher in the Methodist Church.

Issue of April 6, 1816

    Died on the morning of the 3d inst., Mrs. Jennet Smart (of Charleston), in the 38th yearof her age....
    All persons who are indebted to Mr. Thomas Barr, late of Georgetown, are called on for payment....
Willtown, April 1st 1816   Thomas McConnell, Executor.

Issue of April 17, 1816

    All persons indebted to the Estate of John Lawson, late of Georgetown (mariner) Deceased, are requested to make payment....
Charleston, March 19   Michael McGrath, Admr.
    Obituary of Bishop Francis Asbury....
Departed this life at Cambridge, on the 26th of March, 1816, the Rev. Mr. James Laird, Rector of Great Choptank Parish....
    All persons having any demands against the Estate of Harry Greggs, deceased, will please hand them in to J. L. Wilson in Georgetown or the subscriber on Waccamaw.   Thomas Alston, Admr.
April 17

GEORGETOWN GAZETTE

Issue of April 20, 1816

Died on Thursday last, in the 75th year of his age, Mr. John Smith, a worth and highly respected inhabitant of this town.
At his lodgings in Georgetown, (Col.) yesterday, the Hon. Richard Stanford, a Representative in Congress from the state of N. C., aged about 47 years.
Died at Baltimore, on the morning of the 9th inst., the Rev. Francis Charles Nagot, first superior of the Catholic seminary, aged 82 years.
Died at Mobile on the 5th February, last, Capt. John Alexander Watson...a native of Balden county, N. C....(eulogy and account.)

Issue of April 27, 1816

Married on Wednesday evening last by the Rev. Mr. Lance, Mr. John W. Shackelford of the House of John Shackelford & son, to Miss Elizabeth S. Tati, all of this town and
On Thursday evening last, by the same Reverend gentleman, Mr. Stephen Ford to Miss Hellin Walter, all of this district.
Died at Ipswich, (Mass.) on the 1st inst., Major Joseph Swaley, aged 65--an officer of the revolutionary army....
on the 3d inst., at his residence in Schoharie county, New-York, Capt. Thomas Machin, member of the order of Cincinnati, aged 72 years....
at his residence in Georgia, on the 5th instant, General John Twiggs, the oldest Major General in the U. S.....

Issue of May 1, 1816

Died lately at Havelberg, in Prussia, Field Marshal Mollendorff, aged 92....
Died, last evening, James, aged 7 years, youngest son of Mr. J. Whitehurst of this town.

Issue of May 4, 1816

Died at Clough Creek, Hamilton co., Ohoi., Mrs. Margaret Eichelberger, aged 109 years. She was born in Germany, A. D. 1707.
At Paris (found dead in bed) Count Momer, one of the peers of France.

Issue of May 8, 1816

Notice on estate of Edward Thomas....Francis Withers, Exrs.
May 4   Edwd. G. Thomas
All persons having any demands against the estate of James M'Donald, deceased....   Sarah McDonald, Adm'x.
May 8
Died in Germany, the celebrated General Count Bulow.
In England, the Dowager Lady Hamilton, at age 90. Also Lord Vincent Fitzwilliam.
In Paris, M. Bartholemy, engineer....

GEORGETOWN GAZETTE

Issue of May 11, 1816

Died, at Indian Town, Williamsburgh District, on the 16th ult., Mrs. Mary Port Snow, aged 23 years and 7 months...leaving husband, father, mother, three small infants....
Died at Augusta, (Geo.) on the 23d ult., the Rev. John Garvin, in the 54th year of his age...in the Methodist connection ....

Issue of May 15, 1816

Died in this town, on Friday last, in the 42d year of his age, Mr. Anthony Pawley.
Died in Athens, in New-York, on his way home from Washington with his family, the Hon. Samuel Dexter of Mass.
Nat. Intelligencer
Died in Abbeville District, on the 28th ult., Mr. James W. Cotten, aged 47...left wife and eight children. (eulogy)
Charleston Times

Issue of May 18, 1816

Died in this town on Wednesday last, aged twenty months and 15 days, Miss Mary Ouldfield Heriot, youngest daughter of Robert Heriot, Esquire.

Issue of May 22, 1816

Married on Thursday evening last by the Rev. Mr. Knox, Mr. Anthony Potts, of this town to Mrs. Hannah Davisson of Williamsburgh Dist.
 in the village of Newberry, on the 9th inst., Dr. James E. Shell to Miss Rebecca H. Berry, both of the same place.
 on the 16th inst., near Fayetteville, Mr. Henry Blake, merchant, to Miss Polly Tommy.
 in Elizabethtown, Bladen county, on the 16th ult., Mr. Samuel B. Andres, to Miss Mary Ann Cumming.
 In Chatham co., N. C., Mr. Aaron Bryan, aged 82, to Miss Patsey Groce, aged 18.
Died at his residence in Williamsborough, Granville co.,(NC) col. James Vaughan, a high respect and worthy citizen...capt. in the Rev. war.
 in Hagerstown, in the 36th year of his age, Col. John Ragan ....

Issue of May 25, 1816

Died at his residence near Baltimore, on the 3d inst., in the 63d year of his age, James M'Henry, Esq...in the revolutionary war....
 at the High Hills of Santee, on the 15th inst., Thomas Eveleigh, Esq., formerly of Charleston, in the 69th year of his age.
 in England, Thomas Oliver, aged 82, Lt. Gov. of Mass. in 1774.
 at Springfield, Capt. John Bryant, aged 73, of Boston...an officer in the Revolutionary war....

Issue of May 29, 1816

Married at Savannah, on the evening of the 15th inst., Mr. John King, to Miss Jane Achord, both of that place.

GEORGETOWN GAZETTE

Died in Norfolk (Vir.), on the 16th inst., Peter Forde, a native of France...left no relation.   Norfolk Herald
in New Jersey, Elder David Brown, aged 82, of the Society of Friends....   Bost. Cent. 18th
in Fairfield District, on the 11th inst., Doctor Alexander Wylie. (eulogy).

Issue of June 2, 1816

Died lately at Fort Johnson (S.C.), Captain Andrew Lewis Madison, of the 4th Regt. United States Infantry. He was a native of Virginia and served during the late war....
at Camden S. C. on the morning of the 22d inst., Captain Isaac Dubose of that town....
at Clarksborough (Geo.) on the 9th inst., Major Edwin Mounger of that place--he was formerly Treasurer of the State and afterwards Collector of the customs at Savannah, Ga.

Issue of June 8, 1816

Richmond yesterday lost one of her most beloved Citizens, William Marshall, Esq. the Commonwealth's Attorney for this city....(eulogy).
All persons having demands against the Estate of Mary Gasque, deceased, of Georgetown District.... Thomas G. Scott, Admr. June 8

Issue of June 12, 1816

Died at Boston, on the 8th ult., Mr. William Ellison, in the 75th year of his age. (long eulogy).

Issue of June 15, 1816

Died at Bennington (Vt.), Anthony Haswell, Esq. one of the earliest Printers in Vermont.
in Boston, Mr. Abijah Adams, aged 62, senior editor and proprietor of the "Independent Chronicle," published in that town....
a short time since, Mrs. Eliza Brent, late wife of Daniel Brent, of Washington....   Phil. paper
at Groton, widow Eunice Sullard, aged 106.
in Dorchester country(sic), Md., Mr. John Mitchell, aged 105.
in Talbot co., Md., a black woman, commonly called Old Deborah, aged 120.

Issue of June 19, 1816

Died on her way from Wilmington to Hillsborough, N. C., on the 23d ultimo, Mrs.Rebecca C. Moore, the wife of Alfred Moore, Esq. of Brunswick county...about 30 years of age....
at Leeds Castle, Kent, Eng., Mrs. Martin, a maiden lady, aged 86, sister to the present general Martin, and niece to the late Lord Fairfax.
Lately at Chatham, N. C., two gentlemen named Bell and Wilson, hunting turkies....on B's arriving at the rendezvous alone, W. was there imitating the call, and B. discharged the contents into B.'s head, who soon after died....

GEORGETOWN GAZETTE

Issue of June 22, 1816

Died in this town, on Wednesday morning, Mr. John N. Taylor. in the Creek Agency, on the 6th inst., Col. Benjamin Hawkins, Agent for Indian Affairs.

Issue of June 26, 1816

All persons indebted to the Estate of Thomas Scott, late of Williamsburgh District, deceased.... John M. Witherspoon, June 22   Samuel Scott, Administrators.
Married in Fayetteville on Thursday the 13th inst., by the Rev. Mr. Turner, William B. Mears, Esq. attorney at Law, of Wilmington, to Miss Catharine G. Davis, daughter of Gen. Thomas Davis of the former place.
    at the same place, Mr. John MacDonald to Miss Margaret Chisholm.
    in North Carolina, on the 13th inst., John B. Robbitt, Esq., Principal of the Louisburg Male Academy, to Miss Harriet B. Partridge, Principal of the female Academy of that place.
    in England, Simon Marrott, cordwainer to Sarah Thomas, both of Wisbech....
    Died lately at his seat in Nash County (N.C.), the Rev. John Atkinson--Pastor of the Baptist Church at the Falls of Tar River, a venerable and high respected character.
    at Laurel Hill, N. C., on the 26th of May last, Mrs. Mary McFarland, consort of Duncan MacFarland, Esq.
    in Ashby on the 3d inst., Widow Tabitha Pearson, in her one hundred and first year....

Issue of July 3, 1816

Married at New-York, Mr. George W. Fairfax, to Miss Isabella K. M'Netle; on the same evening Lietu. Joseph Easterbrook, of the British Navy to Miss Mary C. M'Neall, daughter of Dr. D. M'Neill, lately from Wilmington, N.C.
    in Wilmington on Wednesday the 19th ult., Mr. Julius H. Walker, to Miss M. M'Neill, daughter of Col. A. F. M'Neill, all of that place.
    at Rockingham (Vermont), Mr. Ebenezer Allen, aged 83 to Miss Hannah Johnson, aged 84. and at Georgetown (Col.), Mr. Jacob Fusteney, Sen'r aged 75 to Miss Priscilla Hickey, aged 84.
    at the northward, a short time since, Mr. Sphraim C. Crace to Miss Abigail Blodget, after a courtship of 35 years.
    in London, May 2d, His Serene Highness Leopold George Frederick, Duke of Sace, Margarve of Meissen, etc. to Princess Charlotte Augusta of Wales, daughter to the Prince Regent.
    in Russia, His Royal Highness Frederick-William-Charles, to Her Imperial Highness Catharine Paulowna, of Russia, sister to the Emperor Alexander.
    Died in Charleston, on the 17th ult., after a few days illness, Captain Frank Hampton, late of the U. S. Army, and son of General Wade Hampton, of Richland district.
    at his residence in Union District, in this State on Monday, the 17th ult., John Haile, Esq. in the 70th year of his age.
    at Russelville (Ken.) on the 20th May, Mrs. Abigail Morgan, aged 73, widow of the celebrated General Morgan.
    at Addison (Vt.) on the 10th ult., General John Strong, aged 79 years, a soldier in the Revolutionary War.
    in Raleigh (N.C.), on the 25th ult., the Rev. Wm. Glandinning, in the 69th year of his age....

GEORGETOWN GAZETTE

at his residence in Dorchester Country, E. S. Md., Mr. John Mitchell, at the very advanced age of 105 years and 9 months.
in Philadelphia, James Fennell, Teacher of Elocution, etc....

Issue of July 6, 1816

Died at Beaufort on Sunday 30th ult., the Hon. Paul Hamilton, late Secretary of the Navy of the U. S.
in Columbia (S.C.) on Wednesday morning the 26th ult., Mrs. Sarah Faust, wife of Mr. Daniel Faust, Printer.
in Newtown, New-Hampshire, June 8, Mr. Francis Chase, jun'r aged 32....

Issue of July 13, 1816

Died in this place, on Wednesday morning last, Frederick Rogers Fort, aged 13 months and 12 days, only child of Moses Fort, Esq.
on Tuesday, June 25th, 1816, between 3 and 4 o'clock in the morning, at Carlisle, Pa., the Hon. Henry Hugh Brackenridge, one of the Judges of the Supreme Court of Pa. at the age of 67.
Departed this life at Philadelphia, on Saturday the 29th ultimo, in the 36th year of his age, Mr. Thomas Hawkins, a Minister of the M. E. Church and a highly respected Merchant of that city.

Issue of July 20, 1816

Married at Peedee, on Wednesday evening last by the Rev. Mr. Wayne, Mr. Robert Oliver, to Miss Theresa E. Flicx.
Married in Savannah on the 22d inst., by the Rev. B. Scriven, Mr. John Howard to Miss Harriot Chaplin, of St. Helena Island, Beaufort Dist., S. C.

Issue of August 3, 1816

Died on the 29th of July, at his place of residence near Port's Ferry, on Pee Dee, in Marion District, Benjamin Davis, Senior, Esquire, aged 56 years. (eulogy)

Issue of August 10, 1816

Died on Thursday the 8th instant, Mr. Daniel Patterson, in the 18th year of his age.

Issue of August 31, 1816

Departed this life, at North Inlet, on the 30th inst., Mrs. Ann Carnes, in the 65th year of her age.
Died near this place, on Wednesday the 14th inst., Julia Anna, daughter of Ransom Sessions, aged 2 years and one week.
At Croom, his seat in Prince George's County, on Friday the 2d inst., The Rt. Rev. Thomas John Claggett, Bishop of the Protestant Episcopal Church in the state of Maryland...73 years of age.... (eulogy)   National Intelligencer.

Issue of September 7, 1816

Died at his country seat in Williamsburgh, on the 24th ult., John Canter for many years a respectable merchant of Georgetown.

GEORGETOWN GAZETTE

In New York, Robert Barnes, aged 35, suicide by opuim--leaving a wife and seven children.
in London, in June, Lady Asgill, aged 82....
in Seabrook (Conn.), Mrs. Phoebe Dow aged 101, relict of the late venerable Abraham Dow. Her descendants are 260, several of the fifth generation.

Issue of September 11, 1816

Died on the 18th ult., near this place, in the 26th year of his age, Mr. Nathan Bates, late of the firm of Bates & Perkins of Charleston. He was a native of Abington (Mass.)
Died, in Richmond co., N. C., on the 27th ult., Duncan M'Farland, Esq., late a representative in Congress from that state.
Died in London, on 4th July, Rt. Rev. John Watson, D. D., at a very advanced age....
in London, Miss Eleanor Saunders, aged 62, who put a period to her existence by hanging....

Issue of September 14, 1816

Married at Georgetown (Col.) on the 3rd inst., the Hon William Gaston, a representative in Congress from N. C. to Miss Eliza Worthington, of that town.
in this town, on Monday evening last, Mr. Thomas Tarbox, to Miss Mary M'Ginney.
Died in Charleston, on the 16th inst., General Joseph Alston late Gov. of this State, aged 38 years. His remains were deposited in the family burial place at Waccamaw on Thursday last. (eulogy).
In London, the Hon. Richard B. Sheridan, aged 65 (eulogy).

Issue of September 18, 1816

Died in Fairfield district, Mr. James Newton, in the 93 year of his age. He was a native of Virginia, and was one of the earliest settlers on the Congaree (eulogy)
yesterday, in this town, Dennis Duprat, aged 67, a native of Mirande (Gascon(France, but for three years past a journeyman baker in this place.

Issue of September 21, 1816 [at USC]

(long obituary of Gen. Joseph Alston).
Died at North Inlet, on Thursday morning last, Mrs. Esther Cheesborough...left a son and several grandchildren.

Issue of September 25, 1816

Married a few days past, in Chesterfield District, S. C., Mr. Benjamin Hendricks of that district aged 86, to Mrs. Sarah Smith of Anson County, N. C., aged 66 years.
Died on Saturday evening last, aged 5 years and two months, David W. Howren, son of the Rev. James Howren, of this town.

Issue of September 28, 1816

Died in New-York on the 9th inst., Gen. K. Van Rensselar. He distinguished himself in the revolutionary war, in an engagement at Fort Ann in 1777 received a wound....

GEORGETOWN GAZETTE

on the 12th inst., at Hillsborough, on the Eastern Shore of Md., in the 59th year of his age, the Revd. Jesse Lee, late Chaplain in Congress, and for 33 years a Methodist preacher....
in Italy, Paesiello, the celebrated composer of music, aged 84.
in this town, on Wednesday last, in the 23d year of his age, Dr. John Futhey....
in this town, on the same day, Miss Elizabeth Wooden, in the 15th year of her age.
Married in Charleston, on the 17th instant, Capt. John R. Grason of Washington, to Miss Frances-Ann Harvey of this place.

Issue of October 5, 1816

Died at Society Hill on the 19th ult., Mary Ann Elizabeth Haws, aged 4 years and 6 months, daughter of Dr. Oliver Haws, of that place.
at the same place on the 27th ult., Wm. E. M'Intosh, AE 14 years son of the late William McIntosh of that place.
at the same place on the 29th ult., after an illness of 4 days, Mr. _____ Watson, for many years past a useful citizen of that place....left a wife and three children.
All persons to whom the estate of Gen. Joseph Alston deceased is indebted....   John A. Alston   ) Ex'rs.
Oct. 5.   William A. Alston)

Issue of October 9, 1816

Died in Germany, her Royal Highness Marie-Louise-Frederique-Alexandrine-Elizabeth-Charlotte, Archduchess of Mecklenburg.
in England, John Hazerentine, whitesmith, aged 56....

Issue of October 12, 1816

Died in this town, yesterday morning after an illness of 18 days, in the 34th year of his age, Ebenezer Runtlett, seamon, a native of Lincoln co., Mass.
in Duplin co., N. C., on the 21st ult., John E. Spicer, of Wilmington AE 34 years.
in the same county on the 28th ult. by the fall of a horse, David Waterman, aged 12 years, youngest son of Mr. Wm. Waterman of that county.

Issue of October 19, 1816

Died at Baltimore, on the 4th inst., Col. Nicholas R. Moore, aged 62 years, late a member of Congress.
at Washington, on the 11th inst., Col. Tobias Lear, accountant of the war department.
in this town, on Tuesday last, John Mason, seamon, aged 45 a native of Philadelphia.
on Thursday evening last, Mr. Robert Carr, aged 45 years.
at Willtown, on Monday evening last, James Zuill McConnell, the only son of Thomas McConnell of that place, in the 4th year of his age.

Issue of October 26, 1816

Died at Society Hill, on the 5th inst., Miss Louisa M'Intosh, aged 17 years and

GEORGETOWN GAZETTE

at the same place on the Monday following, Miss Mary M'Intosh, daughters of Capt. Alexander M'Intosh of that place.

Issue of November 2, 1816

Died at Mulberry Hill (All Saint's Parish) on Friday the 29th ult., Mrs. ____ Hemingway, consort of Mr. Thos Hemingway of that Parish.

Issue of November 6, 1816

Died at Paris (Ken.) on the 21st ult., George W. Madison, Esq. Gov. of Kentucky.
on the 1st inst., at the residence of Christopher Gadsden Hasell, on Waccamaw, Mrs. Mary Provaux, in the 50th year of her age.
in this town on Monday last, James Lawrence Bogle, aged 21 months, only son of Dr. James Bogle.
Died in Washington co., Md., Mammy Lucy, a woman of colour, aged at least 130 years.
in Hungary, Michael Krauss, a farmer aged 125 years. He had been married three times. At the age of 114 he was married for the 3rd time.

Issue of November 13, 1816

Married at Columbia, on the evening of the 31st ult., by the Rev. John Capers, the Rev. William Capers of Sumter Dist., to Miss Susan M'Gill, of that place.

Issue of November 16, 1816

Married on the 5th inst., near Wilmington, William Anderson, Cashier of the Bank of Cape Fear, to Miss Mary B. Howard.
at Columbia, on the 5th inst., Dr. David W. Cuttino, of this town to Miss Susan S. Park, of Columbia.
in this town, on Thursday evening last, by the Right Rev. Theodore Dehone, the Rev. Maurice H. Lance to Mrs. Anna M. Allston.
All persons having demands against the estate of Robert Carr, millright, deceased..... Thomas Skrine, Ex'r
Nov. 16
All persons indebted to the Estate of Robert Hodges, late of Marion District, deceased. John J. Hodges, Administ.
Marion, Nov. 16

Issue of November 20, 1816

Died in this town on the 12th instant, Capt. Abner S. Brewer, aged about 40 years. He was a native of New-York....

Issue of November 23, 1816

Died at Philadelphia, on the 11th inst.,aged 73 years, Matthew M'Connell, Esq., and one of the few surviving officers of the Revolution.
at the same place, Mrs. Catharine Shelter, in her 99th year, a native of the city of Hanover, in Germany....
at Cheltenham, Sept. 16, Richard Rynolds, a Quaker....
Mathew Holroyd, murdered by his wife Susannah, who also murdered her own son, aged 8 years, and an infant child, aged 15 weeks....

GEORGETOWN GAZETTE

Issue of November 27, 1816

Died in Nagpore, India., the Rajah (Prince) of Beran. about the same time, the Brown Begum (a celebrated princess of India .)
in England, Sir Chaloner Ogle, aged 88, the oldest admiral in the British navy.
Died in Morrissania, N. Y., the Hon. Gov. Morris, aged 65...

Issue of November 30, 1816

Died in the Havans, Dr. Valli, the celebrated physician....
An old man (83 years of age) of the name of Ashby, of Yalding, in Kent, pur a period to his existence by hanging himself.

Issue of December 4, 1816

Married in Chesterfield district on the evening of the 24th ult., the Rev. Joseph H. Cook, of Sumter district ot Miss Obedience Strother of Chesterfield.

Issue of December 7, 1816

Married in New-York, Mr. Henry Va. Sith, aged 80 to Miss Susan Lewis, aged 30, the daughter of Mr. Cesar Cart, Oysterman, all of that city.
Died at Augusta (Geo.) on the 1st ult., in the 41st year of his age, Mr. Nathan Gasque, for many years a resident of Black River, in this District...left a widow and numerous relatives....
at Smithville, on the 14th inst., Mr. Benjamin Blaney, aged 50 years...a native of Roxbury, Mass.

Issue of December 11, 1816

Married at Workington, England, Mr. Wm. Bennet,of Senton, to Mrs. Sarah Twentyman, being the fifth time the happy couple have been married...the bridgerrom is 73, the bride 68.
Died at the Lower Borough walks, Bath (Eng.) in the 32d year of his age, George Gerson, the converted Jew.
in Pembroke-street, Deck. (Eng.) at the advanced age of 104 years, Mrs. Martha Evans...born in London, June 19th, 1713....

Issue of December 18, 1816

Died near this place, on Saturday last, Capt. John Screven ...leaves widow and children....
in Roynham (Mass.) Nov. 27th, Capt. Joshua Leonard, in the 92d year of his age. He was the eldest of 14 children....

Issue of December 28, 1816

Married on Thursday evening last by the Rev. Wm. Capers, Mr. Robert Howren to Miss Martha Simmons, all of this place.

Issue of January 15, 1817

All persons having any demands against the estate of Dr. John R. Futhey, late of Georgetown, deceased....
January 7, 1817   Sam'l I. Thurston, Admr.

GEORGETOWN GAZETTE

Died at his residence in York District, onthe 1st inst., Col. William Hill, in the 75th year of his age. He commenced his military services with the revolutionary war, in which they were continued....served in the Legislature.... **State Gazette**

Issue of January 18, 1817

    Married at New York, on the 6th inst.,by the Rev. Dr. Bomeyn, Mr. Azor S. Marvin, of the house of A. & A. S. Marvin, of this place, to Miss Delia Maria Penny, daughter of Mr. Samuel Penny, of that city.
    Died in Rockingham county, N. C., on the 29th of November, the Rev. Thomas Mullins, in the 80th year of his age...a member of the Baptist Society about 60 years....

Issue of January 22, 1817

    Married at Chateaugay, Deacon Andrew Blackman, aged 77, to widow Relief Alvorf, aged 71.
    at Parish (Maine) on new year's day, Gen. Isaac Rolster, of Paris, aged 76, to Miss Aphia, daughter of Mr. J. J. Greder, late of Switzerland, aged 33.
    Died at New-Bedford, Elisha Thurston, aged 70--a minister in the Society of Friends.   **Mercury**.
    at his residence at Hamilton College, in New-York State, the Rev. Dr. Backus, President of that Institution....
    at Hartford (Con.) Rev. Nathan Strong, D. D. aged 69....
in the Mediterranean, Capt. Downes, of the U. S. Navy, also Lt. Kahn, of the marines, killed in duel.
    at Ipswich, Jan 3, Mr. Henry Spiller, aged 84, and Jan. 4, Mrs. Spiller, aged about 70....
    in Robertson county, N. C., Martha Rowland, widow of the late John Rowland, Esquire, aged 83...for 30 years a member of the Baptist Church.
    at New-Haven, the Rev. Timothy Dwight, LL. D. President of Yale College.
    in this town on Sunday evening last, Mr. William Croft, aged 61 years, Register of Mesne Conveyance for this district.

Issue of January 25, 1817

    (long obituary of Timothy Dwight)
Died early in the morning of the 16th inst., the Hon. Alexander J. Dallas....

Issue of January 29, 1817

    Died on the 20th inst.,at the residence of Mrs. Hannah Capers, on Black river, Col. John Postell, Servant Syphur....

Issue of February 1, 1817

    All persons indebted to the estate of the late Mr. John Smith....   W. W. Trapier, Admr.
January 18
    Married on the 18th ult., under the painted rock, in Buncombe co., N. C., by a Magistrate, Mr. Lewis Sawyers, sen. aged 80 years, to Mrs. Hannah Postn aged 90 years, both of Greene co., Tenn. The lady who waited on the bride was 100 years old.
    Died at Roxford (Mass.) widow Rebecca Stiles, aged 72....

GEORGETOWN GAZETTE

Issue of February 5, 1817

Married in this state, on the first inst., Mr. Stephen Lyon, to Miss Rebecca Lamb.

Died at Baltimore, Mrs. Riggins, killed by her husband, in a controversy.

At the residence of the honorable Theodore Gourdine, in Williamsburgh District, on Friday evening last, Mr. Joseph Erwin, a native of N. C.

Issue of February 8, 1817

Married on Thursday the 31st instant, on Black River, by the Rev. Wm. Capers, Mr. John White to Miss Sarah E. Green.

in this town, on Thursday evening last, by the same Rev. gentleman, Mr. thomas Ballow to Miss Ann Swanston.

GEORGETOWN GAZETTE

[This is apparently a new series, resuming the simple title Georgetown Gazette.]

Issue of January 9, 1824 (Vol I, #24)

All persons having demands against Murdock M'Lennan, deceased, are deisred to render statements...   Alexander M'Kab,
December 12   Administrator indiv. estate.

Issue of February 17, 1824

All persons having any demands against William Leger, late of this district, deceased, are requested to render them....
December 30.   E. Waterman, Ordinary

All persons having any demands against the estate of Mrs. Elizabeth Singleton, late of All Saints Parish...
February 17   John Singleton, Administrator.

All persons having any demands against the estate of Alexander Collins, late of this District, deceased, will render them....
December 2.   Elizabeth Collins, Administratrix.

Issue of February 20, 1824

Death of Miss Mary Linereux, aged fourteen....

The notes and accounts of the late Jeremiah Wadsworth deceased, are left with me by the Administrator.   J. C. Coggeshall.

Issue of March 23, 1824

Departed this life on Tuesday the 9th of March, Mrs. Margaret Merceir, in the 48th year of her age. (widow of the late Capt. John Merceir) of Georgetown, S. C., but recently of this city.
                                        Charleston paper.

All persons indebted to the estate of A. D. Dyre, deceased, are requested to pay....
March 5   James Coggeshall,
                         Attorney of the Administrators.

Issue of April 13, 1824

Died on Saturday last, Mrs. Elizabeth, consort of Francis Withers, Esq...a member of the Episcopal Church.

All persons having demands against John Oliver, late of this District, deceased, are requested to render them...
April 20   William T. Thompson, Administrator.

Issue of May 7, 1824

All persons having demands against the estate of Mr. James Green, lately deceased, will render them to Benjamin Green, Esq.
March 26.   John F. Green, Executor.

Issue of October 19, 1824

All persons having demands against John Shackelford, late of Georgetown, deceased, are called on to render them....
September 28.   J. W. Shadkelford, Administrator.

GEORGETOWN GAZETTE

Estate sale of the estate of Mrs. Flora Emanuel, deceased.
October 19.   Simon Emanuel, Administrator.

Issue of November 12, 1824

Died in Williamsburgh District, lately, Mr. Allen Norton, aged about 30.

Issue of December 3, 1824

Married in Marion District, by the Rev. Collin Woodbury, Mr. James Martin, to Miss M. Britton, daughter of Dr. T. Britton.
Died on the 2d inst., Sarah, aged 2 years and 3 months, daughter of Mr. Joseph Joseph. (sic)
On the 30th ult., Mr. Anson Wood, aged 62, a native of Massachusetts...buried with Masonic honors.
In Marion District, on Little Pee Dee, Mr. Ezekiel Chimes, aged 72, an active soldier in the Revolution.

Issue of January 4, 1825 [Duke University]

Sale of negroes belonging to the personal estate of the late Edward R. Taylor....John Cox, Adm'r.
Dec. 24.
From the National Journal
Died at his lodgings at Tennison's, on Thursday, the 23d ult., at about 12 o'clock, in his 60th year, Push-Ma-Ta-Ha, one of the Choctaw Delegation....
Married at Little Pee Dee, on the 21st ult., by the Rev. Collins Woodbury, Mr. John P. Rice to Miss Rachael Rowell.
Died in this town, this morning of the croup, Mathias Fowler, an apprentice to Mr. A. Christian, aged about 14 years--a native of North-Carolina.
Elizabeth M'Clinchy has made suit for Letters of Administration on the Estate of her husband, Alexander M'Clinchy, late of this District....28 December 1824.
All persons having debts or accounts against the estate of Mary L. Belin, late of Georgetown, deceased are called on to render statements....   Ebenezer Flagg, Executor
Nov. 9

GEORGETOWN GAZETTE

[The issues for October 21, 1825 through October 13, 1826 are located in the Charleston Library Society.]

Issue of October 25, 1825

Married at St. Pauls Church, New-York, by the Rev. M. Schroder, the Hon. John L. Wilson of south Carolina, to Miss Rebecca Eden of Washington City.

Married at Groton, Conn., on the 2d inst., Captain Alfred H. Wood to Miss Margaret Lester.

At New-London, Conn. on the 12th instant, Mr. Edward Stanton to Miss Charlotte Spencer.

George Mitchell was a man of color, but no shade of his complexion fell upon his character. He was born a slave and bought his freedom by his merit. He felt himself a man, but was too humble to grasp for privilege which it were wrong for him to reach....George was the sexton of the Episcopal Church in this place.... He died on the evening of the 21st inst., aged about 60 years. (eulogy).

Issue of October 28, 1825

Died on Santee, the 17th ultimo, Mary Axson, youngest daughter of Louis and Elizabeth Deschamps, aged 13 months.

Died in Charleston, on the 22d inst., Mr. John Billing, aged about 45 years, a native of Bennington, Vermont, but for many years a worthy and respectable citizen of Charleston. He had just returned from a visit with his aged mother.

Final Notice on the estate of Dr. George Irving, late of Williamsburg, deceased....   William Cooper, administrator Williamsburg District, Sept. 25, 1825.

Issue of November 1, 1825

All persons indebted to the estate of the late William M'Kenzie, are requested to make immediate payment....
Oct. 18, 1825   M. Calverly)
                                          M. Fort   ) Executors

Quaker Marriage. At the friends' Meeting House, Durham, Me. on the 29th ult., Elijah and Reuben Cole, twin brothers, married Elizabeth and Mary Jones, twin sisters, and daughter of Edward Jones, of Brunswick.

Died on Sampit, on the 30th ult., Susan Elizabeth, youngest daughter of the late Mr. James H. and Mary Eliza White.

Estate sale at Withersville, the late residence of the Rev. John S. Capers, deceased.... October 28.

Issue of November 4, 1825

All persons having demands against the estate of Capt. Willaim Taxbox, Pilot, late of Georgetown, deceased are desired to render them....   Sarah P. Tarbox, Admx.
October 7

Died at Bowling Green, Ky., on his way home, Robert Withers, Esq., after a few days illness of the typhus fever. Mr. W. was a native of Waccamaw....

GEORGETOWN GAZETTE

Issue of November 8, 1825

All persons having demands against James Herrington, late of this District, deceased.... Mary Ann Herrington, Adm'rx. November 8, 1825

Issue of November 15, 1825

By permission of E. Waterman, Esq., Ordinary, will be sold... at the store lately occupied by George Mitchell, deceased....
Nov. 13   J. W. Shackelford

Issue of November 18, 1825

Died at Serenity, near Georgetown, on Tuesday the 15th inst., Mrs. Elizabeth Davidson Blount, consort of Thomas M. Blount, aged 30 years.

Issue of November 29, 1825

All persons having demands against George Mitchell, late of Georgetown, deceased....   John Wilson, Qualified Ex'r. Nov. 22.

Issue of December 2, 1825

Married at Williamsburg, on Thursday, the 24th ult., by the Rev. E. J. Mills, Doctor William Dollard to Miss Jane Louisa, daughter of David M'Cleary, Esq.
Died in Caroline County, Md., after a short but painful illness, Mr. James Pearce, in the 56th year of his age; he had survived seven wives and married to the eighth.
On Monday evening last, Rebecca, consort of the late Thomas Dowdney, in the 37th year of her age.

Issue of December 6, 1825

Will be sold 8th of December, a set of Blacksmith's tools, the property of Joseph R. Rogers, late of Georgetown, deceased....
Dec. 2   J. W. Shackelford, Auctioneer.

Issue of December 13, 1825

Died on Sunday the 5th inst., at Sandy Island, near this place, Mr. John A. Constant, aged about 33.

Issue of December 16, 1825

Died near this town on the 9th inst., Mrs. Ann Garnier. She was 70 years old; had always been a resident of this District.... (eulogy).
Near Georgetown last night, Mr. Harbert Dubose, aged about 36 years.

Issue of December 20, 1825

Our lamented friend Harbert Dubose has been suddenly snatched from our Society....born in Darlington District--his body lies in the Baptist Church Yard of Georgetown....(eulogy).
Died at Kingstree, on the 16th inst., Dr. William Dollard, aged about 40 years.

GEORGETOWN GAZETTE

Issue of December 30, 1825

Died in Williamsburg District on the 16th inst., Dr. William Dollard...left wife and daughter....(eulogy).

Issue of January 6, 1826

Died yesterday, very suddenly, Mr. Hugh Dubose, aged about 45.
All persons indebted to the Rev. William Palmer, deceased, are requested to render their demands....
January 6, 1826   B. Bard, administrator

Issue of January 10, 1826

Died last evening on Waccamaw, Mrs. Rachael Palmer, consort of Mr. Asa Palmer.
On Santee, Mr. David Rice.
Charlotte C. Dubose has made suit for letters of admn. on the estate of Harbert Dubose, late of Pee Dee, deceased...10 Jan 1826.

Issue of January 13, 1826

Died Today, Mr. John S. Jacks, aged about 45 years, a native of Charleston.

Issue of January 20, 1826

Died at his residence in Horry District, on Tuesday, the 10th instant, Bethel Durant, Esq. aged 50.
At Natchez, on the 13th Dec. the Rev. S. F. Gallagher, aged 69.

Issue of January 24, 1826

Married on the evening of the 19th inst. by the Rev. E. J. Mills, Mr. James Phillips of Georgetown District, to Miss Mary Eliza Cantley of Williamsburgh.
Died last week in Williamsburg District, Mr. John Matthews, a highly respectable Painter of that District.

Issue of January 27, 1826

Died lately in Norwall, Conn., Mr. Nathan Lockwood, aged 40.

Issue of January 31, 1826

All persons having demands against the Estate of Mrs. Henrietta Rothmahlder, deceased, are requested to render them....
Jan. 31   S. S. Gasque
                                     E. B. Rothmahler

Issue of February 3, 1826

Married last evening by the Rev. E. J. Mills, Mr. George Griffin, of Connecticut to Mrs. Mary Rich of this city.
Died in Charleston, Captain James Mausle(?) Elford, in the 56th year of his age...a native of Bristol, England, and had resided for the greater part of his life in Charleston. (eulogy)

GEORGETOWN GAZETTE

In Charleston, on the 16th ult., after a lingering illness, Theodore Gourdin, Senior, in the 62nd year of his age. (eulogy)

Issue of February 7, 1826

Married in Marion District, on the 18th ult., by the Rev. Mr. Kerton, John Macrae, Esq. Postmaster at Fayetteville, N. C. to Miss Mary Ann Shackleford, daughter of John Shackleford, Esq.

Departed this life at the residence of her father, Richard Woodberry, Esq., Marion District, on the 18th ult., Mrs. Elizabeth B. Gause, consort of Mr. John J. Gause, in the 21st year of her age....(eulogy).

Died last night on Black River, very suddenly, the Rev. Jeremiah Russell.

William Nesbit Mitchell died at Bamboritta, in St. John's Berkley, on Thursday, 19th ultimo; and on the Sunday following his body was burnt in an iron coffin purchased for the occasion in 1803. (eulogy).

All persons having claims against the late Hugh Dubose, of Georgetown, deceased, are required to redner them....
February 7, 1826   James C. Coggeshall
                         John Ingraham
                Agents for administratrix.

Issue of February 10, 1826

Died last Thursday near Smithville, N. C., Mr. John J. Gause of Little River, in the 26th year of his age. He survived his wife only a fortnight.

In Charleston, on Wednesday last, Francis Kinloch, Esq., aged near 70.

By permission of W. M'Cleary, Esq.,Ordinary for Williamsburg District will be sold at the late residence of Dr. William Dollard....   W. S. Brockington, Administrator.
February 10, 1826

Issue of February 14, 1826

Sale by order of the Court of the Ordinary...on Tuesday the 7th of March, all that land belonging to the Estate of Caleb C. Lenud, deceased, near the Rope Ferry, on Black River, adj. land belonging to John Brockington and estate of Anthony White, originally granted to George Henderson.
February 14.

Issue of February 21, 1826

John J. Gause, Esq. departed this life on the 2nd inst., at the residence of Samuel Frink, Esq., Brunswick County, North Carolina, in the 27th year of his age....

Issue of February 24, 1826

Married last evening by the Rev. Paul Trapier Keith, Stephen Charles Ford, Esq. to Miss Hannah Wilson, all of this place.

Issue of March 7, 1826

Died on Pee Dee, on Wednesday last, Mrs. Elizabeth Holmes, consort of Mr. Joseph Holmes, in the 42d year of her age. For the last eight years she has been a member of the Methodist Church.

GEORGETOWN GAZETTE

A few weeks since, Mr. Jesse Wiggins, of Marion District, a Revolutionary Soldier of great worth, aged about 70.
On the same day, his wife. They were both interred in the same grave.
In this town, on Sunday last, Mrs. Lydia Gridlis, aged about 50.
On Sunday last, Miss Elizabeth Rothmahler.

Issue of March 10, 1826

Estate sale on Thursday, the 28th inst., at Colonel Alston's Clifton Plantation...estate of William Brackingberry, deceased...
March 10   W. G. Linerieux, Executor

Issue of March 17, 1826

Married in Sumter District, on the 2d inst., Mr. Henry Spann to Miss Louisa Chandler, all of that district.

Issue of March 21, 1826

Married in Newstead, N. Y. by the Rev. Mr. Crrook, Mr. Ichabod Crane to Miss Susannah Hook....
Died in Gloucester, Mass. on Thursday, Feb. 23, Captain William Damrel, of Portsmouth and master of the Sloop Boston of that port, aged 36....
In Westford, Ms. widow Betty Flecther, aged 95....

Issue of March 24, 1826

Died lately at Philadelphia, Commodore Richard Dale, in the 70th yearof his age, one of the distinguished naval officers during the revolution....
At Greenfield, Massachusetts, lately Mrs. Mary Newcomb, wife of the Hon. Richard E. Newcomb and the only surviving daughter of General Warren, who fell at Bunker Hill.

Issue of March 31, 1826

Died on Thursday night last, Mrs.Daniels, wife of John Daniels, Esq. of a long and tedious illness....

Issue of April 4, 1826

Capt. Robert Sutton departed this life on 24th January last, at his residence in Williamsburg District, on Santee, in the 71st year of his age. (eulogy).

Issue of April 7, 1826

Married in Williamsburg District, on Thursday evening, the 30th March, by the Rev. John Cousar, Mr. William Staggers, to Miss Susan Gamble.

Issue of April 10, 1826

Married this evening, by the Rev. M. H. Lance, Peter W. Fraser, Esq. to Miss Mary A. Pawley.
Died in this town, on Saturday last, Mrs. Margaret E. Coggeshall, wife of James C. Coggeshall, Esq., aged 24 years... leaves an aged mother and an afflicted husband (eulogy).

GEORGETOWN GAZETTE

Died on the 3d inst.,Mrs. Elizabeth Palmer, consort of Mr. David Palmer, in the 26th year of her age...left a husband and 2 children.

Issue of April 14, 1826

Died in Marlborough District, on the 24th March, Mr. Sandy Scott, aged 53 years and 6 months, a native of Williamsburg District.
In Camden on the 6th inst., William Ennis, Printer, a native of Newbern, North Carolina, aged 32 years.

Issue of April 18, 1826

Departed this life, on Sunday morning last, Mrs.Rebecca Henderson, an aged and respectable inhabitant of this District.
Died on Saturday last, Mr. Stephen Roque, a native of France, and inhabitant of this City.
Departed this life in Williamsburg District, on Sunday morning, the 2d, Mrs. Joanna Ferdon, aged 56 years and 4 months... for 20 years a member of the Methodist Church.
Died at Bridgeport, Conn., the Hon. Pierpont Edwards, Dist. Judge of the U. S. for the Dist. of Connecticut....born at Northampton, Mass., April 1750...last surviving child of the celebrated Jonathan Edwards.

Issue of April 21, 1826

Estate sale of William Brackinfberry, decd....
Wm. G. Linerieux, Exr.

Issue of April 25, 1826

Died on Sunday the 23d inst., Thomas Henning, Esq. (eulogy)

Issue of April 28, 1826

Died on Black River, on Tuesday last,Mr. Burrell Burd, in the 35th year of his age, leaving two small children, who lost their mother a few months since. (eulogy).
Loame Palmer applied for letters of admn. of Burrell Burd, late of Black River, deced...28 Apri 1826.

Issue of May 2, 1826

Died on North Santee, on the 25th ultimo, Capt. Asa Clarke, aged about 60 years, a native of New England.

Issue of May 9, 1826

Died in Washginton co., Ala., on the 28th March last, Mrs. Elizabeth Godfrey, consort of the late William Godfrey, Esq. of this town. Mrs. Godfrey, whose maiden name was Dozier, was a native of Marion District, S. C., and daughter of Mr. John Dozier decd. of Pee Dee. Of her father's family, her brother Capt. John Dozier, of Williamsburg, remains the sole representative. (eulogy)
Died last week in Williamsburg District, Mr. Gilbert Johnson, aged about 50 years.
All persons having any demands against the estate of John Gota, Senior.... William A. Calhoun, Gdn.
May 9, 1826

GEORGETOWN GAZETTE

Issue of May 12, 1826

Anna B. Henning, and Benjamin Green applied for admn. of Thomas Henning, late of Georgetown, Merchant, decd....11 May 1826.

Issue of May 16, 1826

Died in Georgetown, on Monday, the 15th inst., Allen Fort, third son of Daniel D. and Sarah Scott Fort, aged 5 months.

Issue of May 19, 1826

Married on the 11th inst., at Pendleton, by the Rev. A. W. Ross, Mr. W. C. Smith to Miss Sarah N. Smith, daughter of Benjamin Smith, Esq.

At **Indiantown**, on the 27th ult., by the Rev. Mr. James, Mr. John T. Scott, to Miss Elizabeth A. M'Gill, daughter of Samuel M'Gill, Esq.

By the same reverend gentleman, on the 20th ult., Mr. I. G. M'Knight, to Miss Julian T. Bereneau, daughter of Isaac Bareneau, Esq.

Died at Lynch's Lake, Williamsburg District, on the 11th inst., Mrs. Sarah Thompson, consort of Mr. William Thompson.

Died and was buried on the 2d of May, in the Roayl burial place of the Mohegans, in Norwich, Conn., Ezekiel Mazeen, aged 27 years, great grandson of the Great Uncas....

Issue of May 26, 1826

Married last evening, by the Rev. P. Ludlow, Mr. Robert Pollock to Mrs. Charlotte Christian.

At Marion, on Thursday last, by the Rev. Jesse Leggett, Jesse Palmer, Esq., to Miss Ann Leggett of Marion.

Issue of June 2, 1826

Estate of Isaac L. Keyes, late of Horry District, decd....
June 2   Margaret Keyes, Admx.

Issue of June 6, 1826

Married on Sunday evening last, by the Rev. P. Ludlow, Mr. St. John Cambridge, to Miss Martha Carr, both of this city.

Died on Saturday night, last, Mrs. Mary Howren, consort of Capt. James C. Howren.

Ann Clarke applied for admn. on the estate of her husband, Asa Clarke, late of Santee, decd....30 May 1826.

Mary Jane Hartley applied for admn. on the estate of her husband, Joseph Hartley, late of Santee...6 June 1826.

Issue of June 13, 1826

Andrew B. Jayroe applied for admn. on Daniel Rice, late of Santee, decd....12 June 1826.

GEORGETOWN GAZETTE

Issue of June 30. 1826

Died in this town last evening, Master William Steele, in the 15th year of his age.
Died, on St. James Parish, Santee, on Thursday last, Frances Ann, aged 2 years, daughter of John H. and Harriet M. Allston.

Issue of July 4, 1826

Died at Black River, on Saturday last, Mr.Cornelius Howe, aged 45, a native of Ireland.

Issue of July 7, 1826

Married in the Episcopal Church at North-Brandford, Conn., by the Rev. Mr. Garfield, Mr. John S. Small, of this town, to Miss Sarah Walker, of Guildford, Conn.

Issue of July 11, 1826

Death of Thomas Jefferson.

Issue of July 14, 1826

Death of Capt. Alexander M'Knight, who departed this life at his residence in Williamsburg District, on Monday, the 10th inst., in the 52d year of his age. (eulogy).

Issue of July 18, 1826

Died at Augusta, on Saturday last, Jacob Myers, Esq. of this town.

Issue of July 25, 1826

Died in Georgetown, on 21st July, Mr. Samuel D. Cuttino, in the 22d year of his age. (eulogy).

Issue of July 28, 1826

Married on Thursday, the 20th inst., by Dr. B. P. Fraser, Mr. William Dooer to Miss Ann Hewet.
Departed this life in Marion District, on Friday, 21st inst., Mrs. Julia Ann Davis, consort of Francis Davis, Esq.
Died on Waccamaw, on the 25th inst., at the plantation of Dr. B. P. Fraser, Mr. Duncan Carmichael of North Carolina.
John A. Simons applied for admn. of Eleanor Simons, of Georgetown....28 July 1826.

Issue of August 1, 1826

Departed this life on the 22d ult., Ann Maria, youngest daughter of Rev. James C. Postell, in the 3d year of her age.
Died in New York, Mr. Joseph Rickard, Druggist, of this town.

Issue of August 11, 1826

Died lately in Sumter District, Capt. John R. Murrell, late of Santee, aged about 50 years.
In this town, Mr. John Cox, Overseer of the Poor House, aged about 45.

GEORGETOWN GAZETTE

Issue of August 15, 1826

Died in this town, on Sunday evening last, Mr. John Steele, a native of Monaghan co., Ireland, formerly merchant of Charleston, aged 50 years.

At her residence in Williamsburg District, on the 3d inst., Mrs. Margaret Burgess, in the 51st year of her age.

Issue of August 18, 1826

Married on Thursday last, Mr. Stephen Evans to Mrs. Ann Holmes, both of this town.

Died on Wednesday last, after four days illness, Sarah T. T. Hoddy, aged 7 years, youngest daughter of Mrs. Lucretia Hoddy.

Issue of August 22, 1826

Died in this town on Thursday last, Mr. William Hall, a native of Nova Scotia, aged about 37 years.

Died at Spring Bank, Williamsburg District, on the 2d inst., Mrs. Margaret Burgess, relict of James Burgess, Esq. (eulogy)
                                        Charleston Courier

Issue of August 25, 1826

Died on Black River, on Sunday last, Margaret Hannah, only daughter of Christopher James and Elizabeth Ann Atkinson, aged 1 year, 6 months and 27 days.

Issue of August 29, 1826

Died in Kingstree, on the morning of the 20th inst., Mr. Samuel Dayton Bostwick, in the 21st year of his age. (eulogy).

Issue of September 1, 1826

Married in Marion, on the 24th inst., Mr. Hugh Giles, to Miss Mary Baker, daughter of Mr. John Baker.

Died in this town, on Tuesday last, Christopher, only son of Mr. Stephen Beach, aged about 11 years.

Issue of September 5, 1826

Married in Waye(sic) co., N. C., on the 8th ult., by the Rev. John Howell, Mr. Hobhead Speight, of Green co., aged 77½ years, weight 99¼ lbs., to Mrs. Sally Peacock, of the former county, aged 44 years, weight 333¼ lbs.

Issue of September 8, 1826

Died, yesterday, James, aged 2½ years, son of Mr. John Knox.

Issue of September 15, 1826

Died near this town, on Monday last, Mrs. Palmer, consort of Mr. Jesse Palmer.

On Tuesday last, Miss Ann Gorman, aged 20.

Last night, Mr. William Ferguson Brown, aged 25, a native of Charleston.

GEORGETOWN GAZETTE

Issue of September 19, 1826

Died near Georgetown, on Saturday last, Mrs. Margaret Hales, conosrt of Mr. Alexander Hales.

Issue of September 22, 1826

Died this morning, Col. Robert Andrew Taylor, in the 35th year of his age.
On Tuesday last, Mr. John Waldo, aged 64.
Died in Kingstree, on the 24th day of August, Capt. Samuel Malcomson, aged about 55 years...a native of County Down, Ireland, emigrated to this country about 30 years ago.

Issue of September 26, 1826

Died on Friday last, Mr. Moses Solomon, aged 27.
On Sandy Island, on the 20th inst., Mary Ann, only child of John P. and Rachel Rice, aged about 3 months.

Issue of September 29, 1826

Died in Sumter District, on the morning of the 5th of September, in the 22d year of his age, Mr. Robert Burgess.
Sampson Solomon applied for admn. of Moses Solomon, late of Georgetown...29 Sept 1826.
Estate of Capt. Alexander M'Night, late of Williamsburg District., decd....   John G. McKnight, Administrator
Sept. 26   Jane McKnight, Administratrix

Issue of October 6, 1826

Died in this town, Mr. James Steele, son of Mrs. Sarah Steele, aged about 18 years. (eulogy).
Died at the residence of Maj. Harrell, in Marion District, Charlotte Elizabeth, aged 2 years and 10 months, only child of John J. and Sarah Raphill.
At Lebanon Springs, on the 22d ult., William Crafts, Esq., late of Charleston.
At the residence of Col. M'Kinne, in the Sand Hills, Ga., Dr. John Powell, of Louisville, in the 79th year of his age.
In Marlborough, S. C., John McFarland, Esq., aged about 65, late of the firm of Course and McFarland, of Georgetown.

Issue of October 13, 1826

Died yesterday, Thomas Arthur, son of the late Mr. Arthur Christian, aged 2 years and 8 months.

Issue of January 26, 1827 [American Antiquarian Society, Worcester, Mass.]

Thomas Hartley applied for letters of admn. on the estate o fhis brother Amos Hartley, late of Santee, deceased....
                        25 Jan 1827

THE HARVEST

[The only known issues of this newspaper are in the American Antiquarian Society, Worcester, Mass.]

Issue of October 17, 1828 (Vol. I, #9)

All persons having demands against Major Joshua Ward, late of Waccamaw deceased....   Joshua John Ward, Qual. Exr. Aug 5, 1828

All persons having any demands against William M. Wilson, late of Georgetown deceased....   William G. Linerieux, Exr. Sept 9, 1828

All persons having demands against Daniel G. Williams, late of Georgetown, deceased....   John Hawkins, Junr, Admr. Aug 15

Issue of December 19, 1828

Clara Withers, daughter of Francis R. and his late wife Mrs. Clara Shackelford, died in this town on the 17th aged 3 years 9 months and 8 days....

WINYAW INTELLIGENCER

Issue of November 15, 1817 (Volume 1, #11)

Married in Charleston, on Monday 29th September last, by the Rev. Mr. Galuchat, Mr. Robert A. Paisley, late of this town, to Miss Charlotte J. Will of that city.
Married at Philadelphia, on the 28th October, by the Rev. Mr. Carr, at the residence of Stephen Girard, Esq., Gen. Henry Lallemand, to Miss Harriet Girard, niece of Stephen Girard. There were present Messrs Cte. de Survilliers, Marshal de Grouchy, and son, Generals Vandamme and Charles Laileland sen....
in this town on Thursday evening last, by the Rev. William Capers, James Hardwick, Esq. to Miss Mary Susan Malvina Skrine, all of this place.
Died on the 13th ult. in Sumter District, Mr. Thomson Hargroves Hanks, aged 21 years, late deputy Sheriff of that and Darlington District. (eulogy).
In Edgefield District, on September last, Benjamin C. Yancey, attorney at law, of Charleston, S. C....representative in the legislature of this state. Telescope
Died in Pendleton District, on the 16th inst.,Mr. John Gilleland, aged 116 years, 85 of which he had lived in America. He has left a numerous offspring of children and grandchildren.
Died in Iredell Co., N. C., on the 1st September, an African names Titus, celebrated for his arden warmth in the cause of religion (long eulogy). Raleigh Minerva
Recently in N. C., Col. John Mercer, of Fredericksburg, Va. He was the son of Gen. Mercer who fell in the fields of Princeton in the cause of American liberty....Raleigh Minerva
Departed this life at Savannah on the 29th ult., Mrs. Ann Prince, aged 66.
At Columbia, S. C., on the 30th ult., Mrs. Mary Ann Hart, consort of Capt. Benjamin Hart.
At Marion Court House on the 11th inst., Mr. Neill Hughs, a native of N. C., but for 7 years past a resident of Marion District.
Persons indebted to the Estate of John Carnes, deceased, for Boarding and Schooling....
Nov. 12   H. L. Carnes
All persons indebted to the estate of Dr. John R. Futhey....
October 11   Saml. I. Thurston, Adm'r.

Issue of April 4, 1818

On Monday the 20th inst., at the late residence of Jesse Windham, deceased, near China Grove, will be sold all persons estate of said deceased.
April 1   Robert Cotten, adm'r.

Died on the 4th of February, near New-Milford (Conn.), aged 87 years and 2 months, Mrs. Hanna Waldo, mother of Mr. John Waldo of this place, and widow of the Rev. Samuel Waldo, former pastor of the Bpatist Church in Paulings Town (New York) (eu-ogy).
at Charleston, on the 18th of March, in the 69th year of her age, Mrs. Hannah Walker, relict of Mr. Richard Walker, late of Georgetown district, and sisters of Messrs. John and Samuel Smith late of this town...member of the Baptist Church...left children and grandchildren. (eulogy).

WINYAW INTELLIGENCER

Issue of January 13, 1819

All persons having any demands against the Estate of Mrs. Martha Grier (late of Pee Dee) are requested to render them....
January 9, 1819   Benjamin Grier.

All persons having demands against the Estate of George Smith, individually, or as survivor of George & Savage Smith, are requested to furnish statements....
November 27   S. S. Smith, in Charleston)
                               P. Cuttino, in Georgetown) Adm'ors.

All persons indebted to the Estate of David Prior deceased, are requested to make payment....
December 30   E. Waterman, Ordinary.

Issue of January 16, 1819

All persons having demands against the Estate of the late Capt. John Bossard, are hereby requested to render them....
January 16, 1819   John Withers,   ) Ex'rs.
                               Joseph S. Bossard)

All persons having demands against the Estate of Colonel Lamuel Benton, late of Darlington district, are requested to render them....
Darlington Ct. House,   Lawrence Prince) Administ'rs.
January 16, 1819   Isaiah Dubose)

Issue of January 23, 1819

Married near this place on Wednesday evening last, by the Rev. M. H. Lane, Rector of this Parish, Henry A. Middleton, Esq. of Charleston, to Miss Knoloch, daughter of Cleland Kinloch, Esq.
    in this place, on the same evening by the Rev. Hugh Fraser, Mr. Walter K. Penny, of New-York, to Miss Mary C. Anderson, of this place.

Issue of January 27, 1819

Died, in England Mr. Griffith Wright, aged 87 years. He was perhaps, the oldest proprietor of a newspaper in the kingdom, if not in the world, having established <u>Wright's Leeds Intelligencer</u> in 1751, nine years before his Majesty came to the throne.
    We regret to learn (says the Franklin Gazette) that Captain Gamble, that gallant and accomplished officer, died at Pisa on the 10th October last.

Issue of January 30, 1819

Married on Thursday evening last, by the Rev. Mr. Lance, Mr. James C. Coggeshall of the House of N. Coggeshall & Son, to Miss Margaret Prior, youngest daughter of the late David Prior.
    Died, in Baltimore on Friday night last, the 22d inst. the Rev. John Wesley Bond, in the 35th year of his age...a useful minister of the Gospel in the itinerant connection of the Methodist Episcopal Church....
    Those to whom Adam McDonald late of Williamsburg district, deceased are indebted, are requested to send in a statement....to Mr. Samuel N. McDonald at Murray's ferry on Santee...
June 20   Catharine McDonald, Administratrix.

WINYAW INTELLIGENCER

Issue of February 6, 1819

Married, near Conwayborough, a short time since, by the Rev. E. Bird, Mr. Bethel Durant, to Miss Hannah Hankins, all of Horry District.

Issue of February 10, 1819

Died, in Christ Church Parish, on the 26th ult., Joseph Dubose, Esq. in the 42d year of his age. This gentleman had resided with his brother at South Santee ferry during the last year, and left that place about a month since....

Issue of February 13, 1819

All persons who have any demands against the Estate of George Pawley, late of All-Saints Parish, deceased, are requested to render them....
February 10   John Withers, Jun'r, Executor.

Married, on Thursday evening last, by the Rev. Mr. Lance, Samuel Smith, Esq. Attorney at Law, to Miss Emma Waring--all of this place.

Issue of February 17, 1819

Died, near Bladensburg on the 9th inst. Gen. A. T. Mason, representative to congress from Virginia. He was killed in a duel fought with muskets at ten paces distance.

Issue of February 20, 1819

Married on Wednesday evening last, by Solomon Cohen, Esq. Mr. Sampson Solomons, to Miss Molsey Joseph, daughter of Mr. Lizar Joseph, all of this place.

Issue of February 24, 1819

Married at Society Hill, on Thursday the 11th inst. by the Rev. Mr. Dossey, Mr. Joseph R. Gilbert, of Fayetteville, N. C. to Miss Eliza Wilds Punch, eldest daughter of the late John Punch.
    at Black Mingo, on Thursday evening last, by the Rev. Jer. Russell, Mr. John Graham, jun'r to Miss Elizabeth Smith, daughter of Adam Smith, of Williamsburgh.
    Died, in this place on Satruday last, of a pulmonary disease, Edmund Park Botsford, only son of the Rev. Edmund Botsford, aged 17 years.
    ____ yesterday morning, at Mr. Green's residence on Black River, Mrs. Mary Coachman, the amiable consort of John Coachman, Esq. of that place.
    ____ on Waccamaw, on Sunday last, Capt. Samuel Allston.

Issue of February 27, 1819

All persons in any way indebted to the Estate of James Sparkman, deceased, are required to make immediate payment....
Feb. 27   Moses Miller, Executor.

WINYAW INTELLIGENCER

Issue of March 3, 1819

Married on the 25th ult. Wm. R. Maxwell Esq. to Miss Anna Maria Johnston, eldest daughter of Wm. Johnston, Esq. of North Santee.

Issue of March 10, 1819

Married, in Bloomfield, Pickaway county, on the 7th July by Christian Brotherin, Esquire, Mr. William Montgomery, aged 54, to Mrs. Sarah Short, aged 68 years.
In Hamstead, Mass. Mr. Job Eaton, to Miss Ruth Sawyer, after an undisturbed courtship of six years.
In the same place, Mr. Michael Shute, to Miss Olive Johnson, after a plasant(sic) and undisturbed courtship of only 8 years, 7 months and 6 days.
In Newburyport, Mr. Samuel Somerby, to Miss Hannah George, after a pleasant, undistrubed and uninterrupted courtship of 17 years, 8 months and 23 days.
In Boston, Mr. Nathaniel Nottage, aged 62, to Mrs. Harriet Witherbe, aged 29, after a courtship of 3 weeks and 6 days.
On Sunday the 27th of December last, Mr. John Miller, of Brothers Valley township, to Miss Susannah Didy, of Alleghany, Pennsylvania, after an agreeable courtship of 30 minutes.

Issue of March 13, 1819

Died, in this town, on Wednesday last, Mrs. Catharine Carville, aged 43 years.

Issue of March 17, 1819

Married, in Edgefield District, on the 25th of Feb. last, Col. James Postell, aged 74, to Miss Jane Bertwhistle, aged 18, a native of London.
At Verona, on the 9th inst. by the Rev'd Elijah Stebbins, Mr. Daniel Butts, of Augusta, aged 15, to Miss Elizabeth Matoon, of the former place, aged 11 years. Two brothers, the eldest 8, the other 15, married mother and daughter, the mother 35, the daughter 11.   Utica N. Y. paper.
Died, in London (in prison), on the 7th December last, Daniel Lovell, Esq. Editor of the London Statesman. His death was occasioned by a long imprisonment.

Issue of March 31, 1819

By permission of Eleazer Waterman, Esq. Ordinary for Georgetown District, will be sold all the perishable articles belonging to the estate of Mrs. Martha Jaudon....   Isaac Jaudon,
March 31   Administrator.

Issue of April 10, 1819

Married at Charleston, on Wednesday evening last, Ezra Benjamin, of this town, to Miss Susan M. Poyas, of the former place.
Married at Philadelphia, 20th ult., Mr. Robert S. Coffin, Esq. (Boston Bard) to Miss Sarah Moore, of Philadelphia.

WINYAW INTELLIGENCER

Issue of April 24, 1819

Died, at Portsmouth, N. H. of the dropsy, Mrs. Polly Blasdell, wife of Mr. Daniel Blasdell, aged 46....

Issue of April 28, 1819

Married in Franklin county, N. C. on the 11th inst., General Calvin Jones of Raleigh, to Mrs. Temperance Ones.
Died in Frederickburg county (sic) Va. in the month of October last, Mr. Richard Mastin, in the 98th year of his age. And on the 3d of January last, Mrs. Ann Mastin, in the 100th year of her age. They were both steady members of the Church of Christ upwards of 40 years and lived together as man and wife more than 70 years.

Issue of May 1, 1819

Died, on the 26th April, at the residence of major Keith, on Black River, major Charles Brown, an officer of the revolutionary army, aged 57. (eulogy).
All persons indebted to the late Mr. Samuel Allston, of All-Saints Parish, deceased, are requested to make immediate payment....
Waccamaw, April 23   Jos. Allston)
                          J. H. Allston) Adm'rs.

Issue of May 5, 1819

Died on the 30th ult., near Avant's ferry, on Black river, (Georgetown District), Mrs. Sarah Ann Davis, late consort of John C. Davis, Esq'r...left a disconsolate husband and three small children.

Issue of May 8, 1819

Died, at Belmont (Maryland) on the 23d ult., Alexander C. Hanson, formerly Editor of the Federal Republican, and late a senator in Congress from that state.
At Lanark, in Scotland, on the same day, William Dauglass and his wife. They were born within the same hour, both baptized together in the same church, and have never been separated. At the age of 19 they were married with the consent of their relatives, in the church where they had been baptized...age of 100 years, buried beneath the baptismal fount....
At Westport (Ms) Peleg Tripp, aged about 20....

Issue of May 12, 1819

Died at New-York on the 1st inst., P. Leseinger, a native of Germany, who resided at 74 Bar___ street...was 70 years old and had no family.

Issue of May 15, 1819

Married on Thursday the 6th inst., by the Mr. Henry Gibbs, at the residence of Major Ward on Waccamaw, Mr. Joseph P. La Bruce, to Miss Catharine, daughter of Major Ward--all of All Saints Parish.
in this town on Thursday evening last, by the Rev. Mr. Lance, Mr. Charles Munnerlyn to Hannah Shackelford, all of this place.

WINYAW INTELLIGENCER

Issue of May 19, 1819

Married on the 3d inst., at the house of Benjamin Prescott, Esq. Cochesville, near Waterford, (N.Y.), Mr. Laurent Clerc, of La Balme (France) to Miss Eliza C. Boardman, of Whitesborough, N.Y. both deaf and dumb. Mr. Clerc is one of the principal instructors in the Asylum for the Deaf and Dumb at Hartford, Conn.

Issue of June 2, 1819

Married on Thursday evening last, by the Rev. Mr. Gibbes, Mr. Benjamin P. Fraser of Waccamaw, to Miss Agnes Kirkpatrick, of Pee Dee

Died, on this town, on Sunday evening last, Augustus Britton, aged 5 months, son of Mary and Gabriel W. Wayne.

Issue of June 5, 1819

Melancholy Accident! On Thursday last as Mr. Jacob Cohen was bringing up from Charleston, his sister, niece, Miss Minis and Mrs. Minis the elder, of Savannah, to his place, the carriage was upset in entering the flat at North Santee, where notwithstanding the exertions of Mr. Cohen, the carriage sunk before Mrs. Minis could be got out, and she together with the horses was unfortunately drowned....in the 74th year of her age...on a visit to her daughter Mrs. Levi Myers of this place....

Issue of June 9, 1819

Married on Thursday evening last, by the Rev. Mr. Fraser, Mr. Samuel Pedreaux, to Mrs. Esther Lawson, all of this district.

Married at Farley, in Culpepper, on Thursday evening last, by the Rev. Mr. Woodville, Samuel Appleton Storrow, Esq. an officer of the army of the U. S., to the much admired Miss Eliza Hill Carter, only daughter of William Champe Carter, Esq....
Fredericksburg (Va.) Herald, May 26.

Died in Sumter District, Clarendon county, a few days since, Widow Hicks, aged 104 years.

in Georgia, on the 17th ult. in the 43d year of his age, the Hon. William Hawkins, late Governor of North Carolina.

Issue of June 12, 1819

Died in Augusta, Rackeline Paccarotti, aged two months and 26 days. This child was conceived in Italy and born in Africa has been to the Havana and Savannah, and died in Augusta, 28th May 1819.

At Dudley (Mass) January 30th, Mrs. Mary Day, wife of Col. Johnathan Day, aged 74--they had lived in a married state upwards of 50 years.

Issue of June 23, 1819

Died in this town on Friday evening last, Ann, aged 18 months; and on Monday last Henry, aged 2 months, children of Hannah and Thomas Chapman, Collector, of this place.

WINYAW INTELLIGENCER

Issue of June 30, 1819

Married at Columbia, on the 15th inst. by Rev. Mr. Clifton, Rev. Samuel Dunwoody, to Miss Elizabeth H. Harrison, all of Columbia.

Died, on Friday last, on Sampit, Martha Elizabeth Ann, aged 12 months, daughter of Charlotte and Harburton Dubose.

Issue of July 3, 1819

Died on Thursday last, after a short illness, Mr. Peter Vreeland (sic), bricklayer, aged 23 years, a native of New Jersey.

Issue of July 24, 1819

Married on Thursday last, by the Rev. Mr. Hill, Mr. John Knox to Miss Molsey Davis, daughter of the late Wm. Davis--all of this place.

Issue of July 28, 1819

Died on the 1st inst. at Penn Yann, Ontaior County (N.Y.), Jemima Wilkinson, commonly called the "Universal Friend"...aged 66 years....   Philadelphia Paper.

Issue of August 7, 1819

Died in this town on Wednesday evening last, after a short illness, in the 22d year of his age, Mr. James Rafferty, a native of Dublin, Ireland.

same evening, Hannah Martha, daughter of John W. and Elizabeth S. Shackleford aged 14 months.

Died on Thursday evening last after a short illness, Dr. James Bogle. He was a native of Virginia and has resided little more than two years in this town...left a wife and three infant children. (eulogy).

Issue of August 14, 1819

Married on Thursday evening last, by the Rev. Mr. Hill, Mr. John Tarbox, to Miss Sarah F. Avant, all of this place.

Died, at North Inlet, on the 9th, Mr. John M'Lorinan, a native of Belfast, Ireland.

Died at the sea-short, near this place, on Wednesday morning last, Capt. Joseph Pyatt.

Issue of August 18, 1819

Died on Wednesday last, at his residence on the sea-short, Captain Joseph Pyatt, in the 32d year of his age. The deceased had experienced in early life that orphanage which springs from the grave...a graduate of the South-Carolina college (eulogy).

on Black River on Wednesday last, John Coachman, eldest son of William and Hannah Green, aged 3 years and 8 months.

on Waccamaw on Saturday last, Eleanor Caroline, only daughter of Mr. A. Palmer, aged 17 months.

Died on the 17th ult. at the Vale of Jocasso, in Pendleton District, South Carolina, Mrs. Eliza Pratt Daniel, daughter of the late Mr. Richard Weightman, of Alexandria, and consort of Chisley Daniel, Esq. aged 28 years.

WINYAW INTELLIGENCER

Issue of August 25, 1819

Died at Long-Branch, state of New-Jersey, on the 9th of August, the Hon. John F. Grimke, Senior Associate Judge of the Courts of Sessions and Common Pleas of this State, in the 67th year of his age....
at Bath, (Eng) Dr. Solomon, patentee of "the Balm of Giliad" in Dennis (Mass), Mrs. Betsey, relict of Mr. Edward Crowell, who died a few years since. They both lived together in the marriage state 70 years, and both departed in the 95 year of their age. No less than 375 have descended from them of whom 307 are now living ...
Lieut Ira Connor, was killed on the 21st of August 1817(sic) in the third attack upon fort Hat. in Mexico. He sailed from New-Orleans about the 6th February 1817 for Galveston, in company with generals Mina and Young...(eulogy).

Issue of September 1, 1819

Married in Boston, 15th inst., by the Rev. Dr. Baldwin, Mr. Edward H. Jenkins, to Miss Nancy Brown. This is the 2000th couple married by Dr. B. in less than 29 years.
Died on Waccamaw, on the 26th ult. in the 55th year of her age, Mrs. Martha Rebecca Green, consort of Mr. John Green. (eulogy)
in this town on Friday evening last, Mrs. Elizabeth Brown, a native of New-York, and consort of Mr. William Brown, tailor.

Issue of September 5, 1819

Died, in Charleston on Wednesday evening last, Col. Keating Lewis Simons. (eulogy). Courier.
in this town yesterday morning, Mr. Patrick Gould, aged about 60 years, a native of Ireland.
in Princeton (N.J.) on the 21st ult., the Rev. Samuel Stanhope Smith, D. D. late President of Princeton College.

Issue of September 11, 1819

Married at Woodbury, Mr. Aaron Hurlbut, of Danbury to Mrs. Laura L. Smith...married on the 11th of July.
Died in this town, on the morning of the 8th inst., Mrs. Mary Walker, in the 48th year of age...leaving a numerous family of children....(eulogy).
on Tuesday morning last, Thomas William, second son of Thomas and Ann Henning, at the age of four years, one month and fourteen days.
on Thursday evening last, James, aged about 2 years, son of the Rev. James C. Howren.
All persons having demands against Patrick Gould, late of Georgetown, deceased, are requested to render them....
September 11   John Patterson, Adm'r.

Issue of September 15, 1819

Married in Buzrah, Conn on Wednesday evening last, Mr. John Bate, of Williamstown, Mass. to Miss Mary Ann Bass, of the former place, after a courtship of one hour.
(long obit. of Mrs. Mary Walker).
Died on last Monday night, on Waccamaw, at the age of 23 years, Mrs. Sarah W. Allston, consort of Joseph W. Alston, Esq. and

WINYAW INTELLIGENCER

daughter of the late Captain David Prior. (eulogy).
    at North-Inlet, on Monday last, in the 20th year of his age, Mr. Philip Rafferty, a native of Dublin, Ireland.

Issue of September 18, 1819

    Died, at his residence in Williamsburgh District, on the 2nd inst., Capt. John Gulton, an old and respectable inhabitant. (eulogy).
    Died at Philadelphia, on the 1st inst. of dropsy in the chest, aged 53, Gen. John Rutledge, of South-Carolina. (eulogy).

Issue of September 22, 1819

    Married, at Camden, Mass. Mr. Peling Smith, aged 68 years, to Miss Lucy Cotherel, aged 21.
    (Died) recently and suddenly, Mrs. Sarah W. Allston, consort of Joseph W. Allston, Esq. of Waccamaw, whose death was announced on Wednesday last. (eulogy)
    Died in Marion District, on the 7th instant, Esther Trezerant; and on the 10th Eliza Charlotte: children of Francis A. & Elizabeth Wayne, the eldest about 7 years and youngest about 3 years of age.
    in Marion district, on the 10th instant, Mrs. Mary Grice, late consort of William H(?) Grice, Esq. of said district.
    Died at Sampit, on Friday evening last, in the 17th year of her age, Mrs. Sarah A. DuBose, wife of Mr. Hugh DuBose.
    Died in upper Canada, on Saturday Aug. 28th, the Duke of Richmond, Gov. General of the Canadas. The Duke of Richmond was the heir of one of the natural sons of Charles II who was created Duke of Richmond, 1675. He was born 1764, and succeeded his uncle the late Duke, in 1806...left a family of 14 children, Charles, his eldest son and heir, was born in 1791.

Issue of September 25, 1819

    Died on Wednesday last, at St. James'Santee, Thomas Clark Mitchell, Esq. son of the late Edward Mitchell, in the 25th year of his age...left a wife and child.
    in this town, on the same day, Mrs. Sarah Cock, aged 78 years.
    same day, Catharine Ann Hudson, aged 5 years and 9 months, daughter of Davia(sic) & Ann Davies.
    in Charleston, on the 17th inst. of the prevailing fever, the Rev. Henry T. Fitzgerald, in the 22d year of his age, one of the officiating ministers of the Methodist Church in that city, having been appointed to that station at the last So. Carolina Conference. (eulogy).

Issue of September 29, 1819

    Died, in Missouri Territory after six day's illness, Edward D. Smith, M. D. Prof. Chem and Min: in the South Carolina College. (eulogy).
    Died in Marion District on the 22d inst., Mary, aged 1 year and 9 months, daughter of Francis A. Wayne.
    in this town on Monday last, Abn Catharine, aged 9 years 4 months and 20 days, eldest daughter of Clement Broquer.
    Died of a fever, on Saturday the 18th inst. in Little Ogechee district, Chatham County (Geo.), Mr. Moses Carter, aged 93. This gentleman was born in one of the Carolinas, to which States, with

65

that of Georgia, his residence has always been confined. His wife, an old lady, died 10 days previous.
Died in Upper Seymour street, Lond, 13th of July last, in his 75th year Rev. Wm. Percy, Rector of St. Paul's Church, Radcliffeborough, and formerly of Queen's Squre Chapel, Westminster.

Issue of October 2, 1819

Died at Portsmouth, N. H. on the 18th ult., the Hon. John Langdon, formerly senator in Congress, and more recently governor of New Hampshire.

Issue of October 6, 1819

Married at Smithville, Grunswick County, N. C. on the 23d ult by the Rev. Wm. M. Kennedy, Nicholas Talley, Methodist stationed preacher at Fayetteville, to Miss Amey Ann Potter, of the former place.
Mr. Isaac A. Cohen, merchant, of Kingstree, who died at that place in the 22d year of his age. (eulogy)
Died at Port Spain, in the Island of Trinidad, on the 22d of august last, in the 34th year of his age, Commodore Oliver Hazard Perry, the hero of Lake Erie. (eulogy).

Issue of October 9, 1819

Married, at Savannah, on the 30th ult., by the Rev. William Capers, Mr. Jacob Bryan, merchant of that city, to Miss Margaret Bedout of this place.
Died at Waccamaw on the 26th ult., William, aged 3 years 4 months and 13 days, only son Dr. William J. and Elizabeth Buford.
at Santee the same day, Francis S. Lawson, aged 4 years, 2 months and 13 days, youngest son of the late John Lawson.

Issue of October 13, 1819

Died in Charleston, on the 4th inst. after a painful illness of nine weeks, aged 23 years, Miss Harriet Spindler. (eulogy).

The subscribers having obtained letters of administration on the Estate of Dr. James Bogle, late of Georgetown, deceased, request all payment immediately....
Oct. 13   John W. Jeanerett, Adm'r
                    Sarah Bogle, Adm'x.

Issue of October 16, 1819

Died on the 4th inst. in Sumpter District, near Sumpterville, at Capt. Leonard White's residence, after an illness of three days, Mr. David P. Owens, of Williamsburgh District, but a native of Marion District, S. C.
____ near Wiltown, on Saturday last, after an illness of many months, John Zuill, son of the late Capt. James Zuill of that place, in the 12th year of his age.
Died at North Inlet on Wednesday last, the 12th inst., Mr. Morris L. Henry (of the house of M. L. Henry & Co. of this place) a native of London, but for many years a resident and valuable citizen of this town...left an amiable wife and three children....

WINYAW INTELLIGENCER

Issue of October 20, 1819

Died, in this town, on Saturday evening last, Robert, aged about 7 years, only son of Mr. Charles Munnerlyn, of this place.
Died, in Salem, on the night of the 28th of August, one hour after she had given birth...a loving son, Agnes Eliza M'Faddin, the amiable consort of John M'Faddin, in the 31st year of her age. (eulogy).
At his seat in Williamsburgh on the night of the 26th August, R. Sidney Witherspoon, in the 25th year of his age...left wife and two small children. (eulogy).

Issue of October 23, 1819

Married, in this town, on Sunday evening last by the Rev. Mr. Hill, Mr. Thomas G. Fincklay to Miss Tabitha Ann Stewart, all of Black River.
Died in this town on Thursday last, after an illness of some months, in the 48th(?) year of her age, Miss Sarah Cock...a member of the Baptist Church. (eulogy).
on the evening of the same day, after a short illness, Sarah, aged about 7 years, daughter of Mr. P. Cuttino, of this town.
The subscribers having obtained Letters of Administration on the Estate of Morris L. Henry, late of Georgetown, deceased, request all persons having claims against said estate to render them ....
Oct. 23   Levy Salomon) Adm'rs
                           Benj'n Salomon)
                           Meriam Henry, Adm'x.

Issue of October 27, 1819

Married at North-Inlet, on the 24th inst by the Rev. Mr. Fraser, Mr. Francis P. Rolando to Miss Mary Provaux, both of Charleston, So. Ca.
in Wilmington, N. C. on the 10th inst., Rev. William M. Kennedy, stationed preacher of the Methodist Episcopal Church in that town, to Miss Ann Jones.
We are again called to place in this department of our paper, the name of John Withers, who bid adieu to time on Sunday morning last....(eulogy).
Died, on the 12th ult., at the house of capt. Simeon Timmons, Jeffries creek, Marion district, S. C. Doct. John Johnson, formerly of Lancaster district, much regretted....

Issue of October 30, 1819

Married at North-Inlet, on the 24th inst by the Rev. Mr. Fraser, Mr. Francis G. Rolando to Mrs. Mary Provaux, both of Charleston So. Ca.
Died in this town on Thursday morning last, in the 66th year of his age, Mr. Robert C. McDaniel...left an example worthy of imitation by his children and friends.
Died on Thursday evening last, Richard, aged 1 year and 8 months, youngest son of Mr. Richard Shackelford, of this town.
All persons having demands against the Estate of Mrs. Elizabeth Pawley, late of Georgetown deceased, are required to render them....
Oct. 30   John W. Pawley, Adm'r.

WINYAW INTELLIGENCER

Issue of November 3, 1819

All persons having demands against the Estate of Mrs. Susan Pawley, late of Georgetown, deceased, are required to render them ....
Oct. 30   John W. Pawley, Adm'r.
Died at his residence in Newark, N. J. on the 17th inst., Hon. Elisha Boudinot, a venerable patriot....
All persons having demands against Elizabeth Cock late of Georgetown, deceased, are requested to render them....
Nov. 3   Richard Shackelford, Adm'r.

Issue of November 6, 1819

Married, at Society-Hill, on Sunday evening, last, by the Rev. Mr. Ellis, Mr. William White, of BlackMingo, and tax collector for this district, to Miss Elizabeth R. Hale, daughter of Dr. William Hale, of the former place.
Died in Virginia, Mrs. Dorothea Baughn, aged 103 years, lacking nine days....had ten children, nine of them she raised to be men and women; the other died about eight years of age.
Obituary notices and biographical sketch of Thomas Miller, Esquire, deceased late Clerk of the Branch of the Bank of the State of South Caroline at Georgetown. On Tuesday last this amiable young man closed his eyes upon time...son of the late Abner Miller, of Marlborough district. During the war, and for a year or two after, kept a school in Darlington distirct...in the 26th year of his age.

Issue of November 10, 1819

Married in Pottstown (Pa.) Mr. Frederick Berkhart, cooper, to the charming, tender, fascinating Mrs. Nancy Herbet, being both about four score year old, and she having buried her former husband not longer than eight weeks ago.
On the 24th ult by the Rev. John M'Intyre at his residence, Mr. Archibald M'Intyre of Chatham, S. C. to Miss Ann Graham, eldest daughter of Archibald Graham, Esq. dec'd.
Died in Scriven county (Georgia) on the 25th ult., in the 23rd year of her age, Mrs. Susan Bryan, consort of the Rev. Solomon Bryan, late a stationed Methodist preacher in this town. She left an infant son and affectionate husband.
Died in Williamsburgh district on the 12th of October last, Col. John D. Burgess. (eulogy).
Died on Monday evening last, near this place, Mr. Daniel McDonald, a native of Scotland, aged about 38 years. (eulogy)

Issue of November 13, 1819

Died at Fredericktown, on the 26th ult., Thomas Johnson, Esq. the first Governor of Maryland aged 88 years.
Married on board the schooner Little Emily, in Winyaw bay, on Monday evening last, by the Rev. M. H. Lance, Capt. John White, of this town, to Miss Jane Keys of Conwayborough.
Died on Wacamaw, on the 6th inst., John Francis Robert, infant and only child of John Withers Junr. Esq. deceased.
Died at Walterborough, on the 3d inst., Major General William Fishburne, in the 60th year of his age. At the onset of the American Revolution, when only sixteen year of age, he took up arms... member of the State Legislature....

WINYAW INTELLIGENCER

Departed this life at Savannah on Sunday the 31st October, at half past 12 o'clock A. M., Mr. Henry Denison, Co Editor of the Georgia Republican and son of Judge Gilbert Denison, of 3 Rattleborough (Vt.) in the 24th year of his age....

Issue of November 24, 1819

Married in Charleston on Thursday evening last, by the Rev. M. H. Lance, of this place, Mr. Francis Lance to Miss Elizabeth S. Ball, daughter of the late Archibald Ball, of John's Island.

Died at Portsmouth (Va.) Col. Bernard Magnien, another of the revolutionary worthies, who came to this country with the Marquis La Fayette.

suddenly at Northampton (Mass.) on Sunday the 11th inst., the Hon. Caleb Strong, late Governor of that state.

at Poughkeepsie, N. Y. the Hon. Matthias B. Tallmadge, late a Judge of the U. S. Circuit Court for New-York.

In Rowley, the 5th inst., Mr. John Pearson, aged 29....

at Selen's Grove, Pennsylvania, on the 20th inst., at an advanced age, his Excellency Simon Snyder, late Governor of Pennsylvania.

Marshal Blucher died in Silesia on the 12th September.

Issue of December 1, 1819

Married at Wadesborough on the 11th ult., Mr. Thomas P. Ellerbe of Chesterfield district, S. C. to Miss Louisa Lowry, of the former place.

Died on Sunday morning, Nov. 14th, at his residence in Stratford (Conn.) in the 93d year of his age, William Samuel Johnson, L. L. D., late Presidence of Columbia College, &C. Dr. Johnson was the eldest son of the Rev. Dr. Johnson, the first President of the College of that city...born at Straford in 1727, and was educated at Yale College, where he received the degree of A. B. in 1744.

Those persons who have demands against Robert R. M'Daniel, late of this district deceased, are requested to render them....
Dec. 1   John B. M'Daniel, Adm'r.

Issue of December 8, 1819

Married, at Charleston on Thursday evening last, by the Rev. Gadsden, John Axson, Esq. of St. James, Santee, to Miss Mary Gibbes, daughter of the late Benjamin Gibbes, of that city.

All persons having demadns against Mrs. Mary Walker, late of Georgetown, deceased, are requested to render them....
Dec. 4   Benjamin Walker)
                          L. G. Walker) Ex'rs.

Issue of December 11, 1819

Married, near China Grove, on Thursday evening last by the Rev. Jeremiah Russell, Mr. William Ballox of this town, to Miss Mary Jones of the former place.

Married at Society-Hill on Sunday evening last, by the Rev. William Dossey, Mr. Martin Dewitt, Esq. of Darlington district, to Mis Pris------- of the former place.

Married on Sunday the 14th ult., by the Rev. Reubin Pinnell, Mr. Joseph Caldwell, Jr. Editor of the Virginia Reformer, to Miss Ann, daughter of the late Captain John Mitchell, of Shenandoah, near Front Royal.

WINYAW INTELLIGENCER

Died, at Pee Dee on the 3d inst., Martha Gamble, only daughter of James M. & Eliza W. Grier, aged 9 months and 9 days.

Persons holding claims against Col. John D. Burgess, late of Williamsburgh, deceased, are requested to send statements....to P. Cormick, Kingstree.
Kingstree, Dec. 8   William Dollard, Executor.

Issue of December 15, 1819

Died yesterday, Anna, infant daughter of Eleazer and Anna Waterman.

Issue of December 18, 1819

All persons having demands against John B. La Rebour, late of Georgetown, deceased, are requested to render them...
Dec. 18   John M. Larebour, Adm'r.

Issue of December 22, 1819

Married on the 16th inst., by the Rev. Mr. Lance, John Porter jun'r Esq. to Miss Esther Ann Toomer, daughter of Anthony Toomer Esq. deceased....

Issue of December 29, 1819

Will be Hired before the marker on the 1st of January 1820, two Negro Women, field hands, belonging to the Estate of the late James Belin.
December 22.   William Lester.

Died on Sunday last, in the 75th year of his age, Rev. Edmund Botsford, pastor of the Baptist Church in this place. (eulogy).

Died on Sunday last, Mr. James McRae, of Marlborough district, in the 56th year of his age.

Issue of April 5, 1820

Will be sold at the House of Mrs. Sarah King, in All saints Parish, ...Estate of Wm. Sessions, deceased.
March 29th 1820   Solomon McColl, Administrator.

All persons having demands against the late Mr. John Withers Junr. are hereby requested to render in their accounts....
Reb. 12   Francis Withers) Qualified
            Robert Withers) Executors.

All persons having demands against the late Maj. Joseph Allston, of All-Saints, deceased, are required to render their demands...
                    J. H. Allston,
March 22, 1820   Qualified Executor.

All persons having demands against the Estate of Allard Belin, late of Waccamaw deceased, are requested to render them....
Feb 26   Francis Withers, Ex'r.

Issue of July 21, 1824

All persons having demands against the Estate of Major John Keith, deceased, are requested to render them... to B. F. Trapier, in Charleston or to the subscriber.
Dec. 13, 1823.   Paul Trapier, Executor of John Keith.

WINYAW INTELLIGENCER

Issue of September 18, 1824

Died, on Waccamaw, on the 13th inst., Elizabeth Ann, aged 2 years, 11 months and 5 days, youngest daughter of David and Elizabeth Palmer.
in this town on Tuesday night last, Mr. Josiah Ball, printer, aged about 48 years, a native of Massachusetts.

[The issues for the year 1825 are located in the Charleston Library Society.]

Issue of January 1, 1825

Married in Marion District, on the 28th ultimo, by the Rev. Philip Kirton, Mr. Tilman Kalb of Darlington to Miss Eliza, youngest daughter of Valentine Rowell, Esq.
By permission of E. Waterman, Ordinary, will be sold part of the Estate of the late Joseph Allston.
December 24.   John W. Shackelford, Auctioneer.

Issue of January 5, 1825

Died in Philadelphia, on the 24th ult., Mrs. Harriet Lucas Huger, wife of Col. F. K. Huger and daughter of Gen. Thomas Pinckney.
In this town yesterday morning of the croup, Mathias Fowler, aged 24 years, a native of North Carolina.
All persons indebted to the Estate of Paul Trapier, Esq....
January 5, 1825   W. W. Trapier, Admor:

Issue of January 8, 1825

Married at New York on the 21st ult., Mr. Henry A. C. Sturges, to Miss Jane Matilda Cargill.

Issue of January 15, 1825

Died in this town on Wednesday last, Mr. Anthony Potts, in the 32d year of his age...left a wife and four children.
All persons having any demands against the estate of Alexander M'Clinchy, late of Santee, deceased....
January 15.   Elizabeth M'Clinchy, Adm'x.

Issue of January 22, 1825

Died in this town, on Wednesday night last, Mr. James O. Gasque, in the 36th year of his age.
All persons indebted to the estate of Mrs. Charlotte Ann Allston, late of Georgetown, deceased....
January 22.   Joseph W. Allston) Executors.
                                Robert F. W. Allston)

Issue of January 26, 1825

Died on Friday night last, Mr. James B. Berry, in the 26th year of his age.
on Saturday night, Mary Celia, only child of William and Celia McCollough, aged 15 months and 12 days.
At New-Haven, Conn. on the 8th inst., Eli Whitney, Esq., aged

WINYAW INTELLIGENCER

59. (eulogy.)
James C. Postell having made suit for letters of administration on William Glenn Green, deceased....25 Jan.

William M'Collough made suit for letters of administration on the estate of James O. Gasque.

Estate sale...Caleb C. Lenuel, deceased, near the Rope Ferry, on Black River...   Charlotte Lenuel, Administratrix.

Issue of February 2, 1825

Married in this town on Sunday evening last, by the Rev. Lewis Myers, Mr. John Dicks, to Mrs. Mary S. Linerieux, all of this place.

on Thursday evening the 27th ult., by the Rev. Jas. Sinclaire, Mr. D. C. Rowell, of Waccamaw, to Miss Susanna Willton of Marion District.

Died in this place, on the 1st inst., Dr. Henry Denison....
Died in this town, on sunday night last, Mrs. _____ Sanderlin, aged about 60.

Died suddenly, on Sandy Island, on Saturday, 29th ult., the honest William R. Brooks.

Issue of February 5, 1825

Died in this town, on Wednesday last, Mrs. Lucretia Hopkins, aged 46 years, consort of Capt. Charles Hopkins.

Obituary of Dr. Henry Denison, a native of Conn....

Issue of February 9, 1825

Married in Horry District, on the 3d inst., by the Rev. Thomas Durant, Col. Thomas A. Beaty, to Mrs. D. Johnson, all of that place.

On the 27th ult., by the Rev. Henry Gibbes, Dr. John D. Magill, to Miss Mary E. Vereen, all of this District.

Issue of February 12, 1825

Hannah C. Denison, John Waldo, and LeGrand G. Walker... letters of administration of Dr. Henry Denison. 10 Jan 1825.

Issue of March 19, 1825

Died at Northampton, on the 12th inst., Le Grand G. Walker, son of Peter Walker, aged 14 months.

Issue of April 2, 1825

Died in this place on the 31st inst., Miss Mary Green, daughter of the late Joseph Rogers, Esq., in the 22d year of her age.

Issue of April 9, 1825

Died on Santee on Thursday last, after a short illness, Mrs. Mary Small, consort of Mr. William Small.

Issue of April 16, 1825

(eulogy on Mrs. Mary Small)

WINYAW INTELLIGENCER

Issue of April 20, 1825

Married last evening, at Black River, by the Rev. M. H. Lance, Anthony B. Shackelford, Esq., attorney at law, of this place, to Miss Elizabeth Law, of New-London (Conn.)

Died in this town, on the 15th inst., Mrs. Elizabeth Palmer, consort of Jesse Palmer, Esq.

On Sunday last, the 17th inst., Henry, aged 15 months, youngest child of Israel and Eleanor Solomons, of this place.

Issue of April 23, 1825

Married on Thursday evening last, by the Rev. William Capers, John F. Green, Esq. of Black River, to Miss Esther Shackelford, daughter of the late Francis Shackelford, Esq. of this place.

All persons indebted to the estate of Francis Green, deceased ....
April 23, 1825   John Coachman, Executor.

Issue of April 27, 1825

Died at Baltimore, Lt. Joseph Wragg, of the U. S. Navy, in the 36th year of his age.

Issue of April 30, 1825

Married on Thursday evening last, by the Rev. Mr. Hardy, Mr. James H. White, to Miss Mary Capers, all of this place.

Issue of June 4, 1825

Died in this town on Monday last, Sarah, youngest child of Robert and Martha Howren.

Issue of June 8, 1825

Married in this town on Sunday evening last, by the Rev. Mr. Grosvenor, Mr. Alexander Thomas to Miss Rhoda Rice, all of Marion District.

Died on the morning of the 3d inst., Mrs. Mary Shackelford, conosrt of the late John Shackelford, Esqr., of this town.

Issue of June 11, 1825

Married on Thursday evening last, by the Rev. Mr. Hardy, Mr. Anthony Lewis Mariano, to Miss Ann Catharine Hanion, all of this place.

Died in this town, on the evening of the 9th instant, Mr. Samuel M'Collough.

Issue of June 15, 1825

Married on Monday evening last, by the Rev'd Archibald Purifoy, Capt. Charles Hopkins to Mrs. Mary Harvey, all of this place.

Issue of June 25, 1825

Died at New-York, on the morning of the 13th instant, the Rev. John Summerfield, in the 27th year of his age, and 8th year of his ministry.

WINYAW INTELLIGENCER

Died in New York Hospital, on the 12th May 1825, Madam Helene Victoire Aimee Soliance, daughter of St. Alphonse Raymond Espagnol. Death of Daniel D. Tompkins.... N. Y. National Advocate, June 14.

Issue of June 29, 1825

Died on the evening of the 27th inst., Mrs. Henrietta Rothmahler, an old and respectable inhabitant of this town.

In Lincoln County, N. C. on the 15th ult., Rev. Daniel Asbury, aged 64.

At New Orleans on the 27th ult., James Sterrett, formerly a Capt. in the U. S. Army and late Naval Officer of that port.

Issue of July 9, 1825

Married on Thursday evening last, by the Rev. Mr. Hardy, Mr. Richard Singleton, to Mrs. Catharine C. Patterson, widow of the late Mr. John C. Patterson, of this place.

Issue of July 13, 1825

Departed this life at his residence in Marion District, Gen. Thomas Godbold, in the 53d year of his age. (eulogy).

Died, at Kingstree, a short time since, Mr. Francis Siau, aged about 30 years, formerly a citizen of this place.

Died near this town, on the 9th inst., Robert, youngest child of John and Mary Exum.

Issue of July 23, 1825

Died on the 17th inst., at his residence on Waccamaw River, Horry District, Benjamin Gause, Esq., in the 63d year of his age. (eulogy).

Death of Thomas Jefferson Lee, scarce 18 years of age. (eulogy)

Died in Beaufort, S. C., on the 23d May last, the Rev'd Mason L. Weems, of Dunfries, Va., well known as author of Life of Washington.

Issue of August 3, 1825

Died in this town on Monday evening last, Mr. David Irvin, a native of Coothhill, Ireland, but for the last 5 years, a respectabel mechanic of this place.

Issue of August 17, 1825

Died at Withersville, the summer retreat of some of the inhabitants of our town, on Friday last, the 12th inst., Rev. John S. Capers, of the Methodist Episcopal Church.

On Sampit, a short time since, Mr. Thomas Brit, aged about 115 years.

Issue of August 20, 1825

Died yesterday, in the 28th year of his age, Mr. Arthur Christian, a native of Ireland, an inhabitant of this town...left a wife and children.

At Cox's Ferry, Horry District, on the 25th ult., Mr. Joseph Cox, in the 60th year of his age.

WINYAW INTELLIGENCER

Issue of August 24, 1825

Married at Roadstown, N. J. on the 10th inst., by Rev. H. Smalley, Mr. David A. Bokee of N. Y. to Miss Sarah Ann Dowdney, of this place.

Issue of August 27, 1825

Married near Bradford Springs, on the 16th inst., Col. William H. James, aid-de-camp to Gov. Manning, to Miss Mary Ellen, daughter of Col. Wm. H. Capers, all of Sumter District.

Issue of August 31, 1825

Died in Charleston, on the evening of the 24th inst., Mr. Thomas Jefferson Paisley, in the 22d year of his age, youngest son of Mrs. Ann Paisley, of this town.
At the same place, on the 25th, the Rev. Dr. Furman, Pastor of the Baptist Church of that city.

Issue of September 3, 1825

Died suddenly at Greenville (S.C.), on the 11th ultimo, Miss Mary, daughter of the Rev'd. Wm. B. Johnson, formerly of this place.

Issue of September 7, 1825

Died on Black River, on the first instant, Andrew aged about 4 years, youngest child of Thomas and Ann Westbury.
At Camden on the 23rd ult., John Adamson, Esq., aged 24 years. He died of a gunshot wound....

Issue of September 10, 1825

Died in this place, on Wednesday morning last, Mary Agnes, only daughter of Mr. John J. Green, aged 1 year, 2 months and 15 days.

Issue of September 14, 1825

Married at Oyster Bay, Long Island, N. Y., by the Rev. Mr. Fowler, Mr. Thomas Hilson, to Miss Eleanor Augusta Johnson, both of the Park Theatre.
Died on Monday night last, Mrs. Mary White, consort of Mr. James H. White of this town.
At Charleston, on the 6th inst., Mrs. Sarah Tucker Simons, relict of Maj. James Simons.
At the same place, Mr. Benjamin S. Hart.

Issue of September 17, 1825

Died at Columbia, on the night of Friday, 26th ultimo, Rev. James Norton, having charge of the M. E. Church in that place, in the 38th year of his age, and 18th year of his ministry.

Issue of October 1, 1825

Died at Mr. Kinloch's plantation, near this place, on the 26th ult., John, only child of John and Mary Exum.

WINYAW INTELLIGENCER

At Lafayette, North Island, on Wednesday evening last, Mr. William Tarbox, aged about 40.

In this town on Thursday last, George Washington, youngest child of Mrs. George Skinner.

Issue of October 5, 1825

Died, in this town, on Monday the 3rd inst., Dr. Francis Marion James, in the 22d year of his age, 3rd son of the Hon. W. D. James.

Died at Charleston on Sunday the 2d inst., Capt. Francis Brodut, a native of France, but for many years an inhabitant of this town. (eulogy).

on board the Ship Sarah & Caroline, from Liverpool to Charleston, Samuel McNeel, Esq., many years a respectable merchant of the latter city.

Issue of October 15, 1825

Died in this town, on Wednesday last, Mr. William McKenzie, aged about 50 years, a native of Scotland, but for the last 20 or 30 years, a respectable merchant of this place.

Issue of October 22, 1825

All persons indebted to the late William M'Kenzie....
October 22   M. Calverly)
                M. Fort   ) Executors.

Issue of October 29, 1825

Married at St. Paul's Church, New-York, on the morning of the 20th inst., the Hon. John L. Wilson, of this Town, to Miss Rebecca Eden, of the former place.

Issue of November 2, 1825

Married on Sunday evening last, by the Rev. Tho's H. Taylor, Mr. William Rantin of this place to Miss Mary Smith of New York.

On the same evening, by the Rev. Charles Hardy, Mr. William Sherrell, to Miss Mary Capron, all of this town.

Issue of November 16, 1825

Death of Robert Withers, Esq. (eulogy).

Issue of November 23, 1825

Died at Serenity (near Georgetown), on Tuesday, the 15th inst., Mrs. Elizabeth Davison Blunt, consort of Mr. Thomas M. Blunt, aged 30 years.

Issue of December 3, 1825

Married in Williamsburg District, on Thursday the 24th inst., by the Rev. E. J. Mills, Dr. William Dollard to Miss Louisa, eldest daughter of David McCleary, Esq.

Died at Black River, on Monday the 28th inst., Mrs. Rebecca Dowdney, relict of the late Thomas Dowdney.

WINYAW INTELLIGENCER

Issue of December 7, 1825

Died at Charleston, on the 2d inst., Mr. Isaac Ball, aged 40.

Issue of December 17, 1825

Died near this town, on the 9th inst., Mrs. Ann Garnie, 70 years old, always a resident of this District. (eulogy).

Issue of December 21, 1825

Died on the 16th inst., at Pee Dee, Mr. Harbart Dubose....

Issue of December 28, 1825

All persons indebted to the estate of Capt. Brodut....
Nov. 30.   Francis G. Deliesseline) Exors.
                              W. W. Trapier   )

Issue of August 12, 1826

Married at Tallahassee, Achille Muray, Esq. of Florida, formerly of Italy, eldest son of his late Majesty King Joachim of Naples to Mrs. Catharine Dangerfield Gray, of Tallahassee, formerly of Fredericksburg (Va.) and daughter of Major Byrd C. Willis.
Died in this town, on Thursday last, Mr. John Cox, Keeper of the Poor House, aged 63 years.
All persons indebted to the Estate of Stephen Rouquie, late of Georgetown, deceased, are requested to make immediate payment.... to Gabriel Rouquie.
May 24, 1826.   Hannah Rouquie, Executrix.

Issue of December 27, 1826

Persons having demands against Jacob Myers, deceased, late of Georgetown, are requested to present them....
Nov. 22, 1826.   Abram Myers, Admor:
All persons having demands against the Estate of Thomas Henning(?), deceased, late of Georgetown, are requested to hand them in....
Nov. 1, 1826   B. Green, Adm'r.
All persons indebted to Peter Michau, Jun'r, deceased, late of Santee, are required to amke immediate payment....
Nov. 4   Peter Walker, Administrator.
All persons having demands against the estate of Moses Solomons, deceased, are requested to render them....
Dec. 16.   Sampson Solomons, Admor.
Persons having demands against the late Mr. Joseph Rickard, are requested to render them....
Nov. 4   Robert A. Sands.
All persons having demands against Richard G(?) Green, deceased, are called upon to render them...   Isaac Carr, Admr.

WINYAW INTELLIGENCER
[issues for 1827 located in the Charleston Library Society]

Issue of January 3, 1827

All persons having demands against the Estate of Thomas Henning, deceased, late of Georgetown....B. Green, Adm'r
Nov. 1, 1826.

Issue of January 10, 1827

Married on Thursday evening, the 14th ultimo, by the Rev. Mr. Harrington, Mr. Charles DeLorme, of Charleston, to Miss Elizabeth, second daughter of Mr. Henry Britton, of Sumter District.

Departed this life, on the morning of the 7th inst., after an illness of three weeks, the Rev'd Isaac Hartley, aged 26, pastor of the Methodist Church in this town. (eulogy).

Final notices on the estate of Henry Denison...H. C. Denison Admor, L. G. Walker, Admor. Jan. 10th, 1827.

Issue of January 24, 1827

Married at Charleston on Thursday evening last, by the Rev. Mr. Phillips, William Wilson Godfrey, Esq., Post master of this city to Miss G. V. Harvey, daughter of Capt. Samuel Harvey, of Charleston.

Issue of February 3, 1827

Married on Thursday evening last, by the Rev. Mr. Ludlow, Mr. Moses Tuttle to Mrs. Mary Evans, widow of the late Mr. Thomas Evans, all of this town.

On the same evening at Sampit, by E. Waterman, Esq., Mr. Benjamin F. Shaw, to Mrs. Elizabeth McClinchy, widow of the late Alexander McClinchy.

All persons indebted to the late Samuel Cuttino are requested to make payment.... A. Marvin.
February 3

Issue of February 14, 1827

Married on Thursday evening the 1st instant, by the Rev. Archibald Purifoy, Benjamin Gause, Esq. of Horry District to Miss Sarah B., daughter of Samuel Frink, Esq. of Brunswick co., N. C.

Issue of February 24, 1827

All persons having demands against Amos Hartley deceased are requested to render statements, and those indebted are desired to make payment to William Remley, of Santey....
Feb 17   Thomas Hartley

Issue of March 7, 1827

All persons having demands against the estate of Major John Keith will please render them.   W. W. Trapier
March 7, 1827   Admor debonis non.

Issue of April 14, 1827

Married at Waccamaw on Wednesday evening last, by the Rev. Paul Trapier Keith, Mr. Thomas G. Rice, to Miss Esther Ann Verner, daughter of Mr. John Verner.

WINYAW INTELLIGENCER

At Santee, on Thursday evening last, by the same Reverend Gentleman, Mr. Raphael Rembert to Miss Elizabeth Bailey, daughter of Mr. John Bailey.

On Thursday evening of the 5th inst., by the Rev. J. H. Robertson, Thomas Hemmingway, Esq. to Miss Anne, daughter of the late Benjamin Gause, Esq. of Horry District.

All persons having demands against the late Mrs.Sarah Ford, are requested to render statements and those indebted to make payment to Stephen E. Ford, Qualified Executor.
April 14, 1827

Issue of April 21, 1827

Departed worth is seldom more generally regretted than in the death of Doctor Charles F. Godbold, who departed this life on Sunday the 15th inst. in the 28th year of his age, at his mother's residence in Marion District after an illness of seven days....

All persons having demands against the estate of the late Joseph P. LaBruce are requested to render statements to Le Grand G. Walker..... Catherine LaBruce, Qual Extx.
April 21, 1827 LeGrand G. Walker, Qual. Exr.

Issue of April 28, 1827

Married on Tuesday evening of the 24th inst., by the Rev. Paul Trapier Keith, George T. Ford Esq. to Miss Mary Warham, third daughter of the late Anthony Toomer, Esq. all of this town.

Issue of May 2, 1827

Married on Thursday evening the 26th ultimo by the Rev. N. Morgan, Capt. Thomas J. Smith of Santee, to Miss Elizabeth A. R. Barnette of Darlington.

Died at Marion Court House on the 2nd inst., Eliza Jane, the daughter of Robert J. and Zilpha Gregg, aged 8 years and 3 months.
Marion, April 28, 1827

Issue of May 9, 1827

All persons having demands against the late James Denly Esq. are required to render statements.... LeGrand G. Walker
May 9 Qualified Executor.
All persons having demands against Robert F. Withers....
April 26, 1827 Caroline Withers, Executrix.

Issue of May 12, 1827

Died on the 30th of Jan. last at the island of Syra, Mr. William Henry Potter, aged 29 years, formerly in the Navy of the U. S. and second son of John Potter, Esq. of Charleston, S. C. Mr. Potter volunteered his services in the cause of Greece and accompanied Capt. Gregory in the ship "Hope" from New York to Napoli.

Peter Corbz made suit for letters of adminstration on the Estate of Sampson Holmes, a coloured man, late of Sampit, decd....
5 May 1827

WINYAW INTELLIGENCER

Issue of May 23, 1827

Married on the 17th inst., near Little River, Allsaints Parish, by the Rev. Mr. Purifoy, Mr. William B. Rowell, of Sandy Island, to Miss Martha Brantley, of the former place.
Died in Rowley (Mass.), on the 7th instant, Mr. Robert S. Coffin, the Boston Bard.
All persons having demands against the estate of Capt. Asa Clarke, decd....   Jared R. Clarke, Admor.
North Santee, May 22, 1827.

Issue of May 26, 1827

Married on Tuesday evening last, by the Rev. Paul Trapier Keith, Mr. Joseph Johnson to Miss Martha Rogers, all of this place.
At Waccamaw, on Thursday evening last, by the Rev'd Thomas L. Winn, Mr. William M. Wilson, to Miss Elizabeth Kirton, all of this town.

Issue of June 2, 1827

Died in this town on the 29th ultimo, aged 24 years, Mrs. Clara Elizabeth Shackelford, wife of Francis R. Shackelford, Esq. (eulogy).

Issue of June 6, 1827

Died on the 10th inst., on Waccamaw, All Saints Parish, in the 39th year of her age, Mrs. Mary Ann Vereen, consort of John E. Vereen....left a husband and six small children....

Issue of June 16, 1827

Married in this town on Wednesday evening last, by the Rev. T. Lawson Winn, Mr. William Porter, to Miss Abigail G. Wilson, both of this District.
Married in this town, on Thursday morning last, by the Rev. T. L. Winn, Mr. William Finson to Miss Joannah Watts, all of Sampit.
John F. Green applied for admn. with the will annexed of Elizabeth Withers, late of Sampit decd....   12 June 1827.

Issue of June 23, 1827

Married at Santee, on Thursday evening last, by the Rev. Thomas L. Winn, Mr. Isaac J. Singletary, to Miss Mary C. Michau, both of Williamsburgh District.

Issue of June 30, 1827

Francis R. Shackelford applied for letters of admn. on the estate of his father, Francis Shackelford, late of Georgetown, decd....   29 June 1827.

Issue of July 7, 1827

Died in Guilford (Conn.), on the 22d ultimo, Capt. George Kimberly, of the schr. LaBruce in the 43d year of his age.

WINYAW INTELLIGENCER

Issue of July 11, 1827

Died on Friday the 6th inst., Gen. Thomas Carr, in the -- year of his age....Major General of the 4th Division South Carolina Militia.... (eulogy).

Issue of July 14, 1827

Married on Thursday evening last, by the Rev. Peter Ludlow, Mr. Benjamin Westberry to Mrs. Hannah Potts.
on the same evening, at Serenity, near this town, by the Rev. Thomas L. Winn, Mr. Moses S. Leger, to Mrs. Mary Herrington.

Issue of July 28, 1827

Died in this town on yesterday afternoon, James M. **Grier**, Esq.
Married on Thursday evening last,by the Rev. T. Lawson Winn, Mr. Samuel S. Ballow, to Miss Margaret Skinner, all of this town.

Issue of August 1, 1827

Married in Williamsburgh District on Thursday the 28th June last, by the Rev. E. I. Mills, William James Pressley, Esq., to Miss Elizabeth Gamble.
Died in this town on Monday last, Mr. John W. Pawley, aged about 30.
Died, lately, in Charleston, Daniel T. Heriot, a native of this place, but for the last six years a resident of Charleston.
All persons having demands against the estate of General Thomas Carr..... Joseph W. Allston, Qualified Exr.
July 28, 1827.

Issue of August 15, 1827

Married at Balck River, on Thursday evening last, by E. Waterman, Esq.,Mr. John Hawkins, to Miss Susan Bird, all of this district.

Issue of August 18, 1827

Died in Williamsburg District, on the 5th inst., in the 26th year of her age,Mrs. Margaret R. Rogers....(eulogy).
Died in New York on the 6th inst, Mr. William Jackson Ludlow, son of Peter Ludlow, Esq. and a member of the Senior class in Union College, Schenectady, N. Y.

Issue of August 22, 1827

Died in this town on Monday night last, in the 12th yearof his age, master John Briggs, an apprentice to this office, and youngest son of Mrs. Ann Briggs.

Issue of August 29, 1827

Married on monday the 13th inst.,by the Rev. Mr. Read, John G. North, Esq. of this town, to Miss Jane G., eldest daughter of James Petigru, Esq. of Abbeville District.

WINYAW INTELLIGENCER

Issue of September 1, 1827

Died in Sumter District, on Friday the 17th ult., in the 26th year of her age, Mrs. Ann Smith, consort of Henry I. Smith, Esq. of said District. (eulogy).

Issue of September 5, 1827

Married in Providence, R. I., on Monday evening the 20th ult., by the Rev. Dr. Gano, Mr. Benjamin T. Cuttino to Miss Eliza I. Spooner, of the former place.
Departed this life on the morning of the 30th ult., in the 6th year of her age, at Red Bluff Springs, St. James Santee, Juliann Ellen, daughter of John H. and H. M. Allston.
Died in this town on Monday last, Mrs. Holt, of Allsaints Parish.

Issue of September 12, 1827

Died in Charleston, on the 30th ult., Dr. Matthew Irvine, formerly a practitioner of medicine in this place. (eulogy)
Died on Monday evening the 2d inst., in the 73d year of his age, Mr. Levi Salomon, a native of Germany, but a citizen of Carolina, and resident of Georgetown since the Revolution....a firm believer in the Jewish faith.   S. Patriot.

Issue of September 15, 1827

Married on Thursday evening last, by the Rev. Mr. Winn, Mr. John G. Wilson to Miss Rachel Piggot, eldest daughter of Mr. Joseph Piggot of this place.
Died on Thursday night, Miss Ann Bond, aged about 53 years... member of the Methodist Church in this town.
Died in this town on yesterday morning, Mrs. Tabitha Avinett, aged about 46 years.
At Withersville, near this place, on the 12th inst., Mr. Richard Green, aged 73 years, a member of the Methodist Church.
At the same place, on the 7th inst., Mr. William C. Shackelford, Junr.

Issue of September 19, 1827

Benjamin Salomon applied for letters of adminstration on the estate of his father, Levy Salomon, late of Georgetown...10 September 1827.

Issue of September 22, 1827

Married on the 9th ultimo, at Easton (Penn.), by the Rev. Mr. Pomp, Mr. Abraham Kind, to Miss Susan Queer.
In Lewiston, by James Smith, Esq.,Mr. David B. Finch, to Miss Sally____ of that place.... Finch has been married to three respectable women, all of whom are now living.... Albany Adv.
Died on Black River, on Saturday the 15th inst., Mr. Thomas M. Blount, in the 37th yearof his age. (eulogy).
Died in this town, on Tuesday night last, Eliza Ann, youngest child of Mrs. Ann Briggs.
On Thursday night, John James, son of John and Mary S. Dicks.

WINYAW INTELLIGENCER

Issue of September 29, 1827

Long obituary of Mr. Richard Green, a Revolutionary Soldier, who died at age 72. (see issue of Sept. 15, 1827)
Died in Pendleton, on the 16th inst., Dr. Henry W. Davis, in the 23d year of his age.

Issue of October 3, 1827

Died at the residence of John O. Heriot, Sumter District, 23d ultimo, in the 69th year of her age, Mrs. Agnes Kirkpatrick, for many years a resident of this State near Georgetown. (eulogy).

Issue of October 6, 1827

Married on Thursday evening last, by the Rev. T. Lawson Winn, Mr. Thomas Wilson, of Santee, to Miss Elizabeth, youngest daughter of Mr. John Thompson, of this place.
In Seneca county, on the 13th inst., after a courtship of 25 years, Mr. Gilbert Honeywell of Locke, to Miss Polly Ewen of Scipio....   New York Enq.

Issue of October 10, 1827

Died in this town, on the 6th inst., Mrs. Mary W., consort of Mr. Wm. Sherell, of this place, in the 29th year of her age.
on Saturday last, Miss Jane Brown.
on Monday last, Miss Mary E. Smith, youngest daughter of Major Savage Smith.

Issue of October 13, 1827

Died on the 6th inst., at the house of Benjamin Gause, Horry District, the Rev. John Gamewell, an aged minister of the Methodist Church.
In Horry District, Mrs. Purifoy, wife of the Rev. Archibald Purifoy, of the Methodist Church.
The Rev. Thomas Charlton Henry died on Friday last, the 5th inst., in the 38th year of his age. (eulogy).
Died in this city, on the 25th ult., Col. William Paine, Military Store Keeper in the service of the U. S., aged 84 years and 2 months, a native of Pennsylvania....left four children....
    Charleston C. Gazette
Died on the 11th of August, at the seat of her uncle, the Earl of Albermarle, Mrs. Wm Wakefield, wife of Mr. William Wakefield, a prisoner in Lancaster Castle, for being concerned with his brother, Mr. E. G. Wakefield, in carrying off Miss Turner... daughter of Sir John Sidney...left infant daughter 6 months old ....   Ibid.

Issue of October 20, 1827

Married Thomas Buler Chinn, Esq. of the Close, Litchfield, to the daughter of the late secretary of the navy.... St. James Place, July 26, 1827.
At Lunenberg (N.S.), George Wolfe, aged 82 years, to Miss Barbara Hahm, aged 73 years, after a courtship of nearly 50 years.
Died in Charleston, Miss Joanna M. England, sister of the Rt. Rev. Bishop England of the Roman Catholic Church.

WINYAW INTELLIGENCER

Issue of October 27, 1827

Mrs. Henry Joseph died in this town on Wednesday, the 24th inst., in the 26th year of her age....
Died in Twinsburg, Portage co., Ohio, on the 21st of Sept., Moses and Aaron Wilcox, aged 50 years, twins...Cleveland Herald

Issue of October 31, 1827

Died on Sunday morning last, Mra. Ann Catharine Mariano, aged 21 years, wife of Mr. Anthony Lewis Mariano.
Yesterday morning, Mrs. Rachel Flowers, in the 82d year of her age.
At Cheraw, on the 18th inst., Benjamin Huger, son of Dr. W. H. Fleming, formerly of this place.

Issue of November 10, 1827

Died in this town, yesterday, Mrs. Elizabeth Smith, relict of the late Major Savage Smith....
On yesterday, Mr. William H. Ford, 3rd son of the late Dr. George Ford.
In Wraggsborough, on the 29th October last, Mary Wragg Rothmahler, a native of Georgetown, S. C....Charleston Mercury

Issue of December 15, 1827

Married on Wednesday evening last, by the Rev. Paul Trapier Keith, Mr. Thomas Lynch Shaw to Miss Nanette Walker, youngest daughter of the late James Walker, Esq.
On the same evening, by the above Rev. Gentleman, Mr. Wm. J. Malden, of Greenville, to Miss Martha L. F. Colmar, of this place.

Issue of December 22, 1827

Married at Maccamaw, on the 20th inst., by the Rev. P. T. Keith, Mr. Shadrach Rice to Miss Louisa E. Linerieux, only child of W. G. Linerieux.
At Willtown on the same evening, by the Rev. Peter Ludlow, Doctor John Jay Clark to Miss Jane Pzuill (sic).

Issue of December 29, 1827

John Wragg applied for letters of admn. on the estate of Caroline Cooper, late of Georgetown...   28 December 1827.

[No issues have been located for 1828]

Issue of January 3, 1829

Died, at Sandy Island on Saturday evening 27th ult., Mr. Joseph Holmes, aged about 46 years.
All persons having legal demands against Col. John Porter Junr., deceased....   Esther Ann Porter, Qualified Extx
                                    John Porter)
                                    L. G. Walker)Qualified Executors
                                    A. W. Dozier)
Georgetown, Nov. 19, 1828

WINYAW INTELLIGENCER

Issue of January 7, 1829

Died, on the 22d December last, at the plantation of her son, Capt. C. W. Vereen, on Long Bay, All Saints Parish, Elizabeth Commander, in the 53d year of her age. (eulogy).

Issue of January 10, 1829

Married, in this town, on Thursday evening last by the Rev. P. Trapier Keith, Mr. Anthony Mariano, to Miss Maria N. Church.
All persons having any demands against the estate of Asa Clark deceased....   Jared R. Clarke, Admr.
Jan. 7
Persons having demands against the Estate of Samuel Smith, deceased....   W. W. Trapier) Admors.
Nov. 19   James Smith)

Issue of January 17, 1829

Died in Horry District on Wednesday last, Mr. Stephen P. Keys, son of the late Pebody Keys, aged about 21 years...left an affectionate mother and many fond relations....
All persons having any demands against the estate of the late Thomas Dowdney....   Coggeshall & North, Attorneys
January 17

Issue of January 21, 1829

Married in Greenesborough (Georgia), on the 19th ultimo, Mr. Willis Alston, of Sparta, to Miss Elizabeth Sarah, daughter of the Rev. John Howard, of the former place.
All persons having any legal demands against the estate of Jeremiah Russell, late of Georgetown District, deceased....
January 21   John R. Easterling, Admor.

Issue of January 31, 1829

Died, in this town, on Tuesday evening, the 27th inst., Capt. Enoch Wilcox, a native of Westerly, Rhode Island, aged about 42 years.
Died, yesterday at Pee Dee, after a short illness, Mr. Alexander M'Kab, for many years a respectable and highly useful citizen of this District.

Issue of February 14, 1829

Married, in this town, on Tuesday evening last, by the Rev. Gabriel W. Wayne, Mr. Thomas C. Fearwell to Miss Mary A. Broquier.
Married, on Thursday evening last, by the Rev. Joseph B. Cook, Col. James C. Coggeshall of this town, to Miss Jane M. Scriven--daughter of the late John Screven.
Died on the 10th inst., in this Town, aged about 33 years, T. Burrington Thomas, Esq.
Died on the same day, Mrs. M'Kab, widow of the late Mr. A. M'Kab, whose death was recorded a few days since...a communicant in the Protestant Episcopal Church in this place....
Mary Philips has made suit for Letters of Administration on the estate of her husband James Phillips, late of Black River, deceased...14 Feb 1829.

WINYAW INTELLIGENCER

Issue of February 18, 1829

Married on Thursday the 12th inst., by the Rev. Thomas King, Capt. James Beaty to Miss Louisa Pawley, daughter of John Servis, Esq. all of Horry District.
On the same evening by the same Rev. Gentleman, Mr. Benjamin Freeman of Bladen county, N. C. to Miss Ann Todd, of Horry District.
On the same day by the Rev. James Singleton, Mr. Robert McCrackin to Miss Sarah M'Crackin, all of Horry District.

Issue of February 21, 1829

Married on Saturday evening last, the 14th instant, by the Rev. Paul Trapier Kieth, Mr. John M. Screven to Miss Margaretta Coggeshall.

Issue of February 25, 1829

Died on Sunday last, the 22d inst., Mr. John Taylor, Senr. an old and respectable inhabitant of this Town.
Died, suddenly, on the same day, at Pee Dee, Mr. Solomon Sessions.

Issue of February 28, 1829

Married in Marion District on Thursday evening last, the 27th inst., Dr. John Cherry to Mrs. Rachal Crawford.
In Marion District on Thursday evening the 19th inst., by the Rev. T. Moody, Mr. James Hazleton to Miss Mary Godbold, youngest daughter of the late Gen. Thomas Godbold.
Died in this town on Wednesday the 25th inst., in the 31st year of his age, Anthony Bonneau Shackelford, Esquire. (eulogy)

Issue of March 4, 1829

All persons having demands against James Phillips late of Black River, deceased, ...   Mary E. Phillips, Executrix
March 4, 1829   Hugh W. Cantley, Executor.

Issue of March 11, 1829

Died on Santee, on the 29th January, Mrs. Margaret Small, consort of Mr. Francis Small, in the 59th year of her age...a member of the Methdosti Church for many years.
Died, near this place, on the 3d inst., Mrs. Anne Atkinson, aged about 21. left a tender husband and one child....
Departed this life at Norfolk, Va., on the 10th ult., Mrs. Eliza Hales, consort of Capt. Edward Hales in the 36th year of her age...belonged to the Episcopal Church...left a husband and two children....

Issue of March 14, 1829

John P. Rice applied for Letters of administration of his brother Joel Rice, late of Peedee, deceased....13 March 1829
George Watts applied for Letters of Administration on the estate of Christopher Watts, lateof Sampit, deceased....13 March 1829....

WINYAW INTELLIGENCER

Issue of March 18, 1829

Died on Tuesday morning last, Dr. John Wragg, in the 44th year of his age. (eulogy).

Issue of March 21, 1829

Edward T. Heriot applied for Letters of Administration on the estate of Thomas B. Thomas, lately deceased...20 March 1829

Issue of April 18, 1829

All persons having demands against LeGrand C. Walker, late of Georgetown, Merchant, deceased....
                                        Mary E. Walker, Adm'x.
                                        Benj. Walker)
April 18, 1829   Peter Walker) Admors.

Issue of April 25, 1829

Married, at Catfish, on Wednesday evening last, by the Rev. Mr. M'Millan, Jonah C. Rogers, to Miss Ann Davis.

Issue of April 29, 1829

Died in Marion District on the 17th inst., Mr. Baker Wiggins ....(eulogy).
All persons having demands against the estate of the late Dr. John Wragg....   S. S. Gasque, Qualified Exr.
April 29

Issue of May 6, 1829

Died, at North Island, on Thursday last the 30th ult., Capt. Robert Marsh, aged about 52 years, a native of New-Jersey... Pilot of the Georgetown Bar and Keeper of the Light-House... left wife and six children....
Died on the night of the first instant, at her residence on Waccamaw, Mrs. Elizabeth Ward, consort of the late Major Joshua Ward.

Issue of May 9, 1829

Married on Thursday evening last, by the Rev. P. T. Keith, Mr. Elias J. Etheridge, to Miss Susan Gallivant--all of this place.
Died in this town, on Thursday evening last, Mr. Peter Bartholomew, Baker, aged about 30 years, a native of France.

Issue of May 20, 1829

Married in Horry District, on Thursday last, the 14th inst., by the Rev. William Skinner, the Rev. James C. Howren, of this Town, to Mrs. Hannah Durant, of the former place.
Married, on Thursday evening last, at the Rev. Mr. E. Owens, by the Rev. Archibald Purifoy, Rev. Josiah Lewis, aged 76, to Miss Martha Owens, aged 16.

Issue of May 27, 1829

William Sherrill applied for Letters of Administration on

WINYAW INTELLIGENCER

the estate of Otho Thorp, late of Halifax county, Virginia, deceased....23 May 1829

Issue of May 30, 1829

Died on the 27th inst., Mrs. Elizabeth Willson, relict of the late Mr. William M. Willson.

On Sampit, on the 21st inst., William Alexander Finson, aged 1 year, 4 months and 21 days.

All persons having demands against the Estate of Thomas P. Davis, deceased....   Magdalen L. Davis, Qual Extx.
May 16

Issue of June 6, 1829

Mrs. Elizabeth M. Willson, widow of the late Mr. William M. Willson, died 27th May 1829 (eulogy).

Issue of June 13, 1829

Died, on Thursday, the 11th instant, Aaron--the infant son of Dr. A. Lopez, aged 13 months and 13 days.

Issue of June 17, 1829

Died, yesterday morning, Mrs. Rachel Lockhart, aged about 65 years....

Issue of June 27, 1829

Married in this Town, on Thursday evening last, by the Rev. Jacob S. P. Powell, Mr. Augustua Siau, to Miss Sarah Elizabeth, second daughter of the late George S. Taylor.

Issue of July 4, 1829

Married on the 11th ult., in Richland District, Dr. Samuel D. Grant, of Sumter, to Mrs. Martha Glascow, of the former place.

Died, yesterday morning, Isabella, second daughter of Sampson and Molsey Solomons, aged 4 years.

Issue of July 8, 1829

Died in this town on Monday morning last, William John James, only child of Mr. Christopher J. and the late Mrs. Elizabeth A. Atkinson, aged one years ten months and 20 days.

Issue of July 22, 1829

Died in this Town, on Sunday morning last, Sarah-Ann, infant daughter of John and Mary Louisa Matthews, aged five months and 21 days.

Issue of August 5, 1829

Persons indebted to James Dealy, deceased....
Aug 3, 1829   Samuel Green, Executor.

Issue of August 26, 1829

Died on Monday last, Mr. Bannester Lester, in the 34th year

WINYAW INTELLIGENCER

of his age.
On the same day, John Wragg, son of Dr. S. S. Gasque, of this place.

Issue of August 29, 1829

Departed this life, in Williamsburgh District, on the 9th day of July last, Mrs. Sarah Mills, wife of Rev. Elam J. Mills, in the 51st year of her age. (eulogy).

Issue of September 2, 1829

Died on the 20th ult., at Leggett's Mills, Marion District, Mr. Daniel M'Lean.
In this town, on 29th ult., John S., son of Robert and Martha Y. Howren.

Issue of September 5, 1829

Died, in Allowaystown, New Jersey, on the 9th ultimo, Frederick William, eldest son of D. A. Bokee, Esq.
In this town, on the 2d instant, Ann Murray, youngest child of Mr. A. Marvin.

Issue of September 9, 1829

Died at Withersville, on Thursday last, Mary Ann Elizabeth, aged 6 years, only daughter of Hannah C. and Charles Munnerlyn.
Died, in this town, on Monday last, the 7th instant, Josiah youngest child of Hugh and Elizabeth Bufkin.

Issue of September 16, 1829

Died at Milton ferry, near Charleston, on the 11th inst., George Washington, son of John A. and Sarah D. Bruorton, aged ten months and 19 days.
Died at Charleston, on the 14th inst., in the 22d year of his age, Mr. William R. Daniell, late a compositer in this office ....

Issue of September 23, 1829

Died in this Town, on Friday night last, after a painful illness, Mr. William Sherrell.
at North Island, on Monday morning last, Mr. John Hall, aged about 36 years.

Issue of September 26, 1829

Died at North Island on the 22d inst., William H., oldest son of the late Mr. John Hall, aged 12 years and 5 months.
All persons having demands against the estate of the late Banister Lester, deceased.... Margaret Lester, Administratrix. Sept 26

Issue of October 3, 1829

Married, on Thursday evening last, by the Rev. G. W. Wayne, Mr. Stephen Samuel Wallace, to Miss Martha Elizabeth, daughter of Capt. Henry Smith.

WINYAW INTELLIGENCER

Those indebted to the estate of Gilbert Johnson, deceased.... China Grove, Sept. 29, 1829   John Graham, Admor.

Issue of October 7, 1829

Died, in Williamsburgh District on the 23d ultimo, Mr. Manasseh Michau...a member of the Methodist Episcopal Church....

Issue of October 14, 1829

Married in Washington city on Wednesday, 7th instant, by the Rev. R. H. Neals, the Rev. Archar B. Smith, of this place, to Miss Mary, daughter of Col. Wm. Dewees, of the Treasury Department.

Issue of October 21, 1829

Died, in this place, on the 13th inst., Mary Maria, eldest daughter of James and Susan Corson, aged three years and 13 days.

Issue of October 31, 1829

Died, on Wednesday last, Mrs. Eleanor Wragg, an old and respectable inhabitant of this town.
On Thursday last, in the 22d year of his age, Mr. John Potter...left a mother and several brothers and sisters....
On the same day Mrs. Mary Marsh, relict of the late Capt. Robert Marsh.

Issue of November 14, 1829

Departed this life, on Waccamaw, on the night of the 9th inst., John Benjamin, only child of Thomas G. and Esther A. Rice, aged one years, three months and 20 days.

Issue of November 21, 1829

Married at Potatoe Ferry, on Wednesday evening last, by the Rev. T. S. King, Mr. Thomas Johnson to Miss Ann Marshall, all of Birch Creek, Williamsburg Dist.
Died in this place, yesterday morning, in the 37th year of his age, Mr. Joseph M. Puche, a native of New Orleans, but for several years a resident of this place.
Of an inflamation of the lungs, on the 12th inst., at the house of J. C. Granger, Horry District, Moses Harralson, Esq., in the 61st year of his age....

Issue of December 12, 1829

Married in this Town, on the evening of the 5th instant, by the Rev. P. Trapier Keith, Anthony W. Dozier, Esq., Attorney at Law, to Miss Mary C., daughter of Capt. P. Cuttino.

Issue of December 16, 1829

Died at Mrs. Swanston's, in this Town, on Sunday morning, the 6th instant, Capt. Joseph Greaves, of Pee Dee (Marion Dist.) aged 52 years, 4 months and 1 day....
Dr. William Burnett, who died about the year 1786, was possessed at the time of his death of Lot #57 in this town...His heirs are required to come forward....

WINYAW INTELLIGENCER

All persons having demands against the estate of Mrs. Eleanor Wragg, late of Georgetown, deceased.....   John G. North, Admr. Dec. 16

Issue of December 23, 1829

Died at Wacamaw, on the evening of the 19th, Benjamin Porter Fraser, eldest son of the Rev. Hugh Fraser, aged 52 years, 3 months and 19 days.

Issue of January 2, 1830

Married in this town, on Tuesday evening last, by the Rev. Jacob S. P. Powell, Mr. Nimrod Howren of New Orleans, to Miss Maria Margaret Tarbox.
    At Black Mingo on the evening of the same day, the Rev. James C. Postell, Mr. Goodwin Wal(ker?) to Miss Ann Kesiah Smith, daughter of C-- Henry Smith.

Issue of January 27, 1830

Married on the 21st inst., by the Revd. Charles Betts, on Pee Dee, Mr. Joseph A. Brown, of this District to Miss Mary E. C. Horton, late from Sumpter District.
    All persons having demands against the Estate of David Phillips, deceased....   Wm. L. Phillips, Administrator January 27
    Stephen Farrow applied for letters of Administration of his father, Thomas Farrow, late of Georgetown, deceased...25 Jan 1830.
    James Smith, applied for letters of administration on the estate of Dr. William Burnett, late of Georgetown, deceased....

Issue of February 24, 1830

Christiana Bates (widow of Thomas Bates) and James Parker applied for Letters of Administration on the estate of Thomas Bates, late of Georgetown, deceased....22 Feb 1830

Issue of February 27, 1830

Married on Thursday last, the 25th inst., by the Rev. Paul Trapier Keith, Thomas B. Clarkson, Esq. of Charleston, to Sarah Caroline, the eldest daughter of Robert Herior, Esq. of this place.

Issue of March 3, 1830

Married at Lynch's Creek, on Wednesday evening the 24th ult. by the Rev. J. C. Postell, Mr. Benja. Walker to Miss Margaret Swanston, daughter of the late David Swanston.

Issue of March 13, 1830

Died in this town, on Saturday evening last, Mrs. Ann Taylor, aged 45.

Issue of March 20, 1830

Married in Horry District on the 11th inst., by the Rev. G Williams, Mr. Samuel M'Cracken, of Black River, to Miss Thirza

WINYAW INTELLIGENCER

Williams, of the former place.

Issue of April 3, 1830

Stephen Elliott, Esq., died a few days since very suddenly in Charleston. (eulogy).
Married on Wednesday evening last, by the Rev. James C. Postell, Mr. John S. Crane, of Ireland, to Miss Martha A. Westbury, daughter of Mr. Benjamin Westberry, of this District.
All those indebted to Wm. Bellune late of Marion District, dec'd....   John C. Davis, Admor.

Issue of April 17, 1830

Departed this life on the 21st inst., at 8 o'clock, the Rev. Thomas Avant, aged 64 years....
Departed this life on the 30th ult., Eli Avant, in the 25th year of his age....

Issue of April 21, 1830

All persons indebted to John Keele, late of Waccamaw, deceased, are requested to make payment....   Wm. B. Rowell, Admor.
April 21, 1830

Issue of May 15, 1830

Married in Williamsburg District on Wednesday evening last, by the Rev. James C. Postell, Samuel Vinson King, Esq. of this town to Miss E. M. O. M'Connell, daughter of Thomas M'Connell, Esq.

Issue of June 2, 1830

Death of Mr. Daniel C-mbie....

Issue of July 7, 1830

Died in this town on Friday last (the 2d inst.), Mr. Andrew Peterson, aged 28 years, a native of Ireland.
Died at his mother's residence in this town, on the 3rd inst., Mr. George Potter in the 17th year of his age, son of the late Obadiah Potter, Esq. (eulogy)

Issue of July 10, 1830

All persons having any demands against the estate of Isaac Baneneau, late of Williamsburgh District, decd....
Kinstree, July 2, 1830   Sam'l E. Graham, Admr.

Issue of August 11, 1830

Died in this Town, yesterday morning, Mrs. Margaret Hall, relict of the late Mr. John Hall.
On Monday night last, Mr. Israel Solomons.

Issue of August 14, 1830

Marinda R. Wayne applied for Letters of Administration on the estate of her husband, the Rev. Gabriel W. Wayne, late of Georgetown, deceased...13 Aug 1830

WINYAW INTELLIGENCER

Issue of August 18, 1830

Eleanor J. Solomons applied for letters of administration on the estate of her husband Israels Solomons late of Georgetown, deceased....18 Aug 1830

Issue of August 25, 1830

Mr. John Dozier was a member of the State Legislature from the District of Williamsburg....death announced in issue of Saturday last....

Issue of September 15, 1830

Died on Sampit, on the 7th inst., Ann Kirton, youngest child of Daniel and Jane Kirton, aged 1 month and 25 days.
Died on his plantation in Horry District, on the 15th ult., James Gould Cochran, Esq., a native of Scotland, but for many years a resident of that district.
At Black River, on the 11th instant, Mr. James Leger, aged about 40 years.
In this town on Monday evening, Mr. Michael Calverly, a native of Cork (I.) but for the last 30 years a resident of this town.
At his summer residence on Mill Creek, on the 4th inst., the Hon. Robt. Stark, secretary of state, in the 66th year of his age.

Issue of September 18, 1830

Died on Waccamaw on the 23d ultimo, Martha L. P. Horton, daughter of Mr. J. W. Horton, aged 8 years and 3 months,
Departed this life on the 1st inst., Mrs. Mary Eliza C. Brown, consort of Joseph A. Brown of Pee Dee...aged 17 years and 25 days.

Issue of October 6, 1830

Departed this life on the 27th ult., at his residence in Georgetown, Isaac Carr, Esq., in the 40th year of his age...a native of this place and was educated at Yale College....
Henry Benjamin, in the 7th year of his age, only son of Capt. Peter Cuttino of this town, lost his life on Monday the 4th by drowning....
Oct. 6, 1830

Issue of October 9, 1830

Died on the 30th ult., at his plantation, All Saints Parish, Samuel Wilson, Esq., in the 53d year of his age. (eulogy)

Issue of October 16, 1830

Died in this town on Thursday evening last, Mrs. Ann McCracken, in the 63d year of her age, leaving nine children...member of the Methodist Episcopal Church....

Issue of October 20, 1830

Sarah Carr applied for Letters of Administration on the estate of her husband Isaac Carr, late of Georgetown, 20 Oct 1830

WINYAW INTELLIGENCER

Issue of December 1, 1830

James Morrow applied for Letters of Administration on the estate of Ann(?) M. Morrow, deceased, late of this District... 30 Nov 1830

Issue of December 22, 1830

Died in Marion, on Friday, the 17th inst., Mrs. Elizabeth Davis, formerly of this town, aged about 21 years, leaving a husband, mother and stepfather....

Issue of January 1, 1831

James Beaty applied for letters of administration on the estate of Wm. R. Daniell, late of Georgetown deceaed, 31 Dec 1830

[Issues of January 4, 1832 through June 27, 1833 are located in the Charleston Library Society]

Issue of January 4, 1832

Married at Darlington C. H. on Thursday evening the 29th ultimo, by the Rev'd Noah Laney, Mr. Samuel Ferdinand Gibson, to Miss Mary Rachael Godfrey, of Marion.

Issue of January 7, 1832

Married on Thursday the 15th ult., in the county of Hanover (Va.), at the residence of the Rev. William Wood, by the sd. Rev. Wm. Wood, Mr. Matthew M. Toler, to Miss Lucy, daughter of the said Rev. Wm. Wood and at the same time and place, by the said Rev. Wm. Wood, Mr. Benjamin H. Toler to Miss Eliza, another daughter of the sd. Rev. Wm Wood--the two ladies being sisters and the two gentlemen brothers.

Issue of January 14, 1832

Married on Wednesday evening last, by the Rev. Mr. Beaty, S. B. Wilkins, Esq. of Darlington to Miss Mary E. King, daughter of Mr. Eli King, of this town.
Died at his residence in St. James, Santee, on the night of the 10th inst., General R. Vanderhorst, aged about 45...left a wife and several small children.
All persons having demands against the estate of John Swinton late of Georgetown.... Jan 14   John D. Watts, Adm'or.

Issue of January 18, 1832

Married in Charleston, on the 10th inst., by the Rt. Rev. Bishop Bowen, Robert J. Turnbull to Miss Ann B. M'Call, daughter of the late Hext M'Call, Esq.
Died, recently on Waccamaw, Col. John A. Alston, aged about 52 years.
In Charleston, on the 11th inst., Thomas Mitchell, Esq., aged 63 years....
All persons having legal demands against the estate of Dr. James Doughty....   Sarah B. Doughty
Dec. 31, 1831   S. T. Gaillard
                                           Qual. Extx & Exr.

94

WINYAW INTELLIGENCER

Issue of January 21, 1832

Persons having demands against the estate of Col. John A. Alston....   John Izard Middleton, Jr.)Admrs.
Thomas Alston, Jr.   )

Issue of January 25, 1832

Died in this town on Sunday last, Mr. Wm. G. Palmer, about 33years of age.

Issue of February 4, 1832

Died at the Poor House, in this town, on Thursday evening, Mr. James Rose, by trade a painter, a native of Richmond, Va....

Issue of February 11, 1832

All persons having demands against the estate of John A. Daniel....   John Hawkins, Admor.
Feb. 11

Issue of February 15, 1832

Died in this town on the 13th inst., Mrs. Ann Matthews, aged 61 years--mother of John Matthews, Esq., Proprietor of the Georgetown Union.
Daniel Pipkin hath made suit for letters of administration on the estate of John J. Raphill, late of Santee, decd....
11 Feb 1832

Issue of February 22, 1832

All persons having demands against the late William G. Palmer....   Laommi Palmer, Administrator.

Issue of February 29, 1832

Married in this town on the evening of the 24th inst., by the Rev'd. Mr. Ellison, Mr. Daniel McWilliams to Miss Eliza Christian.
On Britton's Neck, Marion District, on Wednesday the 22d inst., by the Rev'd. Benjamin Holt, Mr. Benjamin Gause of Horry, to Miss Martha Woodbury, of the former place.

Issue of March 3, 1832

Died on Waccamaw on Saturday the 25th ult., Mr. Elijah Exum, aged 21 years, 1 month and 22 days.

Issue of March 7, 1832

Died on the 23d ult., at the residence of his mother in Upper All Saints Parish, Mr. Thomas Livingston, aged about 26 years. (eulogy).
George Gibson applied for administration on the estate of William G. Grier, decd...5 March 1832.

Issue of March 10, 1832

Thomas G. Avant applied for admn. on the estate of Elijah T.

WINYAW INTELLIGENCER

Exum, late of Waccamaw, decd... 6 March 1832

Issue of March 28, 1832

Died on the 20th inst.,Mrs. Mary Warham, in her 75th year. (eulogy).

Issue of April 7, 1832

Married in this town on Tuesday evening last, by the Rev. P. Trapier Keith, Edward Thomas Esquire to Mrs. Mary Elizabeth Walker.

Issue of April 11, 1832

Married in Charleston, on the 5th inst.,by Rev. Dr. Dalcho, Col. R. F. W. Allston of this District, to Miss Adeline Petigru, of the former place.

Issue of April 18, 1832

All persons having demands against the estate of the late William S.Thomson, of Williamsburg.... Elizabeth Thomson, Williamsburg, April 14, 1832   Qua. Admr'x.

Issue of April 25, 1832

Died on the 10th inst., at her residence on Lynch's Creek, Mrs. Ann Swanson, aged 54....
At the Thirty-Two Mile House, on the 22d ult., Mrs. Elizabeth Bufkin, consort of Mr. H. F. Bufkin, in the 35th year of her age

Issue of April 28, 1832

Married in Charleston, on Tuesday the 24th inst., by the Rev. James C.Postell, Mr. Thomas McConnell to Mrs. Jane Clark, of Williamsburg District.

Issue of June 2, 1832

Married on Thursday evening last, at Rose Hill, Waccamaw, by T. Pinckney Alston, Esq., Mr. Nathaniel Nesmith, to Miss Elizabeth Marlow, all of All Saints Parish.
Died in this town, on yesterday, Mr. Joseph Salomons, Merchant of Charleston.

Issue of June 6, 1832

Obituary of General Thomas Sumter.

Issue of June 13, 1832

Married on Tuesday evening the 5th inst.,by the Rev. Thomas Ledbetter, Robert Nesbit, Esq. of Georgetown, S. C. to Miss Mary, daughter of John Hamilton, Esq. of Charleston.

Issue of June 20, 1832

Long obituary of Joseph Solomon from the <u>Charleston Evening Post</u>.

WINYAW INTELLIGENCER

Died at Sumter, 29th ult., Mrs. Martha Ann Heriot, aged 42, consort of John O. Heriot, Esq.

Issue of June 27, 1832

By shipwreck of the brig Edwina...Mrs. Rachel Cohen, Priscilla aged 10 and Abram aged 6 years--the wife and children of Jacob Cohen, Esq. of this District. (eulogy).

Issue of June 30, 1832

Married in this Town on Tuesday evening last, by the Rev. James C. Postell, Mr. John G. Calwell, to Miss Mary Anna, daughter of Capt. Charles Lehue.

Issue of July 11, 1832

Married on the 4th inst., by David Bokee, Esq., Mr. Elias Tields of New-York, to Miss Sarah E. Hawkins, of this town.

Issue of July 18, 1832

Married on Tuesday the 19th ult, George W. Addison, Esq., formerly of this place, and now Ed. of the Opelousas Gazette, to Miss Martha Bell, of Louisiana.
Died on North Island on Sunday the 15th inst., Esther B., infant daughter of George T. Ford, Esq.
All persons having demands against Leonard Avant, late of Black River deceased or Francis Small late of Santee decd....
William Small
Admr. of L. Avant and F. Small

Issue of July 21, 1832

Died on 29th June, at the residence of her husband, Mrs. Martha Ann Heriot, conosrt of John O. Heriot, in the 42d year of her age...(eulogy).
Stateburgh, July 13.

Issue of July 28, 1832

Died in this town on the 25th inst., Mr. Elias Field, a native of New Jersey, in the 21st year of his age. (eulogy).
Died, suddenly, on Santee, at the residence of her son (Mr. James White), Mrs. Hannah Roquie, relict of the late Stephen Roquie of this town.

Issue of August 1, 1832

Died on Monday last, at the residence of his adopted father, Mr. Samuel Green, Samuel Green Dealy, youngest son of the late Mr. James Dealy, aged 7 years and 8 months.
Died near Milledgeville (Ga.) on the 20th inst., Rev. S. B. Townsend of the Presbyterian Church, a native of Rhode Island.

Issue of August 4, 1832

Died on the North Santee on Tuesday the 24th ult., Mary Elizabeth, infant daughter of C. I. and T. T. Atkinson.

WINYAW INTELLIGENCER

Issue of August 11, 1832

Died on Tuesday morning, the 7th inst., on Waccamaw, Oatland, Mary Ruth, eldest daughter of Mr. and Mrs. Francis B. Durant, aged 4 years 1 month and 21 days.

Died on the 00 (sic) ult., in New Brunswick, the Rt. Rev. John Croes, D. D., Bishop of the Protestant Episcopal Church in the state of New Jersey, in the 70th year of his age.

Issue of September 22, 1832

Married on Wednesday evening last, in the Methodist Episcopal Church in this town, by the Rev'd. Wm. H. Ellison, Mr. Joseph R. Rogers to Mrs. Miranda Wayne.

Issue of October 3, 1832

Died on North Island on Thursday last, the 27th of Sept., W. W. Trapier, Esq. President of the Branch Bank of the State of S. C. at this place. (eulogy).

Issue of October 6, 1832

Died at the residence of Maj. James C. Billune (sic), at Marion Court House, on Thursday the 11th inst., Mr. James Hinds, in the 19th year of his age. (eulogy).

Sale of 50-60 Negroes belonging to the estate of Thomas F. Goddard....   Elizabeth C. Goddard, Admx. of T. F. Goddard, Georgetown, S. C., June 29, 1832.   decd.

Issue of November 28, 1832

Died at Col. Joshua John Ward's on Waccamaw, on the 23d inst., Mr. Simon Parker, in the 43d year of his age.

Issue of December 1, 1832

Died on Black River, the 27th inst., Anna, only daughter of Thomas and Mary Ford, aged 16 years. (eulogy).

Issue of December 12, 1832

All persons having demands against the estate of W. W. Trapier, of Prince George's Parish, Winyaw....   B. F. Trapier, Extr. Georgetown, Nov. 21, 1832

Issue of February 9, 1833

All persons having demands against the estate of William S. Thompson, late of Williamsburg....   Elizabeth Thompson, Admx. February 2, 1833

Issue of February 13, 1833

Married at Waccamaw on Thursday evening last, by the Rev. Mr. Glennie, Mr. Francis Weston to Miss Elizabeth Blyth, eldest daughter of Mr. John H. Tucker.

WINYAW INTELLIGENCER

Issue of February 16, 1833

James Smith applied for Letters of Administration on the estate of John Smith, late of Georgetown, deceased...16 Feb 1833

Issue of February 20, 1833

Married on Sunday the 10th inst., by Squire D. Gibson, Mr. Jos: L. Brown, to Miss Elizabeth, eldest daughter of Mr. J. Richardson, all of Brittons Neck, Marion District, S. C.

Issue of March 6, 1833

W. Litchfield applied for admnistration on the estate of Rosena Peyong... 27 Feb 1833

Issue of April 3, 1833

Married on Sampit, on Saturday last, by W. S. Harvey, Mr. Wm. F. Pauls, to Mrs. Lydia E. Walker, widow of the late Mr. James Walker.

Issue of May 4, 1833

Henry Cuttino applied for admn. on the estate of his sister Mrs. Elizabeth Smith, late of Georgetown, deceased...3 May 1833

Issue of May 23, 1833

Died at Waccamaw on the 2d ult., Mrs. Harriett Tucker, wife of John H. Tucker, Esq. (eulogy).

Issue of June 13, 1833

Died on Friday last, the 7th inst., Joseph L. E. Easterling, Sheriff of this District.

Issue of June 20, 1833

Died on Waccamaw, on the 9th inst., M. C. Ward, Esq.,in the 22d year of his age. (eulogy).
Isaac Sessions applied for admn. on the estate of his father Ransom Sessions, late of Georgetown District, decd....7 June 1833

Issue of June 27, 1833

Wm J. Cryer applied for administration on the estate of his brother Joseph Cryer, late of Georgetown District, decd...25 June 1833.

[Issues of July 11, 1833 through January 21, 1834 are located at Duke University]

Issue of July 11, 1833

Married on Monday evening last, at Harlaem Heights, by the Rev. Dr. Bogart, Col. Aaron Burr to Mrs. Eliza Jumel.
On the 4th inst., at Mount Gillead, Allsaints, by the Rev. Charles Wilson, Mr. Samuel L. Oliver, to Miss Ann R. Stevenson, all of the above parish.

WINYAW INTELLIGENCER

Issue of July 30, 1833

Dr. Daniel V. Berton departed this life on Thursday the 25th inst.... (eulogy).

Issue of September 10, 1833

Married on Tuesday evening last, by the Rev. Charles Betts, Mr. Henry C. Davis, to Miss Harriet Roach McGregory, all of this place.
Died lately at Black River, Mr. Henry Smith, aged 48 years. With his consort he left 8 children.
on Black River, Mr. Samuel W. Smith.
at New York on the 4th inst., Mr. Thomas Hall, of this town.
at New Orleans, on the 4th ult., Mr. James D. Ellis, formerly of this place.
in this town on the 4th inst., Hannah Catharine, 4th daughter of E. Waterman, Esq., aged 5 years.
on the 10th inst., Nannette, aged about 14 years, and eldest daughter of Jacob Wayne, Esq.
On the 1st inst., Wm. Archibald Walker, son of Mr. Peter Walker.
Died in this town, on Tuesday 1st, the 3d inst., Susan Ann, third child of John and Mary Louisa Matthews, aged eleven months and three days....

Issue of September 17, 1833

Died, in this town, on Thursday night, last, Mr. John M. Davis, aged about 40 years.
on the Waccamaw Sea Shor, on the 12th inst., Mr. Joseph Taylor, a native of Charleston, aged 19.

Issue of October 1, 1833

Died, in this Town on Thursday the 19th ultimo, Mr. Augustus L. Wragg, aged about 27 years.
on the 23d ult., Mr. Sampson Solomons, aged 39 years.
at Charleston, recently, Capt. John Deas, of the schooner Martha Piatt, of this town.
to-day, Mr. Wm. Coalman, overseer of the Poor House, aged about 50.

Issue of October 15, 1833

Master Joseph G. Taylor...leaves his bereaved mother....

Issue of November 19, 1833

Died, near this place, on the night of the 16th inst., Mr. William B. Shum, in the 38th year of his age.

Issue of November 25, 1833

Died in this town on Saturday last, Mrs. Hannah Tait, aged about 70.
at Black River, on Monday evening last, Mrs. Margaret Ford, an aged and respectable Lady, relick (sic) of the late Stephen Ford, Esq.
on the same day, Mr. Francis G. Coachman.

WINYAW INTELLIGENCER

on Pee Dee, last week, Major ____ Perry.
   Death of Col. Thos. Taylor. The Telescope says: "Our town has just followed to the grave its Patriarch. The venerable Thomas Taylor died on Sunday morning at the residence of his son, Mr. Benjamin Taylor...." born on 10th Sept., 1743, in Amelia County, Va....

Issue of December 10, 1833

   Death of Hon. T. D. Singleton.
The Raleigh N. C. Star of the 7th inst., says" died in this city on Wednesday morning last, 5th inst., Dr. T. D. Singleton a Representative in congress from S. C....
   All persons having any demands against the estate of the late A. L. Wragg, deceased....
Dec. 10
   All persons having any demands against the Estate of Francis G. Coachman, late of Black River, deceased....
Dec. 10   Jas. J. Coachman) Executors
                                 J. W. Coachman)

Issue of January 7, 1834

   All persons having any demands against the late Mrs. Margaret Ford....
Jan 7   S. Ford or Thomas Ford, Jr.

Issue of January 21, 1834

   Married on the 13th inst., in the M.(?) E. Church, by the Rev. Charles Holt(?), Wm. Croft of this place, to Miss ____ Baily, the only daughter of Mr. John Santee.
   Died on Black River, on the ____, Mr. Charles McGinny, aged ____. He has left a wife and eight helpless children....
(Issue in poor condition.)

Issue of March 11, 1834

   All persons indebted to the late Dr. Tho. D. Singleton, are requested to make payment.... Thos. D. Singleton, Executor.

Issue of September 9, 1834

   All persons having any demands against the estate of the late Col. Wm. Salters of Williamsburgh District, decd....
February 22   Sarah Salters, Admi'x.

Issue of September 16, 1834

   Died in this town yesterday 15th inst., Patrick Magrath, a native of Queens County, Ireland, in the 33d year of his age.
   Departed this life on the 2d inst., at his residence in Horry District, Daniel C. W. Conner, Esq., in the 23d year of his age.
   Departed this life at Flat Rock, N. C., on the 16th ult., Mrs. Elizabeth Frances Gourdin, consort of Dr. Theodore Gourdin, and only daughter of Dr. Wm. Allston of this place.
   Died at Charleston, on the evening of the 9th inst., Mr. Henry G. Young, of this place, in the 22d year of his age.

WINYAW INTELLIGENCER

Issue of October 7, 1834

All persons having demands against the Estate of the late Patrick Magrath of Georgetown (Mechanic)...John Harrelson, Oct. 4th, 1834   Qualified Executor.

Issue of November 7, 1834

Married in Charleston on Wednesday 22d inst., by the Rev. Mr. Cohen, Mr. Jacob Cohen of North santee to Miss S. Barrett of that city.

Issue of November 21, 1834

Died, on Monday the 3d inst., William Charles, only child of John G. and Mary Caldwell, aged 19 months.
All persons indebted to the Estate of Gen. J. W. Allston, late of All Saints deceased....   Mary Allston, Executrix.
Nov. 20   R. F. W. Allston, Executor.
All persons having demands against Paul Jaudon, late of this district deceased.....
Nov. 6th, 1834

Issue of December 18, 1834

All persons having demands against the Estate of Matthew Allen, late of Georgetown district, deceased....
Nov. 12   Thos M'Connell, Qual. Exr.

Issue of January 15, 1835

Died on Black River, on the 7th ult., Mrs. Elizabeth L. Keith, after a long and painful illness, consort of Mr. Thos. J. Keith.

Issue of January 22, 1835

Married on Thursday evening the 8th inst., in Brownsville, by the Rev. Mr. Ware, Dr. Robert Harllee of Marion District, to Miss Ann J. Gourly, of ths same.
Died on the 12th inst., at Laurel Hill, Waccamaw, Paul W. Tillman, in the 24th year of his age.

Issue of January 29, 1835

Departed this life, in this place, on the 14th inst., Mr. Asa Palmer, an old and experienced manager in the culture of Rice, in his 42d year...left three small orphans....

Issue of February 12, 1835

Died on the 31st ult at his plantation on Santee, Thomas J. Smith, Esq.

Issue of February 19, 1835

All persons indebted to A. Palmer deceased....
Jan 29   S. A. Hawkins, Executrix.

Issue of March 5, 1835

Married in Georgetown, Feb. 26th, by the Rev. Mr. Bowles,

WINYAW INTELLIGENCER

Mr. Caleb H. Nettles of Darlington S. C. to Miss Mary Elizabeth Cox, of the former place.

W. J. Dawsey applied for Letters of Administration on the estate of Adam Doar, late of Santee deceased....4 March 1835.

Issue of March 19, 1835

Henry Bailey applied for Letters of Administration on the estate of Daniel V. Berton, late of Georgetown deceased...14 March 1835.

Jonah W. Collins applied for letters of Admn. on the estate of John C. Harrington, late of Santee, deceased...14 March 1835.

Issue of April 2, 1835

All persons having any demands against the estate of William Small.... Susannah Small, Admi'x.
April 2

GEORGETOWN UNION

Issue of September 23, 1837 (Vol. 8, #19)

Married at Burlington, New Jersey, on the 4th inst., by the Right Rev. Bishop Doane, Capt. John T. Newton of the U. S. Navy, to Adela D. Lancey, daughter of the late Ralph Izard, of South Carolina.

At the same place, and on the same evening by the same Rev. Gentleman, Mr. Ralph Izard Middleton, of South Carolina, to Georgiana, youngest daughter of the late Ralph Izard, of South Carolina.

Died lately at the residence of Mr. Wm. J. Gause, on waccamaw, Mrs. Mary Small, aged about 56 years.

On Santee, on the 20th inst., Mrs. Eliza Shaw, consort of Mr. Benjamin F. Shaw.

In this town on Thursday morning last, youngest child of Thomas C. and Mary A. Fearwell, aged one year and nine months.

Issue of September 30, 1837

Died, on the morning of the 15th inst., in All Saints Parish, Mr. William Rowe, formerly a resident of Georgetown, in the 70th year of his age...left a widow and two young children....

Issue of October 14, 1837

Notice. All persons believing that they are the heirs of the late Mrs. Elizabeth Hanion of All Saints Parish, S. C., are informed that Mr. Charles Lewis of the Parish aforesaid has proved that he is a first cousin to the deceased and if there are others equally related with him, they are requested to prove it.... Mrs. Hanion was the Daughter of Mr. Nathaniel Dwight, of the Parish aforesaid, and she departed this life on the sixth of August 1836.   Jas. L. Belin, Admr.
Oct. 14

Issue of October 21, 1837

Died, in this place, on Monday the 18th inst., DR. S. S. Gasque, in the 38th year of his age. (eulogy)

Died, at North Inlet, on the 8th inst, Mr. Howel M. Christopher a native of Tennessee, but for the last 16 or 18 years, a resident of this town.

All persons having demands against the Estate of the late John Woody, of Williamsburg District, deceased....
Sept. 9   Benjamin King, Executor.

Issue of November 4, 1837

Married, on Pee Dee, on the 24th ultimo, by the Rev. Mr. Whitby, Mr. Robert H. Collins, to Miss Mary Jane, eldest daughter of Samuel Grier, Esq.

On the 27th, by Mr. Justice Carr, Mr. Isaac Morris to Miss Martha Britt, all of Sampit.

On the 31st, by Mr. Justice Carr, Mr. Isaac Singleton, Post Master at Poinsett, to Mrs. Elizabeth Milliken.

John Beaty died on the 24th ult., in his 73d year....
Horry, Oct. 28

GEORGETOWN UNION

Issue of November 11, 1837

Persons indebted to the late Dr. Samuel P. Dunbar, deceased
....   Mary Ann Dunbar, Executrix.
June 3, 1837
All persons having any demands against the Estate of Thomas R. Mitchell, deceased....   N. Mitchell, Qua'd Exr.
Feb. 25

Issue of November 18, 1837

All persons having demands against the Estate of Dr. S. S. Gasque....   E. B. Rothmahler, Adm'r.
Nov 4

Issue of December 16, 1837

Married on Britton's Neck, on the 7th ultimo, by the Rev. James Singleton, Mr. Richard G. Williams, to Miss Ann Rodgers, all of the above place.

Issue of May 26, 1838

Married on the 21st inst., by the Rev. P. T. Keith, Mr. C. F. Smith to Matilda Tucker, all of this place.

Issue of June 2, 1838

Married in Charleston, on the 24th ult., by the Rev. Paul Trapier, the Rev. Paul Trapier Keith, to Anna, daughter of Dr. W. Wilkinson.
All persons having claims against the estate of Thomas J. Smith, late of Georgetown District, deceased...
                          Henry J. Abbot, Admr.
Willow Grove Post Office, Sumter District.
April 21, 1838

Issue of June 9, 1838

Married in Kingstree, on Thursday evening the 24th inst., by the Rev. Lewis, Capt. Samuel P. Matthews to Miss Jane Bell, all of that place.
Heriot Tucker applied for Letters of Admn. on the estate of her husband Benjamin W. Tucker, deceased....6 June 1838

Issue of June 16, 1838

E. B. Rothmahler applied for letters of Admn. on the estate of Dr. John Wragg, late of Georgetown deceased, with his will annexed....15 June 1838

Issue of June 30, 1838

Departed this life on the 5th inst., in New York, Mr. William Brown, for many years a resident of this Town...left a widow....

Issue of July 11, 1838

Died in this town on the 29th ult., Mrs. _____ Hucks, consort of Mr. J. S. B. Hucks, aged 36 years.

GEORGETOWN UNION

in Marion District, on the 25th ultimo, Mrs. Allston Palmer, consort of Mr. David Palmer, in the 28th year of her age. Mrs. Palmer was the daughter of Capt. Alexander Taylor, of North Carolina. Deprived of both her parents in early life. In 1827 she married Mr. David Palmer of South Carolina....

Issue of July 21, 1838

Died on North Island on Monday, Archibald T. Ford, in the 20th year of his age....

Issue of July 28, 1838

Married on Sampit, on Thursday the 26th inst., by the Rev. Jno. R. Coburn, Mr. William Watts to Miss Rebecca Durant, all of Sampit.

Issue of September 1, 1838

Died on the night of the 28th inst., Capt. David Steel, in the 76th year of his age; a native of Scotland, for the last 20 years an inhabitant of this town.

Issue of September 8, 1838

Married on the 6th inst., by the Rev. J. W. M'Coll, Dr. Jos. M. Simmons, of Charleston, to Miss Eliza Ann, eldest daughter of the late Thomas Evans of Winyaw Bay.

Issue of September 22, 1838

Died, in this Town, on the 21st inst., Francis S. Matthews, in the 8th year of his age.

Issue of September 29, 1838

Died on Monday the 24th inst., at Charleston, S. C., Mrs. Marietta Munnerlyn, wife of Mr. William C. Munnerlyn, formerly of this place, in the 24th year of her age.

Issue of October 6, 1838

Died in this Town on the 17th ult., Mrs. Elizabeth Prior, in the 74th year of her age....
On Monday last, Mrs. Mary E. Magill, consort of Dr. Wm. Magill, aged 35 years and 5 months.

Issue of October 13, 1838

Departed this life on the 28th ult., at her residence in Williamsburgh, Mrs. Ann Haselden, in the 68th year of her age.

Issue of October 20, 1838

Deaths at North Island--on the 14th ult., Mrs. Anne Simmons, in the 49th year of her age, a native of swancy (R. I.), but for the last 8 years a resident of Charleston.
On the 16th Jane Simmons, in the 10th year of her age.

GEORGETOWN UNION

Issue of November 3, 1838

Died, in This Town, yesterday, Ann Eliza Waterman, aged 12 years, third daughter of E. and E. G. Waterman.

Issue of November 17, 1838

Married on Pee Dee on the 11th ult., by the Rev. John Woodward, Mr. Owen G. Kennedy, of Horry District, to Mrs. Christianna Bates, of the former place.
Died in Charleston, on the 7th inst., Benjamin Foissin Trapier, of this District, in the 65th year of his age.
Died at New York, on the 25th ult., Mr. Saul M. Boas, a native of Amsterdam Holland, but for the last 18 years a respectable and honest citizen of this town.
Died on Black River, on the 29th ult., Ezra Green, son of John J. and Clementina Green, aged 2 years 6 months and 2 days.
Died in this town on 24th ult., Eleanor, daughter of Nathaniel and Mary Patch, in the 13th year of her age.

Issue of December 8, 1838

Died, in this Town, on the 24th Nov., Mr. Joseph Lesesne, in the 69th year of his age. He was the oldest surviving male resident of this place.
All persons having claims or demands against the Estate of the late Mrs. Mary Huger, are requested to render them in....
Sarah M. Waring, Executrix
Wm. B. Bullock)
M. G. Gibbs)
H. A. DeSaussure) Executors
C. M. Furman)
Nov. 24   C. J. Colcock)
John Ralston applied for letters of Admn. on the estate of of Saul M. Boas....7 Dec 1838

Issue of December 15, 1838

Married, in this Town, on Wednesday evening last, by the Rev. J. W. McColl, Mr. Robert Leeper, to Mrs. Ann Gibbs.

Issue of December 22, 1838

Died, in this town, on the 29th ult., Ellen and on the 18th inst., John, each in the 7th year of their age, children of Eleazer and Eliza G. Waterman.

Issue of January 6, 1839

Married on the 26th December, by the Rev. Jas. Singleton, Samuel Grier, Esq. to Miss Mary Bath, eldest daughter of Capt. Daniel Bath, of Carver's Bay.

Issue of January 20, 1839

Died, on the first inst., in West Tennessee, Mr. Francis Greaves, formerly of Marrion district in the 56 years of his age.
in this town on the 6th inst., Mr. John R. Frisbie, of Guilford (Conn.) in the 25th year of his age.
Julia Ann Sellers applied for letters of admn. on the estate of Samuel S. Sellers, her deceased husband...8 Jan 1839

GEORGETOWN UNION

Issue of January 27, 1839

Died, in this Town, on the 20th instant, Emma Anna, youngest daughter of Samuel N. and Frances Marsh, aged 2 years 7 months and 14 days.

Issue of February 3, 1839

Married on the evening of the 31st ult., by the Rev. P. T. Keith, Mr. L. G. S. Middleton of Society Hill to Miss M. P. Gallavant, of this Town.
Departed this life on the night of the 28th ult., William Denison, in the 39th year his age, who was born, raised and educated in the State of Connecticut, but for many years a resident of this town....

Issue of February 17, 1839

Married at Lirins, near Wilmington, N. C., on Wednesday, 24th January, S. Gratz Moses, M. D. of Bordentown, N. J., to Mary P., daughter of the late Col. Samuel Ashe, of the former place
All persons having demands against the Estate of the late Mrs. M. Keyes deceased, of Horry Dist., S. C....   W. Whitby Feb. 3, 1839

Issue of February 24, 1839

Elijah Owens applied for admn. on the estate of his son Jesse Owens, late of Carver's Bay, deceased...23 Feb 1839

Issue of March 3, 1839

All persons having demands against Thomas W. Brightman, late of Santee, decd....   Sarah A. Brightman, Admx.
March 3

Issue of March 17, 1839

Married on Thursday the 15th inst., by the Rev. Paul T. Keith, Majr. John W. Coachman to Miss Mary H. daughter of Stephen Ford, Esq., both of this district.

Issue of March 31, 1839

Married on Thursday evening 29th inst., by the Rev. P. Trapier Keith, Mr. John Ralston to Miss Elizabeth Giles Dozier, daughter of the late Col. John Dozier of Williamsburg.
Married, at Waccamaw, on Tuesday 27th inst., by the Rev. Mr. Glanis, Mr. John Ashe Alston to Miss Francis Buford, youngest daughter of the Rev. Hugh Fraser.

Issue of April 14, 1839

Died, on Sunday Morning 1st inst., Silena Caroline, daughter of A. S. & Ellen E. Grosvenor, aged 1 year and 4 months.

Issue of April 21, 1839

Died, at Caproman on the 19th March last, Mr. W. H. Skrine, aged thirty two yeras and 7 months.

GEORGETOWN UNION

T. Galliard applied for letters of admn. on the estate of Sarah Pawley, late of Georgetown deceased with her will annexed 17 April 1839

Issue of May 12, 1839

Married at Kingstree on Thursday evening 3d instant, by the Rev. James Lewis, N. Gustavus Rich, esq. to Miss Magdalen M. Singleton, youngest daughter of the late Col. Thomas D. Singleton, of Williamsburg.

Issue of January 5, 1839

Married on the 26th ult., by the Rev. P. T. Keith, Mr. Wm. E. Sparkman, to Miss Elizabeth Burgess, all of this district.
 In Sumter District on the 27th ult., by the Rev. Mr. Converse, Major Abraham Van Buren (eldest son of the President) to Miss Sarah Angelica Singleton, daughter of Richard Singleton.
 At. Fort Hill, S. C., on the 12th ult., by the Rev. Mr. Potter, Mr. Thomas G. Clemson, of Philadelphia, to Miss Anna, daughter of the Hon. J. C. Calhoun.

Issue of January 26, 1839

Peter W. Fraser applied for letters of admn. on the estate of his father the Rev. Hugh Fraser.... 18 Jan 1839
 All persons who have any demands against the Est. of the late B. F. Trapier....   W. H. Trapier, Exor. Dec. 29
 All persons having any demands against the estate of John Harrelson, late of Georgetown District....   Daniel Bath, Admor. Dec. 22

Issue of February 9, 1839

Married on Wednesday evening last, by the Rev'd Mr. Forster, Mr. F. W. Munnerlyn to Miss Sarah A.Wright, all of this place

Issue of March 2, 1839

All persons having any demands against the Estate of Celia Rozier, late of Georgetown District, deceased...   Feb. 16 P. M. Davis, Exor.

Issue of March 23, 1839

Married on Sampit on Tuesday the 10th inst., by the Rev. Mr. Foster, Mr. Charles P. Matthews to Miss Esther Ann Sullivan.
 Died, on the 21st inst., at daylight, at his father's residence on Pee Dee, Robert Allston, 2d son of R. F. W. and Adelle Allston, aged 4 years 2 months and __ days.
 David Crosland applied for letters of admn. on the estate of Matthew Allen, late of this district, decd...22 March 1839

Issue of April 20, 1839

Married in this town on Tuesday evening last, by the Rev. A. M. Forster, Mr. George S. Taylor, to Miss Susan A. Marsh ,all of this place.

GEORGETOWN UNION

Issue of May 25, 1839

Died in this town on the 20th inst., Wm. Peter, son of Nannette and Tho's L. Shaw, aged 3 years.

Issue of June 8, 1839

All persons having demands against John Green, Esq., late of All Saints Parish, deceased....   Solomon King, Qualified Exr. June 8

Issue of July 13, 1839

Died in this town on the 8th inst., Henry Jackson Dunster, aged 31 years, a native of Boston, Mass.

Issue of July 27, 1839

In New York, on the 3d inst.,by the Rev. S. H. Cone, M. Richard O. Bush to Miss Caroline Amelia, youngest daughter of Capt. Samuel Aimy, all of that town.

Issue of August 31, 1839

Married, in this town, on Thursday evening last, by the Rev. Mr. McCloud, Mr. Henry F. Detyens to Miss Margaret Wall.

At Paris, July 22nd Wm. Young, Esq., youngest son of Rear Admiral Young, to Harriet Elizabeth, only child of A. S. Willington, of Charleston, S. C.

Died in this town on Saturday last, Asa D. Shaler, a native of Connecticut, aged 26 years.

GEORGETOWN AMERICAN

Issue of November 9, 1839 (Volume I, #1)

All persons having demands against the Estate of J. G. A. Anderson, late of Georgetown Dist., Deceased....Thomas G. Finklea, Admr. Nov. 2

J. S. B. Hucks applied for letters of administration on the estate of Mary Elizabeth Singleton, minor...18 Oct 1839

All persons having demands against the estate of Col. William Alston deceased....
    Wm. A. Alston   )
    T. Pinckney Alston) Executors
    Charles Alston   )

All persons having demands against Wm. T. Thompson, late of Waccamaw deceased, are requested to render statements....
    C. J. Atkinson, Executor

Issue of November 23, 1839

Died at Port's Ferry, on the 9th inst., John David B. Mendenhall, a native of Guilford County (N.C.), aged about 22 years.

In this town, on the 11th inst., Thomas Heriot, Esquire, Post Master in the 50th year of his age.

Also, on the 12th inst., Capt. John Miller, a native of Germany, aged 35 years.

Issue of January 4, 1840

Mary Vernon applied for letters of administration on the estate of Henry Vernon...11 Oct 1839

Issue of January 28, 1840

Died in this Town on the 4th instant, Mrs. Esther Cogdell, in the 97th year of her age, widow of the late John Cogdell, Esq. She died of old age.

On the 14th instant, George S. Taylor, in the 25th year of his age... Mr. T. was the last proprietor of the late Georgetown Union.

On the 19th instant, Mrs. Elizabeth F. Blyth, in the 78th year of her age, widow of the late Dr. Joseph Blyth.

All persons having legal demands against John Chapman, dec'd, ...   William Chapman, Admr.

William V. Brown, applied for letters of administration on the estate of Isaac Brown, late of Black River, deceased.... 25 January 1840

Issue of February 4, 1840

Died in this place on the 19th instant, Mrs. Elizabeth Frances Blyth. (eulogy).

Died on the 30th ult., Eliza Victoria Keith, daughter of Thomas J. and M. L. T. Keith, aged one year 6 months and 5 days.

Issue of March 3, 1840

Died at North Santee, on Sunday morning, the 23d inst., Anne Elizabeth, infant daughter of Dr. Joseph M. and Eliza A. Simmons.

GEORGETOWN AMERICAN

Issue of March 6, 1840

Married in this Town, on Thursday the 23rd of January last, by the Rev. P. T. Keith, James G. Henning, Esq., to Emma--daughter of the late Dr. Edward G. Thomas.
on Thursday evening last, by the Rev. Mr. Forster, Dr. O. M. Roberts of Charleston, to Miss Martha, daughter of the late Peter Cuttino, Esq.
Died in this Town on the 1st ult., Mr. William Moody, in the 55th year of his age, for some time past a Merchant.

Issue of March 13, 1840

Married at the seat of Mrs. M. L. Davis on Black River, on Thursday evening the 5th inst., Thomas BEnnett, to Mrs. Jane M. Gordon, relict of the late John Gordon, Esq. both of Charleston.

Issue of March 20, 1840

Died in this Town on the 6th inst., Mr. Wm. Dicks, in the 56th year of his age.
in this Town on the 13th inst., James Corson, aged about 16 years.

Issue of March 27, 1840

Died on the 26th inst., Annette Louisa Corson, aged 3 years 10 months and 7 days, youngest daughter of the bereaved parents.

Issue of April 3, 1840

Died, at Darlington, on the 20th of March, Peter C. Coggeshall Esqr., a native of Newport R. Island, but from childhood, a resident of South Carolina. (eulogy).

Issue of April 24, 1840

Died on the 12thinst., after 9 days of painfull illness, Margaret Ann Desdamona Hawkins, daughter of Mrs. Mary Hawkins, of this Town, aged 4 years and 5 months.

Issue of May 1, 1840

Married in this Town on Tuesday evening last, by the Rev. A. M. Forster, Mr. Thomas R. Sessions, to Miss Jane E. Davies, all of this place.

Issue of June 12, 1840

Died in this Town on the 24th inst., Magdalen W., aged about two years, only daughter of Thomas L. & Annette Shaw. This is the third child this estimable couple have lost within twelve months...

Issue of June 19, 1840

Died on Sampit, on the 14th inst., Robert Atkinson, third son of R. W. and Mary H. Sullivan, aged 2 years and 13 days.
Died at Planters Ville on Monday Morning the 15th inst., Joan Joseph, oldest son of Mr. & Mrs. Jas. J. Coachman in the 7th year of his age.

GEORGETOWN AMERICAN

Issue of July 3, 1840

Died near Durhamville, Tenn. on the ___ of May last, Isaac D. Coachman, Esqr., lately a citizen of this Town.

Issue of July 17, 1840

All Persons having any demands against the estate of Thomas Jinkins late of Horry District deceased....Benj. Gause, Admr. July 17

Issue of July 29, 1840

Married on the 16th inst., by the Rev. David Legett, at the residence of David J. Taylor, Esq., Major J. P. Doyle to Miss Ann Taylor, both of Marion District.
Died in this town on the 20th inst., Mrs. Ann Bosman, aged 40 years.
Died on North Island on the 18th inst., Mr. Robert Leeper, in the 23d year of his age.
John Booth applied for Letters of Administration on the estate of Ann Bosman, as next of kin...23 July 1840

Issue of August 5, 1840

Married on Black River on the 26 inst., by the Rev. Paul A. M. Williams, Mr. James D. Ham, to Miss Mary F. K. Miller.
Died on the 31st ult., Miss Susan E. Shum, of this Town. On the 1st inst., Mr. William M'Collough, aged about 40 years.

Issue of August 12, 1840

Died, in this town, on the 3d instant, of dropsy, Mr. Jesse Palmer, aged 66 years.
All persons having demands against Jesse Palmer, late of Georgetown, deceased....   Rebekah Ann Palmer, Executrix. August 12

Issue of August 19, 1840

Married at Withersville, on Thursday the 13th instant, by the Rev. Mr. Williams, Arthur Vanderhorst, Esq. of Charleston, to Miss Susan E. F., eldest daughter of the late Wm. Shackelford, of this District.

Issue of September 2, 1840

Died, at Marion Court House, on Tuesday the 11th ulto., George McKay, a native of New York, aged 26 years. He was a resident of this State about two years. (eulogy).
On the 24th ultimo, on Black River, near Georgetown, Mrs. Mariah L. F. Keith, consort of Mr. Thos. J. Keith, and only daughter of Mr. Saml. Fraser, formerly of Darlington. (eulogy)
In this Town on the 19th ultimo, Benjamin, youngest child of Eleazer and E. G. Waterman, aged 13 months.
On Pee Dee, on the morning of the 25th ulto., Mr. Henry C. Smith, a native of Scotland, aged about 35 years.
W. S. Forsyth applied for Letters of Administration on the estate of Henry C. Smith, foreigner, late of this place, deceased, as next friend....29 Aug 1840

GEORGETOWN AMERICAN

Issue of November 18, 1840

Departed this life on Wednesday 18th in the 52 year of his age, Mr. David Davies, a native of Wales, but for many years a resident of this town and district. (eulogy).

Died at his seat on Black River, on Sabbath morning, on the 15th inst., Thomas Ford, Esqr., in the 58th year of his age....

Issue of December 9, 1840

All persons having any demands against the estate of Thomas Ford, late of Black River, deceased....   Stephen Ford, Exr. Dec. 2

Issue of December 16, 1840

Ann C. Davies applied for Letters of Administration on the Estate of her husband David Davis....16 Dec 1840

Issue of December 23, 1840

Married on Black River, on Thursday last, by the Rev. Mr. Phillips, Mr. H. F. Detyens, to Miss Sarah M'Ginney, all of this District.

Died at her residence near Society Hill, on the 17th ult., Mrs. Elizabeth Williams, relict of the late Gen. David R. Williams.

at Darlington Court House, on the 7th inst., John Gibson, an old and highly respected citizen.

Issue of December 26, 1840

Died at Mattapoisett Massachusetts, on Friday evening the 11th inst., Miss S. T. M. Barstow, daughter of Capt. James Barstow, aged 18 years.

All persons having any demands against Percival E. Vaux, late of Georgetown Dist., deceased....   John P. Ford) Qual. Exrs.
                                                    W. P. Vaux)

Issue of December 30, 1840

Married in Mobile, on the 2d Dec., by the Rev. Jefferson Hamilton, Mr. D. R. W. Davis, formerly of this City, to Miss Mary W. Norris, daughter of Jno. B. Norris, Esqr.

All persons having demands against Thomas Evans, late of Winyaw, deceased....   Mary Ann Evans, Admix. Dec. 23

Issue of January 6, 1841

All persons having demands against the Estate of Mrs. Rebekah Smith, deceased....   James Smith, Qual. Exr.

Issue of January 13, 1841

Died, at his residence on Black River (Brown's Ferry) on the 6th inst., in the 48th year of his age, Mr. William V. Brown.

Issue of January 27, 1841

Married in this town on 19th inst., by The Rev. Paul A. Williams, Mr. William Williams, to Miss Louisa Matilda, daughter

GEORGETOWN AMERICAN

of Zacariah and Elizabeth Cogdell, all of this place.

Issue of January 30, 1841

Married in this Town on 19th inst., by the Rev. P. A. Williams, Mr. Maesheck S. Williams, to Miss Louisa Matilda, daughter of Zacariah Cogdell, all of this place.

Issue of February 3, 1841

Jane C. Linerieux applied for letters of Administration on the estate of her husband Joseph C. Linerieux....29 Jan 1841

Issue of February 6, 1841

Died in this town on the 3d inst., Mrs. Sarah L. Coachman, relict of the late Francis G. Coachman, aged about 32 years. (eulogy)

Issue of February 17, 1841

Married in this district, on Thursday night last, Mr. Benj. F. Westberry, to Miss Ann Cumbie.
Died on the 13th inst., Mrs. Mary B. Davis, consort of Mr. L. W. W. Davis, of Waccamaw, aged 28 yeras and 11 months, for twelve years a member of the church...leaving a husband and three infant children....

Issue of February 20, 1841

Died at the Georgia Female College, on the 26th January, Jane P., daughter of Francis R. Shackelford, late of this place in the 15th year of her age. (eulogy)
Died on the 19th inst., John Alway, of the brig Juno, a native of New-York, aged 35 years.

Issue of March 3, 1841

Susannah Brown applied for Letters of Administration on the estate of her brother Isaac Brown...3 March 1841

WINYAW OBSERVER

Issue of March 10, 1841 (Vol. I, #1)

Married at Lucknow, Pee Dee, on Wednesday evening, the 3d inst. by the Rev. Mr. Gallagher, Francis Deliesseline Richardson, Esq. of Charleston to Miss Agnes on ly Daughter of the late Benjamin P. Fraser, of Georgetown District.

All persons having any demands against the Estate of Mrs. Sarah Coachman, late of Georgetown dec'd will render....
March 10   J. W. Coachman, Qualified
                                        Ex'or.

All persons having demands against Joseph C. Linerieux, deceased, are requested to render Attested statements....
Feb. 17   Jane C. Linerieux, Administrator.

All persons having any demands against Percival E. Vaux, late of Georgetown Dist., deceased....
Dec. 23   John P. Ford) Qualified Exors.
                         W. P. Vaux)

Persons having demands against the Estate of Mrs. Rebekah Smith deceased....
Dec 9   James Smith, Qualified Executor.

Issue of March 13, 1841

All persons having demands against Isaac Brown, deceased, late of Black River, are requested to render statements....
March 13, 1841   Susannah Brown, Administratix.

Issue of March 17, 1841

Died, at New-Haven (Con.) Catharine Waldo, aged 85 years, relict of the late John Waldo of this town. She was a discendant (sic) of the same family, we understand, who were the first settif not first proprietors of the soil on which Georgetown now stands

Issue of March 20, 1841

Information Wanted. If William Ayres, who married Margaret Brown, in Lower All Saints Parish Georgetown district in 1801 or 1802, or any child of the issue of that marriage, will address a letter to me at this place, to the care of Mr. Wm. S. Croft, they will hear of something to their advantage. They are heirs of one third of the estate of Isaac Brown deceased late of Black River. Mr. Ayers lived on Cooper River from 1804 to 1809 and moved thence to Alabama, and has not since been heard of.
March 13   Susannah Brown, Administratrix of
                         Isaac Brown.

Issue of April 3, 1841

Married in this Town, on Sabbath evening, the 28th ult. by the Rev'd. Mr. Leard, Mr. Charles H. Faulkner, of Guilford, Conn. to Mrs. Martha Folk, of this place.

At Marion Court House, on Thursday the 25th ult by the Rev'd. T. R. Walsh, Mr. Richard Woodberry, eldest son of Gen'l W. Woodberry, of Brittons Neck, to Miss Joanna Bellune, eldest daughter of the late Major J. C. Bellune of Marion village.

Issue of April 7, 1841

Married on Pee Dee, on Tuesday evening, the 16th inst., by the Rev. James Singleton, Benjamin Bruton, Esq. Sheriff elect of Horry

WINYAW OBSERVER

District, to Miss Elizabeth L. Sarvis.
in Charleston, on the evening of the 1st inst., by the Rev. W. T. Brantly, Mr. B. A. Coachman, of this place, to Miss E. O. Taylor, of Charleston.
Died in Charleston, on the 29th ult., John Hume, Esq. one of the oldest and most respectable planters of this district. He must have attained the age of 80 years.

Issue of April 10, 1841

(Death notices of Pres. Harrison)
Married in the City of New York, on the 5th ult., by the Rev. E. P. Rogers, Albert G. Colwell, Esq. of this place, to Miss Sarah P. Rogers, of the former place.
Died in Charleston on Friday last, Rev. Jehu G. Postell, a native of this district.
Died last evening, suddenly, Wm. ;. Heriot, Esqr. aged about 40 years, a native of this place.

Issue of April 14, 1841

Persons indebted to Michael Young, lately deceased, are requested forthwith to make payment to A. W. Dozier....
Test. G. W. Christee   her
                               Hannah X Young
April 14   mark

Issue of April 21, 1841

Married on Sunday morning the 24th January 1841, by Dr. Kokon, Mr. William Edwin Miller, a Teacher of School of Wilmington, New Hanover County, N. C. to Miss Elizabeth Massey, youngest and only daughter of Mr. Jonas Suggs, of All Saints Parish, So. Ca.

Issue of April 24, 1841

Married in Marion Village, on Sunday evening the 4th inst. by the Rev'd. F. R. Walsh, Mr. Thomas A. Smith, to Miss Caroline M. Brown, daughter of C. B. Brown, Esqr.

Issue of May 1, 1841

Citation on Estate of Cain Lockey...Moreland Williams applied for letters of admn. 24 April 1841.
Citation on Estate of Francis Kinloch, Esqr. late of this district deceased...Henry A. Middleton applied for letters of admn, 23 April 1841.

Issue of May 4, 1841

Died in Charleston, on the 28th March last, John Hume, of Santee, aged 78 years and 5 months. As a soldier, in the tent of Marion, he acquired the confidence of his General....left 7 children, 44 grand children, and 4 great grandchildren. (eulogy).

Issue of May 19, 1841

Persons having demands against the estate of William V. Brown, late of Black River deceased, will render them in....
May 19   Hannah Brown, Qualified Executor.

WINYAW OBSERVER

Issue of May 22, 1841

Died in Charleston on Tuesday last, deeply regretted, Mr. Robert Thurston, of the House of Robertson & Thurston of that city. Mr. Thurston was a native of this town.

Issue of May 26, 1841

Married in Cheraw, on Thursday evening last, by Rev. A. M. Forster, Mr. S. C. Sessons, of this town, to Miss Caroline Campbell, of the former place.

Issue of June 9, 1841

Died in Charleston, on Thursday last, Mrs. Jane Thurston, relict of the late Samuel I. Thurston, late of this town.

Issue of June 23, 1841

...death of Colonel William Timmons, in the 42d year of his age. He died at his residence in Darlington on the 6th inst. of a congestive or bilious fever, contracted, perhaps by his visit to Charleston and this place, a short time previous...a member of the Baptist Church more than 18 years.

Issue of July 7, 1841

Married at Rockingham, Richmond county, N. C. recently, Dr. C. Zimmerman, of Columbia, to Mrs. Hannah Green, late of this town.

Issue of July 14, 1841

Died on the 9th inst., Isaiah Lawrance, aged 53 years, a native of Boston. He had been residing here two seasons, a fisherman and sportsman in winter, and a carpenter in summer.

Issue of July 27, 1841

All persons having demands against William Timmons, late of Darlington District, deceased, are requested to present them....
July 21   John M. Timmons, Administrator.
P. S. Address the subscriber at Effingham, Darlington District, S. C.
All persons having demands against Mr. A. Lawrence late of this place deceased, are requested to render attested statements....
July 21   E. Waterman, Ordinary.

Issue of August 4, 1841

Married on Pee Dee, 29th July 1841, by the Rev. Mr. Woodward, Mr. James Howell of Horry, to Miss Elizabeth Anderson, only child of Mrs. Rachael Holmes.
Died at North Island, on Thursday last, of congestive fever, Mrs. Anna B. Henning, relict of the late Thomas Henning....member of the Protestant E. Church. (eulogy).

WINYAW OBSERVER

Issue of August 11, 1841

Died at North Island, on Thursday last, of Bilious fever, Maj. William Chapman, the Post-Master of our town and eldest son of the late Thomas Chapman, aged 46 years. (eulogy).

___ in this town, on the 5th inst.,Mr. James Murphy, a native of Ireland. Mr. Murphy was a mechanic and has resided here for two years....

All persons indebted to William Harrington, late of Georgetown merchant, deceased, are requested to make payment immediately....
Martha A. Harrington, Administratrix.

All persons having legal demands against the Estate of the late Dr. Samuel Hodges, deceased, will please present them....
Marion C. H. Aug 11   R. H. Reaves, Executor.

Issue of August 18, 1841

All persons having demands against Jane Thurston, late of Georgetown deceased are requested to render the same....
Aug 11   Stephen Ford, Executor.

Issue of August 25, 1841

Died in this town on the 22 inst. Mr. Charles Johnson, a native of Norway (S.) aged about 27 years. He was master of the Sloop Reliance of this place, and an honest and industrious man.

All persons having demands against Thomas Heriot, late of Georgetown deceased, are requested to render attested statements....
Aug 25, 1841   E. Waterman, Ordinary.

Issue of September 1, 1841

Married on Pee Dee on the 12th inst. by the Rev. John Woodward, Mr. John C. Lester, to Miss Louisa eldest daughter of Mr. Alfrid(sic) Wilson.

Married at Tabernacle, Marion Diss. S. C., on the 22d inst. by the Rev. W. A. McSwane, Mr. David J. Taylor, to Miss Eugenia E. Potter, daughter of the late Obadiah Potter of this place.

___ in this town on the 26th inst., by the Rev. Mr. Leard, Mr. Hansford Jennings Morris to Mrs. Hannah Brown, all of this District.

Issue of September 8, 1841

Died, at North Island, on the 26th ult., Henry Stevens, son of Capt. James Corson, aged 2 years.

at North Island, on Friday last, Capt. Constant Corson, aged 75 years, a native of New Jersey. He was remarkable for his industry, and the even tenor of his life.

in this town, on the 5th inst., John Hardwick, aged 49 years, a native of this town, and second son of the late John Hardwick surveyor--whose plats are principally relied upon as best locating the real estates on this and the adjoining districts.

at Smerdon, the residence of J. H. Read, Jr. Esqr. on Pee Dee, on the 6th inst., William S. Forsyth, of this town. (eulogy).

Issue of September 15, 1841

Died at his residence on North Island, in the 20th year of his age, Mr. John Porter, eldest son of Col. John Porter, deceased. (eulogy)

WINYAW OBSERVER

Died in Williamsburg Dist. on the 11th inst. Henrietta Louisa, youngest daughter of John G. and Margaret A. Cross of this town aged two years and five months.

By permission of James Beaty, Esq. Ordinary for Horry District, will be sold at the late residence of Isaac Parker dec'd, of said District, near the Mineral Spring, all the personal property ....
C. B. Sarvis, Adm'r.

Issue of September 22, 1841

Died on Wednesday last of bilious fever, in the 16th year of his age, Archible McClenan Brightman, second son of the late Thomas W. Brightman, of Santee.

on Thursday last in the 80th year of her age, Mrs. Elizabeth Campbell, relict of the late Alexander Campbell. Mrs. Campbell was born at Hampstead in the immediate neighborhood, and with the exception of two years, may be said to have resided here from her birth. She was the second oldest female native of this place ....

at North Island on the same day, in the 60th year of her age, of cancer, Mrs. Emily Thomas, relict of the late Dr. Edward G. Thomas....

Issue of September 29, 1841

Died on Black River on the 22d inst., Francis James Sparkman, aged 2 years, youngest son of F. L. and Sarah Siau.

In this town yesterday morning, Andrew Roney, Carpenter, a native of New York but for the last two years a resident of this town.

In New Orleans, lately James A. Hart, late of Darlington district.

Issue of October 6, 1841

Married in this town on Thursday evening last by the Rev. Mr. Leard, Mr. James B. Anderson to Mrs. Eliza Denison.

On Black River on Thursday evening last by Rev. Mr. Williams, Mr. John Blunt to Miss Mary Howard.

Died at the residence of W. J. Dawsey, on Santee on the 2 ult. D. A. Seitz, aged about 27 years, a foreigner, believed to be German. He landed in New York in July 1840 came to this place in July last, and was journeying to Charleston on foot....

In this town on Monday last, aged about 19 years, Mr. Edward Kedney, a native of the city of New York, and attached to the brig Ann of that port.

Citation on the estate of William F. Heriot, late of Georgetown Deceased...Edward T. Heriot applied for letters of admm.... 4th October 1841.

Citation on Estate of William S. Forsyth, Carpenter, late of Georgetown deceased...Eleanor Forsyth applied for letters of admn.... 4th October 1841.

Issue of October 13, 1841

Died on the 7th inst after a short illness, at her residence on Waccamaw Seashort, Mary K., widow of the late Gen. Joseph W. Allston.

WINYAW OBSERVER

Issue of October 27, 1841

Died in this town on Wednesday last, Mr. Charles S. Megargee, carpenter, and late deputy Marshall, aged 22 years, a native of Philadelphia.
Died at her residence on Waccamaw sea short on the 7th of October, Mrs. Mary Allston, wife of the late General Joseph W. Allston. (eulogy).
Citation on the estate of Anna B. Henning...Jas. G. Henning applied for letters of admn.... 26th October 1841.

Issue of November 3, 1841

Died on the 4th Oct. on Pee Dee, at Smyrdon Plantation, Mrs. Mary H. McDonald, consort of Enos McDonald, Esq. aged 54 years, leaving a husband and three children to mourn their loss.
in this town yesterday, Casper Marra, aged about 30 years, an Italian.
At St. Augustine on the 24th ult. Col. Charles Downing.
In Pendleton, on the 25th ult., Rev. Jasper Adams, late President of the Charleston College.

Issue of November 10, 1841

Died in this town this morning, in the 64th year of her age, Mrs. Mary Alston, wife of Wm. A. Alston, Esqr. of Waccamaw. (eulogy).

Issue of November 17, 1841

Died in this town on Wednesday last, Mr. Robert Wilson, aged about 26 years, second son of the late Robert Wilson of this District.
On Pee Dee, at the plantation of Francis Weston, Esqr. on the 12th inst. Mr W. W. T. Rogers, formerly of All Saint's Parish.
Citation on the Estate of William Windham Trapier Rogers... Elizabeth Rogers, his widow, applied for letters of admn.... 15th November 1841.

Issue of November 24, 1841

All legal demands against the late William Chapman of Georgetown, are requested to be handed to E. Water Esqr....
Charleston, Nov. 24   James Chapman, qualified Executor.

Issue of December 1, 1841

State of South Carolina, Williamsburgh District, Citation on Estate of Jacob Johnson, late of this district deceased... Jacob J. Howard applied for letters of admn. with the will annexed...26 Nov 1841. Samuel G. McClary, O. W. D.

Issue of December 4, 1841

Citation on estate of George. R. Congdon, late of Georgetown, deceased....Charlotte C. Congdon applied for letters of admn.... 4 December 1841.
Citation on estate of Emily Thomas, widow, late of Georgetown, deceased....Edward Thomas applied for letters of admn....3 Dec 1841.

WINYAH OBSERVER

Issue of December 11, 1841

All persons having demands against William Denison, late of Georgetown deceased....
Dec 11   Jas. B. Anderson, Admor.
All persons indebted to the estate of Henry Vernon....
Dec 8   Mary Vernon.

Issue of December 15, 1841

Died on Pee Dee on the 11th inst. Mr. James Murrow, aged about 45 years.
in this town yesterday, Mr. Benjamin H. Christian, aged about 25 years.

Issue of December 22, 1841

Died on Waccamaw on the 15th inst Mary Elizabeth youngest daughter of L. W. W. and Mary B. Davis, aged 10 months and 21 days.
At the summer retreat of William Lester, Esq. on Black River, in Sept. last, Mr. John Brockington, aged 83 yeras. a Soldier of the Revolution. With the exception of 10 years in Sumter he has resided in this distrct.

Issue of January 12, 1842

Estate sale...Williamsburgh District...estate of the late John Wooddy.
Jan. 12   Benjamin King, Exor.

Issue of January 15, 1842

Married in this town on Wednesday evening last, by the Rev. Mr. Howard, Dr. George Heriot to Mrs. Marilda Smith, all of this place.

Issue of January 19, 1842

Departed this life at Rockingham, N. C. on the morning of January 2nd, Christiana Coachman, infant daughter of Daniel P. and Margaret A. M'Donald.
All persons having demands against Emily Thomas, widow, and her son Washington Thomas, each late of Georgetown deceased....
Jan. 19   Edward Thomas, Admor.

Issue of February 2, 1842

Died at his residence Lucknow, on the Pee Dee River, January 29, 1842, Davison McDowell Esqr. in the 59th year of his age. He was a native of Newry in the County of Armagh, Ireland, and for upwards of 37 years a resident of this District. At a tender age he was left by his parents under the care of his Grandfather and Grandmother....At the age of 22 he came to this country to see his mother, and found her a Widow, with two daughters: he came their only protector. (eulogy)

Issue of February 10, 1842

Citation on the Estate of Andrew Carville...Sophia Pigott

WINYAH OBSERVER

applied for letters of admn. with the will annexed. 9 Feb 1842.

Issue of February 12, 1842

Died, near Darlington Court House on the 22d ult., Mr. Samuel Frisbe, aged 25 years, a native of Connecticut, and one of the House of Charles & Frisbie.

Issue of February 16, 1842

Died, last evening in the 38th year of his age, Capt. J. R. Porter. He has been engaged in the coasting trade between Charleston and this place for the last 18 years-...

Issue of February 19, 1842

on Thursday, the death of our townsman Mr. John Ralston... in 1838 married the second daughter of our lamented Col. John Dozier....Mr. Ralston was about 32 years of age...left widow and two small children.
Died in this town on Thursday last, Mr. Thomas Lynch, aged about 27 years.

Issue of February 26, 1842

Died near Bucksville, on the 19th inst., Josephine Haseltine Norton, aged four years and 10 months.
Citation on Estate of John Ralston...A. W. Dozier applied for letters of admn...25 Feb 1842.

Issue of March 5, 1842

Married in this town on Thursday evening last by the Rev. Mr. Leard, Isaac C. Croft, Esqr. to Miss Martha Wright, all of this place.
on the same evening, by the same gentleman, Mr. James M. Hunter of Darlington to Miss Sarah Waterman, of this place.

Issue of March 16, 1842

Married in this town on Thursday evening last, Mr. Benjamin Ellis, of Charleston to Miss Elizabeth Pigott, of this place.
On the same evening, Mr. James H. White, to Miss Mary Bunch.
Died in Charleston yesterday, of cancer in the stomach, Hon. Jacob F. Mintzing, Major of that city.

Issue of March 23, 1842

Citation on the estate of Robert James Dealy, late of Georgetown, deceased...Benj. W. Dealy applied for letters of admn.... 15 March 1842.

Issue of March 30, 1842

Married in Charleston, on the 18th January last by the Rev. Dr. Backman, Cleland K. Huger, to Miss Mary A., eldest daughter of Chancellor Sunkan, both of Charleston.
on 22d February in St. Mathews Parish, Thos. P. Huger, to Miss Anna, eldest daughter of Hon. Langdon Cheves.

WINYAH OBSERVER

Issue of May 7, 1842

Married at Rose Hill, Waccamaw, by the Rev. A. Glennie on the 4th inst. Dr. S. Deas to Miss Alston, daughter of Wm. A. Alston Esqr.
Died at Rocky Point, on Black River on Tuesday last, Mr. William Sessions, aged 20 years.

Issue of June 4, 1842

Married at St. Peter's Church in Charleston, on the 26th inst. by the Rev. Mr. Branwell, Col. Allard H. Belin, of this district, to Miss Virginia Wilkinson, daughter of Dr. Willis Wilkinson, late of this town.
in the same city, on Tuesday morning, 31st ult. at the residence of Gen. James Hamilton, Dr. William Alexander Sparks, of Society-Hill, Darlington district, to Miss Alvira Middleton, youngest daughter of the late John Middleton of St. James, Santee.
Died in this town on Saturday last, Miss Sarah Taylor, aged 58 years.
On the same day, Capt. Zachariah Cogdell, a native of Wayne County, N. C. in the 58th year of his age.
on Santee, on Wednesday 25th ult., Mrs. C. Lenud, aged 49 years, relict of the late Caleb C. Lenud.
at the residence of Mr. Wm. J. Dawsey, on Saturday last, Mrs. Martha L. Smith, aged 39 years, relict of the late Jesse Smith.

Issue of June 11, 1842

Married at Society Hill, on Thursday the 2nd instant, by the Rev. F. M. Hubbard, William H. Evans, Esq., son of the Hon. Josiah J. Evans, to Miss Jane, youngest daughter of Col. J. D. Witherspoon, all of that place.
Died on the 2d inst. at her residence in Williamsburg, near China Grove, Mrs. Susan Snow, consort of James Snow, Esq. A devoted husband, an aged and affectionate mother, a fond sister and brother are left to mourn....member of the Methodist Episcopal Church. (eulogy).
at his residence in Marion district, on Saturday last, Mr. David Palmer, aged 59 years, late of this District, and one of the representatives in the State Legislature from Marion.
on Santee on Sunday last in the 65th year of his age, John Perdriau, Esq., greatly respected and much lamented.
Citation on the estate of Elizabeth Campbell, late of Georgetown deceased...Anna Hall applied for letters of admn....11 June 1842.

Issue of June 18, 1842

From the New York Spirit of the Times....
decease of Mr. William Ashe Alston, son of Mr. William A. Alston, of Georgetown District, S. C. who died in thie city on Monday last (May 30th), in the 30th year of his age....returned from Europe in October last, and immediately repaired to Oak Lawn, the seat of his father-in-law in Louisiana....(eulogy and a long account).

Issue of June 28, 1842

Departed this life on Pawley's Island, on Monday night last,

WINYAH OBSERVER

at the residence of his Son in Law, Mr. R. Nesbit, Mr. John Hamilton, in the 58th year of his age....

Issue of July 2, 1842

Departed this life on the 4th instant, at his late residence in Marion District, Mr. David Palmer, in the 53d year of his age, a son of the Rev. Wm. Palmer, who was for many years, a faithful minister of Christ in the Baptist Cause...left an affectionate wife and nine children. (eulogy).

Died at Camden (So. Ca.) on the 24th instant, Mrs. Elizabeth Jenkins, consort of the Rev. James Jenkins, in the 64th year of her age.

Issue of July 16, 1842

Died at the Camps, near town, on Thursday last, in the 17th year of her age, Mrs. Olevia L. Coachman, consort of Mr. Benj. A. Coachman. The funeral was solemnized last evening at the summer residence of Maj. John W. Coachman, and the corpse removed to Rock Point, on Black River, for interment...left husband and infant son.

All persons having demands against William W. Sessions, late of Georgetown deceased are requested to render statements....
July 9   William G. Linerieux, Adm'r.

Issue of July 23, 1842

Died in this town on Monday last, Mr. William Courtney, a native of London, aged 23 years.

Issue of July 30, 1842

Died at Marion Court house, on Friday the 1st inst., Mrs. C. K. Bellune, in the 36th year of her age.

at Poplar Hill on the 27th inst. Mary Emeline, aged 2 years and 2 months, daughter of Mr. and Mrs. A. W. Dozier.

Issue of August 6, 1842

Died on the 1st inst. at the residence of James Snow, Esq. Williamsburg district, Mrs. Nancy Easterling, about 66 years of age; and

at the summer residence in Georgetown district, Mrs. Mary Bellune, consort of William G. Bellune Esq. and daughter of the above named Mrs. Easterling.

Departed this life in Sumterville, on the 21st July of congestive fever, Thomas, second son of the late Davidson McDowell Esqr. aged 4 years 10 months and 6 days.

Issue of August 13, 1842

Died in this town, on Monday last, Charles James, aged 4 years, 2 months and 18 days eldest son of Maj. James M. and Eliza Commander.

On Wednesday last John James, infant son of Benjamin A. Coachman. This child survived its mother only one month.

WINYAH OBSERVER

Issue of August 20, 1842

All persons to whom the Estate of the late David Palmer of Marion is indebted are requested to render the same....
Aug 20   William F. Richardson, or David J. Taylor.

Issue of August 27, 1842

Died in this town, yesterday Mrs. Priscilla McDaniel, aged 36 years, consort of Mr. John B. McDaniel...left a large family of children.
____ John Simpson aged three years, son of Emily Anderson.
____ this morning, Benjamin aged 4 years, son of Mrs. Elizabeth Morris.

Issue of September 3, 1842

Died at his residence in Williamsburg district in the neighborhood of Indiantown, on the 7th August Mr. Hugh Hanna, in the 83d year of his age. The deceased was in our district, we believe the last survivor of that noble band of patriots who fought under Marion. (eulogy)
at Bucksville, on the 25th ult., Mr. William Last, aged about 22 years. He was first mate of the birg Caroline E. Platt of New York.

Issue of September 17, 1842

Died in this town, on Monday last, aged 5 months, Solomon King, son of John B. and Priscilla McDaniel.
____ yesterday at Sandy Island, Hariet Malvina, only daughter of Mr. and Mrs. Jas. A. and Eliza Jane Hemingway....
____ in this town, yesterday, Mr. Charles H. Faulkner, a native of Guilford, Connecticut, aged about 40 years. This was his first season with us.
The Hamburg, S. C. Journal mentions the death of Col. Samuel Hammond of this State, at his residence a short distance from Hamburg in the 87th year of his age.

Issue of October 8, 1842

Died on the 5th inst., at Sandy Island, Edward, youngest son of Joseph A. and Eliza J. Hemmingway.

Issue of October 22, 1842

Died on the 17th inst., Mrs. Louisa Mathews, relict of the late John Mathews, aged about 30 years.

Issue of October 26, 1842

Married at Newark (N.J.) on Tuesday evening, 11th instant, by the Rev. Dr. Boinsmade, Col. Edgar Charles, of Darlington (S.C.) to Jane M., daughter of the late Jacob Gray.
All persons indebted to the Estate of the late Davison McDowell Esqr. will please make early payment....
Oct. 15   Richard O. Anderson,
                                Alex. Robertson,
                                    Qualified Executors.

WINYAH OBSERVER

Issue of November 2, 1842

Departed this life on the 2d ult. at Marion Court House, in the 80th year of her age, Mrs. Elizabeth Wheeler relict of the late Wm. Wheeler. (eulogy).
at his residence in Jones County (Geo.) on the 18th of October, 1842, the venerable citizen and patriot John Lamar, Esq. in the 81st year of his age...a soldier of the revolutoin...under Genls. Marion and Pickens...a descendant of the Huguenots, born in South Carolina, and emigrated to the State of Georgia, at the close of the Revolution. (eulogy).

Issue of November 12, 1842

Died at the Mariners Hospital, in this town, on Wednesday last, Mr. David Hughs, a native of Scotland. He came ashore from the three masted schooner Hannah, Capt. Taylor, on the 27th Sept.

Issue of November 16, 1842

Died, yesterday morning, Mrs. Mary M. Perry, aged 35 years, a native of Lyme, Connecticut...resided here for the last four years, and survived all her children. The husband of her youth still survives.

Issue of December 10, 1842

Died on the 8th instant after a short but painful illness of one week, at the 32 Mile House, Saint James Santee, Mr. Joseph Norman, in the 23d year of his age. He was a native of North Carolina, but for the last five years, a resident of this place. He has left a helpless wife and one child.
in this town on the 7th instant, Mr. James M. Morris, aged about 23 years, eldest son of Mrs. Elizabeth Morris. He was a native of this town.

Issue of December 21, 1842

Died in this town on Friday last, Mrs. Sarah Anderson, aged 55 years.

Issue of December 24, 1842

Married in this town on Thursday evening last, by the Rev. Mr. Leard, Mr. William Gregg, of Marion, to Miss Eleanor Wayne, only daughter of Mr. Jacob Wayne of this place.

Issue of December 31, 1842

Died in this town on Saturday the 24th inst., Mrs. Ann Westberry, in the 50th year of her age.

Issue of March 1, 1843

Married in Williamsburgh on Thursday 28 inst. by Justice Blakely, Mr. Richard Pope jr. to miss Mary Haselden, also on the same evening by the Rev. Mr. Stone, Mr. Austire Stone to Miss Mary C. Barr, all of Williamsburgh.

WINYAH OBSERVER

All persons having any demands against the Estate of Miss E. A. Taylor late of Georgetown deceased....
Feb. 25   Jno. Alex. Keith, Admr. will annexed.
    All persons having demands against the estate of the late John F. Pyatt, are requested to render them...
Feb. 22   Benj. Allston, Exor.

Issue of May 17, 1843

    All persons having any demands against the estate of Henry Alexander Culpepper late of Georgetown District deceased....
May 17   B. A. Coachman,
                        Attorney for Administratrix.

Issue of May 24, 1842

    Died in Charleston on Sunday last, in the 32d year of her age, Mrs. Eleanor Black, a native of this town...leaves a husband and five children....

Issue of June 7, 1843

    Death of Noah Webster, in New Haven, about 8 o'clock, on Sunday evening, in the 85th year of his age...born in West Hartford, Oct. 16th 1758 (long account of his life)...New Haven Daily Herald

Issue of June 14, 1843

    Died on Brittons Neck on the 7th inst., Mrs. Elizabeth R. Marlow, iwfe of Vardaman Marlow, in the 52nd year of her age.
    in this town on Monday last, Mary Matilda, only daughter of George and Hary(sic) Hopkins.

Issue of June 28, 1843

    Died at Santee on the 18th inst., after a painful affliction of 10 days, Mr. Jesse Harrelson, aged about 45 years.
    in this town on the 20th inst., Martha Emma, daughter of James G. and Emma A. Henning, aged 10 months.
    on Thursday last, Mrs. Sarah Butts, consort of Mr. Jahiel Butts, aged about 55 years.

Issue of July 5, 1843

    Married in this town on Thursday evening, the 29th ult., by the Rev. T. Huggins, the Rev. S. P. Taylor of the South Carolina Conference of the Methodist E. Church to Mrs. Jane Walker, daughter of Mr. Archibald McClennan of Santee.

Issue of July 12, 1843

    Died, at his residence in Marion district on the 26th ult. Mr. William Richardson, aged 80 years. He served with Gen. Green through the war of the Revolution.....

Issue of July 19, 1843

    Died in this town on Wednesday last Miss Josephine Forte, grandaughter of Mrs. C. M. Durant of this place, aged seven years and seven months.

WINYAH OBSERVER

Issue of August 2, 1843

Married on Sampit on Wednesday last by the Rev. T. Huggins, Mr. Andrew Thompson to Miss Elizabeth Ham, all of this district.
Died on the 4th of July at his residence near Brownsville, Tennessee, Mr. Benjamin Walker, aged 47 years. Mr. W. was a native and for many years, a resident of this District.
Departed this life, on the 7th of July, Miss Elizabeth Ann Leggett of Marion Dist., aged 15 years, 8 months and 7 days... member of the Methodist Church...(eulogy).
at his late residence at Poplar Hill, on Saturday 29th July, Mr. John Hughes, in the 55th year of his age. (eulogy).
Died in this town on Saturday evening last, July 29th, Mrs. Ann Murray, formerly of this place, aged 71 years, widow of Major Wm. Murray...member of the Methodist Episcopal Church... (eulogy).

Issue of August 9, 1843

All persons having any demands against Samuel Fraser, late of Georgetown deceased, are requested to render in attested statements....   R. E. Fraser, Admix.or.
Aug 9

Issue of August 16, 1843

Died in this town on Thursday last, Mrs. Mary N. Hawkins, consort of Mr. John Hawkins, formerly of this place, aged about 40 years...member of the Methodist E. Church in this town...
Persons indebted in any way to Mary N. Hawkins deceased, will please settle the same....   W. S. Croft, Exor.
Aug 16th
All persons having demands against the Estate of the late Emily H. Singleton, will render them in....
Aug 16   C. B. Sarvis, Administrator.

Issue of August 23, 1843

Died, at Poplar Hill, on the 17th inst., Wilhelmina, aged 13 months and 17 days, daughter of M. & O. M. Roberts.

Issue of August 30, 1843

Died at South Island on Saturday the 21st inst., Mrs. Sarah B. Keith, wife of Major Jno. A. Keith, aged 40, leaving a devoted husband, three orphan daughters and a numerous circle of relatives and friends.....

Issue of September 13, 1843

Died at Sumterville on the 19th ult of Inflammatory sore throat Davidson, youngest son of the late Davidson & Catharine D. McDowell, aged 4 years, 6 months and 12 days.
Died on Black River on the 5th inst. Mr. James Row, aged 58 years.
in this town, on Friday last, Mrs. Ann Paisley, aged about 60 years.

Issue of October 25, 1843

All persons having demands against Mrs. Ann D. Murray, late

of Georgetown, deceased, are requested to present them....
Oct 4   W. R. T. Prior, Executor.
   Died in this town on the 20th inst., William Sanders, aged about 23 years, a seaman and from on board brig Tremout, Woodside master.
   in Charleston, on the 20th Capt. Isaac Henry, of the Steamer congaree, Capt. H. took the fever up the PeeDee River.
   on Waccamaw, at the plantation of Mr. Charles Alston Esr., on the 20th Mr. Joseph T. Capps, Mr. C. was a pious, good man and has not doubt gone to a country where pain and fever never can come.
   Died in this town on the 16th inst. Mr. Robert Cooper, in the 76th year of his age. Mr. C. was a native of Pennsylvania, and for 52 years a resident of this place. (eulogy).
   Persons having demands against the late Samuel V. King, are requested to hand in statements...
Oct. 18   Benjamin King, Quallified Executor.
   All persons having demands against Ann Paisley, late of Georgetown....
Oct 4.   E. Waterman, Executor.

Issue of November 1, 1843

   Died on the 31st ult. of croup, William Archibald, elder son of R. W. and S. W. Shackelford, of this district, aged two years and two months....
   at Waccamaw, on the 25th ult., Mr. Edward R. Taylor, and on 2d inst. his widow Mrs. E. Taylor.
   On the 2d inst., in this town, Mrs. Catharine Wells, late of Charleston, an old and respectable lady.
   All persons having any demands against Joseph T. Capps, late of Waccamaw, Deceased....to Mr. John C. Porter, of Georgetown.
Nov. 1   Ann Capps, Executrix.

Issue of November 8, 1843

   Died at Baltimore, on Friday night, 21st ult., John Babcock, printer, in the 91st year of his age...of the house of Babcock & Son. He was a fellow-workman of Benjamin Franklin, and at the time of his death, the oldest surviving printer in the U. S....

Issue of November 11, 1843

   Died on North Santee the 7th inst., Hannah Josephine, eldest daughter of Frances W. and Sarah A. Munnerlyn, aged two years, five months, and thirteen days.

Issue of November 18, 1843

   Died at Col. Read's plantation on Pee Dee, on the 3d inst. Mr. Enos McDonald, aged 55 years.
   at the same place on the 4th inst. Mr. James McDonald, aged 23 years, son of Enos McDonald.
   at the same place, on Monday last, Mrs. Elizabeth McDonald, aged 35 years, relict of Enos McDonald, all of influenza.

Issue of November 25, 1843

   Married on Tuesday the 21st instant at Brittons Neck, Marion District, by the Rev. Thomas Munnerlyn, Mr. Alexander McWhite to Mrs. Elizabeth Graves.

WINYAH OBSERVER

All persons having demands against Robert Cooper late of Georgetown deceased are requested to hand them in....
Nov. 25   James G. Henning.

Issue of December 6, 1843

Died at Marion Court House on Saturday last, in the 55th year of her age, Mrs. Elizabeth Wayne, consort of Mr. Jacob Wayne, of this town.
in Darlington on Saturday evening last, Maj. Wm. H. Cannon, aged about 60 years. (eulogy).

Issue of December 16, 1843

Married on Wednesday evening last, by the Rev. Mr. Howard, Mr. Benjamin A. Coachman, to Miss Caroline Ford, second daughter of Stephen Ford, Esq. all of this place.
on Thursday evening by the Rev. Mr. Huggins, Mr. William M. Anereas, of New York, to Mrs. Elizabeth Christopher, of this place.
Died at his residence on Pee Dee, on the 2d inst., Mr. Alfred Wilson, aged about 50 years. He was an honest and industrious citizen.

Issue of December 20, 1843

Married on Sampit on Sunday evening last, by the Rev. Mr. Williams, Mr. Isaac Taylor of Williamsburg to Miss Elizabeth Airs, of this district.
Died at Marion Court House on the 15th inst., Thomas Gregg, youngest son of Robert J. Gregg, Esq.,aged nine years nine months and three days.

Issue of January 3, 1844

Died of dropsy, in St. James Santee Parish on Wednesday 20th ult. Mrs. Mary McClellan, in the 67th year of her age. Mrs. McClellan was born of highly respectable parents in Georgetown, where she was married to her beloved husband Mr. Archabald McClellan of the above parish. (eulogy).

Issue of January 6, 1844

D. L. McKay applied for letters of admn. on the estate of Mary Vereen deceased....5 Jan 1844.
Estate sale at the Counting House of the late Mr. Robert Cooper....
Estate sale on Monday 8 Jan. for the purpose of making division among the heirs at law of the late Robert Marsh.
Dec. 20   Saml. N. Marsh, Executor of Robert Marsh.

Issue of January 10, 1844

Married in Williamsburgh on Wednesday 20th ult. by Rev. A. G. Peaden, Mr. Sam'l M. Matthews to Miss Mary S. Fluitt.
Married on Thursday 4th inst. by Rev. A. G. Peaden, Mr. J. A. McCollough to Miss Margaret the eldest daughter of Mrs. Jane M. Miller of Williamsburgh District, S. C.
Estate sale of Alfred Wilson, on Pee Dee....Dec. 30.

WINYAH OBSERVER

Issue of January 17, 1844

Died on the 8th inst. at the residence of his parents near Kingstree in Williamsburg District, S. C., Leonard W. Mouzon, in the -- year of his age.
Died on Friday last, Mrs. Martha Dicks, aged 40 years, widow of the late Wm. Dicks.
Died on Saturday last, after a redious illness of dropsy, Mr. James S. B. Hucks, aged 50 years. Hucks was coroner of this district for several years, and resigned the office in Nov. last owing to bad health.
Marion District, in the Court of Ordinary, Mary Fore, applicant vs. Joel Fore and 3 others, Defendants...William Fore, Daniel Fore and James Fore, three of the defendants reside without the limits of this state...division of the real Estate of John Fore....   E. B. Wheeler,
Nov. 29   Ordinary of Marion District.

Issue of February 3, 1844

Marion District, in the Court of Ordinary, James Waters, applicant against Kiddy Waters, Esther Waters and others, defendants. William Waters, Moses Waters, John Waters, Hugh Shumake, Mary Shumake, Levi Blackman (and wife Ish Blackman) six of the defendants reside without this state.... 4 Dec 1843.

Issue of February 10, 1844

Marion District, Court of Ordinary, Gideon Powers and wife applicatsn vs Sarah Perrit and others, Defendants.... Sarah Daniel, Boswell Daniel, Gamewell Daniel, Martha Jane Daniel and Perry Daniel, five of the defendants reside without this state...estate of John Perrett....4 Dec 1843

Issue of February 21, 1844

Departed this life on the 13th inst. at the house of Capt. Samuel J. Snowden at Indiantown in Williamsburg District, Mr. Levi Durand in the 68th year of his age. Mr. D. had been for many years a successful teacher....

Issue of March 9, 1844

Died in this town on the 5th inst. Mrs. Martha McGinney, aged 85 years. She was among the oldest natives of this district, and had the best recollection of the incidents of the Revolutionary war....
recently in Connecticut, Dr. Joseph Manning, thrith years ago a permanent practioner of medicine in this town.

Issue of March 16, 1844

Married on Thursday the 7th inst. at Socastee by D. B. Sarvis, Esq. Mr. John Brown Senior to Will Wealthy Say of Brunswick County, North State.
on State on Thursday evening the 14th inst., by W. J. Howard, Mr. J. D. Doore, to Mrs. Mary Norman, all of this district.
All persons having demands against the estate of W. J. Dicker, late of Williamsburgh will please hand them in....
March 9   W. J. Howard, Administrator.

WINYAW OBSERVER

Issue of March 23, 1844

Died in this town on Wednesday last, in the 36th year of his age, Dr. Solomon Etting Myers. (eulogy).

Issue of March 30, 1844

Married at Dover, the residence of Mrs. S. H. Mayrant, near Georgetown, on the evening of the 23d inst., by the Rev. Mr. Howard, Major Wm. E. Richardson, of Sumterville, to Miss Sarah Ann eldest daughter of the late william Mayrant, Esqr.
Died at his residence in Williamsburg district on Saturday last, George W. Burrows, Esq., aged about 65 years.
All persons having legal demands against the late Doctor Ettiny Myers, will hand them in....
March 30.   A. C. Myers   ) Qualified
                             E. B. Rothmahler) Executors.

Issue of April 6, 1844

Departed this life at his residence in Williamsburg District, S. C., on Saturday the 23d ult., George W. Burrows, aged about 65 years....(eulogy).
At Fayetville (N.C.) on the 1st instant, Mr. T. C. Fay, a native of Bennington (Vt.) formerly for some years editor of a paper in this place.
All persons having demands against the Estate of John McClenaghan deceased will please render them in....to Mrs. M. McClenaghan Adm.x and H. M. Clenaghan, Admr.
March 30, 1844

Issue of April 13, 1844

Married on Tuesday 9th by Rev. Mr. Huggins, Mr. Robert Anderson Jr. of Charleston, to Miss Eliza Jane Cogdela of this town.

Issue of April 20, 1844

Estate sale...estate of Levi Durant, late of this place, deceased,   C. M. Durand, Admx.
April 20.

Issue of April 27, 1844

Died on the 17th inst. Nathan Huggins, the last son of Col. Charles Huggins, at the residence of the latter on Santee. (eulogy).

Issue of May 11, 1844

Died on the 5th instant at the residence of his Grandfather, Judge Richardson, Maynard Davis, only child of Francis De Liesseline and Agnes Richardson aged 20 months and 16 days.
at his residence on Black Creek, Darlington District, S. C., on the 27th ult., George H. Pawley, Esq., aged 32 years, 7 months and 10 days, leaving an affectionate wife and two small children. (eulogy).
in Darlington on the 30th ult. the Rev. Jacob Nipper, missionary on Pee Dee River. (eulogy).

WINYAH OBSERVER

Issue of May 18, 1844

Married on Thursday last by the Rev. W. Rodgers, Mr. Francis Marion Harrell to Miss Mary Jane Susan Elizabeth Clementine Rodgers, all of Georgetown District.

Issue of May 25, 1844

Married on Thursday evening last, by the Rev. Robert T. Howard, Mr. J. J. Dickison to Miss Mary M. Lester, daughter of the late Bannester Lester, all of this place.
on the same evening, by the Rev. Theopilus Huggins, Mr. J. Alston Croft, to Mrs. Mary H. Caldwell, all of this place.

Issue of June 8, 1844

Died on Saturday 25th ult at his residence in Marlborough district John Murdock, Esq. aged about 45 years. He served as a member of the Legislature from his native district.
recently, near Camden, S. C., Mrs. Elizabeth Josephine Lloyd, late of this town.

Issue of June 15, 1844

Married on Thursday evening last, by the Rev. R. T. Howard, Dr. John F. Lesesne, to Miss Hannah E. Porter, youngest daughter of the late Col. John Porter, all of this town.
on the same evening by the Rev. T. Huggins, Capt. David A. Sperry, to Miss Sarah Evans, daughter of the late Thomas Evans, of Cat Island.
on the same evening by the Rev. S. Procter Tayler, Mr. Wesberey to Miss Hannah Potts, all of this district.
Margaret Mitchell applied for Letters of Admn. on the estate of her Mother Elizabeth Collins, widow of Elias Collins, late of Santee, deceased....14 June 1844.
Estate sale of Negroes, on the death of Hannah Morris, to the legatees under the will of the late Wm. V. Brown....
        Hannah Morris,
        H. J. Morris
Horry District, Court of Ordinary. Lewis H. Floyd applicant vs James E. Newsom and wife and others, Defendants. James L. C. Floyd, and Benj. R. Floyd two of the defendants reside without the State, and that Sarah A. Floyd resides without the jurisdiction of this Court...estate of Lewis Floyd decd.
James 15   James Beaty, Ordinary H. D.

Issue of June 29, 1844

Married on Black River, on Wednesday evening last, by the Rev. Thos. G. Rogers, Mr. Moses Tuttle, to Mrs. Susan A. Hawkins, all of this District.
John W. Jeanerett applied for letters of admn. on the estate of Elias J. Etheridge, late of Georgetown....28 June 1844.

Issue of July 6, 1844

Married at Washington City, on the 27th ult., the Hon. John Tyler, President of the U. S., aged 55 to Miss Julia Gardiner, aged 22 years of New York.

WINYAH OBSERVER

Issue of July 20, 1844

Died on Black River on Tuesday the 2d inst., after a short, but painfull illness, George C. Bufkin, only son of Hugh F. and Herriot Bufkin, aged eleven months.
in this place on Sunday the 14th inst., Josephine Denison, daughter of Mrs. J. B. Anderson, aged 8 years and 7 days....

Issue of July 27, 1844

Departed this life on sunday morning, 7th instant, at the residence of her husband, near Darlington, S. C., Mrs. Margaret A. P. Sims, wife of A. D. Sims, Esq.

Issue of August 3, 1844

Died of apoplexy on the 3d inst., at the residence of Capt. R. G. Green (Withersville), Mrs. Mary consort of the late Moses Miller, of Williamsburgh District, in the 82nd year of her age. Mrs. Miller has left numerous relatives and friends....member of the Methodist Episcopal Church...left two daughters. H. L. B.

Issue of August 17, 1844

Died in this town on the morning of Tuesday last (the 13th inst), in the 19th year of his age, Mr. Thomas W. son of the late Thomas Henning of this place...leaving a kind brother and two affectionate sisters. (eulogy).
in this Town, on the 16th, Miss Sarah Cannon Wakefield, in the 75th year of her age.

Issue of August 25, 1844

Married on Monday evening the 12th inst., by Thomas H. Holmes Esq. Lieut John D. Brutom, to Miss Ann eldest daughter of Charles Murrell Esq. all of Horry District.
in this town on Monday evening last, by the Rev. Mr. Huggins, Mr. Lewis Rebb of Charleston, to Miss Francis A. Bernon, daughter of the late Henry Vernon, of this place.
by J. R. Sparkman Esq. at his residence in Plantersville, S. C. on the evening of the 22nd inst., Mr. Wm. Roberts to Mrs. Drucilla Moore all of these diggins.
Died at South Island, on Tuesday last of congestive fever in the 36th year of his age, Mr. William A. Williams...superintending Maj. Wm. B. Pringle's North Santee plantation.

Issue of September 7, 1844

Departed this life at Marion Court house on the fourth ultimo, Mrs. Ann Waties Donnelly, aged 78 years. (eulogy).

Issue of September 28, 1844

Married on Thursday evening last, by the Rev. Mr. Huggins, Mr. John B. McDaniel of Pee Dee, to Mrs. Sarah Harrelson, of this town.
Died in this town on Tuesday last, Miss Mary Danford, aged ninety nine years. Some persons have estimated her age of 106, but from good authority, we have more correctly stated it.

WINYAH OBSERVER

Issue of October 19, 1844

Died at Chanceller Dunkin's plantation on Pee Dee, on Thursday evening last, Mrs. Maria Blount, aged about 22 years, consort of Mr. John Blount.
John Cribb applied for letters of admn. on the estate of Mrs. Grif Cribb....30 Sept 1844.

Issue of October 12, 1844 (incorrectly printer October 21)

Married on the 26th ultimo by the Rev. Mr. Huggins, Mr. John B. McDaniel of Pee Dee to Mrs. Catharine G. Harrelson of this town.
John F. Lessesne hath made suit to grant him Letters of Admn. on estate of George C. Gotea, late of Sampit, deceased...10 Sept 1844.
All persons having demands against Robert B. Grouter, late of Black River deceased.....
Oct. 12   Henry Cumbie, Admor.

Issue of November 16, 1844

Died at his residence, All Saints Parish on the 4th inst., Mr. Samuel Bruton, in the 72d year of his age.
on the 10th inst. in All Saints, Horry District, Solomon King, Esq., and on the 11th inst., his wife Mrs. E. M. King, both deeply regretted.
at Black River ferry on Thursday last, Mrs. Sarah A. Siau, aged about 36 years, consort of Mr. A. L. Siau...left husband and a large family of affectionate children.
All persons having demands against Mary Danford, late of Georgetown deceased....
Nov. 16   E. Waterman, Ordinary.
Edward Thomas hath made suit to me, to grant Letters of Admn. on Estate of Sarrah C. Wakefield, late of Georgetown, as next of kin...13 Nov 1844.
Nov. 16
James M. Commander hath applied for letters of admn. on the estate of George C. Gotea...10 Sept 1844.

Issue of November 27, 1844

Died in this town on Saturday last, Mr. Wm. G. DuBose, aged 57 years.
in the evening of the same day, Dr. George Heriot, aged about 40 years, second son of Robert and Maria E. Heriot, late of this town.
On the same evening a valuable servant belonging to Mrs. Mary A. Carr, called Sampson Dunmore, or carpenter Sampson, also departed this life. His funeral was attended by more than 500 persons of his color. His age was 51 years.
All persons having demands against Samuel Whitman, of Horry District, deceased, are requested to hand in their accounts....
Nov. 29   J. R. Whitman, Admo'r.
William B. Pringle applied for letters of admn. on the estate of William A. Williams...4 Nov 1844.

WINYAH OBSERVER

Issue of November 30, 1844

Died at Capt. J. H. Allston's, Breakwater plantation, on Tuesday last, Mr. William Wall, of Marion District.

Issue of December 7, 1844

All those persons having demands against William G. DuBose, late of Georgetown deceased...
Dec. 7   Isaac D. Whitworth, Qualified Exr.

Issue of December 14, 1844

Married in this town on Thursday evening last by the Rev. S. P. Taylor, Mr. John Siddons to Miss Jane Pigott of this place.
All persons indebted to William S. Gaillaird deceased, are requested to make payment....
Dec. 14.

Issue of December 21, 1844

Died on Sunday morning Dec. 15, at Oatland, Waccamaw, Elizabeth Ann, aged 11 days, the infant daughter of Richard W. and Mary H. Sullivan.
Died on the 10th inst. at Society Hill, S. C., Mr. David G. Sparks, son of Mr. Alexander Sparks, in the 26th year of his age.
Died on Friday the 6th instant, at the late residence of his father, near Bennettsville (S.C.), in the 25th year of his age, Dr. Wiley W. Sutbbs....

Issue of December 25, 1844

Horry District, in Ordinary. William B. Graham and wife applicants vs Sarah Conner, J. W. Pickett, Dennis Hankins and wife and others Defts. Summons in Partition.
Sarah Conner, John W. Pickett, Dennis Hankins and Nancy, Edward C. Reaves, George Reaves and Solomon Reaves, children of George Reaves who married Mary Conner, Wm. Braver as guardian of Laura D. Conner and Sarah E. Conner children of D. C. Conner dfts in this case reside without the state...real estate of Edward Conner decd.
Dec. 25   James Beaty, Ordy. H. D.
Departed this life on Thursday 12th inst. at the Plantation of Col. Joshua Ward, Waccamaw, Mr. Samuel Man Gilman, aged 33 years, a resident of Charleston...left a widow and two children, a mother grandmother and brother....(eulogy).

Issue of January 1, 1845

Died in this town on Saturday last, aged 36 years, Miss Hannah Anderson.
at the Lazaretto, on Monday, Peter Druro, one of the crew of the birg Juno, aged about 25, a native of Curracoa.
Benj. H. Wilson applied for letters of admn. on the estate of Matthew Allin, late of this district deceased with his will annexed...1 Jan 1845.

Issue of January 15, 1845

All persons having demands against Wm. Wall, late of Pee Dee....
Jan. 15   E. Waterman, Ordinary.

WINYAH OBSERVER

Issue of January 29, 1845

Died at his residence on Black river on Saturday last, Mr. Andrew B. Jayroe, aged about 45 years.

Issue of February 1, 1845

Married near Bucksville, on Thursday afternoon 30th ult., by C. B. Sarvis, Esq., Mr. Jonathan J. Riley of Horry, to Miss Percy Keyes Moore of Georgetown District.
Died at John Izard Middleton' Clay-Mount plantation on Thursday last, Mr. Charles P. Matthews, printer, aged 35 years, a native of this town, and youngest son of the late John Matthews... a widow and three children survive him.

Issue of February 8, 1845

Married on Brittons Neck on Thursday the 30th ult., by the Rev. James Singleton, Mr. Richard B. Pope, of Williamsburg district, to Miss Ann Rebecca Williams, only daughter of Henry Williams, Esqr., late of the former place.
Died on Black River on Saturday morning the 1st inst., Mrs. Mary Bates, aged 30 years, wife of Mr. Thomas Bates.
in this town on Tuesday night last the 4th inst., Richard David, aged 2 years two months and 25 days, son of George W. and Sarah Tarbox.

Issue of February 12, 1845

Married in Williamsburgh on Sabbath evening 3d inst., by the Rev. Mr. Culpepper, Benjamin Moses Nesmith, to Mrs. Sarah Jacks, widow of the late John W. Jacks of Georgetown, S. C., and youngest daughter of Mr. John Brockinton, Senr., of the former District.
All persons having demands against the Estate of A. B. Jayroe, Esq. deceased...to J. R. Eastering....
Feb. 5   J. R. Easterling,
                                Francis Green, Executors.

Issue of February 15, 1845

Married in this town last evening by W. J. Howard, Esqr., Mr. John McDaniel to Mis. (sic) Harriet A. Morris, of this place.

Issue of February 19, 1845

Rebekah Howell applied for letters of admn. on the estate of Allen Henecy...15 Feb 1845.

Issue of March 5, 1845

Died in Charleston on the 28th ult., Thomas Hardwick Waterman, a native of this town, and of the House of Porter & Waterman, aged 20 years, 11 months and 14 days. (eulogy).

Issue of March 15, 1845

All persons having demands against Percival E. Vaux, late of Sandy Island deceased...   W. P. Vaux) Executors.
March 5.   John P. Ford)

WINYAH OBSERVER

Issue of March 19, 1845

Died in Jefferson county (Pa.) on the 20th ult., John Bellamy, Esq., aged 68 years and 4 months. He was born in Horry District (S. C.) in 1776, and resided in South-Carolina until 1818, when he went to East Florida...He was appointed by President Monroe, in 1822, one of the members of the Legislative Council of Florida which held its session in St. Augustine.

Issue of March 22, 1845

Married on Sunday last the 16th inst., by the Rev. John Woodward, Mr. John Smith to Miss Eleanor Singleton of Horry District.

Issue of April 5, 1845

Died on Sampit near Georgetown on Saturday last, Mrs. Frances Porter, widow of the late Francis Porter, aged 75 years.
at Sampit Bridge, on Monday last, Mrs. Harriet Kales, aged 36 years.
at Augusta Georgia on the 28th ult., the Rev. W. T. Brantley.
in Charleston, on Thursday last, James Jervey, Esq.
Departed this life at Black Mingo on the 3d ult. Mrs. Mary Knox, consort of Mr. John Knox, aged about 38 years...left an affectionate husband and three small children.

Issue of April 12, 1845

Married at Friendfield the residence of Francis Withers, Esq., on Thursday evening last, by the Rev. A. M. Forster, Dr. Alexius M. Forster, to Miss Elizabeth Warham, all of this place.

Issue of April 19, 1845

Married at Mr. E. H. Miller's on Thursday 13th ult. by the Rev. Mr. McPherson, Mr. John B. Miller, to Miss Sarah E. McConnell of Williamsburg, South Carolina.

Issue of April 26, 1845

Married in this town on Wednesday evening last by the Rev. Mr. Crook, Rev. Wm. H. Fleming of the So. Ca. Conference to Miss Agness Ann Magille, daughter of Dr. Wm. Magill of this place.
at Sandy Island on the same evening, by the Rev. Mr. Glennie, James R. Sparkman, M. D. to Miss Mary Heriot, eldest daughter of Dr. Edward T. Heriot.
in this town on Thursday evening last by the Rev. Mr. Crook, Dr. Charles Williams of Darlington, to Miss Mary E. Laval, of this place.
Died at Aiken on the 18th inst., Emma Georgianna, youngest daughter of William R. and Anna Maxwell, aged 16 years and 7 months.
at his residence on Cooper River on Sunday evening last, in the 92d year of his age, Dr. William Read, the father of John H. Read, Esq., of this place. Dr. R. at the time of his death was believed to be the oldest revolutionary officer in this State. He was a member of Gen'l Washington's staff....
in this town on Wednesday last, Capt. William Thyne, aged 65 years. Capt. T. was a native of Sumter District, passed the

WINYAH OBSERVER

morning of his life in the mercantile business in Charleston, and from that city retired to Monk's Corner....(eulogy).

Issue of May 24, 1845

Died on Friday 2d inst. at the residence of his parents at Indiantown in Williamsburgh Dist., S. C., William McCutchen, just I think entered on his eighteenth year. (eulogy).

Issue of June 7, 1845

Georgetown District, in the Court of Ordinary: Thomas Bates, John Bates, S. Kirton, B. M. Grier, applicants vs Owen G. Kennedy defendant. Owen G. Kenedy the defendant resides without this state.
May 24.

Issue of June 14, 1845

The last mail from Cheraw, brought us a letter saying that William Wingate, late sheriff of Darlington had died...left wife and children.
Died in this town, last evening, Naomi Elizabeth, infant child of Robert and Eliza Jane Anderson.

Issue of June 21, 1845

Obit. of Gen. Andrew Jackson...a native of S. C., born at Waxsaw (sic) in 1767. (long account).

Issue of June 28, 1845

Died in Conwayborough on Thursday the 19th inst., after a month of severe affliction, Mrs. Charlotte C. Congdon, in the 30 year of her age.

Issue of July 5, 1845

Died at South-Boston, on the 10th ult., Mr. Henry S. P. Gulliver, aged about 38 years. He resided in this town several years and has left a widow and child....several years engineer on the steamer Osceola, and was at one time Captain of the steamer Utility.
at his residence on Black river on Monday last, George W. Heriot, Esq. aged about 65 years.

Issue of July 19, 1845

Married in this town on the 12th inst., by the Rev. Mr Crook, Mr. Benjamin Rumney of Alabama, to Mrs. Susan E. T. Vanderhorst of this neighbourhood.

Issue of July 26, 1845

Died on the 19th ult., Mrs. Margaret J. Wilson, consort of Robt. F. Wilson of Williamsburgh District in the 21st year of her age, leaving an affectionate husband, a fond mother and kind sister.... four short years since the nuptials. Black Mingo, 21 June 1845.

WINYAH OBSERVER

Issue of August 9, 1845

Departed this life on Sunday last on Black River, Mr. Richard Singleton, aged about 19 years, son of Richard and Catherine Singleton.

Issue of August 16, 1845

Died at his residence on Santee, last evening, Mr. Levin Pipkin, aged about 56 years.

Issue of August 23, 1845

Departed this life at Effingham on the 11st (sic)inst. Mr. Cyrus Ham...kind husband and father....
Departed this life at Wadesborough N. C. on the 2d inst., Mrs. Susan M. Leard, consort of the Revd. Samuel Leard. (eulogy).

Issue of August 30, 1845

Married on Wednesday evening 27th inst. by Rev. S. P. Taylor, Mr. Jno. J. Anderson to Miss Irvinia Hamlin, daughter of Mr. Thos B. Hamlin of Pee Dee.
on Thursday evening 28 inst., by the Rev. S. P. Taylor, Mr. Wm. Small, to Miss Sophronio Sanders.
death of Mr. J. W. Cheesborough, departed this life yesterday. a native of Georgetown District, many years since he removed to Charleston....
Died at South Island on the morning of the 25th ult., Francis W. youngest child of James K. and Amelia Munnerlyn, aged 1 year and 21 days.
Death of Hon. Thomas Evans, formerly a Senator of this district departed this life in Granville county, N. C. on the 10th inst., in the 55th year of his age. (long eulogy). Marion Court House, Aug. 23, 1845.

Issue of September 6, 1845

Died in Charleston on the 28th of August, Mrs. Susan Anna Lord, second daughter of the late Capt. Rob't Marrh (sic) of this town. (eulogy).
in this town on Tuesday last Miss Amelia King, aged 23 years.
at Mr. Withers, Springfield plantation, on Tuesday night last, Mr. Samuel T. Sessions, aged 26 years, a native of Sumpter District.

Issue of September 13, 1845

Died at Sumerville, vicinity of Darlington village, on the 10th Aug. last, Augustus H. son of Calib H. and Mary E. Nettles, aged 10 months and 3 days.

Issue of September 20, 1845

Died at his residence in Cambridge, Mass. on the 10th inst., Judge Joseph Story...65 years of age. (account and eulogy).
Died at Woodford, Black River, on the 19th inst., John H. A. Miller, son of M. S. and S. G. Millor, after 3 days illness, aged 2 years and 12 days.
Mary Fearwell applied for letters of admn. on estate of Thos. C. Fearwell, late of Georgetown decd....5 Sept 1845.

WINYAH OBSERVER

Issue of September 27, 1845

Married in this town on the 23d inst., by the Rev. S. P. Taylor, Mr. John Stell of Santee, to Miss Sarah Ann Davis, second daughter of the late David Davies, of this place.
Died in this town on the 18th inst., Ann Elizabeth infant daughter of the late Wm. A. Williams deceased and A. E. Williams, age eleven Months and 16 days.
in Darlington, at the residence of Dr. E. W. Green on the 18th inst., Miss Mary Green, aged 54 years, eldest daughter of Samuel Green, late of this district deceased. She was interred at the old family burying ground on Black River on Monday last.
at Black River yesterday Thomasine Maria, aged two years, youngest daughter of Dr. W. R. T. and Martha Prior, of this place.

Issue of October 4, 1845

Married on Thursday evening 2nd inst., by the Rev. S. P. Taylor, Mr. Wm. Capers Waterman to Miss Mary E. eldest daughter of the late Wm. Skinner, all of this place.
Departed this life at South Island on the 22nd September, Mrs. Ann E. R. Fickling, consort of J. J. Fickling, and daughter of the late Samuel A. Taylor of this district, aged 22 years, and 3 months...left husband, a child and sister....
on Sampit on the 25th inst., Benjamin H. Christian aged 3 years 7 months, youngest son of the late Benjamin H. Christian.
on Saturday the 27th Sept. Francis infant son of Jos. D. and S. M. Rogers aged 6 months ad 27 days.

Issue of October 11, 1845

We failed to announce on the second week in August the death of Mr. Samuel Blakeney, and are pained today to have to record the death of his eldest son and youngest daughter who have died in the present week.
Died in Guilford county, N. C., on the 19th ult., in the 54th year of his age, Mr. John M. Howren.
in Marion, on the 4th inst., William, aged one year, son of William and Elizabeth Hyman, late of this place.

Issue of October 18, 1845

Died at Springfield on Pee Dee the 10th inst., John B. Cockfield, after four days illness, in the 15 year of his age... leaves three orphan sisters and a brother....

Issue of October 25, 1845

Died at Capt. Petigrue's plantation at Sandy Island, on the 8th instant, Mrs. Frances Wiggins, consort of Mr. J. W. Wiggins.
on the 18th inst., on Santee, Mrs. Mary Elizabeth Hyman, consort of Mr. L. Hyman, aged 28 years, 1 month 8 days...a native of Marion Dist. So. Ca....two years since she removed with her husband to Santee....remains were deposited in the church yard. of Santee Ferry.

Issue of November 1, 1845

Died on the 23d ult. Stafford, the eldest son of the Revd.

WINYAH OBSERVER

S. P. Taylor, aged 11 years. (eulogy).
    at his residence on Black river, on the 3d inst., Mr. Kinsey Brown, in the 60th year of his age.
    Married at Santee, on the 23 ult., Mr. John D. Barnett to Miss Catherine E. Pipkin.
    John B. Gorman applied for letters of admn. on the estate of Levi Pipkin, late of Santee decd...28 Oct 1845.
Nov. 1

Issue of November 5, 1845

    Thomas B. Hamlin applied for letters of admn. on the estate of Samuel G. Munnerlyn, late of Pee Dee, deceased...5 Nov 1845.

Issue of November 12, 1845

    Died at her residence on Black River on Thursday evening last, Mrs. Sarah Shackelford, relict of the late Capt. Wm. Cartwright Shackelford, aged about 90 years....
    at his residence in Williamsburg, on Saturday last, Dr. Wm. J. Buford, senator from that district. He was about 60 years of age. (eulogy).

Issue of November 15, 1845

    Died in this town on Monday last in the 16th year of her age, Martha Elizabeth daughter of Mrs. M. A. Cross.
    All persons having demands against Miss Mary Green, late of this district deceased, are requested to render statements...
Nov. 15   J. White)
                             E. W. Green)Executors.
    Richard W. Shackelford, applied for letters of admn. on the estate of Richard Withers, late of St. James' Santee, deceased, with the will annexed...14 Nov 1845.

Issue of November 22, 1845

    Married on Thursday evening the 20th inst., by the Rev. S. P. Taylor, Mr. C. J. Coe to Miss Mary Frances Taylor, all of this place.
    on the same evening Mr. Jno. P. Thompson to Miss Ann Brown, of Williamsburgh district.

Issue of December 3, 1845

    Married on Wednesday 26th ult., by the Rev. T. Adams, the Rev. W. W. Childers, Pastor of the Baptist Church of Georgetown, S. C. to Miss A. N. Hasvin, of Clarendon, Sumter District.
    Magdalen Blakely hath made suit for letters of admn. on the estate of Samuel M. Blakely, late of Sampit, as next of kin....
29 Nov 1845.

Issue of December 6, 1845

    Married on the 20th ult., by Rev. Mr. Rolling, Dr. James E. Byrd, to Miss Mary L., daughter of J. Keith Esq. of Darlington District.

WINYAH OBSERVER

Issue of December 10, 1845

D. L. McKay applied for letters of admn. on the estate of George W. Heriot, late of this distirct decd...2 Dec 1845.

Issue of December 13, 1845

Died in this town on the 2d inst., Capt. William L. Thomas, a native of North Carolina, aged 56 years. He had resided in this neighborhood for the last ten years. He was master of the schooner Harvest wrecked on our bar in 1839.

Issue of December 20, 1845

Died on Sampit on Thursday evening last, Mr. David Durant, a native and resident of Horry. He was on a visit to his friends on Sampit.
All persons having demands against the late Sarah C. Shackelford....
Dec. 20   Richard W. Shackelford, Exo'r.

Issue of January 3, 1846

Archabald J. McClellan applied for letters of admn. on the estate of Sarah Ann Steele deceased...30 Dec 1845.

Issue of January 7, 1846

Married in this town on the 1st inst., by the Rev. A. M. Forster, Mr. Julius D. Pestch of Charleston to Miss Elizabeth A. Price, only child of Isham Price, late of thie district, deceased.
Died on Black River, on the 28th ult., Mrs. Rebekah Easterling...left husband and children.
Died at Judge Dunkin's plantation on Waccamaw on the 30th ult., Mr. Nicholas F. Johnson of Williamsburg District, aged about 29 years....

Issue of January 10, 1846

All persons having claims against the estate of Geo. T. Lathrop....
Dec. 31   E. B. Rothmahler)
                     J. W. Coachman) Executors.

Issue of January 21, 1846

Died, near Cheraw, on the 13th inst., Miss Mary Ann Campbell, second daughter of Angus and M. Campbell, deceased, of Cheraw. (eulogy).
Wm. P. Congdon applied for letters of admn. on the estate of Mrs. Charlotte C. Congdon, 13 Jan 1846. Horry District.

Issue of February 4, 1846

Died, at his residence near Muddy Creek Church, Williamsburg district, S. C., on the morning of the 24th January 1846, Stephen C. Heaseldon, in the 44th year of his age, leaving a wife and a numerous circle of friends...member of the Methodist E. Church....
                                    Leonard Stone.

WINYAH OBSERVER

Died on the 29th of January, Mary Rebecca, eldest daughter of Francis W. and Sarah Munnerlyn, aged 2 years 5 months and 23 days.

Died at his residence on Black River on Sunday evening last, Mr. William F. Sparkman, aged about 38 years...leaves wife and three children. (eulogy).

Issue of February 11, 1846

Asaph Waterman departed this life at two o'clock yesterday (Augusta Sentinel, 4th inst.)...in the 76th year of his age... resided in Augusta for maore than 50 years...member of the Methodist Episcopal Church...He was of the old Pilgrim stock, being the fifth in lineal descent from one of the original settlers of Plymouth, Mass. He was born in Franklin, Connecticut, on 23 Nov 1770....

Died in Charleston, on Monday last, William Bond Read, aged about 20 years, youngest son of the Hon. John H. Read, of this neighborhood.

Issue of February 18, 1846

Married on Wednesday evening last, in Charleston, Mr. Henry F. Heriot, of this town, to Georgianna P. youngest daughter of the late Dr. William Chisolm of that city.

Died in this town on Thursday morning last, the Rev. Elijah Sinclair, aged about 58 years.

Issue of February 25, 1846

All persons having demands against Dr. W. J. Buford, late of Williamsburg district...   Elizabeth Buford, Executrix. Feb. 24

Mrs. Elizabeth Sparkman applied for letters of admn. on the estate of Wm E. Sparkman, deceased...24 Feb 1846.

Issue of March 4, 1846

All persons having demands against Sarah E. Steel, deceased, are requested to make payment....   A. J. McClennon, Admo'r. March 4.

Issue of April 8, 1846

Died at his residence in Bridgeport, Conn., on the 25th March last, Samuel Wilmot Snr., in the 69th year of his age, and on the 16th January last his wife Mary Wilmot, aged 71, and in this place on the 19th February last, Thomas Townsend, son of Samuel Wilmot, Jr., aged 11 months....

Issue of April 15, 1846

Died on the 3d inst., at Newport, R. I., Archibald, aged 14 months, son of George C. and Elizabeth Thurston Munro.

Issue of May 13, 1846

Died at the plantation of Judge Dunkin, on Pee Dee on Saturday last, Mr. Archibald Liggett, aged about 39 years....

William Lester applied for letters of admn. on estate of William C. Shackelford...2 May 1846.

WINYAH OBSERVER

Issue of May 27, 1846

Departed this life in Horry District on Monday, Mrs. Mary Ann Hemmingway, consort of Thos Hemmingway, aged about 30 years... left husband and four small children.

Issue of June 3, 1846

Married on Thursday evening last, by the Rev. W. W. Childers, Rev. T. W. Mellishamp of Sumter to Miss Sarah L. Cuttino, of this town, youngest daughter of the late Capt. Peter Cuttino.

Issue of June 10, 1846

Died in this town on the 1st inst., Martha Smith, aged 60 years, a native of North Carolina but for the last 14 years a resident of this town.

All persons having demands against Archibald Ligett, late of Pee Dee, deceased....
Jun 16 (sic)   James Green) Executors.
                          E. Waterman)

Issue of June 17, 1846

Died in this town on the 12th inst., Mary Martha, first and only child of Sarah E. and David A. Guerry, aged 11 months and 27 days.

Died at his residence in Charleston, on Sunday evening last, Hon. Henry Middleton, in the 76th year of his age...Governor in 1810 and 1811, and for many years our minister to Russia.

Issue of June 24, 1846

Married at Kingstree on Thursday 14th inst., Capt. Samuel Sampson of this place to Mrs. C. Joseph of Charleston, S. C.

Died on Waccamaw on Wednesday morning Jan. 17, Joshua John Ward, aged 1 year 3 months and 11 days, a son of Dr. John D. Ward(?).

At his residence on Monday last, John Gasque, aged about 76 years.

Issue of July 1, 1846

Died on the 17th inst., at Debordieu Island, Miss Mary Rutledge Smith, in the 42nd year of her age.

Died on Wednesday last the 24th inst. Mr. Asahel Slate, in about the 50th year of his age. He was a native of ____, but a reside of this state upwards of 30 years.

Issue of July 8, 1846

Married on the 2d July (at the Summer residence of her father) by the Rev. G. K. Tally, Richard Dozier, Esq. to Miss Elizabeth Jane Exum, all of Georgetown District.

Died on Sampit on the 3d inst., Mrs. Lucy Gause, a native of Marlborough district, and consort of Mr. Saml. Gause from North Caroline.

at Serenity, on Saturday last, Mrs. Robert W. Bone, aged about 55 years.

WINYAH OBSERVER

Issue of July 15, 1846

Died at his residence on Santee on Saturday last, Mr. Joseph A. Glass, aged about 50 years.

All persons having demands against A. Slate late of Horry District will render them....
Conwayborough   James Beaty, Ordinary H. D.
July 15

Issue of July 22, 1846

Married near the Blue Springs in Williamsburg District, on Wednesday, the 15th inst., by the Rev. Samuel M. Green, Mr. Samuel J. Singletary to Mrs. S. T. McCrea, widow of the late T. Armstrong McCrea, of said district.

Died, at Darien, Georgia, last week, Mrs. Mary Shackelford, aged 81 years, a native of this town, for more than 60 years a permanent resident.

at Midway plantation on Waccamaw on Tuesday last, Mr. Samuel M. Bryan, aged about 23 years, eldest son of the late Samuel M. Bryan, late of Santee, deceased...leaves mother, his younger brother and sisters.

Rebecca Watts applied for letters of admn. on the estate of William D. Watts, late of Sampit deceased...20 July 1846.

Issue of August 12, 1846

Died on Black River on the 1st inst., Sarah Tabithy, aged 20 months, youngest child of Wm. S. and Sarah Rebekah McDaniel.

Issue of August 26, 1846

Died at Elizabethtown, Bladen County, N. C., on the 6th inst., Mrs. Charlotte W. Cowan, consort of Gen. W. J. Cowan, aged 63 years. Mrs. Cowan was born in this district, and married in this town in 1814. She was a daughter of Paul Villepontiex, of Huguenot decent(sic).

Died at Horry Court House on Sunday the 16th inst., Bushrod M. Singleton, in the 24th year of his age. (eulogy).

Issue of September 2, 1846

Married on Santee on Thursday the 20th inst. by the Rev. William Patterson, Mr. J. W. Collins of Marion District to Miss Susan daughter of the late Joseph Quimby, of Charleston, S. C.

Died on the 22d August near this place, Trisvan Ferrel, infant daughter of Andrew P. and Elizabeth Thompson, aged 2 years 2 months and 22 days.

Died in this town on the 26th inst. David Davies, eldest child of Thomas R. and Jane F. Session, aged 5 years and 5 days.

Issue of September 9, 1846

Departed this life on Enfield, Pee Dee on the night of 1st September, Ann Elizabeth, only daughter of Hugh F. and Harriet Bufkin, aged 4 years 9 months and 18 days.

Died in this town, on the 2d inst., in the 59th year of his age, Mr. John Tollman, a native of Plymouth colony, Massachusetts. Mr. Tollman visited this town some fifteen years since, as a portrait painter....

WINYAH OBSERVER

Cecilia Sinclair applied for letters of admn. on the estate of her husband Elijah Sinclair, late of Georgetown deceased... 4 Sept 1846.

Issue of September 16, 1846

Married in All Saints parish on Wednesday the 2d inst., by the Rev. Wm. Crook, the Rev. Charles Betts, of the South Carolina Conference to Mrs. Ann Green, of Horry.
Married on the 20th ult. by the Rev. J. W. Picket, Mr. John B. Gorman, to Mrs. Magdalen A. Blakely, all of Santee.

Issue of September 23, 1846

Died at his residence in Horry district, on the 3d inst., in the 76th year of his age, John Durant, Esq. (eulogy).
Departed this life in Horry District, on the 13th inst. Mr. Benjamin Singleton, in the 53d year of his age....
Died on the 20th inst., William Algernon, youngest child of F. T. and Amanda E. Dixon, aged 2 years,4 months and 30 days.
Died at Mr. Weston's Hagley plantation on Waccamaw on Sunday last, Wm. Sturges, Snr., a native of Marion, aged about 56 years.
in this town on Monday Mrs. Ann J. Sturges, aged 21 years, leaving an infant and an afflicated husband. It is seldom that a man attends the funeral of his father and his wife on the same day....

Issue of September 30, 1846

Died, in All Saints Parish, on Saturday the 5th September, instant, Mrs. Jane T. Session, consort of DR. I. M. Sessions, and daughter of F. A. and E. M. Wayne, aged 22 years 3 months. (eulogy)

Issue of October 7, 1846

Death of Mrs. Mary Margaret the affectionate consort of Mr. J. J. Dickison on Thursday morning last at 3 o'clock...age 23 years 7 months and 14 days...left a little boy 17 months old, a mother, and three brothers....
Died in this town on the 4th inst. Acquila Cogdell Davis, aged 6 years 6 months and 4 days.
in this town on the 4th inst., Mary Esther Matthews aged 2 years and 14 days.

Issue of October 21, 1846

Married on Thursday evening the 8th inst., near Longwood, All Saints Parish, by Samuel G. Singleton Esq., Mr. Solomon Hines to Miss Mary, and at the same time Mr. Solomon Sellers to Miss Eliza, both daughter of Mr. William Burgess.
Died in this town on Wednesday the 30th September last, Miss Elizabeth Martha Cox, in the 19th year of her age.
Died on board the Alvarada on Thursday last, M---- Harrmon, aged 25 years,a native of Pope, Maine.
Died, yesterday, Alice, daughter of John R. Easterling, Esq...funeral at the Methodist Episcopal Church.

Issue of November 4, 1846

Died in this town on Wednesday last, Mr. David Kidd, aged about 57 years...came to this place some 25 years ago as a mill-

WINYAH OBSERVER

wright. He was the first who introduced the varied skrines for assorting the grains of rice....
   Died at Mt. Elon, Darlington District, on the 28th ult., John Joseph infant son of C. H. and Mary E. Nettles, aged 3 months and seven days.

Issue of November 11, 1846

   Died at Society Hill, Dr. John K. M'Iver on his way home from Newbern, N. C. where he had gone on a visit to his daughter... expired on Friday night, the 30th ult. (eulogy)
Carolina Baptist   T. P. Lide.
   Another Revolutionary Relict Gone.
Died on the 3d November at his residence in St. James Santee, Archibald McLellan, in the 82d year of his age...with Gen. Marion Warden of the Episcopal Church in the parish.

Issue of November 18, 1846

   Died at Black Mingo, on the 7th of November, Mrs. Martha Boone, in the 67th year of her age.
   The following persons were consumed by the burning of the schooner Alvarado in Winyaw Bay on the morning of the 4th inst. Elias Michael, aged 21 years, a native of Munro, Maine.
Jacob Fountain, aged 19 years, a native of Bristol, Maine.
Charles Drinkwater, aged 18 years, a native of Belfast, Maine.

Issue of November 25, 1846

   Married at Bucksville on Thursday the 19th inst., by Rev. John Woodward, Mr. Isaac Martin to Miss Elizabeth Louisa, daughter of the Rev. J. H. Beaty, all of Horry District.

Issue of December 2, 1846

   Died at his residence in Marion district on the 4th ult., Mr. Solomon Owens, aged 60 years.
   Died at Sandy Island, on the 24 ult., Mr. James Powell, aged about 45 years, a native of Marion District. (eulogy).

Issue of December 9, 1846

   All those indebted to the Estate of the late Bushrod M. Singleton, deceased are requested to make payment...
Dec 9   S. G. Singleton, Admor.

Issue of December 30, 1846

   Married on Thursday evening the 17th inst. by C. B. Sarvis, Esq. Mr. Andrew Stevens of New York to Miss Margaret H. Session, of All Saints Parish.
   Married in this town on Monday evening last by the Rev. G. R. Talley, Mr. William Moody, to Mrs. Elizabeth Hawkins.

Issue of January 6, 1847

   Married on Tuesday evening the 22d ult., in Camden, by the Rev. Mr. Shand, Col. David R. Williams, of Society Hill, to Miss Catherine, daughter of the late Stephen D. Miller, of Sumter District.

WINYAH OBSERVER

Issue of January 13, 1847

Died at her residence on Pee Dee, on the 30th ult. Mrs. Christiana Skinner, relict of the late Rev. Wm. Skinner, aged about 47 years.

Death of Maj. Armeline Bryan...well known in Horry District and in Brunswick county in North Carolina. He recently embarked with his family, a few neighbours and his servants about 80 in all, for Florida in the well known steamer Anson, which boat landed the whole about 150 miles up the St. John's river. He was drowned while crossing Lake Griffin.

Robert H. Collins applied for letters of admn. on the estate of Christiana Skinner, late of Pee Dee, deceased...12 Jan 1847.

William S. Croft applied for letters of admn. on the estate of Amanda M. Hawkins...5 Jan 1847.

Amos Seward applied for letters of admn. on the estate of Samuel M. Bryan, Junior...5 Jan 1847.

Issue of February 3, 1847

Married in this town on Tuesday evening 26th ult., by the Rev. W. H. Flemming, Mr. J. L. Johnson, to Mrs. M. A. Farewell.

Died in this town on the 29th ult., Mr. Thomas Hales, aged about 40 years, a native of Kershaw.

Death of an aged Minister. The Rev. James Jenkins, of the Methodist E. Church departed this life in this place, on Sunday night last, at the advanced age of 83 years. He was one of the early pioneers of Methodism in the Southern States, and a regular and constant Preacher of the Gospel for 53 years.
                              Camden Journal, 37th inst. (sic)

Issue of February 10, 1847

Died at Springfield, Waccamaw on Monday morning last, after a short illness, Mr. John G. Wilson, aged about 45 years.

Issue of March 31, 1847

Married in this town on Thursday evening last by the Rev. R. T. Howard, Mr. Robert L. Fraser, to Miss Sarah G. McCollough, all of this place.

Issue of April 7, 1847

Died on Britton's Neck, on Sunday 28th March Mrs. Jane Williams, consort of Mr. A. W. Williams in the 58th year of her age...leaves husband and a numerous circle of friends.

Died in this town yesterday, Mrs. Julia A. Carr, aged about 85 years. Mrs Carr was believed to be the oldets citizen in the district. She was a native of the town and never changed the climate.

Henry Cuttino applied for letters of admn. on the estate of George Mitchell, with his will annexed, late of Georgetown... 15 March 1847.

Issue of April 21, 1847

Married in this town on Wednesday evening last by the Rev. Archer Smith, Dr. William C. Miller to Miss Margaret B., eldest daughter of Mr. Benjamin T. Cuttino, all of this town.

WINYAH OBSERVER

Information wanted. If Howell G. Hales, whose last residence as far as I can learn was Florence, Alabama, who had a son by the name of Thomas Hales, born in Kershaw district in this State in 1796, will address a letter to the subscriber at this place, he can obtain information worth to him $800 or $900.
Georgetown, S. C. April 21, 1817   E. Waterman, Ordinary.

Issue of May 5, 1847

Married by the Rev. A. W. Walker, on Thursday evening the 29th ult., in Marlborough District, S. C., Col. E. P. Ervin to Miss Mary Ann, daughter of John McCollum, Esqr.

Issue of May 12, 1847

Married last evening, in this town by the Rev. R. T. Howard, Mr. James S. Magill to Miss Ella M., youngest daughter of Capt. J. H. Christian of this place.

Issue of May 19, 1847

Died on Wednesday morning last, in the 51st year of her age, Mrs. Eliza Grant Waterman. She was the eldest daughter of John Hardwick, for many years known in this district and others as Surveyor of Lands. He died in 1803, and Mrs. Waterman's early training was confined to her mother and aunt the late Mr. and Mrs. Hannah Botsford. In May 1820 she married the husband who now survives her.

Issue of June 2, 1847

Married in Darlington on the 13th ult., by the Rev. Mr. Napier, Mr. Jos. Nesmith of Williamsburg to Miss Jane S. Hellen, of Marion District.
in Williamsburg on Thursday evening 20th ult., by the Rev. J. P. McPherson, Mr. John G. Wilson to Miss Jane M. Cooper, eldest daughter of Mr. George Cooper of said District.

Issue of June 9, 1847

Married in this town on Thursday evening last by the Rev. H. Durant, Mr. George T. Brightman, to Miss Mary J. Anderson, all of this place.
Benjamin T. Verner applied for letters of admn. on the estate of Sarah Emily Gasque...4 June 1847.
Benjamin T. Verner applied for letters of admn. on the estate of Esther Ann Rice...4 June 1847.

Issue of June 23, 1847

Died at her su-mer residence near town, on Friday last, Mrs. Charlotte A. Coachman, aged about 56 years--relict of the late John Coachman.
in this town on Saturday last, John W. Coachman, Esqr.... (eulogy)...left widow and four children.

Issue of July 14, 1847

Died in Marion District, on the 27th ult., in the 23d year of his age, Dr. James E. Crosswell, the eldest son of E. G. Crosswell, of Sumter Dist., upper Salem, near Bishopville....

WINYAH OBSERVER

Issue of July 28, 1847

Married in Williamsburg district by W. J. Howard, Esq., on Thursday the 15th inst., Mr. Cleland K. Byrd of Georgetown, to Miss Elizabeth Marshall of Williamsburg District.

Frederick W. Ford applied for letters of admn. on the estate of John W. Coachman, late of Georgetown deceased....6 July 1847.

Issue of August 11, 1847

All persons having demands against the late Mrs. C. A. Coachman, are requested to render them....R. F. W. Allston, Exo'r. Aug. 11

Issue of August 18, 1847

Departed this life on the 12th inst., after an illness of 48 hours, Elizabeth Cuttino, daughter of Leonard and Elizabeth S. Dozier, aged 2 years, 6 months and 29 days.

Issue of September 8, 1847

Died at Poplar Hill, Friday morning 3d September, Harvey Leonidas, only son of Dr. Harvey Leonidas and Pamelia Adelaide Byrd, aged one year 5 months and 27 days.

Issue of September 29, 1847

Married on the 31st August by the Rev. Wyndham Malet of Sydeard Church, England, Plowden C. J. Weston of Hagler, in All Saints Parish, Waccamaw, to Emily Frances, daughter of Edward Jeffries Esdale, Esqr., of Cothelestone House in the county of Somerset, England.

Issue of October 13, 1847

Died in Darlington, S. C. on the 3d instant, James Madison, youngest son of J. M. and Sarah Hunter, aged 1 year 6 months and 2 days.

Died in Darlington, S. C. on the 5th instant, Benjamin Allston, second son of J. M. and Sarah Hunter, aged 3 years, 4 months and 16 days.

Issue of October 20, 1847

Died on the morning of the 22d ult., Ralph, youngest son of R. E. and Martha A. Darr, aged 5 months and 13 days.

at Orangeburg on the 9th inst., the Rev. B. M. Palmer, Snr., for many years pastor of the Circular Church in Charleston.

at his residence in Fairfield, on the 10th inst., the Hon. Wm. Harper one among the ablest Chancellors of the State.

in this town, yesterday, Mrs. Mary A. Johnson. She was less than a year ago, the widow of the late Thomas C. Fearwell. Her last husband lived with her but a few months when he suddenly absconded to parts unknown with another woman...she was the only surviving daughter of the late Clement Broqueir. Her infant is living.

Married on South Island on Wednesday the 6th instant by the Rev. H. H. Durant, Mr. Wm. C. Munnerlyn of this place to Miss Rebecca W. Shaffer, of Charleston.

WINYAH OBSERVER

in Williamsburg District on Thursday the 7th inst., by the Rev. J. P. McPherson, Mr. Thomas Board of Missouri to Mrs. Susannah D. Britton, of Williamsburg, S. C.
  in Salem on the 5th inst., by the Rev. P. Pierson, Mr. Wm. R. Burgess to Mrs. Martha Rose, all of Sumter District.

Issue of October 27, 1847

Died on the 17th inst., at his residence, Bear Bluff, Mr. Joseph Dewitt in the 70th year of his age. (eulogy).

Issue of November 3, 1847

Died in this town on Sunday last George Edward, aged one year 11 months and 9 days, youngest son of Jane and Thomas Bragdon.

Issue of November 10, 1847

Departed this life on the 6th ult., Mrs. E. P. Coachman, in the 32d year of her age...left a husband and five small children.

Issue of December 1, 1847

Death of John S. Graham in his 25th year...left wife and aged mother and children. (eulogy).
  Died on the 25th inst., in Charleston, Mr. Francis Withers, at the advanced age of 77 years. (eulogy).
  Death of Benjamin Allston, Esq...of Georgetown, departed this life at the residence of his daughter (Mrs. Pyatt) in this city on Friday night last, having completed his 82d year on the 6th ultimo. C. Courier 29th ult.
  Died in this town on Tuesday mornig the 30th inst., Capt. J. H. Christian, aged 58 years.

Issue of December 8, 1847

Married on Sampit at Friendfield plantation, on Thursday last, the 2d inst., by the Rev. W. H. Flemming, Mr. Alexander C. Anderson, to Miss Georgiana L. Steele, all of this district.

Issue of December 15, 1847

Married on Thursday the 9th inst., near the village of Marion, by the Rev. Mr. Walsh, C. D. Evans, Esqr. to Miss Jane Haselden, both of Marion District.
  Died at Jalapa, Mexico, on the 27th of June last, Col. Thomas G. Carr aged aboug 36 years, eldest son of the late Gen. Thomas Carr of this town...attached to the Palmetto regiment.
  in St. James' Santee, on Sabbath last in the 46th year of his age, Mr. William H. McClellan, eldest son of the late Archibald McClellan.

Issue of December 22, 1847

Catherine Christian applied for letters of admn. on the estate of Jacob H. Christian...14 Dec 1847.
  D. L. McKay applied for letters of admn. on the estate of Francis G. Coachman, with his will annexed...5 Dec 1847.
  D. L. MaKay applied for letters of admn. on the estate of Sarah L. Coachman 5 Dec 1847.

WINYAH OBSERVER

Issue of December 29, 1847

Died at the residence of her husband on Britton Neck on the 19th inst., Mrs. Ann W. Cook, consort of Mr. John T. Cook and daughter of John Rogers, Snr., in the 49th year of her age... left husband and five children some of which are small....

All persons having any claims against the late Francis Withers, Esqr., will present them...
Dec 29, 1847   Sarah P. Withers, Exet'x.
                            J. H. Read Senr.)
                            E. T. Heriot   ) Exe's.
                            A. Robertson   )

Issue of January 5, 1848

Married last evening in this town by the Rev. H. H. Durant, Mr. St. John Ellis of Charleston, to Miss Mary Holmes of this place.

Issue of January 14, 1848

Married last evening on Sampit, at Waterfield plantation, by the Rev. George R. Talley, E. Waterman, Esqr., to Miss Charlotte A. M'Cracken.

All persons having demands against the late Jacob H. Christian, will please render statements...
Jan. 12   Catherine Christian, Adminix.

Issue of January 19, 1848

Died at Savannah, Geo. on the 19th inst. in the 31st year of her age, Mrs. Mary Sullivan, a native of this town, and consort of Mr. Richard W. Sullivan...an affecionate wife and tender mother. Her body was intered in the family cemetery in this place on Saturday last.

in this town, yesterday morning, after a short illness, Mr. Jacob Wayne, aged 62 years. He was the oldest male native of this town. He reared a considerable family but survived all but one daughter. was engaged in the mercantile business with his father the late Rev. WM. Wayne....

Issue of January 26, 1848

Married on last evening by Rev. R. T. Howard, M. Anglo Thos. Coote of Braintree, England, to Miss M. B. Watts, of Slago County, Ireland.

Issue of February 2, 1848

Died on February 1st, Francis Waterman, the only child of Francis & Sarah Munnerlyn, aged 2 years 2 months and 20 days.

Issue of February 9, 1848

Died on Sunday morning last, in the 76th year of his age, Dr. William Allston. He was the eldest native practitioner. He retired from the practice some twenty years since with an ample fortune....

Died on the 6th inst.,Benjamin King, aged 6 months and 16 days, youngest son of William S. and Frances M. Croft.

WINYAH OBSERVER

Issue of February 16, 1848

In Ordinary, Horry District. Cader Hughes, applicant, vs Mary Bellemee, H. C. Williams and wife, Dr. John D. Bellemme and others dfts. Summons in Partition. Dr. John D. Bellemee, John C. White & wife and John Long defendants reside without the State...real Estate of John Bellemee Snr. of All Saints Parish, deceased.   James Beaty, Ordinary H. D. Jan. 13

Issue of February 23, 1848

Died on board the schooner Ann, Capt. BArtlett of Wells. (Me.) on the 21st inst., Thomas Joseph, seaman, aged about 18 years.
Married in this town on Wednesday evening last, by the Rev. R. T. Howard, Mr. JOHN E. ALLSTON of Pee Dee to Miss Rejina Coachman, daughter of the late Ffrancis G. Coachman.

Issue of March 1, 1848

Died near Britton's ferry on Monday the 21st ult., Mr. William S. Stillman, aged about 30 years. He was a native of Massachusetts and had been a year or two carrying on the business of a tinner in this place.
on Friday last, Mr. William W. Taylor, a native of this place, aged about 27 years.
on Monday morning last, William O'Hanlon, only son of the Rev. W. G. and C. C. Connor, aged 16 months. funeral at the Methodist Church.

Issue of March 8, 1848

Married at Oak Lawn, on the 24th February, by the Rev. Stephen Elliott, Andrew Johnson of this neighborhood to Mary Barnwell, daughter of William Elliott.

Issue of March 29, 1848

Married at the residence of her uncle Mr. Robert D. Walker, in Savannah Geo. on Wednesday evening 22d inst. by the Rev. Mr. Mann, Dr. P. C. Goddard, of this place, to Isabella J., daughter of John White, Esq. of Charleston.
Married on the evening of the 26th March inst., at Horry C. H., by the Rev. M. Eady, Mr. Jonathan Greenleaf Littlefield(?) of Bucksville, S. C., to Miss Emma Grant of the former place.
Died at Oatland Waccamaw on the morning of the 20th inst., Daniel T. Durr, in the 31st year of his age.
Mrs. Mary Hillen, on Tuesday the 21st inst., and on Wednesday last her body was put beside that of her late son, Lieut. Dudley, at the burial place in Marion. She lived to the age of 82, and was perhaps the "oldest inhabitant" of the district.

Issue of April 5, 1848

Died at his residence in All Saints Parish, Little River, Mr. Jeremiah Vereen in the 32d year of his age. He has left a widow and five small children....
John M. Scriven applied for letters of admn. on the estate of Rebekah Coggshall, deceased...4 April 1848.

WINYAH OBSERVER

Issue of April 19, 1848

Died in Charleston on Sunday evening last, Mr. Benjamin Keith, aged about 23 years, a native of this district, and for the last 15 years a resident of this town. His remains were taken to the old cemetery at Morris's ferry last evening for interment.

Married in Charleston on Thursday the 13th inst., by the Rev. Whiteford Smith, Mr. John W. Sturges, of this place, to Miss Henrietta R. Cockfield, of Charleston.

Issue of April 26, 1848

Died at R. O. Anderson's Ramsay Grove plantation on the 21st inst., in the 66th year of his age, Mr. Isaac Singleotn.

Died on Sunday last, Theodore Patch, aged about seven years, youngest son of the late Capt. N. Patch.

All persons having demands against Mary Hillen, late of Georgetown deceased....
Apl 12   E. Waterman, Executor.

Issue of May 17, 1848

Married in All Saints, by the Rev. J. A. Minick, 19th April, Mr. James Norton Brown to Miss Sarah Elliott.

in this town on Tuesday the 19th inst.,by the Rev. W. G. Connor, Capt. Leonard B. Pratt, of Bucksport, Me., to Miss Ann C. Glenmore, of this place.

in this town, on Thursday evening last, by the Rev. WM. H. Flemming, Capt. Charles C. White to Mrs. Jane S. Siddons, all of this place.

in this town, last evening by the Rev. Wm. G. Conner, Mr. Jesse Jones of Charleston, to Miss Hannah Evans, of this place.

Thomas Bates applied for letters of admn. on the estate of Isaac Singleton, late of this district...16 May 1848.

In Ordinary, Horry District, E. Cooper & wife by Atty.applicants, vs Wm. N. Ward & Wife, and others, heirs of John Graham, dec., Summons in Partition.
John Graham one of the defendats resides without this state...
         James Beaty, Ordinary H. D.

Issue of May 24, 1848

Died in this town on Wednesday the 17th inst., Elizabeth Adaline Forrester, infant daughter of J. M. and Elizabeth LeRebour.

Married on Wednesday last 17th inst., on Sampit, by the Rev. David R. Seale, Mr. John R. King of North Santee, to Mrs. Rebecca Watts of Sampit.

All persons who are indebted to the estates of Geo. Gibson and John S. Graham deceased....
May 24   John F. Nesmith, Adm'r.

Issue of May 31, 1848

Died near North Santee ferry on the 16th ult., William Irvine alias Patrick McKune, aged about 27 years. He came here as one of the crew of the brig Eliza Jane, Capt. Brown. McKune said he was a native of Limerick, Ireland....

WINYAH OBSERVER

Issue of June 7, 1848

John R. King made suit for Letters of Administration on the estate of William D. Watts, late of Sampit...1 June 1848.

Joseph J. Hamlin hath made suit for Letters of Administration on the estate of George W. Smith...5 June 1848

Thomas Bates hath made suit for Letters of Administration on the estate of Isaac Singleton, late of this district...16 May 1848....

Issue of June 14, 1848

Died, in this place, on the 8th inst., Allard Belin, infant son of Dr. C. and Mary E. Williams....

Died in this town on Sunday last, Mr. George W. Tarbox, aged 45 years, one of the oldest pilots on our bar....

John C. Porter hath made suit for Letters of Administration on the estate of Daniel T. Durr, late of Waccamaw, as creditor... 8 June 1848....

Issue of June 21, 1848

Married on the 8th ult., in Charlotte, Mecklenburg co., N. C., Rev. Thomas M. Farrow of this place, to Miss Mary Elizabeth Harris of the former place.

Issue of June 28, 1848

Died, near Georgetown, on the 16th inst., Helen Augusta, infant daughter of Thomas and Elizabeth T. Wilson, aged one year, one month and twelve days.

On the evening of the 20th inst., Herriet Francis Foster, second daughter of Henry and N. D. Tobey, aged 5 years, 2 months, and 11 days.

on the 25th inst., Hasford Walker, youngest son of Thomas L. and Nannette Shaw, aged 3 years, and 5 months.

Issue of July 5, 1848

Mary Jane Moyd hath made suit for Letters of Administration on the estate of Robert Moyd, late of Sampit, deceased, as next of kin...4 July 1848.

Issue of July 12, 1848

Died in New-Orleans, on the 23d ult., Mr. Samuel Chapman, aged 39 years, youngest son of the late Thomas Chapman, and a native of this town and for some years did an extensive business in New-Orleans. Of this very large family only one of the name survive the grave: Mr. James Chapman of Charleston.

Issue of July 19, 1848

Died, on Waccamaw Beach on the 15th inst., Alcenora, son of John Ashe and Fanny Allston--aged 15 months and 22 days.

Issue of July 26, 1848

Departed this life at Bucksville, on Wednesday, the 19th inst., Joshua L. Norman, Esq. in the 60th year of his age...

WINYAH OBSERVER

Died on Monday, Thomas Lauren Fraser, aged 34 years, eldest son of the late Samuel Fraser. His body was yesterday taken to the upper Chappel on Waccamaw for interment.

Married in Charleston, on the 13th instant by Rev. H. Cohen, Mr. Gustavus V. Ancker of this place ot Miss Hannah D., eldest daughter of Mr. Moses D. Hyams of that city.

Married on Thursday evening last, by the Rev. Wm. H. Fleming, Wm. Joseph Magill of this town, to Miss Mary E., daughter of J. Chapman Percival, of Albany, New York.

John Cheeseborough applied for Letters of Administration on the Estate of Moses Emanuel, late of this district, with his will annexed....19 July 1848.

Issue of August 2, 1848

Died on Thursday evening 27th inst., at the Summer residence of Col. Fraser on Pawley's Island, Mr. Robert Richardson, aged 61 years....a native of England but for nearly 30 years a resident of Philadelphia and Charleston, S. C.

at his residence in Charleston, on Thursday last, Mr. William Matthews, aged 70 years. (eulogy).

Issue of August 9, 1848

Died in Charleston, on the 1st instant, Mrs. Rachel Chapman, aged 33 years, widow of the late Thomas Chapman, a native of this town. Mrs. C. was the last surviving child of the late Thomas Blackwood of Charleston, who had a family of ten. Her husband was the son of the late Thomas Chapman of this town who twenty years ago had a family of ten children also. With the exception of Mr. James Chapman they also have passed the gate of death....

Issue of August 16, 1848

Died at her residence in Williamsburg District, S. C., on the 17th of July 1848, Mrs. Jane McKnight, aged 72 years, 4 months and 10 days.

at her residence in the same District, on the 24th of July, Mrs. Agnes Singeltary, aged 69 years, 4 months and 23 days.

both were members of Indiantown Church....

Issue of August 23, 1848

Died in this town on Tuesday 15th inst., Mary E., daughter of R. M. Sullivan, aged 8 years, 4 months and 6 days....

on Friday, afternoon the 17th of August, Eleazer Waterman, son of W. S. and Frances M. Croft, aged 2 years and 11 months....

Issue of September 6, 1848

A. W. Dozier hath applied for letters of administration on the estate of Mrs. Comfort Baxley, late of Pee Dee...29 August 1848.

Issue of September 13, 1848

Married on the 29th ult., at the residence of Mr. D. J. Keeffe, on Santee, by the Rev. W. H. Fleming, Mr. W. P. Morris of Marion District ot Miss C. A. G. Wish of this place.

Married at the residence of Mr. J. A. Bruorton, on the 11th

WINYAH OBSERVER

inst., by the Rev. J. H. Stone, Mr. G. W. Christie of this place to Miss S. A. Small of this district.

Died at Richmond, Virginia, on the 12th ult., Mr. John Fraser(?) of this town, aged 53 years...on a visit to the Springs of Va....

on Pee Dee, on the 20th ult., Mrs. Mary Foxsworth, aged 27 years.

at Ramsey Grove, Black River on the 27th ult., Thomas Bates, aged 2 years, only son of Thomas and Jane Bates.

Issue of September 20, 1848

Mr. Cleland J. Gilbert responded to the call of his country on the battlefields of Mexico....died at a camp near Pascoguala, Miss., on the night of the 6th of August, in the 26th year of his age....

Died in this place on the 16th inst., Robert Franklin, son of Capt. Samuel N. and Sarah F. Marsh, aged 3 years, 3 months and 22 days.

Issue of October 4, 1848

Died on Sampit on the 11th ult., Mr. Ezekiel P. Moid, aged 51 years.

at Savannah, Geo., on Friday last, in the 40th year of her age, Mrs. Ellis the amiable consort of Mr. G. L. Ellis...left husband and three children and friends in this district and Horry ....

Issue of October 11, 1848

Mr. George T. Brightman died on the morning of Thursday the 21st August...left wife, an infant daughter and a kind widowed mother....

B. Ervin only child of Dr. James E. and Mary E. Byrd, of Marion District died on the 26th of Sept., aged 2 years and 3 days....

Issue of October 18, 1848

Married on Saturday evening last the 7th inst., in All Saints Parish, Mr. E. F. Harrison to Miss Avey Wells.

Married on Wednesday evening last the 14th inst., in Horry District, James Potter, Esq., Mr. Samuel Singleton to Miss Charlotte Causey.

Died at Darlington C. H., on Sunday last, aged 6 months, Thomas W., youngest son of Sarah and James M. Hunter.

Mr. Robert Nesbit, aged 53 years died at his summer residence on the Seashore.

Issue of October 25, 1848

Departed this life on the morning of the 17th instant, Mr. Robert Nesbit--Planter--of All Saints Parish, Waccamaw, in the 48th year of his age. A native of Scotland, Major Nesbit came to Carolina when a boy, and settled with hi uncle, the late Dr. Robert Nesbit on the plantation which he owned and resided on up to his lamented death...(eulogy).

WINYAH OBSERVER

Issue of November 8, 1848

Married on Thursday 2d inst., in Charleston, by Rev. D. Post, Mr. Daniel Gabriel Wayne, of this place, to Miss Harriette Julia Lavinia, youngest daughter of late Major James M'Call Ware, of that city.

Died on North Santee, on the 29th ult., Gabrella M., daughter of D. J. and R. S. Keiffe, aged 1 year, 4 months and 1 day.

On Combahee, St. Bartholomew's Parish, on the 24th inst., Georgianna Thomasoena, infant child of the late George T. and Mary Jane Brightman, aged seven weeks and one day.

Issue of November 29, 1848

Married at the residence of her father, in Marion District, on Thursday the 12th inst., by the Rev. Mr. Stone, Mr. Daniel Bath, Jr., of this District to Miss Mary, eldest daughter of William Johnston, Esq.

Married in Charleston, on Wednesday evening the 22d inst., by the Rev. Thomas Smyth, D. D., Mr. William H. Goddard, of this place, to Miss M. Euphemia, daughter of John White, Esq., of the former place.

Married in this town on Thursday evening last, the 23d inst., by the Rev. W. G. Conner, Mr. John J. Tamplet, to Miss Anna, eldest daughter of Hugh S. Thompson, Esqr., all of this place.

Issue of December 6, 1848

Died at Weymouth, Pee Dee, on the 16th inst., Mrs. Esther Elvira Haseldon, consort of Mr. S. M. B. Haseldon, aged 33 years.

Issue of December 13, 1848

Married on Wednesday evening the 6th instant, at the German Lutheran Church, by the Rev. Dr. Bachman, Mr. J. J. Dickison, of this place, to Miss Mary Elizabeth, daughter of the late Mr. Ling, of Charleston.

Married in this town on Sunday last, by the Rev. Charles A. Walker, Mr. Samuel Blackwell to Miss Mary R. Easterling, all of this place.

Issue of December 20, 1848

Died at the residence of her father on the 21st of Nov., 1848, aged one year 9 months and 23 days, Caroline Lawrence, the only daughter of Mr. and Mrs. W. Porter....

Issue of December 27, 1848

Married in this town on the 21st inst., by the Rev. G. R. Tally, Capt. John B. LeResour to Miss Elizabeth F. W. Shackelford, daughter of the late Wm. C. Shackelford.

Issue of January 10, 1849

All persons having claism against the estate of John Taylor, Esq., late of Chesterfield District, S. C., deceased....
Cheraw, S. C. Nov. 27, 1848.   John Macfarlan) Qualified
                                 Allan Macfarlan) Executors.
                                                  Dec. 20

WINYAH OBSERVER

All persons having demands against the Estate of A. Slate, late of Horry District, deceased....
Jan. 3   James Beaty, Ordy. H. D.

Issue of January 31, 1849

Notice is hereby given to the legal Heirs and Representatives of the late Robert Cooper that there is in the hands of the Admr. a sum of money ready to beo distributed....
Jan. 31   James G. Henning, Admor.

Issue of February 7, 1849

Died on Saturday morning last, Capt. Robert M. Howren, aged 52 years, a native of Guilford county, N. C., and for the last 35 years a resident of this town....leaves a large family....
    on Monday morning last, Edward Eugene, infant son of Richard O. and Caroline A. Bush, aged three months.

Issue of February 21, 1849

Married, at the Episcopal Church, in this place on Sunday afternoon last, by the Rev. R. T. Howard, Mr. John N. M. Merriman, of Cheraw, to Miss Catherine Logan of Upentine, County of Northumberland, England.
    Died at his residence on Lane's Creek, on the 11th inst., Mr. Elias Thompson, aged 36 years. He was born and raised in Marion District and for the last 10 or 14 years has been in the low country in the employment as an overseer on the rice plantations...left a wife and numerous friends....

Issue of February 28, 1849

Married in Marion dist., on the 18th inst., by the Rev. Mr. McCauquedale, Mr. Alexander McWhite, to Miss Margaret Davis, both of that district.
    at the Episcopal Church on Sunday the 18th inst., by the Rev. R. T. Howard, Mr. John M. Merriman, of Cheraw, to Miss Catharine Logan, of Newcastle, Upon Tyne, County of Northumberland, England.
    Died in Charleston on Friday, Feb. 23, 1849, Mrs. Eliza Anderson, wife of Mr. J. B. Anderson of this place....
    John M. Scriven hath made suit for letters of administration on the estate of Rebecca Cogeshell, with her will annexed....27 Feb 1849.

Issue of March 7, 1849

Married near Bucksville, on Wednesday last, by C. B. Sarvis, Esqr., Mr. John Singleton to Mrs. Catharine Ann Goode, all of Horry District.

Issue of March 14, 1849

Estate notice on estate of the late J. B. Jayroe, deceased... Francis, Green, J. R. Eastinglin, Exors. March 14.

Issue of March 21, 1849

Married on Monday the 12th inst., in New York City, by the Rev. R. S. Sorris Dickinson, Mr. Thomas Burden of this place to

WINYAH OBSERVER

Miss Elizabeth Laing, of Edinburgh, Scotland.
 Married on the 13th inst., near Bucksville, by C. B. Sarvis, Esq., Mr. William J. Rhuark to Miss Sarah Singleton, all of Horry District.

Issue of April 11, 1849

Died at North Santee on the 30th March, Mary M. Hume, in the 35 year of her age--Consort of John Hume.

Issue of May 9, 1849

Col. Peter W. Fraser died in Charleston on the evening of the 1st inst...a member of the Indico Society....

Issue of May 16, 1849

Died in this town on the 4th inst., Miss Elizabeth Jacks, aged about 30 years--only daughter of the late John S.Jacks.
 on the 10th inst., Mrs. Harriet Puche, aged about 60 years.

Issue of May 30, 1849

Died on Sunday the 20th inst., at his residence on Pon Pon, Mr. Daniel J. Keefee in the 33d year of his age...left an amiable wife and one little son and numerous friends....

Issue of June 13, 1849

Departed from this transitory scene, at Oatland, on the 21st ult., in the 30th year of her age, Mrs. Sarah A. D. Tillman, consort of Mr. B. Allston Tillman, leaving bereft of a mother's care, three interesting children....

Issue of June 20, 1849

All persons having demands against Mrs. Mary Johnston, late Mrs. Mary Farewell, formerly of Georgetown deceased....
June 13   E. Waterman, Ordinary

Issue of June 27, 1849

Died in Charleston, on the 5th instant, Col. Charles Huggins, of Santee, Georgetown District, in the 57th year of his age... left an only daughter...at an early age he represented his native District in the Legislature....
 at South Island on the 19th inst., Dr. Joseph M. Simmons, aged about 30 years...A widow and two children survive.
 in Charleston, on Friday last, Jonah M. Atkinson, Esq., aged about 58 years...left a widow and a large family of children....

Issue of July 4, 1849

Married on Thursday last, the 21st inst., by the Rev. J. Rosenfeldt, Leon A. Nones, Esq. of New York, to Miss Marion, daughter of Nathan Emanuel Esq. of Charleston.
 at Cedar Island, on the 28th ult., by the Rev. Mr. Little, Mr. Josiah Doar of Santee to Miss Catherine E. Davis of this place.
 in this town on Wednesday evening 20th ult., by the Rev. A.

WINYAH OBSERVER

M. Chritzburg, Mr. John Armstrong, to Miss Elizabeth Bufkin, all of this place.
in this town yesterday morning the 3d inst., by Rev. A. M. Chritzeburg, Mr. S. M. B. Haselden, to Miss Sarah Munnerlyn, of Santee of his place.

Issue of July 11, 1849

Died in this town, on the 4th inst., Mr. Anthony Sweet, a native of Marion District. He was in the 31st year of his age, an industrious good citizen, and leaves in Marion a widow and two or three children....
on the morning of the 5th instant, Mr. Thomas Burden, a native of Liverpool, England...The whole community sympathize with his bereaved family who reside in New-York....
Wm. Sweet hath applied for letters of admn. on the estate of Anthony Sweet...7 July 1849....

Issue of July 25, 1849

Married in this town on the 23d inst., by the Rev. Mr. Christzburg (sic), Mr. William Sweet of Marion, to Mrs. Sarah Hucks of this town.

Issue of August 15, 1849

Died on Sampit on Friday last, Mrs. Mary Marsh, aged 82 years. Mrs. M. was a native of Horry district and removed to this town in 1815....

Issue of August 22, 1849

Died in Conwayborough on the 14th instant, John Obadiah, infant son of James and Mary Potter.
in this town on Thursday last, Mrs. Elizabeth Gause, in the 70th year of her age, relict of the late Benjamin Gause, of Horry. She was among the oldest inhabitants of the town. She was the widow of three affectionate and devoted husband--a practical mariner, an elevated and devoted preacher, and a very respectable planter....
on Firday last, Mr. W. Bird, long known as the mail carrier from Cheraw to this place....

Issue of August 29, 1849

Married on Britton's Neck on Thursday, 16th inst., by the Rev. D. Legett, Gov. John A. Williams, to Miss Harriet, daughter of Dr. Wm. Russ, Sen. late of Horry District.
On the 8th inst., was gathered to the Tomb, one of the "oldest inhabitants" of Horry, Mr. David Anderson, in the 70th year of his age....
at Mr. R. S. Izard's plantation, on Wednesday last, Mr. John W. Swinton, a native of this district, in the 54th year of his age. Mr. Swinton had for more than thirty years been engaged as a manger on rice plantation in this neighborhood and in Georgia....

Issue of September 5, 1849

William McNulty applied for Letters of Administration on the

WINYAH OBSERVER

estate of John Bird, formerly of Darlington deceased....4 Sept 1849.

Estate notice of Mrs. Elizabeth Gause, of Georgetown....
Aug 29   I. C. Croft, Executor.

Issue of September 12, 1849

All demands against the Estate of Jonah M. Atkinson, deceased, must be rendered....   Susan A. Atkinson, Qual. Extx.
Sep. 12

Issue of September 19, 1849

Died at Newport, R. I. on the 12th inst., Mr. Pleg A. Potter, aged about 38 years, a respectable merchant of this town...a native of Newport, but for several years had been engaged in the mercantile business in this place.

at his residence on Pee Dee, on Tuesday morning last, Mr. John Hayse Allston, aged about 60 years. Mr. A. was a native of Darlington district, but for the last 36 years a resident of this immediate neighbourhood....funeral at Prince Frederick's Chapel, Pee Dee....

Issue of September 26, 1849

Died at Venice, 19th ult., Dr. William Sparks, son of Alexander Sparks, Esq. of Darlington. Dr. Sparks we believe graduated in Paris, in 1839, and was appointed by President Polk, U. S. Consul to Florence, I., in 1846.

Departed this life on Tuesday morning 18th inst., John Hays Allston of Georgetown district. Son of Peter Allston of North Carolina and Mary his wife, he was born 30th Jan. 1786, early moved into this State and died in the 64th year of his age.... Commencing almost without capital, on Waccamaw, he removed successively to Colleton district, St. James Santee, and to his late residence on the Pee Dee...(eulogy).

Departed this life, at Mount Gilead, Waccamaw, on Friday the 21st inst., Dr. R. W. Vaux in the 27th year of his age. (eulogy)

Issue of October 3, 1849

(repeat of obit. of Dr. R. W. Vaux)
Died in this town on Wednesday last, Mrs. Mary Willard, aged 61 years, a native of this place.

on the 26th ult., at Mr. F. Rutledge's plantation, St. James' Santee, John G. Westbury, a native of this District, but for the last nine years a resident of St. James', Santee, aged 27 years.

on Sunday last, Louisa, second daughter of the late Jonah M. Atkinson, aged about 13 years.

At Kensington plantation on Tuesday morning, Mr. Hines, aged about 25 years, a native of Horry district, but for several years a resident on the plantation where he died an manager....

Issue of October 10, 1849

Departed this life inCharleston, on the morning of the 27th Sept., in the 30th year of her age, Miss Sarah Jane Shackelford, daughter of the late John W. Shackelford, Esq., of this town... in the Communion of the Catholic Church....

WINYAH OBSERVER

Departed this life, in Charleston, on Monday last, the 1st October, Mrs. Mary Allston Fraser, relict of the late Col. P. W. Fraser of this District, aged 41 years and 11 days...An only daughter survives her to claim and receive the sympathy....buried Chapel of All Saints, Waccamaw.

Died on the 5th inst., in Williamsburgh dist., at the residence of her uncle, T. G. Finklea, Esq., Frances Ellen, daughter of the late B. W. Cokfield, Esq. of Charleston, aged 13 years....

Samuel R. Carr applied for letters of administration on the estate of Peleg A. Potter....9 Oct 1849.

Issue of October 17, 1849

William A. Parker applied for letters of admn. on the estate of Mary Foxworth, as an heir at law....6 Oct 1849.
Oct. 10

Issue of October 31, 1849

Married at the Methodist E. Church in this town on Wednesday the 24th inst., by the Rev. A. M. Chritzeberg, Mr. George P. Eldred formerly of Newport, R. I., to Miss Eliza C. Christopher, both of this place.

All persons having demands against John Atkins, late of All Saint's Parish, deceased....
Oct. 31

Issue of November 7, 1849

Married on the 15th inst., at Carvers Bay by the Rev. Lemuel A. Grier, Mr. Samuel Avant to Miss Margaret Cribb, all of that place.

Issue of November 14, 1849

Robert R. Hines applied for letters of admn. on the estate of Isaac Hines, as next of kin....14 Nov. 1849.
Nov. 14

Died in this place on the morning of the ___ inst., James Green son of James G. and E__ Henning, in the 5th year of his age.

Executors Notice....All persons having claims against the Estate of the late Major Robert Nesbit of Waccamaw,
                              Joshua John Ward) Executors
Nov. 14   A. Robertson   )

Issue of November 21, 1849

Married on the 15th instant, in Marion District, by the Rev. McQuorquadale, Dr. T. J. Dozier of Georgetown, to Miss Sarah B. Gause, daughter of Hon. B. Gause of the former district.

Died at Horry Court House, S. C., on the 5th inst., Abby, the infant daughter of J. Greenleaf and Emmer Littlefield, of Bucksville, S. C., aged 10 months.

Issue of November 28, 1849

Died, in Conwayborough, on the 19th inst., Mrs. Mary Potter, wife of James Potter, Esq., and daughter of John McMillan, of Marion C. H., S. C., aged 29 years, 2 months and 21 days.

WINYAH OBSERVER

Issue of December 5, 1849

John W. Sturges hath made suit for Letters of Administration on the estate of Frances Ellen Cockfield, as next of kin... 26 Nov 1849

Martin Rhodes hath made suit for Letters of Administration on the estate of William G. DuBose, with his will annexed, as heir at law...20 Nov 1849.

Issue of December 8, 1849

Mary Ann Evans hath made suit to me for Letters of Administration on the Estate of her son Thomas Evans, late of Black River... Dec. 5   E. Waterman, Ordinary.

Issue of December 12, 1849

Married last evening by the Rev. Robert T. Howard, W. B. Steadman, of Charleston, to Mary E., only daughter of the late Thomas F. Goddard, of this place.

Catherine Ann Vaux, applied for Letters of Administration on the estate of Dr. R. W. Vaux, late of Waccamaw, deceased...30 Nov 1849.

Issue of December 19, 1849

Tribute of Respect by Winyah Fire Engine Company to Brother Ralph Woolf....

Issue of December 29, 1849

Cordelia Woolf applied for Letters of Administration on the estate of Ralph Woolf...27 Dec 1849.

Issue of January 5, 1850

Died, in Brookly, N. Y. on the ___, Louise, wife of M. H. Hyde, aged 37 years...

18th ult., at Straford, Conn., Mary El--, wife of L. W. Barret, and only daughters of Samuel Wilmot of this place.

Issue of January 23, 1850

W. J. Howard applied for Letters of Administration on the estate of Thomas W. Finklea...22 Jan 1850

Issue of January 26, 1850

All persons having demands against Peter Michau, derelict.... Jan. 23   E. Waterman, Ordinary

Issue of February 2, 1850

Married on the 23d inst., by the Rev. A. M. Chrietzberg, Mr. James T. Sturges of this place to Miss J. J. Cockfield, of Charleston.

on Wednesday evening last, by the Rev. A. M. Chrietzberg, Mr. J. J. Bryant, to Mrs. A. E. Williams, all of this place.

Departed this transitory life at her residence on Sampit, on the morning of the 23d inst., Mrs. Sarah S. Watts, wife of John D. Watts in the 43d year of her age, leaving a husband and 7 small

WINYAH OBSERVER

children....

Issue of March 6, 1850

Died at Green Wood, in this district, on the __ ult., after a few days illness, Sophia Ann only ____ (Daughter?) of G. W. and S. A. Christian.
Departed this life in Horry District, on the 25th ult., Mrs. Elizabeth Bruton in the 7-__ year of her age. For the last half century she was an exemplary member of the M. E. Church....

Issue of March 9, 1850

Married at Black Mingo on Thursday evening 29th ult., by the Rev. M. McPherson, John J. Steele, M. D., to Miss Sarah Ann, youngest daughter of the late Mr. John Miller, all of Williamsburg District.
Departed this life on the 14th ult., in All-Saints Parish, Mary A. Siau, consort of Louis Siau, formerly of Georgetown, S. C., aged about 65 years. she has left one son somewhere in the state of New York.

Issue of March 20, 1850

Married at Sampit Church on Wednesday 13th inst., by the Rev. Mr. Parker, Mr. Richard W. Sullivan to Miss Margaret A. Carter, all of this district.

Issue of March 30, 1850

Died, at Greenwood, in this District, on the 23d inst., Mrs. Susannah Bruorton, wife of Capt. John A. Bruorton, aged 58 years and 5 months. Forty years ago she attached herself to the Methodist Episcopal Church....

Issue of April 3, 1850

Death of John C. Calhoun

Issue of April 17, 1850

Died on the 13th inst., at Lagranage, North Santee, Mr. John R. King in the 26th yearof his age.

Issue of May 15, 1850

Died at his residence in Kershaw District on the 15th April last, Mr. Hugh F. Bufkin, aged 27 years, 6 months and 12 days... leaves his wife and two young children....

Issue of May 29, 1850

Died, on Wednesday 22d inst., on Black River, Mr. Thomas Wilson, in the 52d year of his age..-.

Issue of June 12, 1850

Died, on Waccamaw, on Saturday evening last, Mrs. Georgeanna L. Anderson, wife of A. C. Anderson, aged 22 years and 5 months.

WINYAH OBSERVER

Issue of June 19, 1850

Died on Black River, on Friday 14th inst., Mrs. Jane C. Ford, wife of Stephen Ford, Esq., aged 50 years and 2 months.

Issue of June 26, 1850

Married on the 8th ult., by the Rev. Mr. Bonham, Mr. John J. Green, Jr., of this place to Miss Jane Ellen Smith, of Macon, Ga.

Issue of July 17, 1850

Died in this place on Sunday morning last, Mrs. Rebecca Beckman, wife of Mr. A. E. Beckman....
Departed this life on the 14th inst., at North Island Beach, Mr. Martin Salomon, aged about 30 years, a native of Hamburg, Germany. Mr. S. has been in this country for 12 years, and for the last 8 has resided in this town.

Issue of August 7, 1850

Died in this place on the 31st ult., Mary Martha, aged 4 years, 6 months and 10 days, only daughter of Capt. and Mrs. David A. Sperry....

Issue of August 28, 1850

Married on Thursday the 22d inst., by the Rev. A. M. Chritzeburg, Mr. J. B. Anderson to Miss Martha Ann, second daughter of Mr. Geo. Durant, of this town.
Died in this town, on the 20th inst., Mr. Elias M. Geanerett, aged 30 years, a native of Darien, Ga.
Saturday last, Mr. William Forbes, aged 18 years, a native of Glasgow, Scotland.
We understand that Mrs. Ann Lesesne, the venerated widow of the late Joseph Lesesne, died at the residence of her son, Dr. John F. Lesesne, in this immediate neighborhood, on Monday evening last, at the advanced age of more than 70 years. She was the oldest resident of our town....

Issue of September 18, 1850

Died in this place on the 12th inst., Nimrod Howren, the youngest son of Samuel and Frances S. Marsh, aged two years, six months and 14 days.
at the residence of her uncle in Williamsburg district, on sunday last, Henrietta R., wife of Mr. John W. Sturges of this place. Aged 22 years.

Issue of October 2, 1850

Departed this life on the 26th ult., Mary Anna, youngest daughter of T. R. and J. E. Sessions, aged 1 year, 5 months and 6 days.
Died, in this town on Friday last at Bucksville, Mr. Parker D. Sewell, a native of Bath, Me. He was the second officer in command on board the ill fated brig Fox, at the time she was wrecked on out bar last week.

WINYAH OBSERVER

Issue of October 16, 1850

Married on Wednesday evening the 9th, by the Rev. A. M. Chritzeburg, Mr. John P. ____ to Miss Julia Anna L., second daughter of --- en Farrow, Esq. all of this place.

Married in Christ Church, Savannah, Ga., Thursday evening last, Mr. Henry R. Chris--- of this town, to Miss Elizabeth Losee of the former place.

Issue of October 23, 1850

Married at the residence of her father in Withersville on Thursday evening last, by the Rev. A. M. Chrietzburg, Mr. Paul Tamplet to Miss Hannah Wilson, all of this district.

Issue of November 13, 1850

Married near Bradford Springs, Sumter District, on the 24th ult., by the Rev. Mr. Eliot, Mr. D. H. Smith, of this place, to Miss Ellen Elizabeth, daughter of Mr. Joseph S. Bossard.

Died on the 3rd instant Nanett Maria, infant daughter of Mr. Thomas L. Shaw, in the first year of her age.

Died on Wednesday, last 6th inst., at Bennetsville, S. C., Jane, wife of Jno. McCollum, Esq. of that place, and youngest daughter of the late Hugh McKay, Esq. of Chesterfield.

All persons having demands against the late Thomas Wilson... Oct. 30   C. J. Atkinson, Admr.

Issue of December 18, 1850

Died in this town on the night of the 16th inst., Mrs. Sarah G. Fraser, in the 24th year of her age....

Issue of January 8, 1851

Died at the residence of his brother on Black River, on Saturday, the 4th inst., Mr. James B. Bates, aged 30 years.

Issue of January 18, 1851

Married on the 9th inst., by the Rev. James Stone, Mr. William D. Bostick of Quincy, florida, to Miss Martha Harrell, of Marion District, S. C.

Issue of January 22, 1851

Married on Pee Dee on the 15th inst., by the Rev. L. S. Grier, Mr. Nelson Cooper to Miss Milly Jones, all of this district.

Married on Pee Dee on the 16th inst., by the Rev. L. S. Grier, Mr. Nicholas P. Bone to Miss Mary E. Young, all of this District.

Issue of February 8, 1851

Married in Charleston, on Wednesday evening, the 5th inst., by the Rev. H. Cohen, Mr. Joseph Sampson, of this place, to Miss Esther Cohen, of the former city.

Issue of February 12, 1851

Married on Sunday evening, the 26th ult., at Horry Court

WINYAH OBSERVER

House, by the Rev. Israel Hughes, Capt. Samuel Pope to Miss Sarah Richwood, all of Horry District.
    Estate Sale at the late residence of Ezekiel Owens, deceased, on Carver's Bay, ...   P. M. Grier, Admo'r.
Feb. 12

Issue of March 1, 1851

    Married, near Bucksville, on the evening of the 27th inst., by C. B. Sarvis, Esq., Mr. Ma--- A. Hampton of Randolph co., N. C., to M-- Jane Rheuark of Horry District.
    Died onthe night of the 26th inst., at his residence in All Saints, in the 44th year of his age, Benj. Brutor, Esq., leaving a disconsolate family....

Issue of March 8, 1851

    Married in this place on Thursday evening last, by the Rev. James Stacy, Mr.Henry M. Hiddleson to Miss E. Lucile Marianno, all of this place.
    Died on Pee Dee on the 18th ult., Mrs. Sarah Mitchell, in the 61st year of her age. She was a strict member of the Baptist Church for the last 30 years.

Issue of March 19, 1851

    Married in this town last evening by the Rev. James Stacy, Mr. A. A. W. Siau to Miss Carline M. Cooper, all of this place.

Issue of March 22, 1851

    Esther Jane Tarbox, departed this life in Georgetown, S. C., March 20th, 1851...aged 21 years, 5 months and 24 days, and had been married only a few months...a member of the M. E. Church, South nearly 10 years.

Issue of March 26, 1851

    Married on Black River, on the 13th inst., by the Rev. G. R. Talley, Mr. Benjamin S. Thompson to Miss Elizabeth Bellune, all of this district.
    Died on Sampson Island on 12th inst., 55 miles south of Charleston, Miss Susan Gabraella, aged 14 years, and 6 months, eldest daughter of L. L. W. and Mary B. Davis, formerly of Georgetown, S. C.

Issue of April 16, 1851

    Departed this life April 3d, Mrs. Sarah Session, in the 76th year of her age...a member of the M. E. Church for a period of near 60 years...a native of Nottinghamshire in England.

Issue of April 23, 1851

    Married on Thursday evening 17th inst., at Creenville (sic), S. C., by the Rev. T. T. Hopkins, Capt. Arther Magee, of the Steamer Nins, of Charleston, S. C. to Miss Nancy, daughter of James Goodlett, of the former place.

WINYAH OBSERVER

Issue of May 7, 1851

Departed this life in Britton's Neck, Marion District, on the 29th April, by the accidental discharge of his gun, Mr. Wm. Drayton Gause, in the 19th year of his age. (eulogy).

All persons having claims against the Estate of the late Mrs. Sarah Sessions of Georgetown, S. C.....
May 7   Thomas R. Sessions, Executor

Issue of May 14, 1851

All persons having demands against B. A. Thompson, late of Horry District....
May 14

A. E. Beckman hath made suit for Letters of Administration on the estate of Rebekah A. Beckman...29 April 1851

Issue of May 21, 1851

Married in Conwayboro on the 14th inst., by the Rev. John Woodward, Mr. Bethel D. Beaty, to Miss Martha A. R. Hemingway, all of that place.

on Wednesday evening the 14th inst., in this place, by the Rev. James Stacy, Dr. Wm. D. Rice of Tennessee to Sarah M., eldest daughter of the late Thomas Wilson of this District.

Issue of June 4, 1851

Married on Thursday evening the 29th inst., on Black River, by the Rev. S. P. Taylor, Mr. Oliver J. Butts to Miss Anna R. Siau, all of this District.

Died, at Philadelphia on the 28th May, Abraham Myers, a native and for many years a resident of this town, at an advanced age....

Issue of June 11, 1851

Died at his residence on Santee on the 25th ult., Mr. Raphael Rambert, in the 43d year of his age. He leaves a widow, one son and a great many friends....

Issue of June 18, 1851

Married on the 28 ult., in the Episcopal church by the Rev. Robert T. Howard, Mr. James Smith, to Miss Eugenia Withers, second daughter of the late Dr. Edward Gibbes Thomas.

Sarah E. Rambert hath applied for Letters of Administration on the estate of Raphael Rembert, late of Santee Deceased... 10 June 1851

Estate sale at the late residence of James D. Benbow, on Sampit for the purpose of making a division among the heirs....
                                        H. J. Morris, Admor.

Issue of July 2, 1851

Married on the 26th ult., by the Rev. James Stacy, Mr. Thomas C. Cox to Miss Georgia Anna Calhoun, all of this place.

Issue of July 30, 1851

Married on Thursday the 17th inst., at the Methodist Episcopal Church, by the Rev. James Stacy, Mr. John H. Ford to Mrs.

WINYAH OBSERVER

Elizabeth Taylor, all of this place.
    Died on the 23d inst., at his late residence, eight miles from Wilmington (N.C.), Mr. Timothy Bloodworth, in the 71st year of his age....the last survivor of the children of the Hon. T. Bloodworth, who represented this State in the U. S. Senate from 1795 to 1801...left a wife and nine children...member of the Methodist Church.

Issue of August 20, 1851

    Died, on Wednesday the 13th inst., at Cedar Island, Mr. Elias M. Do---, in the 39th year of his age...one of the best planters in our District.
    in this town yesterday, Mr. Franc-- Durant, aged about 25 years. He was a native of Horry District, and came to this place as a resident some two years since....

Issue of August 27, 1851

    Died on the 20th inst., near Flintville, Marion District, S. C., Mrs. Jane Bragdon, consort of Thomas Bragdon, in the 33rd year of her age...left a husband and three little children.... member of the Baptist Church....

Issue of September 10, 1851

    Died, on the morning of the 4th instant, J. Hayes Alston, eldest son of Jno. E. and R. M. Alston, aged 2 years and 9 months.
    on Waccamaw, on the 6th inst., of Congestive fever, Susan Antenia, daughter of Mr. and Mrs. W. T. Smith, aged 3 years, 4 months and 21 days.
    in this town on Saturday last, Mr. Hasford Walker, of the House of Coachman & Walker...leaves a widow an too(sic) small children.
    on the same day, Mr. Daniel McFarlane, of Boston, second officer of the schooner Phoenix...vessel wreck on the 24th August. We understand he has a wife and children in Boston.

Issue of September 17, 1851

    Died in this town on the 11th inst., Benjamin Franklin, infant son of j. B. and E. F. W. LeRe--ur.
    Mary A. E. Walker applied for Letters of Administration on the estate of her late husband, Hasford Walker, merchant, as next of kin....9 Sept 1851.

Issue of September 24, 1851

    Died on Black River on the 19th inst., Mary Eliza, infant daughter of J. B. and S. J. Harrell, aged 3 months and 10 days.

Issue of October 1, 1851

    Married in Wallingford, Conn., on the 25th ult., Mr. Stephen J. Rembert, of this District, to Miss Laura Hiddeeson of the former place.
    Died on the 29th inst., Francis Asbury, youngest son of Mr. and Mrs. Jno. C. Porter. aged one years and two months.

WINYAH OBSERVER

Issue of October 8, 1851

Died in this town, on the 30th ult., John Davis, second officer of the brig Chief, a native of Dublin, Ireland.
on the 1st instant, Stephen Durant, aged 26 years, a native of Calias, Me....in hospital here 2 months.

Issue of October 22, 1851

Died, very suddenly, on Saturday night 19th inst., in Withersville, Mr. William Wilson, leaving a wife and several children....

Issue of October 29, 1851

Died of inflamation, at Withersville, on the 18th Oct., 1851, in the 47th year of his age, Mr. William Wilson. (eulogy).
Jane T. Wilson hath applied for Letters of Administration on the estate of her late husband William Wilson...29 Oct. 1851

Issue of November 12, 1851

Departed this life on Sunday evening the second Nov., at Murphy's Island, Mr. Josiah Doar, in the 45th year of his age, leaving a bereaved widow and child, brothers and sisters....

Issue of November 19, 1851

Married on Thursday the 13th inst., in Darlington District, by the Rev. Mr. Timmons, Josiah W. Cockfield, Esq., of Williamsburg District, to Mrs. Rosana Dinkings of Darlington.

Issue of November 26, 1851

Married on the 28th October by George W. Myers, Esq., Mr. Henry L. Gainey to Miss Frances Turbeville, daughter of William Turbeville, Esq. all of Marion.
on the 4th of November, by the Rev. J. P. McPherson, Mr. Joseph A. W. Woodbery of Marion to Miss Jannet E. Scott, daughter of Jno. T. Scott of Williamsburgh Dist.
on Thursday evening the 20th inst., on Black River, by Rev. James Stacy, Mr. Stephen W. Rouquie to Miss Margaret E. W. Thompson, both of this District.
on the 20th inst., by George W. Myers, Esq., Mr. Theophelus Lewis to Miss Prudence A. Johnson, all of Marion District.

Issue of December 3, 1851

Stephen D. Doar applied for Letters of Administration on the estate of Elias M. Doar, late of Santee, deceased...2 Dec 1851
William Daniel applied for Letters of Administration on the estate of Stephen M. B. Haselden, deceased....28 Nov 1851

Issue of December 17, 1851

Died, in this town, on Saturday last, Mrs. Caroline M. Siau, wife of Mr. Alexander Siau, in the 18th year of her age....

Issue of December 24, 1851

Married on Black River, on Thursday evening last, by the Rev.

WINYAH OBSERVER

James Stacy, Mr. William J. Thompson to Rebecca Ann, eldest daughter of William S. McDonald, Esq.

Died, on Sampit, on Saturday night last, John D. Watts, Esq., one of those good men whose death is a loss to any community.

on Saturday last in this place, Mrs. Esther A. Jones, aged about 80 years, one of the oldest inhabitants of our town.

on Monday last in this place, Mrs. Rebecca McDaniel, conosrt of John B. McDaniel.

Issue of December 20, 1851

Died on the 12 Dec., at EaGrange(sic), North Santee, Mr. T. K. Morris.

Issue of January 14, 1852

Married in this town last evening, by Rev. Wm. L. Lee, John Wilson, of London, to Miss Harriet Morris, daughter of the late Benjamin Morris, of this district.

Died in this town on the morning of the __ inst., Mrs. Sarah A. Warden, in the 24th year of her age....

Issue of January 17, 1852

Died at Fairfield, Waccamaw, S. C., on the 9th of January, 1852, John J. Steele, in the 29th year of his age...born in St. Thomas' Parish, S. C., March 30th, 1823...left a wife and 3 small children...
All Saints Parish, S. C., Jan. 13, 1852.

in this town, on the 11th inst., Rev. Samuel Proctor Taylor, aged about 44 years...a minister in the Methodist Episcopal Church.

Sarah Ann Steele applied for letters of admn. on the estate of her late husband John J. Steele, late of Waccamaw...16 Jan 1852.

Issue of January 21, 1852

Married on the 15th instant, on (Black River?), by the Rev. J. P. McPherson, James (Mun?)nerlyn of this place to Miss Agnes J. ___ of Williamsburgh.

Died in this place on the 12th inst., in the ___ year of her age, Mrs. Sarah A. Wasdin, ___ Mr. Thomas W. Wasdin...member of the M. E. Church....

Issue of January 31, 1852

Robert B. Chambers applied for letters of admn. on the estate of James W. Chambers, late of Blackmingo...28 Jan 1852.

All persons having demands against John D. Watts, late of Sampit, deceased....   A. D. Watts, Qual. Exr.
Jan. 17

Issue of February 7, 1852

Married, on Thursday evening last, by the Rev. James Stacy, Mr. Wm. W. Ward of Marion Dist. to Mrs. Henrietta Dubose of this place.

WINYAH OBSERVER

Issue of February 11, 1852

John A. Bruorton applied for letters of admn. on the estate of Thomas K. Morris, formerly of this district, late of Georgia. 10 Feb 1852

Issue of February 28, 1852

Died in this town on Thursday last, Mrs. Margaret Croft, widow of the late Wm. Croft, aged about 60 years.
    in Charleston, on the morning of the same day, Mrs. Magdalen E. Keith, widow of the late Maj. John Keith. She has left us at an advanced age....
    on Black River, on the same day, Mr. William S. McDonald, aged about 45 years--an honest and industrious citizen.

Issue of March 6, 1852

Departed this life on the morning of Monday the 1st instant, Mr. Benjamin T. Verner in the 48th year of his age. (eulogy).

Issue of March 10, 1852

On the evening of Friday last at 10 minutes to 9 o'clock, aged 2 years, 6 months and 20 days, Ann Eliza, only daughter of J. M. and S. W. Hunter....

Issue of March 17, 1852

Died at the Plantation of Mr. R. O. Anderson on Pee Dee, on the 12th inst., Mr. DeKalb Swinton, aged 27 years and 27 days....

Issue of March 24, 1852

Death of Capt. W. C. Waterman who died at his residence in this place, on Saturday evening last. On the 17th inst he attained the age of 34 years....left an affectionate wife....

Issue of April 7, 1852

Died at the plantation of Mr. Arther Blake, of St. James Santee, on Saturday morning the 3d inst., Mr. A. N. Westbury, aged 40 years 10 months and 27 days...left a wife and four helpless children.
    in this town on the 1st inst.,Mrs. Lucy S. Tarbox, consort of Capt. Francis G. Tarbox, aged 27 years.

Issue of April 14, 1852

Married on Wednesday evening the 7th inst.,by the Rev. R. T. Howard, Robert H. Clarkson of Charleston, to Mary E., daughter of the late William Mayrant, Esq., of this District.

Issue of April 28, 1852

Married in Wayne co., N. C., on the 30th ult., by the Rev. N. Anderson, Mr. L. H. Moye to Miss Sallie Jane, daughter of T. Hadly, Esqr.
    at the M. E. Church, in this place on Wednesday evening the 21st inst by the Rev. James Stacy, Mr. Villiam H. Lester, to Miss

WINYAH OBSERVER

Frances M. Sperry, of New Haven, Conn.
   in Williamsburg District on the same evening by the Rev. J. P. McPherson, Mr. William Cooper, Jr., to Miss Lenora Steele.
   on the same evening by the Rev. A. Glennie, A. R. Mitchell Esqr. of Charleston to Miss Ann Rebecca, eldest daughter of Dr. John D. Magill, of Waccamaw.
   Died on Black River on the 17th April inst., Mrs. Harriet P. Bruorton, wife of Mr. Henry W. Bruorton, aged 30 years and 3 months....
   at Wadesboro, N. C., on the 18th inst., Agnes, aged about 14 years, daughter of Sam'l L. and Ann R. Oliver of this neighborhood...at Floral College.
   in Horry District on the 22d inst., Major Allen Blount, of Pitt County, N. C., moved to this State in January last...left wife and children....
   All persons having demands against Benjamin T. Vernor deceased ....
April 21

Issue of May 5, 1852

   Died in Charleston on the 5th ult., aged 59 years, Mrs. Sarah Emanuel, consort of Nathan Emanuel, Snr., daughter of Isaac Gomez, of New York, and grand daughter of Aaron Lopez, the distinguished merchant of Newport, R. I.....

Issue of May 19, 1852

   Married in Charleston on Thursday evening 6th inst., by Rev. Dr. Hanckel, Joshua Ward, Esqr., of All Saints Waccamaw, to Miss Elizabeth, second daughter of Col. S. H. Mortimer of Charleston.

Issue of June 2, 1852

   Died on Black River, on the 22d ult., Edward Matthews, infant son of Dr. J. F. and H. E. Lesesne, aged 3 months.
   of consumption on the 21st ult., Mr. Edmund Alston, son of Col. Wm. A. Alston, aged about 31 years.
   suddenly at Chancellor Dunkin's plantation on Pee Dee, on Friday last, Mr. F. M. Davis, aged about 42 years.

Issue of June 9, 1852

   Departed this life on 5th inst., Julia Shaffer, only daughter of Wm. C. and Rebecca W. Munnerlyn, aged two years, seven months and 14 days.

Issue of June 16, 1852

   Died at her residence on North Santee, May the 19th Mrs. Maria Huggins, wife of Capt. Robt. Huggins, in the 64th year of her age ...daughter of Col. Nathan Huggins, the youngest of four brothers, all of whom were attached to Marion's Brigade in the War of Independence...left husband and three children....
   Tribute of Respect to Francis Marion Davis, by I. O. O. F., June 10, 1852....

Issue of June 30, 1852

   Married in Charleston on Tuesday evening the 22d inst., at

176

WINYAH OBSERVER

St. Michaels Church, by the Rev. Dr. Hanckel, Richard S. Porcher, Esq. of St. John's Berkeley, and Esther Charlotte, daughter of the late Dr. Gasque, of this place.

Issue of July 7, 1852

Married on Thursday the 1st inst., at All Saints Parish Upper Church, by the Rev. Alex. Glennie, Nathaniel Barnwell of Charleston, to Jane Rose, only daughter of the late Col. Peter W. Fraser, of this District.

Tribute of Respect by Vestry and Church Wardens of Parish Church of Prince George Winyah, to Rt. Rev'd. Christopher Edwards Gadsden....

Issue of July 14, 1852

Died in this place on Friday the 9th instant, Georgianna Virginia, second daughter of Capt. William C. and Ann H. Uptigrove, aged 4 years, 6 months and 12 days.

on Sunday the 11th inst., Hannah Sarah Ann, youngest daughter of R. J. and Sarah Ann Davidson, aged 3 years, 3 months and 15 days.

Issue of July 28, 1852

Death of Mr. Stephen Ford, who died on Thursday morning at the pine land residence of his son-in-law Col. B. A. Coachman...

Died in this town on Friday last, aged about 50 years, Mrs. Martha Coleman, a native and resident of Marion. She had been on a visit to a daughter at the South....

Issue of August 4, 1852

Died in this town on Wednesday last, Mr. James Dennie, age about 40 years.

Issue of August 18, 1852

Died on the 26th of July in All Saints Parish, Elizabeth Jane, infant daughter of James N. and Sarah Brown, aged 15 days.

Died at Conwayborough on the 9th instant, Mary Frances Przyborowskie, daughter of Mrs. Susannah Przyborowski, aged 5 years, 6 months and 19 days.

Issue of August 25, 1852

Died in this Town on Sunday last, Capt. William Lester in the 68th year of his age...among the oldest natives of the District.

Issue of September 1, 1852

Died at his residence in Williamsburgh District on the 18th inst., Leonard Stone, Esq., in the 40th year of his age...left a widow and three young children....

at North Santee, on Thursday last 26th inst., William Benjamin, only child of Larry and Mary Jane Hyman, aged 1 year and 5 months.

in this town on the 27th ult.,Mrs. Sarah Ann Christie, consort of Mr. G. W. Christie of this place...in the 22d year of her age...left a fond and affectionate husband and an infant child....

WINYAH OBSERVER

in this town on Friday last, Mr. Edward H. Senter, a seaman attached to the Schr. John G. Faxon, aged about 34 years.
in this town on yesterday morning, William Walter, infant son of V. and Sarah Richardson, aged 1 year and 7 months.

Issue of September 8, 1852

Died in this town on yesterday morning, Malachi S., only son of G. W. and Elizabeth Williams, aged 2 years and 27 days.

Issue of September 15, 1852

Died in this town on Wednesday the 1st of September, Julia Rebecca, eldest child of I. C. and Martha H. Croft, aged 9 years, 8 months and 16 days.
also in this town, on the 10th September, Albert Carr, son of I. D. and Martha H. Croft, aged 2 years and 3 days.
in this town, on the 14th September, John David, son of Mr. and Mrs. V. Richardson, aged 8 months.

Issue of September 22, 1852

Departed this life on Wednesday the 15th inst., Mrs. Sa--, wife of James W. Skinner, aged about 34 years....
Died on Thursday morning 15th inst., in the sixth year of his age, Toomer Porter, eldest __ of Dr. E. B. and Mrs. E. C. Brown.

Issue of September 29, 1852

Married in Charleston on the 12th Sept., by the Rev. Whiteford Smith, Mr. J. H. Ashby of Virginia, to Miss ann J. Howren of this place.
Died in this town on Saturday last, Mr. Isaac C. Sessions, son of the late Ransom, aged about 42 years. He was for many years Register in Mesne Conveyance....

Issue of October 6, 1852

Died at the residence of Mr. Thomas G. Fainklea, in Williamsburg District, on the 7th ult., Mr. W. W. Cockfield, aged about 20 years.
at his residence in East Bridgeport, on Wednesday the 22d inst., Minerva, wife of Samuel Wilmot, aged 29 years.

Issue of October 13, 1852

Died in Conwayboro on Sunday the __ October, Samuel Thomas, only son of Mr. D. Britton, aged 7 years 3 months and 22 days....

Issue of October 20, 1852

Died in this town on Monday the 11th inst., William youngest son of Elizabeth and William Hyman, aged 4 years.
Departed this life in this place on the morning of the 15th inst., in the 45th year of his age, Mr. Agustus L. Siau, a planter of this District...left a widow and 7 children.

Issue of October 27, 1852

Died on the 20th instant in Darlington District, Mr. Alonzo

178

WINYAH OBSERVER

J. B. Fraser, a citizen of Charleston....

Issue of November 3, 1852

Died on Monday last in the 56th year of his age, Mr. Benjamin T. Cuttino...a member of the Baptist Church....

Issue of November 17, 1852

Departed this life at his residence in Georgetown, S. C., the 1st November 1852, Mr. Benjamin T. Cuttino, in the 56th year of his age, leaving an interesting family...born, reared, and lived his entire life in Georgetown, and descended from one of the oldest settlers and residents of that Town...(long account)

Issue of November 24, 1852

Married on the 11 inst., at Choppee Church by the Rev. Mr. Carson, Mr. Benjamin T. Wilson to Miss MaryE. Knox, all of this District.

Issue of December 1, 1852

Married on the 25th ult., in Marin District, by the Rev. Elija Hicks, Mr. Henry R. K---- of this place, to Miss Henrietta, youngest daughter of Capt. Cannon Gibbs, of Marion District.

Issue of December 8, 1852

Married on the 25th inst., by the Rev. D. McQueen, M. L. L. Fraser, Jr. to Miss Mary Adelaide, daughter of W. M. DeLorme, Esq. all of Sumpter District.

Issue of December 15, 1852

Richard Oswald Anderson was borne at Ramsy's Grove, on Black River, the residence of his father, 24th Nov 1793--he died at Bath in England, Oct. 11th, 1852, at the residence of his sister ...sent to England for an education....
Died on December 1st, 1852, Mrs. Rebecca W. Munnerlyn, aged 32 years and 3 months...left__ babes, one an infant of days....
Died at his residence on Black river on Friday(?) last, in the 64th year of his age, Mr. William G. Leneriux, one of the oldest managing rice planters in the District...with the Hon. Thos. R. Mitchell at Greenwich, on Eastern part of the town in 1810 and his __ with Col. Hunt at Richfield plantation....
in this town on the same evening, Francis R. Dixon, aged about 42 years, leaving a widow and five children....

Issue of December 22, 1852

Married on Wednesday evening the 15th inst., on Black River, by the Rev. James Stacy, Mr. William H. Dorrill to Miss Alafair D. Hawkins, all of this District.
Married on Thursday the 16th inst., by the Rev. R. T. Howard, A. Toomer Porter, Esq., to Miss Magdalene Atkinson, daughter of the late Jonah M. Atkinson, Esq. of Winyah.
Died in Georgetown District, S. C., on the 9th of December, 1852, Mr. Wm. G. Lenerieux, in the 68th year of his age...joined the Methodist church five or six weeks previous to his death....

WINYAH OBSERVER

Issue of December 29, 1852

All persons having claims against the late Richard O. Anderson....
Dec. 22
      Alexander Robertson) Executors.
      John F. Blacklock)

All persons having demadns against F. M. Davis, deceased....
Dec. 22   J. G. Henning, Administrator.

PEE DEE TIMES

Issue of March 9, 1853 (Vol. I, #9)

Joshua John Ward died Sunday, 27th Feb., in the 53d year of his age...served in the State Legislature for many years from All Saints Parish....
Died in this town on Monday the 28th ult., Mr. Robert Lester, in the 28th year of his age.

Issue of March 16, 1853

Married on the 3rd inst., by the Rev. James H. Stone, Mr. George S. B. Huggins of Darlington, to Miss Elizabeth Timmons, of Williamsburgh District.
on the 3rd inst., by the Rev. James H. Stone, Mr. Clark Eaddy, to Miss Margaret H. Barr, all of Williamsburgh District.
B. C. Pressly hath applied for letters of admn. on the estate of James Lamble, as next friend...12 February 1853

Issue of March 30, 1853

Married on the 17th instant by the Rev. James H. Stone, Dr. David E. Wilson to Miss Mary Jane Britton, all of Williamsburgh District, S. C.

Issue of April 6, 1853

Robert E. Fraser applied for Letters of Administration on the Estate of Edward Thomas...5 April 1853

Issue of April 20, 1853

Married in Wilmington, N. C. on the 12th inst., by the Rev. Dr. Drane, John W. Gregorie, U. S. Coast Survey, to Miss Sallie E. Baker, of that place.
All persons having demands against the Estate of the late W. G. Linerieux deceased....   J. R. Easterling)
                                                Francis Green) Executors.

Issue of May 4, 1853

Died, at the residence of Capt. P. W. McCrea in Williamsburgh District on the 6th of March last, Mrs. Mary Ann Dobson, in the hundred and eighth year of her age.
All persons having demands against Capt. Daniel Bath, late of Craver's Bay, deceased....   Ann Bath, Executrix.
April 27   Thomas Bath, Executor.

Issue of May 18, 1853

Tributes of Respect by Winyah Indigo Society.
Stephen Ford, of Black River, became a member in 1818 and died in June last.
Augustus L. Siau, also of Black river, was elected a member in May 1838, and died in June or July last.
Richard Oswald Anderson united himself with us in April 1824 and died in Bath, England, in August last, in the 54th year of his age...leaving his large fortune to a widowed sister in England.
William G. Lenerieux became a member in 1826 and died in January last in the 63d year of his age.
Joshua John Ward died in March last, in the 54th year of his

PEE DEE TIMES

age.
All persons having demands against the Estate of William L. Phillips deceased....   C. B. Sarvis,
May 11   B. E. Sessions, Exor's of W. L. Phillips

Issue of May 25, 1853

Our District has within the last few weeks been deprived of two of its most venerable, respected and wealthy citizens, in the demise of Dr. Robert Muldrow of Salem, and Capt. Leonard White of Claremont....   Banner.
All persons having demands against Benjamin M. Ville Pontoux, late of Sampit, deceased....   Jacob A. Lockwood, Admor. Charleston, May 1, 1853.

Issue of June 15, 1853

Married on the 30th May last, by the Rev. Daniel DePree, Mr. James W. Skinner to Miss Margaret Ann Green, all of this district.
Married in Conwayboro on the 9th of June, by the Rev. Thomas A. Beaty, Mr. Thomas Nelson Rowe to Mrs. Susan D. Prezbyrowski, all of that place.

Issue of June 22, 1853

Died in St. Paul's Parish, Colleton Dist., June 10th, 1853, Benjamin Capers Coleman, aged about 30 years.

Issue of July 20, 1853

Married on Wednesday 6th July by the Rev. R. T. Howard, Mr. W. W. Shackelford to Miss Hess B. Ford, all of this place.
Married on the 7th inst., by the Rev. J. H. Stone, Mr. Leonard Baxly, to Miss Elizabeth McDaniel, the daughter of Randle McDaniel of Williamsburgh Dist.
Died on the 15th inst., at Pine Grove near this place, Robert Gibson, infant son of J. K. and A. J. Munnerlyn.
Died on Sunday last after a painful illness of ten days, Sarah Edith, infant daughter of David H. and Ellen Smith.
Died, on board the Schr. F. Merwin, Capt. Thomas on Monday last, Mr. John Dent, aged about 22 years--a native of Stamford, Conn.

Issue of July 27, 1853

Died on Friday morning 1st instant, Mrs. Sarah E. Witherspoon, wife of Dr. S. W. Witherspoon, and daughter of Col. D. D. Wilson, in the 31st year of her age...left husband and children....

Issue of August 3, 1853

Married on the 27th July by the Rev. J. L. Shuford, Mr. J. A. Bruorton, to Miss Caroline E. J. Lewis, both of this District.
Died, on Black River on the 18th ult., at his residence on Black river, Mr. Elisha Cumbie, aged 85 years.

Issue of August 10, 1853

Married in this place at the M. E. Church on Wednesday evening

PEE DEE TIMES

last by the Rev. H. A. C. Walker, Mr. Daniel Goldfinch to Mrs. Mary Finklea, both of this place.
   Died, in this town on Saturday last, Mr. Josiah H. Barker, a native of Charlestown, Massachusetts, aged 63 years.

Issue of August 17, 1853

   Died, in Fayetteville, N. C. on the 7th inst., Mrs. Elizabeth Henderson, aged 75 years. The deceased was a consistent member of the Protestant Episcopal Church for the last twenty-three years.
   Died in this town on the 14th inst., Miss Sarah Eliza Siau, daughter of the late Augustua L. Siau, aged seven years and 5 months.
   in Savannah, Ga., Aug. 12th, 1853, Henry Mattie, only son of James S. & Ella M. Magill, formerly of Georgetown, S. C., aged 4 years, 1 month and 6 days.
   on Friday last, Josephine, youngest daughter of N. C. & L. Hickman, aged 14 months.

Issue of August 31, 1853

   Departed this life on the 14th inst., Miss Sarah Eliza Siau, daughter of A. L. and Hannah Mariah Siau, aged 7 years and 5 months....

Issue of September 7, 1853

   Died in this town on Friday last, Mr. William Hayle, a native of England, aged 45 years--a shoemaker by occupation.

Issue of September 21, 1853

   Died, in this place on Thursday last, Charles Walter, second son of J. J. and A. G. Tampler, aged 2 years and 5 months.
   Died on Monday 19th inst., Gurdon Wright, infant son of Francis W. and Sarah H. K. Munnerlyn, aged one year and eight days.

Issue of September 28, 1853

   Married at the M. E. Church in this place, on Wednesday evening, last by the Rev. J. A. Minnick, Mr. Joseph Meier to Miss Mariah Blanchard, all of Wilmington, N. C.
   on the 22d instant, by the Rev. Mr. Grier, Mr. J. R. Bailey, to Miss Elizabeth A. L. K. Goude. All of this district.
   on Thursday the 15th inst., by the Rev. James H. Stone, Mr. Jesse Carter to Miss Julian O. Gaskins. All of Williamsburgh district.
   Within the last week several of our oldest and respectable citizens of Williamsburgh have gone down to the grave. The first, Mr. Thomas McConnell, died on the 19th in the 69th year of his age. He leaves a widow and 8 children. A few days afterwards Mr. James Gamble, aged about 62 years followed-- and on Friday last, Mr. John Brockington died, leaving a widow and seven children. They were each neighbours....

Issue of October 5, 1853

   Married on the first September 1853 by the Rev. J. L. Shuford, Mr. J. J. Hamlin to Miss A. Price, all of Pee Dee.
   (torn....) on the 1st inst., Mr. Ezekiel Owens, aged ninety-two years. a native of this district and lived in retirement on

PEE DEE TIMES

Carver's Bay, Pee Dee. He was at the time of his death the oldest man in the district and the last but one now living who carried a gun in the war of the revolution.

Issue of October 12, 1853

Married on the 6th inst., by the Rev. Frederick Rush, Mr. J. D. B. Hanna to Miss C. A. Anderson, all of Williamsburg District.
on the same evening by Mr. Samuel McGinney, Mr. Henry Griggs to Miss ann Pierce, both of this district.
Died in Newport, R. I., on the morning of the 9th ult., at 11 o'clock, William J. only son of W. J. and E. A. Munro, aged 16½ months.
at his residence in Marion District on the 8th instant, Mr. C. F. White. He leaves a large family....

Issue of October 19, 1853

Died, in Williamsburgh district, S. C., September 28, 1853, Mr. William Tilton Snr., in the 79 year of his age.

Issue of November 9, 1853

Oscar Eugene Ham, son of Thomas A. and Sarah E. Ham, was born on the first day of January 1850, and departed this life Oct. 12th, 1853, aged 3 years, 9 months and 11 days. J. L. Shuford.

Issue of November 16, 1853

Died in Williamsburg District, S. C., on the 18th of September Mr. Thomas McConnell in the 68th year of his age....member of the Presbyterian Church....

Issue of November 23, 1853

Married in Horry District, by the Rev. Mr. Grier, Mr. William Kennedy Grier to Miss Cornelia Mary, daughter of C. B. And M. H. Sarvis.
on the 17th of November, by the Rev. James H. Stone, Mr. Alexander J. McCrea to Miss Margaret G. Flagler, all of Williamsburgh District.

Issue of November 30, 1853

(torn)...the Rev. Mr. Hunter, Mr. J. H. McCon(nell?) to Miss Mary L. Durant all of this place.
on Wednesday evening last, the 23d inst., by the Rev. M. H. Lance, Mr. Robert N. Rouse of Charleston, S. C. to Miss Elizabeth B. Farrow of this place.

Issue of December 14, 1853

Married on the 7th inst., by the Rev. J. L. Shufford, Mr. Jehu Gasque to Miss Mary E. Calhoun, all of this place.
All persons having demands agaisnt the estate of James Gamble, deceased....   John F. Nesmith, Exor.
Dec. 14

PEE DEE TIMES

Issue of December 21, 1853

Married on the 8th inst., by the Rev. James H. Stone, Mr. Robert C. Brown to Miss Susan L. Thorp, all of Williamsburgh District.
on Wednesday the 14th inst., by the Rev. C. H. Prichard, Mr. G. W. Christie to Mrs. H. C. Porter, all of this place.
on the 15th inst., by the Rev. James H. Stone, Mr. Sumpter S. Gasque to Miss Sarah R. Harrel, both of Marion District.
Died in this town on Sunday morning last, Mrs. Charlotte M. Durant, aged 73 years, widow of the late Levi Durand. She was among the oldest native residents of the town, if not the oldest and had never changed her residence in winter or summer.

Issue of January 4, 1854

Married on the 22d ult., by the Rev. Saml. Crapps, Mr. Edward McDonald to Miss E. S. Blakely, all of this District.

Issue of January 11, 1854

Married on the 22d December, by the Rev. R. Nappier, Mr. J. L. Harrell to Miss Hannah J. Hinds, all of Marion District.

Issue of January 18, 1854

Married on the 8th of January 1854, by the Rev. James H. Stone, Mr. William J. Graham to Miss Frances Britton, all of Williamsburgh District.
All persons having demands against Charlotte M. Durand, late of Georgetown deceased....   St. John P. Ellis) Executors
Jan 18, 1854   John Ford   )

Issue of February 1, 1854

Died on the 28th December 1853, at his residence in Williamsburg District, S. C., Mr. James McFaddin, in the 81st year of his age....

Issue of February 15, 1854

Died at Montgomery, Ala., on the 2nd inst., Mr. James Roberts, late of Britton's Neck, in the 38th year of his age.

Issue of March 1, 1854

Married on the 9th Feb. by the Rev. James H. Stone, Mr. James Owens to Miss Rebecca Vause, all of Williamsburgh District.
Died on Black Mingo on the night of the 24th inst., Robert Bell Chambers in the 48th year of his age...left a large salary on the Savannah river two years ago to comfort his aged mother, and whom he has survived but a short time.

Issue of March 8, 1854

The Rev. James Coachman Postell, son of Major Postell, who served in the army of the Revolution, died at his residence in Georgia, on the 25th ult., in the 66th year of his age...
James K. Munnerlyn applied for Letters of Administration on the estate of Robert B. Chambers...7 March 1854.

PEE DEE TIMES

Issue of March 15, 1854

Married on the 6th inst., at Union Church by Rev. H. R. Ogburn, Capt. Stephen Gibson to Mrs. Renolds, widow of the late Edward Renolds, all of Georgetown District.

Issue of April 19, 1854

Died in this town on the 5th inst., Captain Thos. H. Briggs, in the 40th year of his age.

Issue of May 10, 1854

Married on Wednesday 26th April by the Rev. James H. Stone, Mr. James Gerganus to Miss Elizabeth S. Gordon, all of Williamsburgh District at the present time.

Issue of May 17, 1854

Died, at his residence on Sampit, on the 6th inst., Mr. Absalom D. Watts, aged about 38 years. He was the last of three brothers and all sons of the late Christopher Watts. He leaves a widow and two children.
    at North Inlet, on the 7th inst., Mrs. Louisa Cains, consort of Mr. Richard Cains, aged 30 years. She leaves an affectionate husband and six children, the eldest 10 years old is deaf and dumb.

Issue of May 31, 1854

Married on Thursday evening the 11th inst., by the Rev. Donald McQueen, A. White, Jr. and Miss Elizabeth A., second daughter of Dr. Thomas M. Dick, all of Sumter District.

Issue of June 14, 1854

Married on the 24th of May by the Rev. James H. Stone, Mr. Evander M. Woodberry of Marion District to Miss Sarah C. Johnson of Williamsburgh District.
    on the 1st June by the Rev. James H. Stone, Mr. W. R. Vance to Mrs. Frances M. Brown, all of Williamsburgh District.
    on the 1st of June by the Rev. James H. Stone, Dr. W. M. Davis to Miss Mary B. Belin, all of Marion District.
    at Bucksville on the evening of the 9th inst., by C. B. Sarvis, Esq., Cap. John W. Saymour to Miss M. L. Dennis.
    on Thursday evening last, by the Rev. Mr. Crofford, Mr. Thomas M. Britton of Williamsburgh District to Miss Sarah G. Durant, of this place.
    Died in Charleston, April 3d, 1854, James Logan, son of J. N. and Catharine Mc--anan(?), aged 4 years and 5 months.
                                                            J. E. Haynes.

Issue of July 5, 1854.

All persons having demands against Absalom D. Watts, late of Sampit deceased....   Joseph W. Moyd, Exor.
June 28
    All persons having legal demands against the late Benjamin King, ...   E. B. Rothmahler) Qualified
                                 J. C. Porter   ) Executors.

PEE DEE TIMES

Issue of July 26, 1854

Married on the 18th instant, at Bucksville, by the Rev. D. McDonald, Mr. Henry Bell of North Carolina, to Miss Mary Jane, eldest daughter of Capt. H. Buck of the former place.
 on the 21st instant, in this place, by L. Dozier, Esq., Mr. Thomas Crosby of Santee to Miss Emily Squires.

Issue of August 2, 1854

Married in Horry Dist., on the 9th July by Cornelias Sarvis, Esqr., Mr. John W. Joiner to Miss Sarah Ann Newton, all of the above place.
 Married in Horry Dist., on the 23rd July, Mr. William W. Newton, Jr. to Miss Emily C. Branton, all of the above place.
 Married on Wednesday morning the 26th instant, at St. Pauls Church, Radcliffeboro', Charleston, S. C., by the Rev. C. Hanckel, D. D., the Rev. Maurice Harvey Lance to Sarah Laura, youngest daughter of the late Samuel Smith of Georgetown District.
 Married on the 29th July at Socastee Church, Mr. Leonard Bone to Miss Elizabeth E. Stalvey all of All Saints Parish.

Issue of August 9, 1854

Died on Monday evening 3d July at his residence in Williamsburgh, Mr. Josiah W. Cockfield, in the 38th year of his age....
 in this place on Monday, July 31st Mrs. Elizabeth J. Dennis, in the 37th year of her age.
 Departed this life on Lynches Lake, Williamsburg District, on the evening of the 4th inst., Rev. James H. Stone, aged 48 years, 11 months and 28 days.

Issue of August 16, 1854

Married on Wednesday the 9th inst., by the Rev. R. T. Howard, D. L. Stocking, Esq. of Charleston to Miss Emma A., daughter of Mr. Jas. K. Munnerlyn, of this place.
 Departed this life on the 31st of July, Mrs. Elizabeth Dennis, in the 27th year of her age....

Issue of August 30, 1854

Died in this town on Wednesday evening last, Mr. Samuel Kade, of Indian River, Delaware, second mate of the Schooner Mary D. Hayeson (?), aged about 25 years.
 in this town, on Thursday morning last, Mrs. Eliza Carns, aged about 60 years.

Issue of September 6, 1854

Died, on Waccamaw, on Wednesday evening last, Mr. William Millikin, aged about 26 years. He leaves a young wife and child ....

Issue of September 13, 1854

Married at Limestone Springs, in Spartanburg District, on the 31st ult., by Professor D. Curtis, D. D.,Mr. Albert A. McGinney of the house of Waterman & McGinney of this place to Miss Adriel B. Cooper of Williamsburg.

PEE DEE TIMES

Died, in this place on Friday the 8th inst., Henrietta Gabriella, youngest daughter of J. J. and A. E. Bryan, aged about one year.

Issue of September 20, 1854

Departed this life on the 11th inst., in Williamsburg Dist., Mrs. Martha Coward, consort of Capt. Salomon Coward, aged about 55 years. In 1821, united with the M. E. Church at Darlington C. H., then in charge of Rev. M. C. Turrentine. (eulogy).

Died, in this town on Thursday 14th instant, Marion fourth daughter of N. and F. Emanuel, aged 5 years and ten days.

Issue of September 27, 1854

Died, on Sampit, Georgetown District on Monday 18th instant, Ary Ann, daughter of James and Mary Walker, aged about 6 months.

Died on Wednesday evening last, Capt. John Wesle Weymour, late of the schooner Joshua Skinner...had been married but a few weeks....

All persons having demands against William Millikin, late of Waccamaw, deceased.... Frances Ann Smith, Admx. Sept. 27

Issue of October 11, 1854

Married in this place, on Thursday evening last 5th inst., by the Rev. C. H. Pritchard, Mr. Thomas W. Wasdin to Miss Harriet Maria Farewell, all of this town.

Departed this life in the city of Charleston, S. C., September 20, 1854, in the 13th year of her age, Anna Maria, the eldest daughter of John Harleston Read Jr., Esq. (eulogy).

Died in this town on the morning of the 20th September, Mr. John White, in the 68th year of his age.

Died on Richmond Plantation, Sampit, September 30, 1854, John Alexander Gorman, eldest son of John B. and Magdeline A. Gorman, aged 5 years 6 months and 17 days....

Died in Pendleton on Monday the 2d inst., Sarah Edith Smith (of this place), in the fiftieth year of her age. (eulogy)

Died, on Black Mingo on the 6th October, Sarah Elizabeth, daughter of Wm. F. and Sophrona Small, aged three years and twenty-one days.

Issue of October 18, 1854

Married in this town on Thursday evening last, by the Rev. C. H. Pritchard, Mr. A.M. Judon to Miss Henrietta Isabella Bryan, all of this district.

Died in this town on the 20th ult., Mr. John White, in the 68th year of his age....

Died in this town on the 10th inst., Mrs Lydia Jacks, widow of the late John S.Jacks...and daughter-in-law of John S. Jacks the memorable jeweller in Broad street in Charleston.

Died on the 10th inst., Mrs. Susannah Ferari, formerly the widow of the Gen. Robert Conway, in memory of whom as a revolutionary officer, the capital of Horry district took the name of Conwayboro. After the death of her second husband, she kept a tavern in this town--and sustain a good reputation. She was about 76 years of age.

Died, at Wallingford, Con., on the 10th inst., in the 58th

PEE DEE TIMES

Died in this town on Tuesday the 10th inst., John Dallam Wallace, son of Ruben and Ann E. Wallace, in the 17th year of his age....
Departed this life on Wednesday last, the 11th inst., Mr. Robert Thurston Ford, in the 25th year of his age....
Departed this life on Saturday the 14th October in the Parish of St. Johns Berkley, Harris Simons Gasque, aged twenty years, 1 monthand 19 days...a native of this town.
Died in this town, on the 14th inst., Mr. Donald Steuart, a native of Scotland, aged 40 years.
Died on the 14th inst., Mr. Jahiel Butts, aged about 57 years a native of Syracuse, New-York....

Issue of November 1, 1854

Married in Horry District on the 25th inst., Mr. Joseph E. Hearl of this District to Miss Haveliah Irenah Adaline, eldest daughter of Mr. Joel B. Skipper of Horry District.

Issue of November 8, 1854

Married on the 2d inst., at Blackmingo by Samuel McGinney, Esq. Mr. William Forbes of North Carolina to Miss Rebecca Fenters of this district.
Departed this life in this town on Thursday morning last the 2d inst., Mrs. Sarah F. Tarbox, consort of the late Capt. John P. Tarbox, in the 53d year of her age...a member of the M. E. Church for more than 30 years....
All persons having demands against the estate of the late John White deceased....   W. C. White
Nov. 8   R. G. White
                    Qualified Executors.

Issue of November 15, 1854

Married on Pee Dee, on Wednesday evening last, by the Rev. C. H. Pritchard, the Rev. M. L. Banks to Miss Ann Skinner, all of this district.
Married on Pee Dee, on the 8th inst., by Rev. L. Shuford, Mr. Thomas W. Hickson to Miss Anna W. Swinton, all of this district.
Departed this life on Saturday evening October 25th, 1854, Emma Margaret, fourth daugheter of Dr. Wm. R. T. and Mrs. Martha Prior, in the 14th year of her age....
Died in Newport, R. I., on the 1st inst., Annie Throop, daughter of Mr. George C. Munroe, aged 2 years 6 months and 2 days.
Died on the 1st inst., in New Orleans, Mrs. Elizabeth H. Ryan, of New Castle, Me., wife of Capt. D. T. Ryan, of Ship White Falcon.

Issue of November 22, 1854

Died at half past 2 o'clock A. M., on the 15th October, William Thomas, aged six years and nine months, also on the 30th of the same month at half past one p. m., Mary Jane, aged 5 years, both children of Dr. C. and M. E. Williams.
in Lower St. Johns Berkeley, Charleston District, on the 18th ult., at the early age of one year and ten months, James Henry, the only son of L. R. and J. A. Phillips....
on the 15th November, Mary Green, infant daughter of William and Elizabeth Morris, aged 10 months and 12 days.

PEE DEE TIMES

Issue of November 29, 1854

Married at Black Mingo on the 21st inst., by Lemuel A. Grier, Esq., Mr. Henry B. Ham to Miss Sarah J. Britton, all of this district.

Died on Saturday the twenty-fifth of Noevember, at Laurel Hill in the Parish of All Saints, Francis Marion Weston Esq., in the 73d year of his age.

Issue of December 6, 1854

Married on Tuesday the 24th ult., by the Rev. A. Glennie, at All Saints Chappel, Waccamaw, Dr. Arthur B. Flagg, to Georgeanna, daughter of the late Hon J. J. Ward.

Issue of December 20, 1854

Married on the 28th Nov., by the Rev. Mr. Wallace, Mr. Wm. S. Camlin to Miss Sarah Q. Hudson, both of Williamsburgh District.

in this town on Tuesday evening the 12th inst., by Rev. A. M. Chrietzberg, Edward H. Brown to Caroline Taylor.

Issue of December 27, 1854

Married on the 24th December, by the Rev. N. Hyatt, Mr. John W. Bone, to Miss Mary A. Hewit, both of St. James, Santee.

Issue of January 3, 1855

Married in this town on Thursday the 28th ult.,by the Rev. C. H. Pritchard, Mr. John W. Tarbox to Mrs. Hannah M. Siau, all of this place.

All persons having any claims against the estate of the late Francis M. Weston....
Jan. 3   Alexander Glennie,
                          P. C. J. Weston, Qual. Ex'ors.
All claims against the Est. of the late Dr. E. T. Herriot...
                Eliza J. Heriot, Extx.
                F. W. Heriot   )Ex'ors.
                R. S. Heriot   )
                J. R. Sparkman)

Issue of January 17, 1855

Died in this town on the 8th inst., Mrs. Julia A. Bates, wife of Mr. John P. Bates in the 23d year of her age...a member of the M. E. Church.

Departed this life on Thursday the 11th January 1855, captain Richard Green of Waccamaw...aged about 78 years, leaving a large number of relatives....

Issue of January 24, 1855

Frederick W. Ford applied for Letters of Admn. on the estate of Robert T. Ford deceased...10 Jan 1855

Issue of February 14, 1855

Married on the 8th inst., by the Rev. C. H. Pritchard, Mr. C. W. Brightman to Miss M. S. Davis, all of this place.

PEE DEE TIMES

Mary J. Dealy applied for Letters of Admn. on the estate of Benjamin W. Dealy, late of Sampit, as widow. 13 Feb 1855

Issue of February 21, 1855

Died, in Savannah on the 29th, 1855, William Harvey, son of Dr. H. L. and Mrs. Adelaide Dozier Bird, aged three years, 7 months and 29 days....

Issue of February 28, 1855

Died in Falmouth Mass., on the 8th instant, Mrs. Nancey Tobey, wife of the late Capt. Limri Tobey, aged 82 years.
All persons having legal claims against the Estate of the late Richard Green are requested to render them...
Feb. 28   Jos. Ben. Johnson, Admor.

Issue of April 4, 1855

On the 27th ult., Mrs. Caroline Emma Jane Bruorton, consort of Capt. John A. Bruorton departed this life at the residence of her husband near China Grove in this District...in the 22d year of her age...leaves two small children....

Issue of April 11, 1855

Married on the 3d inst., by the Rev. John Hunter at the residence of her uncle, S. T. Gaillard on Black River, Theodora C., only daughter of the late D. A. Gaillard to Edward P. Guerard, all of Georgetown district.

Issue of April 18, 1855

Departed this life at the residence of his uncle, Wm. Henry Cuttino, in this town on the morning of the 4th inst., Mr. George Savage Smith, in the 59th year of his age....
Died in Georgetown, S. C., on the morning of the 3th (sic), Willie N., only son of Paul and Hannah E. Tamplet, aged 2 years, 2 months and 26 days.
Died at the residnece of W. J. Dowsey, on the 6th inst., Mr. william G. Miller, aged 54 years...an overseer in this District, and southern Parish in this state and Georgia....
Died in this town on the 7th inst., Mr. John Pinner, a native of New England, aged about 40 years.
Died in this town on Thursday morning the 12th inst.,Capt. Francis Green Tarbox, aged 33 years and 3 months.
Died on the 13th inst., Mrs. Mary E. GAsque, wife of Mr. Jehu Gasque, all of this place...a member of the M. E. Church. She leaves an infant of a few days old....

Issue of April 25, 1855

All persons having legal demands against the late G. S. Smith....   D. H. Smith, Administrator.
April 25

Issue of May 9, 1855

Departed this life on the 24th of April, at the residence of Mr. T. B. Hamlin of this District, Mrs. Ann Council, aged 69 years, 7 months and 7 days.

PEE DEE TIMES

Issue of May 23, 1855

Married on Paul Swamp, Horry District, Tuesday evening, May 15, by the Rev. J. Woodward Mr. Thomas Martin to Miss Francis Hux, both of Horry District.

on Wednesday evening the 16th inst., by the Rev. R. T. Howard, Mr. Archibald J. Shaw to Mrs. Mary E. Walker, both of this place.

Issue of June 13, 1855

Departed this life on the 4th instant at the residence of his son D. Goldfinch in Georgetown, S. C., Wm. Goldfinch, about 70 years of age, a native of Canterbury, England--he had been a resident of New Jersey about 20 years and for the last 3 years a resident of Centreville, Pa.

on the 8th instant, Mary E., infant daughter of the late deceased Mrs. Mary E. GAsque, and Mr. John Gasque, aged 2 months.

Issue of June 27, 1855

Died in this town on the 21st inst., Susan R., eldest daughter of J. M. Mishaw, in the 14th year of her age....

Issue of July 4, 1855

Died, in this town on the 30th June, Mary Elizabeth, only daughter of J. B. and Elizabeth F. W. LeRebour, aged 20 months and 26 days.

Issue of July 11, 1855

Departed this life on the 5th inst., Henry Mansfield, only son of H. M. and E. L. Hiddleson, aged 1 year and 10 months.

Issue of July 18, 1855

Died in Robertson (sic) County, N. C.,on the 3rd of June, Mr. Willis Barns, aged 57 years...a member of the Baptist Church ....

Died in Georgetown July 6th, Tos. L. Shaw, in the 66th year of his age...for 25 years a member of the M. E. Church..-.

Issue of August 1, 1855

Married on the 25th July, at the residence of her father, in Georgetown, by the Rev. R. T. Howard, Jno. Richard Ford, A. M., of Cambridge, England to Annie, only daughter of L. G. S. Middleton, Esq.

Issue of August 8, 1855

Thomas Milton Cooper departed this life on Saturday, the 28th July, at the early of age twenty years...a member of Indiantown Presbyterian Church....

Issue of August 15, 1855

Married on the 15th inst., by the Rev. Mr. Pritchard, Mr. Stephen Watts, to Miss Sarah E. Hickman, all of this town.

PEE DEE TIMES

Issue of August 22, 1855

Married August 2d by the Rev. Alexander Thomas at the residence of Rev. H. H. Porter, _ R. Davis to Miss M. D. S. Avant, all of Marion District.

Died in Beaufort, S. C.,on the 7th August, Mrs. Martha W. Hucks, leaving a husband and four little children.

Died at Sea on board the U. S. Ship, Falmouth, on the morning of the 12th of August, Midshipman, John Cain, Jr., of Indiana.
....

Issue of September 12, 1855

Died at his summer residence Plantersville, Georgetown District, on the 28th July, Mr. Stephen C. Ford, in the 52d year of his age, leaving a wife and children....

Issue of September 19, 1855

Died, in this town on the 8th inst., William Filburne, a native of Ireland aged about 50 years.

September 8th, 1855, at twelve o'clock, M. George McConnell, son of John F. D. and Mary Britton, aged 8 years 8 months and 9 days.

September 8, 1855, at 11 o'clock, P. M., Gillmore, son of John F. D. and Mary Britton, aged 6 years 11 months and 14 days.

in Snow Hill, Green County, North Carolina, September 9th, 1855, George Augustus, son of S. B. and Virginia Turnage, aged 1 year, 5 months and 3 days.

in this town September 10th, 1855, Mrs. Sarah Thomas, consort of the late Capt. Wm. F. Thomas, aged about 54 years...a member of the M. E. Church

at Poplar Hill, Williamsburg District, on the 11th inst., Mrs. Elizabeth S. Gurganus, wife of Jno. E. Gurganus, and only daughter of John Gordon, aged 29 years and 11 months.

at his residence in this place on Sunday evening last, after a short but painful illness, Mr. John Capers Haselden, aged about 50 years. He leaves a wife and two children...

in Georgetown District on the 16th instant, Pinckney Pleasant, son of M. A. and Jane Ethridge, aged 9 years.

in Williamsburg, on Monday last, Mr. Henry Eady, aged about 80 years--leaving a large family and a large estate.

Issue of September 26, 1855

Married in Marion District, S. C., August 16th, 1855, by the Rev. J. L. Shufford, B. M. Williams, Esq. of Fair Bluff, N. C., to Miss C. J. Munnerlyn, of Marion District, S. C.

Departed this life on the 20th inst., Mr. Edward Inglesby (ship wright) aged forty-three years, formerly of the city of Charleston, where he leaves many relatives....

Died in this town on the 22d inst., Mr. John Curran, aged about 35 years, a native of Ireland.

Wade Mitchell applied for Letters of Administration on the estate of David J. Wilson, tailor, late of Georgetown...17 April 1855

Issue of October 3, 1855

Married on last evening by the Rev. C. H. Pritchard, Mr. John P. Bates to Mrs. Esther Ann Matthews, all of this town.

PEE DEE TIMES

Died, in this town on Friday morning Sept. 21st, Mr. William H. Lester, aged about 30 years.

Issue of October 10, 1855

Died, in Georgetown, S. C., Oct. 4, Ann Maria, infant daughter of Robt. W. and Olive Rowell, aged 6 months and 6 days.

Issue of November 7, 1855

Married on the 6th inst., at the Episcopal Parish Church, Prince George Winyah, Georgetown, by the Rev. R. T. Howard, Rector--R. Starr Heriot, M. D., to M. Helen, daughter of the late Stephen Charles Ford.

Issue of December 5, 1855

Died, on Black River, on Monday evening last, Mr. H. J. Morris, aged about 34 years.

Issue of December 26, 1855

Married on the evening of the 13th ult., by Rev. John A. Minick, Mr. John Brown of Williamsburg to Miss Francis P. Johnson, of Marion.
All persons having claims against Hasford J. Morris, deceased ....   Hannah Morris, Admix.
Dec. 26, 1855

Issue of January 2, 1856

Married on the 25th inst., by the Rev. R. T. Howard, Dr. J. A. Grant, of Cuthbert, Georgia, to Miss Martha A. Tucker, of this town.
in Charleston, on Thursday morning 27th inst., by the Rev. J. W. Wightman, Mr. P. Charleston Lewis to Miss Rosalie Alice, second daughter of the late Peter Rotureau, Esq., all of that city.
Mrs. Sarah E. Gamble died at her residence near Kingstree, on the 24th day of December last. She was the daughter of Capt. Henry Mouzon of revolutionary fame; a presbyterian in faith; and at 74 closed a career of usefulness....
January 1st, 1856

Issue of January 9, 1856

Died in this town on the night of the 2nd inst., Mrs. Maria A., consort of A. L. Marianno, Esqr. in the 60th year of her age.

Issue of January 16, 1856

All persons having demands against the late Samuel T. Guild are requested to hand them in....   Ann D. M. Guild, Qual. Admx.
Jan 16

Issue of January 23, 1856

Married on the 22d Nov., 1855, by the Rev. W. D. Martin, Mr. William Faulk to Miss A. L. Hennecy, all of this District.
On the 20th of December by the Rev. L. A. Grier, Mr. Stephen Rowe, to Miss Kissiah Owens all of this District.

PEE DEE TIMES

in Boston, Texas, on the 31st December, 1855, by the Rev. J. W. Anderson, Major Samuel T. Atkinson to Miss Emily McCright, both of South Carolina.
Died at his residence in Sumter District, S. C., on Monday, December 24th, 1855, Thomas B. White...a member of the M. E. Church for a number of years....
All persons having demands against J. B. Harrell, late of Black River, deceased....   Wm. S. Bellune, Admor.
Jan. 23

Issue of January 30, 1856

Married on the 17th inst., Mr. A. B. Gordon to Miss A. J. Hinds, all of Marion District.
Praire Green, on 1st inst., by the Rev. H. K. Raymond, Dr. J. L. Cunningham of Hamburg, Ala., formerly of Williamsburgh, S. C., to Miss Julia A., only daughter of Mrs. Amanda F. Watson of Dallas County, Ala.

Issue of February 6, 1856

Died, at his residence, on Pee Dee, on Tuesday the 29th ult., Mr. Robert H. Collins, aged about 43 years, leaving a wife and some nine children....

Issue of February 13, 1856

Died, at Pon Pon in Colleton District, on the 22d ultimo, John E. Allston, aged 35 years and 11 months....
in this town on Sunday morning the 27th ult., Mr. Henry Cuttino, aged about 62 years. He was, it is said, the oldest male native of this town, and the last son of the ancient family of the name, who have been for near a century connected with the active business of this place....
On Monday evening the 4th inst., at the plantation of W. B. Pringle, on North Santee, Mrs. Martha Susanah Westbury, consort of W. J. Westbury in the 26th year of her age.

Issue of February 20, 1856

Married in this town on yesterday morning by the Rev. Mr. Mitchell, Mr. Isaac Sidney Lefrage of Williamsburgh to Mrs. Georgiana Cox of this town.
Died at Savannah, Ga., on Wednesday 6th inst., Mrs. Israel Salomons, in the 62d year of her age, a native, and for many years a resident of this place.
All persons having claism against the late Mr. Henry Cuttino
...   D. H. Smith
Feb. 20   W. C. Miller
                        Qualified Executors.
Mary J. Collins applied for Letters of Admn. on the estate of her late husband, Robert H. Collins...15 Feb 1856

Issue of February 27, 1856

Died on the morning of the 12th inst., at his residence on Black River, Mr. John P. Ford, in the 45th year of his age....
C. P. Thompson applied for letters of admn. on the estate of William Pinckney Grimsley....25 Feb 1856

PEE DEE TIMES

Issue of March 5, 1856

Married on the 20th ult., by the Rev. Mr. Mickel, J. T. McConnell, of Williamsburg to Miss Mary Brisgane, daughter of L. P. Hext, esqr., of Barnwell.

Issue of March 12, 1856

Departed this life in Georgetown, S. C., on the 27th day of January 1856, Mr. Henry Cuttino in the 62d year of his age...united with the Baptist Church in this place, on 3d of May 1831 (baptized by Rev. --- Bowles), he was chosen Deacon on the 18th of January 1835....(long eulogy).
Departed this life in Georgetown, S. C., February 16, 1856, Luther Marion, youngest son of Rev. D. W. and Mrs. L. E. Cuttino, aged 1 year, 5 months and 4 days.
Died in this place Feb. 27th 1856, in the 51st year of her age, Mrs. Elizabeth Gasque, wife of J. W. Gasque, Esq...daughter of the late Rev. Philip Kirtion....

Issue of March 19, 1856

All persons having demands against Robert H. Collins, late of Pee Dee, deceased....   Mary J. Collins, Admx.
March 19

Issue of March 26, 1856

Died on Monday the 25th of February 1856, at the residence of Col. J. J. Dickison, Orange Spring, Florida, Mr. C. D. Tamplet. The deceased was born in Charleston, S. C., Sept. 26, 1832...left a sister and two brothers....
Died in Charleston on the 26th February, Dr. Ebin Belin Flagg, in the 35th year of his age....

Issue of April 2, 1856

Married in Charleston on Wednesday evening, the 26th inst., by the Rev. John Forrest, George G. Ford, of Georgetown, S. C., to Miss Elizabeth Chisolm, eldest daughter of Charles Edmonston, Jr., Esq.
Married in this place on 27th ult., by James Potter, Esq., Mr. John K. Lambert to Miss Mary Ward, all of this District.

Issue of April 16, 1856

Married at St. Phillips Church, Charleston, on Wednesday evening April 9th by the Rev. Mr. Gadsden, F. W. Ford, Esq. to Mary M., daughter of the late Dr. Alexander Hume.
died, at Perry, Georgia, on the 30th ult., Mr. David Crosland, aged about 68 years, late a resident of Marlboro District....

Issue of April 23, 1856

Died, at Hagley in the Parish of All Saints on Saturday, April 19th, Mary second wife and relict of Francis M. Weston, Esqr., of that Parish and daughter of Charles Weston, Esqr., of Kinsley Warwickshire, England, aged 76 years, 5 months and 9 days.

PEE DEE TIMES

Issue of May 7, 1856

Married at the Episcopal Church in this town on last evening by the Rev. R. T. Howard, Prof. J. B. White to Miss M. J. Prior all of this town.
Died, in Charleston on Tuesday the 29th ult., at half-past 12 o'clock P. M., Capt. John Magee, in the 68th year of his age.

Issue of May 21, 1856

Married in this town on Tuesday evening 13th inst., by the Rev. J. W. Miller, Mr. James M. Smith to Mrs. Sarah Ann Steele, all of this town.

Issue of May 28, 1856

Died, in this place on the 26th instant, Archibald James, son of Archibald J. and Mary E. Shaw, aged one wekk.

Issue of June 4, 1856

Married on the 28th inst., at the Tuttle Hose by the Rev. D. W. Cuttino, G. W. Robinson, of New Bradford, Mass., to Miss Lizzie Solomons, of London, England.

Issue of July 9, 1856

Married, last evening by the Rev. Mr. Mitchell, Mr. A. J. Smith to Miss Mary E. Corson, all of this town.
Departed this life on the 13th June at his residence on Black River, Samuel D. Thompson, aged 45 years, one month and one day.
Died in Charleston, S. C., on the 26th June, Mr. P. G. Gerard, in the 65th year of his age...born in Boston, Mass., but having been brought to Charleston when an infant, he claimed the latter place as his native city...carried by his father to the Island of Hayti (sic), where he was left in the care of a friend....
Died in this town on Monday 7th inst., Miss Martha Agnes, daughter of Capt. John M. LeRebour....aged 21 years and 9 months.

Issue of August 6, 1856

Died on the 26th of June, in Georgetown District, Mrs. Mary Jane Collins. She was for a number of years a member of the M. E. Church....

Issue of August 13, 1856

Died in Marion District, S. C., on the 14th ult., Mr. Washington B. Wall, in the 44th year of his age, leaving a wife and seven children....
Died at the residence of her son, Mr. Samuel A. Burgess, in Sumter District, S. C., on the 18th July, Mrs. Jennet Burgess, relict of William Burgess, Esq., in the 82d year of her age....
Died on the afternoon of the 5th inst., Mr. Geo. W. Robinson, a native of New-Bedford, Mass., in the 24th year of his age.

Issue of August 20, 1856

Died in Williamsburg District, S. C., August 5th, Mr. B. Barrinoe, aged 84 years....

PEE DEE TIMES

at North Inlet, near Georgetown, S. C.,on Tuesday the 12th August, John Brown, a native of New York. Age about 21 years, leaving a mother and two brothers....
in this place on the 19th instant, Mr. G. W. Richardson, formerly of Marion District, leaving a wife and four children....

Issue of August 27, 1856

Married, August 14th, 1856, by the Rev. G. W. Stokes, Mr. C. E. Stalvey to Mrs. Nancy Ammons, all of All Saints Parish.
Died at Brooksville, Georgetown District, June 27th, Mary Martha, only daughter of J. Henry and Mary L. McConnell, aged 18 months.

Issue of September 3, 1856

Henry Tobey applied for Letters of admn. on the estate of George W. Robinson...2 Sept 1856

Issue of September 10, 1856

Married in Columbia, S. C., on the 30th August, last, by the Rev. D. W. Cuttino, Mr. B. S. Lester to Miss Eliza M. McNulty, all of this place.
Departed this life on the 31st August Anna Rosabella, daughter of W. and E. D. Roberts, aged one year and 3 months.

Issue of September 17, 1856

Married in Britton's Neck, at Mount Vernon on Tuesday evening, 2d inst., by the Rev. James W.Ritchie, Mr. Joseph Benjamin Johnson to Miss Elizabeth Ann Calcut.
Married at Mrs. Sarah M. Graham's, Potts Ferry, Pee Dee River, on the 4th inst., by the Rev. C. H. Pritchard, Mr. Richard F. Woodberry of Marion District, S. C. to Miss Mary E. Verner, of Georgetown, S. C.
Died on the 11th instant, at Mr. Robert Pringle's on Black River, David Porter Calhoun, son of Joseph and Mary A. Hucks, aged two years, five months and twenty-four days.
Died in this town on the evening of 12th September 1856, Mary Elizabeth, youngest daughter of J. C. and H. I. Deal, aged two years, 8 months and 12 days.
Lemuel A. Grier applied for letters of admn. on the estate of Robert H. Collins, late of Pee Dee, deceased...16 Sept 1856

Issue of September 24, 1856

Died in this place on the 15th inst., Sarah F. W. child of Mrs. Mary Durant aged about 8 years.

Issue of October 1, 1856

Married on the 26th June last, by the Rev. Mr. Parker, J. M. McNamee to Miss Mary Jane Mills, all of Williamsburg District.
Died, on Black River on the 26th ult., Miss L. S. S. Goud, aged 27 years, 9 months...

Issue of October 29, 1856

Died, at Anderson C. H. on the 20th instant, William Henry, youngest son of the late Mr. E. M. and Mrs. M. A. Doar, of North

PEE DEE TIMES

Santee, aged 5 years, 7 months and 10 days....

Issue of November 12, 1856

Married in Charleston, S. C., on Tuesday the 4th instant, by the Rev. Dr. Mayer, M. J. Solomons, of Savannah, Ga., to Henrietta S., daughter of N. Emanuel of this place.
on Wednesday the 5th inst., by the Rev. Thomas Mitchell, Mr. W. S. Oliver, to Miss M. A. Easterling, all of this town.
Died in Georgetown District, S. C., on the 5th inst., Mr. Joseph E. Price, aged 43 years 2 months and 5 days...leaves a mother, father, one sister and five brothers....
in this town on Friday last, Mr. R. W. Rowell, formerly of Marion District, aged about 35 years.

Issue of November 19, 1856

Married on Tuesday evening the 11th inst., by the Rev. Thomas Mitchell, Mr. J. T. Dubois, to Miss S. E. E. Potter, both of this District.
At the Episcopal Church, Georgetown, by the Rev. R. T. Howard, Rector, Col. F. W. Heriot to Miss Sarah E. Ford, of this district.

Issue of November 26, 1856

Death of Benjamin Allston Dicks on the 20th inst...born on the 19th of August 1830....
Married on the evening of the 13th inst., at the residence of Col. James Beaty, by Rev. James Mahoney, James H. Norman, M. D., to Miss Carrie M. Beaty, both of Conwayboro, S. C.
on Monday afternoon, 20th ult., in New York, by Rev. Mr. Evans, Mr. J. M. L. Heath of Georgetown, S. C. to Miss Mary P. Hiddleson of Wallingford, Connecticut.
at the Methodist Episcopal Church in this town on last evening, by the Rev. W. T. Capers, Mr. T. J. Sessions, to Miss Mary Maria Marsh, all of this place.

Issue of December 3, 1856

William Manley Palmer, youngest son of the late Jesse Palmer, of this place died in St. Thomas' Parish, on Tuesday night, the 25th ult., at Point Hope, near Charleston, whither he had gone to superintend Mr. Nowell's Mills for the winter...just entered on the 26th year of his age....

Issue of December 10, 1856

Married in this town on Saturday evening, 6th inst., by Mr. James Potter, Esq., Mr. Edward T. Rodgers, of this place, to Miss Sarah L. Robinson, of Charleston.
Died on Monday night, 8th instant, Mary Elizabeth, wife of Alex. J. Cox, aged about 24 years...leaves husband and four small children....

Issue of December 24, 1856

Married on the 18th inst., by the Rev. S. C. James, Mr. Henry Holliday to Miss Martha L., daughter of Mrs. Sarah A. Hughes, all of Williamsburgh District, S. C.
Died on the 7th inst., at the residence of his mother, Mrs. Rebecca Thomas, (near Bennettsville, Marlborough District, S. C.)

PEE DEE TIMES

Capt. John S. Thomas....

Issue of December 17, 1856

Married in this place, on Wednesday evening last, by James Potter, Esq., Mr. W. B. McCormick of all Saints Parish to Miss Sarah Stanley of this town.

Died in the vicinity of Wadesboro, N. C., Fannie Goodwyn, infant daughter of James E. and Martha Elizabeth Easterling, aged 2 years, 4 months and 4 days....

Issue of January 7, 1857

Died in this place on the 29th Dec., at her residence, Mrs. Mary Standly, aged about 62 years...a member of the Baptist Church for the last 40 years, until about three years ago, she joined the M. E. Church...left two daughters....

Issue of January 21, 1857

Died in this town on the 12th inst., after an illness of four months, Mrs. Elizabeth G. Perrett, aged about 19 years....

On Wednesday night last, Mr. Isaac D. Faulk, suddenly fell dead.

in this town on the 16th January, Caroline Elizabeth, daughter of C. J. and M. F. Coe   aged 9 years, 1 month and 8 days.

Issue of January 28, 1857

Departed this life at the residence of Mrs. S. A. Verner, in this place on Tuesday evening 20th inst., Mrs. Catharine Williams, aged about 85 years.

Issue of February 11, 1857

Married at the residence of Mr. O. C. Greeman, on Black River, on Tuesday night, January 27th, by Mr. Samuel McGinney, Mr. John F. Burrow, to Mrs. Martha C. King, all of Black River.

Died Feb. 3, 1857, at Waverly, in All Saints Parish, Waccamaw, Samuel L. Oliver, aged 40 years....

at the residence of E. H. Britton, Esqr., in Williamsburgh District, on 27th January last, Mr. Wm. J. H. Graham, aged 25 years, 8 months and 7 days....

at his residence on Black Mingo, on Saturday morning, 31st December, 1856, Mr. Samuel Small...aged 42 years and 26 days.

Issue of February 25, 1857

Died at his residence on Pee Dee on the morning of the 11th instant, Nathaniel Barnwell, in the 88th year of his age.

in this town on the 7th instant, Mrs. Mary C. Goldfinch, wife of Daniel Goldfinch, aged 32 years...left a husband and four young children.

Issue of March 4, 1857

Ann R. Oliver applied for letters of administration on the estate of Samuel L. Oliver, deceased....4 March 1857

PEE DEE TIMES

Issue of March 25, 1857

James Ravenell applied for letters of admn. on the estate of Nathaniel Barnwell, at the request of his widow...21 March 1857

Issue of April 15, 1857

Married in this District on Friday evening last, by James Potter, Esqr., Mr. Lemuel S. Springs, from Wilmington N. C. to Miss Francis E. Dennis, of this District.

Issue of April 22, 1857

Married on Thursday the 16th inst., at Trinity Church, Charleston, S. C., by the Rev. J. W. Miller, Mr. Benjamin H. Cuttino, of Georgetown, S. C., to Miss Caroline V. Miller, eldest daughter of Jno. C. Miller, of this city.
Died in this place, on Sunday morning last, Emily Leighton, infant daughter of R. O. and C. A. Bush, aged 10 months and 9 days.
In this town on Tuesday last, William Christopher Watts, eldest son of the late John D. Watts, of Sampit, aged 18 years....
In this town on Tuesday morning at 7 o'clock, Mrs. Charles C. Davis, one of our most enterprising and active pilots, aged about 45 years...leaves a widow and five children....

Issue of May 6, 1857

Married in Georgetown on the 29th instant, by the Rev. D. W. Cuttino, Mr. William R. Moore, to Mrs. Frances Ann Millikin.
Mary C. Davis applied for letters of admn. on the estate of Charles C. Davis, mariner....5 May 1857
All persons having demands against the Estate of the late Samuel L. Oliver, deceased....   Ann R. Oliver, Admix.
May 6

Issue of May 13, 1857

Married on Thursday evening, May 14th, by Rev. Wm. T. Capers, Mr. J. B. Thomas, of Marion District, to Miss M. H. Vernon, of this town.
Elveny E. Williams applied for letters of admn. on the estate of Henry F. Williams...13 May 1857.

Issue of May 27, 1857

Died in this town on Saturday evening last, Mr. George D. Willard, aged about 35 years.

Issue of June 3, 1857

Hon. A. P. Butler died on the evening of the 25th May at his residence in Edgefield District....
Joseph R. Tucker applied for letters of admn. on the estate of Sarah Heriot Tucker...27 May 1857

Issue of June 10, 1857

Miss Hannah Jones Atkinson, daughter of the late W. K. Atkinson, Esqr., of Columbia, S. C., and Mrs. Anna Atkinson died in

PEE DEE TIMES

Auburn Ala....
Died June 4th, at her residence in All Saints Parish, Waccamaw, Mary, widow of the late Robert Nesbit, Esq., in her 45th year.

Issue of June 17, 1857

Married on Thursday the 13th inst., by Rev. Thomas Mitchell, Mr. William C. Owens, to Miss Mary Hannah, daughter of Mr. J. B. Johnson, all of this District.
Died in this town on the morning of the 15th inst., Robert Lee, infant son of the Rev. R. T. and H. M. Howard.

Issue of June 24, 1857

Married on Thursday evening last, at the residence of L. A. Grier, by the Rev. Mr. Dubose, Rev. C. E. Wiggins, to Miss Mary E. Grier, of this District.
on the same evening and at the same residence, by the Rev. L. A. Grier, Mr. W. S. Collins, of this District, to Miss Elizabeth B. White, formerly of Marion.
Departed this life in Marion District, on Tuesday, the 16th inst., at hsi residence, Mr. Josiah R. Harrell, in the 48th year of his age.
Death of Col. Matthew Irvine Keith in this city, at 8½ o'clock, ...born at Georgetown in the year 1786, removed to this city when quite a youth...elected to the State Legislature....
C. Courier

Issue of July 1, 1857

Died in this town on Friday last, the 25th inst., Fredrick, only son of H. G. Lohse, aged 18 months....

Issue of July 8, 1857

Died in this town on Saturday last, Maj. R. N. Magill, aged about 60 years....

Issue of July 15, 1857

Died in this town on the 13th inst., William Lorenzo, infant son of Josiah G. and Amander E. Carraway, aged 2 years and 2 months.
Married on Wednesday evening, July 8, by Rev. L. M. Hamer, Mr. Alexander J. Cox, to Mrs. Margaret L. Sarvis, both of this town.
On the 5th of July at the residence of D. J. Pipkin, by Rev. J. L. Rolings, Mr. J. J. Richardson, to Miss Ann Pipkin, all of this District.

Issue of August 5, 1857

All persons having claims against the estate of R. N. Magill, deceased....   W. J. Magill, Admor.
August 5

Issue of August 12, 1857

Mrs. Sarah Vines, aged 58 years, died on the 5th inst., She was a member of the Baptist pursuasion of Christian.

PEE DEE TIMES

Issue of August 19, 1857

Benjamin Henry Cuttino died in this city, at the residence of his father-in-law, Mr. John C. Miller, on Thursday the 6th of August....   C. Mercury.
Died on the 11th inst., at Magnolia, Waccamw, Joshua, infant and only son of Joshua and Elizabeth Ward, aged 3 years, 6 months and 28 days.
in this town August 12th, Benjamin Wallace, infant son of Dr. and M. A. Grant.

Issue of August 26, 1857

Died in Adams Run, 16 August, Anne Maria, youngest daughter of R. J. A. & L. Phillips, aged 1 yeard 11 months and 11 days.
Died at the residnece of her late nephew, W. S. McDonald, on Sunday last, Mrs. Jane Tyler, widow of the late Benj. Tyler, aged 84 years....

Issue of September 2, 1857

Married in this town on Monday evening last, by the Rev. Thos Mitchell, Mr. Walter Stanners, to Miss Catharine Farewell, all of this place.
Died in this town on Monday last, John Hughes, a native of Ireland, aged 39 years and formerly attached to the schr. S. Bruen.

Issue of September 9, 1857

Died near the lighthouse on Monday 7th inst., George Boutelle, a native of Edgecomb, Main, aged about 28 years, first Officer Brig Ranibow.
Died in this place on Tuesday the 8th inst., William Minnick Millikin, aged 4 years and 9 months, only child of Frances A. Moore.

Issue of September 16, 1857

Died in this town on the 3d inst., Miss S. C. Brown.

Issue of September 23, 1857

Departed this life on the 16th inst., at Plantersville, Mrs. Daniel Tucker, wife of Dr. Daniel Tucker.

Issue of October 28, 1857

Died on Friday morning 16th Oct., at Ruinville on Sandy Island, Mary Margaret, wife of Mr. JOhn Bellune, in her 18th year....

Issue of November 4, 1857

Died on the 29th October, Joseph Ross, son of the Rev. Joseph Hunter, aged 2 years and 26 months (sic).
Died on Sunday morning 1st inst., in this town, Mr. Henry G. Davis, in the 51st year of his age...leaves a widow and four children....

PEE DEE TIMES

Issue of November 18, 1857

Died Nov. 4th on board of Brig Sea Bell lying in port of Havana, Capt. Richard Barrow, aged about 30 years, belonging to Mata poiset, Mass.

Issue of November 25, 1857

Married on Saturday last, by the Rev. Phillip Davis, Mr. John D. Harper of No. Ca., to Mrs. Margaret E. Wilson, of this District.

Issue of December 2, 1857

Charles Munnerlyn Sen. died in Decatur county, Ga., on the 8th November in his 71st year...born in Marion District, S. C., moved to Georgetown in early manhood... in 1836 moved to Quincy, Fla., from thence to lecatur county....   S. C. Advocate
Died on Friday evening last, Mr. Walter Willard, aged about 50 years.

Issue of December 16, 1857

Married on the 8th instant, at St. Paul's Church, Charleston, S. C., by ___ Hanckel, D. D., John F. Pya(tt?), ___ Harriet, eldest daughter of the Hon J. L. Nowell, both of this city.
on Wednesday evening 9th inst., at the M. E. Church in this place, by the Rev. W. T. Capers, Mr. W. S. Camlin to Miss Mary E. Dicker, both of Williamsburg District.
on last evening 15th instant, at the Episcopal Church in this town, by the Rev. R. T. Howard, Mr. W. F. Joy of Charleston, Mass., to Miss M. M. Glidden, of Newcastle, Me.

Issue of December 30, 1857

Anthony L. Mariano, a native of Fay--, died in this town, on the 22d inst., in the 6th year of his age. He came to this place in 1812....
Died in this town on Sunday last, in the 41st year of his age, Isaac Carr Croft, Esq., Clerk of the Court of Common Pleas, and Locator and Register of Mesne Conveyance....

Issue of January 6, 1858

Married on the 24th December, by J. J. Richardson, Esqr., Mr. J. J. Marshall, to Miss Elizabeth A. Marshall, all of Williamsburg District.
Died at Georgetown on Thursday night at 11 o'clock, December the 31st, Fredrine, daughter of Benjamin A. and Caroline Coachman, aged 5 years 9 months and 13 days....
Dr. Elias Boudinot Brown died at his residence in this town, the 4th inst., in the 49th year of his age.

Issue of January 13, 1857

Died in this place on the evening of the 5th inst., Harriet M., wife of T. W. Wasdin, aged 20 years and 1 day...leaves husband and two little children....
Martha H. Croft applied for Letters of admn. on the estate of Isaac Carr Croft....12 Jan 1858.

PEE DEE TIMES

Issue of February 3, 1858

Married on Santee, January 21st, by the Rev. Mr. Craps, Mr. H. H. D. Alford to Miss M. G. Jayroe, both of this district.
on Pee Dee, 27th ult., by the Rev. A. J. Evans, Mr. J. H. Sawyer, to Miss Mary H. Jayroe.
Died in Newport, R. I., on the 25th of January 1858, George Henry, second son of Thomas S. and Ann E. Tilley, aged 5 years 9 months and 6 days.

Issue of February 24, 1858

Married at Bucksville, S. C., on the evening of the 23d instant, by Rev. ___ Chrietzburg, Capt. Cephas Gilbert of Northfield farm, Mass., to Miss Lucinda M., daughter of Capt. Henry Buck, of the former place.

Issue of March 10, 1858

Married in this town yesterday by the Rev. Mr. Banks, Mr. William J. Westbury of Santee to Mrs. Mary E. Waterman, of this town.
Died at the Mission House on Waccamaw on Friday, Feby 26, Rev. Jno. A. Minnick of the S. C. Conf....leaves a wife and one child....

Issue of March 17, 1858

Death of W. C. Miller on the 10th inst....
Died on Sunday the 14th inst., at the residence of R. Wallace, in this place, Miss Frances H. Read of Beaufort, N. C. The deceased was a relative of R. W., with whose family she had been spending some months....educated in the M. E. Church.
All persons having claim against the Estate of Henry F. Williams, deceased....   Saml. T. Atkinson, Comr. in Equity.
March 10
All persons having claims against the estate of Walter Willard, deceased....

Issue of March 31, 1858

Married in Charleston, S. C., on Thursday evening 25th inst., by the Rev. Dr. Hamckle, Dr. Lewis C. Hasell, of Brooklyn, N. Y.(formerly of this state) to Catharine, daughter of the late Col. J. J. Ward.

Issue of April 7, 1858

Death of Dr. Wm. Capers Miller, son of John C. Miller, Esq., of Charleston, born in that city in 1821...(long account and eulogy)
Died in this place, on the morning of the 28th ult., Ann Iorona, youngest daughter of W. A. and Mary J. Parker, aged 8 years, 11 months and 12 days.
April 3d, Bacot Allston, infant son of Capt. D. A. and Mrs. A. E. Sperry, aged two months.

Issue of April 14, 1858

Died, April 11th David Anson, son of D. A. and S. E. Sperry-aged two years.

PEE DEE TIMES

Issue of April 28, 1858

Departed this life on the evening of the 18th March 1858, Mrs. Trisvan Terrel Atkinson, wife of Christopher J. Atkinson, residing on Black River. She was born at Mars Bluff, Sept 24, 1806. She came down with her father, to the vicinity of Georgetown in 1817. Her mother died when she was about 14 years old... She was married to Mr. C. J. Atkinson, 6th Oct 1831....
    All persons having claims against the estate of Jesse W. Wiggins, deceased....Saml T. Atkinson, Comr. in Equity.
April 28
    All persons having claims against the estate of Ann Eliza collins, deceased....

Issue of May 5, 1858

Died on Saturday morning the 1st May, Samuel Middleton, the only son of J. J. and A. E. Bryan, aged 2 years, 7 months and 18 days.

Issue of May 12, 1858

Death of Senator Evans.
Married on Black River on Thursday evening last, by the Rev. J. W. Miller, Mr. H. T. McDonald, to Mrs. Sarah Jane Harrall, all of this district.

Issue of May 19, 1858

Married by Rev. D. A. Murdock, Mr. James D. Newton, of Doniphan, K. T., formerly of Allsaints, S. C., to Miss Eliza A. Ledington, recently of Doniphan, K. T., formerly of St. Joseph, Mo., on the 22nd April 1858.
    Died in this town on Saturday morning last, Harriet Mariah, infant daughter of T. W. Wasdin, aged 4 months and 15 days.

Issue of June 2, 1858

Married on the 11th April by the Rev. W. B. Curvie, Mr. Robert G. Wilson to Miss Sarah Ann Smith, all of Horry District.
    on the 23d of May by Rev. W. B. Curvie, Mr. Franklin Hughs, of Whitesville, N. C. to iss Charrity Ann, daughter of Hon. R. G. W. Grissette of Horry District.

Issue of June 9, 1858

Died at Darlington Village, on the 23d Apl, Miss Mary F. Legen, aged 37 years...a member of the M. E. church for 21 years.
    Died at Pawley's Island, on the 27th May, Charles D. infant son of D. D. & H. T. Rosa, aged 7 months and 21 days.

Issue of June 16, 1858

Married on Thursday the 3d inst., by the Rev. William Craps, Mr. Edwin McDonal, of Williamsburg, to Miss Magdalin Agness Blakely, of this District.

Issue of June 23, 1858

Departed this life on the 19th instant by a sudden accident, Samuel W. Fraser, the eldest son of R. E. Fraser, Esq. of this

PEE DEE TIMES

town, in the 11th year of his age....

Issue of June 30, 1858

Died on Wednesday the 9th inst., Mrs. Mary D. Lester, in the 63d year of her age.
Departed this life on Sunday morning the 20th June, Mrs. Elizabeth Eveline Lebour, consort of John M. LeRebour, aged 45 years, 11 months and 3 days.
John R. Beaty, Esq., Comr. in Equity applied for letters of admn. on the estate of Enos Fowler, late of Horry District, deceased...24 June 1858.

Issue of July 7, 1858

Married June 24th by the Rev. A. J. Evans, Mr. Earl C. Ellis, to Miss Agness S. Jayroe, all of this district.

Issue of July 14, 1858

Died at his residence, South Island, North Santee, on the 3d inst., Dr. John M. Brailsford, aged 34 years and 6 months.

Issue of May 4, 1859

John R. Beaty, Esqr., Comr. in Equity, applied for letters of admn. on the estate of Thomas Bessant, late of All-saints Parish, deceased....28 April 1859. (Horry District.)

Issue of November 28, 1860

Departed this life, Mrs. Mary A. Thompson, consort of Mr. C. P. Thompson. She was born in 1820, married 22d Nov, 1840, and died 22nd Nov. 1860, aged 40 years.

Issue of December 12, 1860

Departed this life on the 28th Nov., at his residence on Black River, Mr. Elijah Cox, in the 51st year of his age.
on the 1st day of December, Mrs. A. E. Cox, wife of Elijah Cox, in the 41st year of her age.

Issue of December 19, 1860

All persons having demands against the estate of the late R. D. Evans, deceased....   Benjamin F. Evans, Adm'r. Dec. 5
Robert J. Davidson applied for letters of admn. on the estate of Elijah Cox, late of Black River...11 Dec 1860

Issue of January 2, 1861

Married 20th December by Rev. R. T. Howard, A. Glennie Heriot, Esq. to Anna G., daughter of the late J. W. Coachman, all of this place.
Married, Dec. 23d, at the residence of Mr. L. G. Long, in Horry District, by Jos. J. Richwood, Esq.,Mr. John Jones, of North Carolina, to Mrs. Sarah Cox, of Horry.
on Sampit, the 25th Dec., by Henry F. Detyens, Esq., Mr. Daniel Durant to Miss Telessa Jane Altman.

Addenda:

Winyaw Intelligencer, issue of November 20, 1819

Married on the 11th inst., Mr. John McGill to Miss Selina McClary, both of Williamsburg District.

On the 25th ult. was united in the holy bonds of Matrimony, by John McGehze, Esq., Mr. David Hodge, aged 102, to Miss Elizabeth Vailey, aged 40 years, both of Columbia Co., Ga. Mr. H. was at Braddocks defeat and served through the whole of the Revolutionary War.   Augusta Chronicle

Index prepared by Mrs. Betty Porter, Round Rock, Texas

Aaronson, Wolf 21, 22
Abbot, Henry J. 105
Abercrombie, Sophia Douglas 28
Achord, Jane 34
Adams, Abijah 35
  Jasper Rev. 121
  T. Rev. 143
  Wm. 21
Addison, Geo. W. 97
Aimy, Caroline Amelia 110
  Sam'l 110
Airs, Elizabeth 131
Albermarle, Earl of 83
Aldrich, Geo. Gen. 28
Alexander, Emperor of Russia 36
Alford, H. H. D. 205
Allen, Ebenezer 36
  Matthew 102, 109
Allin, Matthew 137
Allston, Adelle Mrs. 109
  Alcenora 157
  Anna M., Mrs. 40
  B. 5
  Benj. 128, 153
  Benj Jr. 1, 3, 18
  Benj. Sr. 21, 26(2)
  Charlotte Ann Mrs. 71
  Fanny 157
  Frances Ann 53
  Harriet M. Mrs. 53, 82
  J. H. 61, 70
  J. H. Capt. 137
  J. W. Gen. 102
  John Ashe 157
  John E. 155, 195
  John H. 53, 61, 82
  John Hays 164(2), 172
  Joseph 61, 71
  Joseph, Major 70
  Joseph W. 65, 71, 81
  Joseph W., Gen. 102, 120, 121
  Josias 26
  Juliann Ellen 82
  Mary 12
  Mary, Mrs. 102, 164
  Mary C., Mrs. 21
  Mary E. Mrs. 21
  Mary K. Mrs. 120, 121
  Peter 164
  R. F. W. Col. 96
  Robert 109
  Robert F. W. 71, 102, 109, 152
  Samuel Capt. 59, 61
  Sarah W. Mrs. 65
  William 17
  William, Dr. 12, 54, 102, 154
  William Sr. 1
Alston, Charles 111, 130
  Col. 50
  John 17
  John A. 39
  John A. Col. 94, 95
  John Ashe 108
  John Hayes 172
  John E. 172
  Joseph 17
  Joseph Gen. (Gov.) 38(2), 39
  Joseph W. 64
  Mary, Mrs. 121
  Miss 124
  R. M. Mrs. 172
  T. Pinckney 96, 111
  Thomas 32
  Thomas Jr. 95
  William 17
  William Col. 111
  William A. 39, 111, 12, 124(2)
  William Ashe 124
  Willis 85
Altman, Telessa Jane 207
Alvorf, Relief, Mrs. 42
Alway, John 115

Ammons, Nancy Mrs. 198
Ancker, Gustavus V. 158
Anderson, A. C. 167
  Alexander 8, 26
  Alexander C. 153
  C. A. 184
  David 163
  Edmund 171
  Eliza Denison Mrs. 161
  Eliza Jane Mrs. 140
  Emily, Mrs. 126
  Georgeanna L. Mrs. 167
  J. B. 161, 168
  J. B. Mrs. 135
  J. G. A. 111
  J. W., Rev. 195
  James B. 120, 122
  Jane, Mrs. 6, 8
  John E. 172
  John J.141
  John Simpson 126
  Josephine Denison 135
  Mary C. 58
  Mary J. 151
  N. Rev. 157
  Naomi Elizabeth 140
  R. M. 172
  R. O. 156
  Richard Oswald 126, 175, 179, 180, 181
  Robert 140
  Robert Jr. 133
  Sarah Mrs. 127
  William 28, 40
  William A. Col. 176
Andres, Samuel B. 34
Anereas, William M. 131
Archer, William 31
Armstrong, John 163
Aronson, Woolf 21 see also Aaronson
Asbury, Daniel Rev. 74
  Francis, Bishop 32
Asgill, Lady 38
Ashby, 41
  J. H. 178
Ashe, Mary P. 108
  Samuel, Col. 108
Ashman, Richard 13, 16
Askins, George Rev. 32
  Robert 9
Atkins, John 165
Atkinson, Anne Mrs. 86
  Anna, Mrs. 201
  C. I. 97
  C. J. 111, 169, 206
  Christopher J. 206
  Christopher James 54, 88
  Elizabeth Ann, Mrs. 54, 88
  Hanna Jones 201
  John, Rev. 36
  Jonah M. 162, 164(2), 179
  Louisa 164
  Magdalene 170
  Mary Elizabeth 97
  Samuel T. 205, 206
  Samuel T., Major 195
  T. T., Mrs. 97
  Trisvan Terrel, Mrs. 206
  William John James 88
  William K. 201
Avant, Elizabeth 92
  Leonard 97
  M. D. S. 193
  Samuel 165
  Sarah F. 64
  Thomas G. 95
  Thomas, Rev. 92
Avinett, Tabitha 82
Axum[Exum?], John 69
Ayres, William 116

Bachelier, Caleste Prudent 8,21
Backman, Rev. Dr. 123, 160
Bacot, Samuel, Capt. 31
Bacus, Rev. 42
Bailey, Elizabeth 79
  Henry 103
  J. R. 183, 184
  John 79
Baker, John 54
  Mary 54
  Sallie E. 181
Baldwin, Rev. Dr. 64
Ball, Archibald 69
  Archibald S. 29
  Elizabeth S. 69
  Isaac 77
  Josiah 71
Ballantine, James 18
Ballow, Samuel S. 81
  Thomas 24, 43
Ballox, William 69
Baneneau, Isaac 92
Banks, Rev. Mr. 205
  Rev. M. L. 189
Banner, Leonard Capt. 182
Bard, B. 48
Bareneau, Isaac 52, 92
Barker, Josiah H. 183
Barnes, John B., Major 30
  Robert 38
Barnett, John D. 143
Barnette, Elizabeth A. R. 79
Barns, Willis 192
Barnwell, Mary Mrs. 23
  Nathaniel 177, 200, 201
  Nathaniel Col. 23
Barr, Margaret H. 181
  Mary C. 127
  Thomas 32
Barret, L. W. 166
  Mary El (Wilmot) Mrs. 166
Barrett, S. 102
Barrinoe, B. 197
Barron, Thomas 13
Barrow, Richard, Capt. 204
Barstow, James, Capt. 114
  S. T. M. 114
Bartholemy, M. 33
Bartholomew, Peter 87
Bartlett, Capt. 155
Bartin, John 28
Bass, Rev. Mr. 28
  Mary Ann 64
Bassett, Nehemiah "Uncle" 31
Bate, John 64
Bates, Christiana Mrs. 91, 107
  Flemming 7
  James B. 169
  Jane Mrs. 159
  John 140
  John P. 190, 193
  Julia A. Mrs. 190
  Mary, Mrs. 138
  Nathan 38
  Thomas 91(2), 138, 140, 156, 157, 159
  Thomas (Jr.) 159
Bates and Perkins 38
Bath, Ann Mrs. 181
  Daniel 109
  Daniel, Capt. 107, 181
  Daniel Jr. 160
  Mary 107
  Thomas 181
Baughn, Dorothea Mrs. 68
Baxley, Comfort, Mrs. 158
  Leonard 182
Baxter, Jane Mrs. 4
  John Col. 4
Bayard, James A. 28

Beach, Christopher 54
  Stephen 54
Bear, George 31
Beaty, Bethel D. 171
  Elizabeth Louisa 149
  J. H. Rev. 149
  James 90, 120, 134, 137, 147,
    155, 156, 161
  James Capt. 86
  James Col. 199
  John 104
  John R. 207(2)
  Rev. Mr. 94
  Thomas A. Col. 72
  Thomas A. Rev. 182
Bedout, Charles 18, 25
  Margaret 66
Beckman, A. E. 168, 171
  Rebecca, Mrs. 168, 171
Begum, Brown (India) 41
Belin, Allard 19, 70
  Allard H., Col. 124
  Esther Martha 19
  James 70
  Mary B. 186
  Mary L. 45
Bell, ___ 35
  Henry 187
  Jane 105
  Martha L. 97
Bellamy, John 139
Bellemmee, John Sr. 155
  John D., Dr. 155(2)
  Mary 154
Bellune, C. K., Mrs. 125
  Elizabeth 170
  J. C., Maj. 116, 98
  John 203
  Jovana 116
  Mary (Easterling), Mrs. 125
  Mary Margaret 203
  William 92
  William G. 125
  William S. 195
Benbow, James D. 171
Benedict, John, Rev. D. D. 31
Benjamin, Ezra 60
Benton, John Augustus, Capt. 14,
  15
  Lamuel, Col. 14, 15(2), 48
Bennett, Thomas 112
  William 41
Beran, Rajah of India 41
Bereneau, Julian T. 52
Berkhart, Frederick 68
Berry, James B. 71
  Rebecca H. 34
Berton, Daniel V., Dr. 100, 103
Bertwhistle, Jane 60
Bessant, Thomas 207
Besselleu, Charles 23
  Mary Riley, Mrs. 23
Betts, Charles Rev. 91, 100,
  148
Billing, John 46
Billune, James C. Major 98
Bird, Adelaide Dozier, Mrs. 191
  E. Rev. 59
  H. L., Dr. 191
  John 164
  Susan 81
  W. 163
  William Harvey 191
Birden, Thomas D., Rev. 23
Bishop, Abel 26
Black, Eleanor, Mrs. 128
  Jonathan 29
Blacklock, John F. 180
Blackman, Andrew Deacon 42
  Ish, Mrs. 132
  Levi 132
Blackwell, Elizabeth Mrs. 13
  Hannah Mrs. 22
  Michael 13, 16, 21

Blackwell, contd.
  Samuel 160
  Thomas 16
Blackwood, Thomas 158
Blair, Rev. Hugh 17
Blake, Arther 176
Blakely, E. S. 185 —Henry 34
  Justice 127
  Magdalen 143
  Magdalen A. Mrs. 147
  Magdalin Agness 206
  Samuel 142
  Samuel U. 143
Blakeney, Samuel 142
Blanchard, Benjamin 8
  Henry 8
  Mariah 183
Blaney, Benjamin 41
  Polly, Mrs. 61
Blodget, Abigail 36
Bloodworth, T. 172
  Timothy 172
Blount, Allen, Maj. 176
  Elizabeth Davidson, Mrs. 47
  John 136
  Maria, Mrs. 136
  Thomas M. 47, 82
Blucher, Marshall 69
Blunt, Elizabeth Davidson, Mrs. 76
  John 120
  Thomas M. 76
Blyth, Elizabeth Frances, Mrs. 111
  Joseph Dr. 111
Board, Thomas 153
Boardman, Eliza C. 62
Boas, Saul M. 107(2)
Bogart, Rev. Dr. 99
Bogle, James Dr. 40, 63, 66
  James Lawrence 40
  Sarah, Mrs. 66
Boinsmade, Rev. Dr. 126
Bokee, D. A. 89
  David 97
  David A. 75
  Fred. William 89
Bomeyn, Rev. Dr. 41
Bond, Ann 82
  John W. 190
  John Wesley, Rev. 58
Bone, Leonard 187
  Nicholas P. 169
  Robert W. 146
Bonham, Rev. Mr. 168
Boone, Martha Mrs. 149
  T. 3
  Thomas 3
Booth, John 113
Bosman, Ann Mrs. 113(2)
Bossard, Ellen Elizabeth 169
  John Capt. 58
  Joseph S. 59, 169
Bostick, William D. 169
Bostwick, Robert 31
  Samuel Dayton 54
  William M. 31
Botsford, Ann (Deliesseline) 21
  Edmund, Rev. 6, 9, 14(2), 21,
    59, 70
  Edmund Park 59
  Hannah, Mr. & Mrs. 151
  Rev. Mr. 18, 22
Boudinot, Elisha 68
Boutelle, George 203
Bowen, Ephraim 7
Bowen, R. Rev. Bishop 94
Bowles, Rev. Mr. 102
Boykin, Capt. 7
Brackingberry, William 50, 51
Bradgon, George Ed. 153
  Jane, Mrs. 153, 172
  Thomas 153, 172
Brailsford, John M., Dr. 207
Branford, Mary Ann, Mrs. 6

Brantley, Martha 80
  W. T. Rev. 117, 139, 149
Branton, Emily C. 187
Branwall, Rev. Mr. 124
Breckenridge, Henry Hugh 37
Brent, Eliza Mrs. 35
  Daniel 35
Brewer, Abner S. Capt. 40
Briggs, Ann, Mrs. 81(2), 82
  Eliza Ann 82
  John 81
  Thomas H. Capt. 186
Brightman, Archible McClenan 120
  George T. 151, 159, 160
  Georgiana Thomasoena 160
  Mary Jane, Mrs. 160
  Sarah A., Mrs.108
  Thomas W. 108, 120
Brit, Thomas 74
Britt, Martha 104
Britton, Benjamin 11(2)
  D. 178
  E. H. 200
  Elizabeth 78
  Frances 185
  Gillmore 193
  Henry 78
  John 16
  John F. D. 193(2)
  M. 45
  M. George McConnell 193
  Mary Jane 181
  Mary, Mrs. 193
  Samuel Thos. 178
  Sarah J. 190
  Susannah D., Mrs. 153
  T., Dr. 45
  Thomas M. 186
  William 15
Broaderick, Michael 2
Brockington, John 23, 49, 122
  John Sr. 138
  W. S. 49
Brockinton, John 122, 183
  John Capt. 22
  Martha 9
  Martha, Mrs. 23
Broderick, Mary 29
Brodut, Francis, Capt. 76, 77
Brooks, William R. 72
Broquer, Abn Catharine 65
  Clement 65
Broqueir, Clement 152
  Mary A. 85
Brotherin, Christian 60
Brown, Ann 143
  C. 19
  C. B. 117
  Carolina M. 117
  Charles, Major 61
  Daniel, Rev. (A. M.) 29
  David 35
  E. C., Mrs. 178
  Edward H. 190
  Elias Boudinot, Dr. 178, 204
  Elizabeth Jane 177
  Frances M., Mrs. 186
  Hannah, Mrs. 117, 119
  Isaac 111, 115, 116(3)
  James Norton 156, 177
  John 194, 198
  John Dr., 20
  John Sr. 132
  Joseph A. 91, 93
  Joseph L. 99
  Kinsey 143
  Margaret 116
  Mary Eliza C. (Horton) Mrs. 93
  Nancy 64
  Robert C. 185
  Sarah, Mrs. 177
  S. C. 203
  Susannah 115, 116(2)

Brown (contd)
  Toomer Porter 178
  William 64, 105
  William Ferguson 54
  William V. 111, 114, 117, 134
Brownfiled, R. 3
  Robert 5
  Robert Dr. 8
Bruno, Frederick Charles Hans 18
Bruorton, Caroline Emma Jane 191
  George Washington 89
  Harriet P. 176
  Henry W. 176
  J. A. 158, 182
  John A. 89, 175
  John A., Capt. 167, 191
  Sarah D. Mrs. 89
  Susannah, Mrs. 167
Brutom, John D., Lieut. 135
Bruton, Benjamin 116
  Elizabeth (Sarvis) Mrs. 167
  Samuel 136
Brutor, Benjamin 170
Bryan, A. E. Mrs. 188, 206
  Aaron 34
  Armeline, Major 150
  Henrietta Isabella 188
  J. J. 188, 206
  Jacob 66
  Samuel M. 147
  Samuel M. (Jr.) 147, 150
  Samuel Middleton 206
  Soloman, Rev. 68
  Susan, Mrs. 68
Bryant, J. J. 144
  John, Capt. 34
Buck, Henry Capt. 187, 205
  Lucinda M. 205
  Mary Jane 187
Budd, Shivers, Capt. 10
Buddon, Solomon 28
Bufkin, Ann Elizabeth 147
  Elizabeth 163
  Elizabeth Mrs. 89, 96
  George C. 135
  H. F. 96
  Harriot, Mrs. 135, 147
  Hugh 89
  Hugh F. 135, 147, 167
  Josiah 89
Buford, Elizabeth Mrs. 66, 145
  William 66
  William J., Dr.,66, 143, 145
Bullock, William B. 107
Bulow, Count, Gen. 33
Bunch, Mary 123
Burd, Burrell 51(2)
  John 21
Burden, Thomas 161
Burgess, Eliza 148
  Elizabeth 148
  James 54
  Jennet, Mrs. 197
  John D., Col. 68, 70
  Margaret, Mrs. 54(2)
  Mary 148
  Robert 55
  Samuel A. 197
  William 148, 197
  William Dr. 81, 90
Burr, Aaron, Col. 99
  Aaron (VP) 17
  Therdosia 17
Burrow, John F. 200
Burrows, George W. 133
Bush, C. A. Mrs. 201
  Caroline A., Mrs. 161
  Edward Eugene 161
  Emily Leighton 201
  R. O. 201
  Richard O. 110, 161
Butler, A. P. 201
Butters, Abigail Mrs. 23

Butts, Daniel 60
  Jahiel 128, 129
  Oliver J. 171
  Sarah Mrs. 128
Byrd, B. Ervin 159
  Cleland K. 152
  Harvey Leonidas 152
  James E., Dr. 143, 159
  Mary E., Mrs. 159
  Pamelia Adelaide 152

Cain, John Jr. 193
Cains, Louisa Mrs. 186
  Richard 186
Calcut, Elizabeth Ann 198
Caldwell, John G. 102
  Mary, Mrs. 102
  Mary H., Mrs. 134
  W. Charles 102
  Joseph Jr. 69
  Joseph Rev. 30
Calhoun, Anna 109
  Georgia Anna 171
  J.C. 109
  John C. 167
  Mary E. 184
  William A. 51
Calverly,M. 46, 76
  Michael 93
Calwell, John G. 97
Cambridge, St. John 52
Camlin, Wm. S. 190
  W.S.204
Campbell, Alexander 16, 27, 120
  Angus 144
  Caroline 118
  Elizabeth, Mrs. 120, 124
  M., Mrs. 144
  Martha, Mrs. 16
  Mary Ann 144
Cannon,William H., Major 131
Canter, John 37
Cantley, Hugh W. 86
  Mary Eliza 48
Capers, Hannah, Mrs. 42
  John Rev., 40, 41
  John S., Rev. 46, 74
  Mary 73
  Mary Ellen 75
  William,Rev. 40, 41, 43, 57,
    66, 73
  William H., Col. 75
  William R., Rev. 199, 201,
    204
Capps, Ann., Mrs. 130
  Joseph T. 130
Capron, Mary 76
Cargill, Jane Matilda 71
Carmichael, Duncan 53
Carnes, Ann, Mrs. 37
  Eliza, Mrs. 187
  H. L. 57
  John 24, 57
Carr, Charles 14
  Isaac 77, 93(2)
  Julia A.,Mrs. 150
  Justice 104
  Martha 52
  Mary A., Mrs. 136
  Rev. 57
  Robert 39, 40
  Sarah 93
  Stephen 9
  Thomas, Gen. 81(2), 153
  Thomas G., Col. 153
Carraway, Amander E., Mrs. 202
  Josiah G. 202
  William Lorenzo 202
Carrol, ___ Miss 18
  Bishop, 18
  Charles 18
Carson, Rev. Mr. 179
Cart, Cesar 41

Cart (contd.)
  Susan Lewis 41
Carter, Eliza Hill 62
  Margaret A. 167
  Moses 65
  Moses, Mrs. 66
  S. D., Capt. 19
  William Champe 62
Carville, Andrew 122
  Catharine Mrs. 60
Carwaldo, Moses Gomez 31
Cassels, James 5
Catharine Paulowna, 36
Chambers, Jas. W. 174
  Robert B. 174, 185
  Robert Bell 185
  Travis 6
Chandler, Louisa 50
Chaplin, Harriot 37
Chapman, Ann 62
  Hannah Mrs. 62
  Henry 62
  James 121, 157, 158
  John 111
  Rachel (Blackwood) Mrs. 158
  Robert 29
  Samuel 157, 158
  Thomas 7, 8, 11, 14, 22, 25,
    27, 29, 62, 119, 157,
    158(2)
  William 111, 121
  William Major 119
Charles II 65
Charles, Edgar Col. 126
Charles & Frisbe, House of 123
Charlotte Augusta, Princess 36
Charlotte [of Mecklenburg] 39
Cheeseborough, Charlotte 12
  Esther, Mrs. 38
  J. W. 141
  John 12, 158
Cherry, John Dr. 86
Cheves, Anna 123
  Langdon 123
Childers, W. W., Rev. 143, 146
Chillcott, Giant 30
Chimes, Ezekial 45
Chinn, Thomas Buler 83
Chisholm, Margaret 36
Chisolm, Emily Mrs. 24
  Georgianna P. 145
  John 24
  William Dr. 145
Chovin, Alexander 25
  A. M., Rev. 169(2), 190
Chrietzburg, Rev. 205 see also
  Chris---, Henry R. 169 Christ----
Christee, G. W. 117
Christie, G. W. 159, 177, 185
  Sarah Ann, Mrs. 177
Christian, A. 45
  Abda, Rev. 30
  Arthur 55, 74
  Benjamin H. 122, 142
  Benjamin H. (Jr.) 142
  Catherine 153, 154
  Charlotte, Mrs. 52
  Eliza 95
  Ella M. 151
  G. W. 167
  J. H., Capt. 151, 153
  Jacob H. 153, 154
  S. A., Mrs. 167
  Sophia Ann 167
  Thomas Arthur 55
Christopher, Elizabeth Mrs. 131
  Eliza C. 165
  Howell M. 104
Christzburg, M., Rev. 163(2),
    165, 166(2)
  A. M., Rev. 168, 169(2)
Church, Maria N. 85
Claggett, Thomas John Bishop 37

Clark, Asa 85
   Jane (Zuill) Mrs. 96
   John Jay, Dr. 84
Clarke, Ann, Mrs. 52
   Asa, Capt. 51, 52, 80
   Jared R. 80, 85
Clarkson, Thomas B. 91
Clemson, Thomas G. 109
Clenaghan, H. M. 133
Clerc, Laurent 62
Clifton, Rev. Mr. 63
Coachman, Anna G. 207
   B. A. 117, 128
   B. A., Col. 177
   Benjamin A. 125(2), 131, 204
   Caroline (Ford) Mrs. 204
   Charlotte A., 151, 152
   E. P., Mrs. 153
   Francis G. 100, 101, 115, 153, 155
   Fredrine 204
   Isaac 113
   J. W. 101, 116, 144, 207
   James J. 101, 112
   James J., Mrs. 112
   Joan Joseph 112
   John 10, 59, 73, 151
   John James 125
   John W. 151, 152
   John W., Major 108, 125
   Mary (Ford) Mrs. 59
   Olevia Mrs. 125
   Sarah L., Mrs. 115, 116, 153
   Regina 155
Coachman & Walker 172
Coalman, William 100
Coburn, John R. 102, 106
Cochran, John Gould (Scot.) 93
Cock, Elizabeth 68
   Sarah 67
   Sarah, Mrs. 65
Cockfield, Ann 3
   B. W. 165
   Frances Ellen 165, 166
   Henrietta R. 156
   J. J. 166
   John B. 142
   Josiah 3
   Josiah W. 173, 187
   W. W. 178
   William 3
Coe, C. J. 143, 200
   Caroline Elizabeth 200
   M. F., Mrs. 200
Coffin, Robert S. 60, 80
Cogdela, Eliza Jane 133
Cogdell, Elizabeth, Mrs. 115
   Esther Mrs. 111
   J. S. 26
   John 1, 26, 111
   Louisa Matilda 114, 115
   Zacariah 115(2)
   Zachariah, Capt. 124
Cogeshell, Rebecca 161
Coggeshall, J. C. 44
   James 44
   James C. 49, 50, 58
   James C., Col. 85
   Margaret E., Mrs. 50
   Margaretta 86
   Peter C. 112
   Rebekah 155
Coggeshall N & Son, House of 58
Coggeshall & North 85
Cohen, Abraham 1, 6, 14, 15
   Abram 97
   Esther 169
   H., Rev. 169
   Isaac 13
   Isaac A. 66
   Jacob 62, 97, 102
   Priscilla 87
   Rachel, Mrs. 97

Cohen (contd.)
   _____ Rev. Mr. 102
   H. Rev. 158
   Solomon 2, 13, 14, 15, 59
Colclough, Col. 22
Clocock, C. J. 107
Cole, Elijah 46
   Reuben 46
Coleman (see also Coalman)
   Benj. Capers 182
   Martha 177
Collins, A. 25
   Alex 26, 44
   Ann Eliza 206
   Elias 134
   Elizabeth, Mrs. 44, 134
   J.W. 147
   Jonah W. 103
   Martha L. F. 84
   Mary Jane 195, 196, 197
   Robert H. 104, 149, 150, 195, 196, 198
   W. S. 202
Colwell, Albert G. 117
Commander, Charles James 125
   Eliza Mrs. 125
   Elizabeth, Mrs. 85
   James M. 136
   James M., Major 125
   Thomas 23
Cone, S. H. Rev. 110
Congdon, Charlotte C., Mrs. 140, 144
   George R. 121
   William P. 144
Connell, Susannah, Mrs. 31
Connelly, Patrick 10
Conner, C. C., Mrs. 155
   D. C. 137
   Daniel C. W. 101
   Edward 137
   Ira, Lt. 64
   Laura D. 137
   Mary 137
   Sarah 137(2)
   Sarah E.137
   W. G., Rev. 155
   William O'Hanlon 155
Connor, William G., Rev. 156(2), 160
Constant, John A. 47
Converse, Rev. Mr. 109
Conway, Robert, Gen. 188
Conyers, Stran 12
Cook, Ann W. (Rogers) Mrs. 154
   Elizabeth 68
   John T. 154
   Joseph B., Rev. 18, 85
   Joseph H., Rev. 41
Cooper, Adriel B. 187
   Carline M. 170
   Caroline 84
   Caroline M. 170
   F. 156
   Nelson 169
   Robert 130, 131, 161
   Thomas Milton 192
   William 46, 176
Coote, M. Anglo Thomas 154
Corbz, Peter 79
Cormack, Patrick 27
Cormick, P.70
Corson, Annette Louisa 112
   Constant, Capt. 119
   HenryStevens 119
   James, Capt. 119
   Mary E. 197
   Mary Maria 90
   Susan, Mrs. 90
Cotherel, Lucy 65
Cotten, James W. 34
   Robert 57
Council, Ann, Mrs. 191

Course, Charles B. 32
   Isaac 32
   Isaac & Son 32
Course & McFarland 55
Cousar, John Rev. 50
Courtney, William 125
Covan, Eliza 27
Cowan, Charlotte W. Mrs. 147
   W. J. Gen. 147
Coward, Martha Mrs. 188
   Salomon, Capt. 188
Cox, A. E., Mrs. 207
   Alexander J. 199, 202
   Elijah 207(3)
   Elizabeth Martha 148
   Georgiana (Calhoun), Mrs. 195
   John 45, 53, 77
   Joseph 74
   Mary Elizabeth 103
   Mary Elizabeth, Mrs. 199
   Sarah Mrs. 207
   Thomas C. 171
Crace, Ephraim C. 36
Crafts, William 55
Cram, Nancy Gove 32
Crane, Ichabod 50
   John S. 92
Crapps, Rev. Samuel 185
Craps, Rev. Mr. 205
   William Rev. 205, 206
Crawford, Rachel, Mrs. 86
Crawley, Walter 25
Cribb, Griffin, Mrs. 136
   John 136
   Margaret 165
Croes, John Bishop Rt. Rev. 98
Crofford, Rev. Mr. 186
Croft, Albert Carr 176
   Benjamin King 154
   Childermas 25, 27
   Edward 3
   Eleazer Waterman 158
   Frances M., Mrs. 154, 158
   I. C. 164, 176(2)
   Isaac C. 123
   Isaac Carr 204(2)
   J. Alston 134
   Julia Rebecca 176
   Margaret Mrs. 175
   Martha H. Mrs. 176(2), 204
   W. S. 129, 158
   William 42, 101, 175
   William S. 116, 149, 150, 154
Cronce, Solomon 30
Crook, Rev. Mr. 139(2), 50
   William Rev. 148
Crosby, Jane, Mrs. 29
   Moses G. 29
   Thomas 187
Crosland, David 109, 196
Cross, Capt. 23
   Henrietta Louisa 120
   Hester, Mrs. 23
   John G. 120
   M. A., Mrs. 143
   Margaret A., Mrs. 120
   Martha Elizabeth 143
Crosswell, E. G. 151
   James E., Dr. 151
Crowell, Betsey 64
   Edward 64
Cryer, Joseph 99
   William J. 99
Culpepper, Henry Alexander 128
Cumbie, Ann 115
   Daniel 92
   Elisha 182
   Henry 136
Cumming, Mary Ann 34
Cunningham, Alexander Lt. 7
   J. L., Dr. 195
Curran, John 193
Curtis, D., D. D. 187

Curvie, W. B., Rev. 206(2)
Cuttino, Benjamin H. 201, 203
  Benjamin T., 82, 150, 179(2)
  David W., Dr. 40, 196, 197,
    198, 201
  Elizabeth Ann 29
  Henry 99, 150, 195(2), 196
  Henry Benjamin 93
  Jer. 25
  L. E., Mrs. 196
  Luther Marion 196
  Martha 112
  Margaret B. 150
  Mary C. 90
  P. 58, 67
  P., Capt. 90
  Peter 29, 112
  Peter, Capt. 146
  Samuel 78
  Samuel D. 53
  Sarah 67
  Sarah L. 146
  William Henry 191

Dalcho, Rev. Dr. 96
Dale, Richard, Commodore 50
Dallas, Alexander J. 42
Damrel, William, Capt. 50
Danford, Isaac 1, 8
  Mary 135, 136
Daniel, Boxwell 132
  Chisley 63
  Eliza Pratt, Mrs.62
  Gamewell 132
  John A. 95
  Martha Jane 132
  Perry 132
  Sarah 132
  Wm. 173
Daniell, William R. 89, 94
Daniels, ____ Mrs. 50
  John 50
Dargan, Timothy 8
Darr, Martha A., Mrs. 152
  R. E. 152
  Ralph 152
Darrell, Benjamin 8
Dauglass, William 61
  William, Mrs. 61
Davidson, Hannah Sarah ann 177
  James 13
  Mary, Mrs. 13
  Robert J. 177, 207
  Sarah Ann, Mrs. 177
Davies, Ann, Mrs. 65
  Ann C., Mrs. 114
  Catharine Ann Hudson 65
  Davia 65
  David 114, 142
  Jane E. 112
Davis, Acquila Cogdell 148
  Ann 87
  Benjamin Sr. 37
  Catherine E. 162
  Catharine G. 36
  Charles C. 201(2)
  David 114
  D. R. W. 114
  Eleanor 14
  Elizabeth, Mrs. 94
  F. M. 180
  Francis 53
  Francis Marion 176(2)
  Henry 1
  Henry C. 100
  Henry G. 203
  Henry W., Dr. 83
  John 173
  John C. 61, 92
  John M. 100
  Julia Ann 53
  L. W. W. 115, 122, 170
  Magdalen L. 88

Davis(contd.)
  Margaret 161
  Mary B., Mrs. 115, 122, 170
  Mary C.,Mrs. 201
  Mary Elizabeth 122
  M. L., Mrs. 112
  M. S. 190
  Molsey 63
  Phillip, Rev. 204
  P. M. 109
  __ R.193
  Sarah Ann 142
  Sarah Ann, Mrs. 61
  Susan Gabraella 170
  Thomas., Gen. 36
  Thomas P. 88
  WM. M., Dr. 186
  William 63
  William Col. 1
Davisson, Hannah Mrs. 34
Dawsey, W. J. 103, 120
  William J. 124
Day, Jonathan, Col. 62
  Mary, Mrs. 62
  Robert 14
Deal, H. I., Mrs. 198
  J. C. 198
  Mary Elizabeth 198
Dealy, Benjamin W. 123, 191
  James 88, 97
  Mary J., Mrs. 191
  Robert James 123
  Samuel Green 97
Deas, John, Capt. 100
  S., Dr., 124
Deborah (a black woman) 35
de Grouchy, Marshal 57
Dehone, Theodore, Rt. Rev. 40
De Liesseline, Agnes, Mrs. 133
  Francis 133
  Maynard Davis 133
Deliesseline, Ann, Mrs. 9
  Elizabeth T. 10
  Emily 31
  Francis G. 10(2), 22, 77
  Francis T. 8
  Isaac 22
Dellet, James 14, 16(2)
DeLorme, Charles 78
  Mary Adelaide 179
  W. M. 179
Denison,Eliza, Mrs. 120
  Gilbert,Judge 69
  Hannah C. 72, 78
  Henry 69
  Henry, DR., 72(3), 78
  Josephine 135
  William 108, 122
Denly, James 79
Dennie, Jas. 177
Dennis, Elizabeth J. 187(2)
  Francis E. 201
  M. L. 186
Dent, John 182
DePree, Daniel Rev. 182
DeSaussure, H. A. 107
Deschamps, Elizabeth Mrs. 46
  Louis 46
  Mary Axson 46
deSurvilliers, Count 57
Detyens, H. F. 114
  Henry F. 110, 207
Dewees,Mary 90
  William Col. 90
Dewitt, Joseph 153
  Martin 69
Dexter, Samuel 34
Dias, Thomas 1
Dick, Elizabeth A. 186
  James Summers 27
  Thomas M. Dr., 186
Dicker, Mary E. 204
W.J. 132

Dicks, Benjamin Allston 199
  John 72, 82
  John Jmaes 82
  Martha, Mrs. 132
  Mary S., Mrs. 82
  William 112, 132
Dickinson, R. S. Sorris, Rev 161
Dickison, J. J. 134, 148, 160
  Mary Margaret (Lester) 148
Dickson, J. J., Col. 196
Didy, Susannah 60
Dinkings, Rosana Mrs. 173
Dixon, Amanda E., Mrs. 148
  F. T. 148
  Francis R. 179
  John 1
  William Algernon 148
Doane, Bishop 104
Doar, Adam 103
  E. M. 198
  Elias M. 172, 173
  Josiah 162, 173
  M. A. Mrs. 198
  Stephen D. 173
  William Henry 198
Dobson, Mary Ann, Mrs. 181
Dollard, Ann, Mrs. 15, 18
  Patrick 12, 15
  William 70
  William Dr. 47(2), 48, 49,
    70, 76
Donnelly, Ann Waties, Mrs. 135
  Charlotte A. 27
Donnolly, P. 5
  Patrick 9
  Patrick, Mrs. 9
Dooer, William 53
Doore, J. D. 132
Dorrill, Wm.H. 179
Dossey, Rev. Mr. 59
  William, Rev. 69
Dougherty, Michael 26
Doughty, James 94
  Sarah B. 94
Dow, Abraham 38
  Phoebe, Mrs. 38
Dowdney, Mary Charlotte 27
  Rebecca Mrs. 4, 7, 76
  Sarah Ann 75
  Thomas 24, 27, 47, 76, 85
Downing, Charles Col. 121 Downes,
Dowsey, W. J. 191   Capt. 42
Doyle, J. P., Major 113
Dozier, A. W. 84, 117, 123, 125,
    158
  A. W. Mrs. 125
  Anthony W. 90
  Elizabeth Cuttino 152
  Elizabeth Giles 108
  Elizabeth S., Mrs. 152
  John 51, 93
  John, Capt. 51
  John, Col. 108, 123
  L. 187
  Leonard 152
  Mary Emeline 125
  Richard 146
  T. J. Dr., 165
Drennan, John 13
  Tabitha Mrs. 13
Drinkwater, Charles 149
Druro, Peter 137
Dubois, J. T. 199
  Philip 28
  Samuel 12, 20(2)
Dubose, Charlotte 63
  Charlotte C., Mrs. 48
  Harbert 47(2), 48, 77
  Harburton 63
  Hugh 48, 49, 65
  Isaac, Capt. 35
  Isaiah 58
  Joseph 59

Dubose (contd.)
  Martha Elizabeth Ann 63
  Rev. Mr. 202
DuBose, Henrietta Mrs. 174
  Sarah A., Mrs. 65
  William G. 136, 137, 166
Dudley, Ed. B., Col. 30
Dunbar, Mary Ann, Mrs. 105
  Samuel P. 105
Duningham, Arthur 19
Dunkin, Judge 144, 145
Dunmore, Carpenter Sampson
    (Colored) 136
Dunnan, Jacob 7
  John P. 7
Dunster, Henry Jackson 110
Dunwoody, Samuel Rev. 62
Duprat, Dorris 38
DuPre -see also DePree
  Cornelius 3(2), 5(2), 6, 7,
          8(2), 15(2), 17,
          21(2), 22
  Elizabeth 10
  Jonas G. 19
  Mary, Mrs. 19, 21
Durand, C. M. 133
  Charlotte M., Mrs. 185
  Levi 185
Durant, Bethel 48, 59
  C. M., Mrs.128
  Daniel 207
  David 144
  Francis 172
  Francis B. 98
  Francis B., Mrs. 98
  George 168
  H. H., Rev. 151, 152, 154
  Hannah, Mrs. 87
  John 148
  Joseph 19
  Levi 133
  Mary, Mrs.198
  Mary Ann 168
  Mary L. 184
  Maru Ruth 98
  Rebecca 106
  Sarah F. W. 198
  Sarah G. 186
  Stephen 173
  Thomas, Rev. 72
Durden, J. S. 30
Durr, Daniel T. 155, 157
Dwight, Isaac B. 2
  Nathaniel 104
  Timothy, Rev. 42(2)
Dyre, A. D. 44

Eaddy, Clark 181
Eady, Henry 193
  M., Rev 155
Easterbrook, Joseph, Lt. 36
Easterling, Alice 148
  Fannie Goodwyn 200
  J. R. 138(2), 181
  James E. 200
  John R. 85, 148
  Joseph L. E. (sheriff) 99
  M. A. 199
  Mary Elizabeth, Mrs. 200
  Mary R. 160
  Nancy, Mrs. 125(2)
  Rebekah, Mrs. 144
Eastinglin, J. R. 161
Eaton, Jacob 60
Eden, Rebecca 46, 76
Edmonston, Charles 196
  Elizabeth Chisholm 196
Edwards, Pierpont, Judge 51
  Simon 15
Eichelberger, Margaret, Mrs. 33
Eldred, George P. 165
Elford, James Mausle, Rev. 48
Eliot, Rev. Mr. 169
Ellerbe, Thomas P. 69

Elliott, John W. 24, 26
  Martha, Mrs. 26
  Martha Mary Barnwell 155
  Sarah 156
  Stephen 92
  Stephen, Rev. 155
  William 155
Ellis, Benjamin 123
  Earl C. 207
  G. L. 159
  Mrs. 159
  James D. 100
  Rev. Mr. 68
  St. John 154
  St. John P. 185
Ellison, William 35
  William, Rev. Mr. 95, 98
Ely, David, Rev. D. D. 31
Emanuel, F. Mrs. 188
  Flora, Mrs. 45
  Henrietta S. 199
  Moses 158
  Marion 162, 188
  N. 188, 199
  Nathan 162, 176
  Sarah, Mrs. 176
  Simon 45
England, Joanna M. 83
  R. Rev. Bishop 83
Ennis, William 51
Ervin, E. P. Col. 151
  John, Col. 22
Erwin, Jos. 43
Esdah, Edward Jeffries 152
  Emily Frances 152
Ethridge, Elias J. 87, 134
  Jane, Mrs. 193
  M. A. 193
  Pinckney Pleasant 193
Evans, A. J., Rev. 205, 207
  Benjamin F. 207
  C. D. 153
  Eliza Ann 106
  Hannah 156
  Josiah J. 124
  Martha, Mrs. 41
  Mary, Mrs. 78
  Mary Ann 114, 166
  R. D. 207
  Rev. Mr. 199
  Sarah 134
  Senator 206
  Stephen 54
  Thomas 15, 78, 106, 114, 134,
          141, 166
  Thomas, Col. 15
  William H. 124
Eveleigh, Nicholas 1
  Thomas 34
Ewen, Polly 83
Exum (see also Axum)
  Elijah 95
  Elijah T. 95
  Elizabeth Jane 146
  John 74, 75
  John (Jr.) 75
  Mary, Mrs. 74, 75
  Robert 74

Fairfax, George W. 36
Farewell, Catharine 203
  Harriet Maria 188
  M. A., Mrs. 150
  Mary, Mrs. 162
Farm, John 12
Farrow, Elizabeth B. 184
  _____ en, 169
  Julia Anna L. 169
  Stephen 91
  Thomas 91
  Thomas M., Rev. 157
Fault, Isaac D. 200
  William 194

Faulkner, Charles H. 116, 126
Faust, Daniel 37
  Sarah, Mrs. 37
Fay, T. C. 133
Fayerweather, Jerusha Mrs. 27,
          28
Fearwell, Mary A., Mrs. 104, 141,
          150
  Thomas C. 85, 104, 141, 152
Fendel, Sarah 1
Fennel, Joseph 37
Fenters, Rebecca 189
Ferari, Susannah Mrs. 188
Ferdon, Joanna, Mrs. 51
Fern, Nancy 31
Fickling, Ann E. R. Mrs. 142
  J. J. 142
Field, Elias 97
Filburne, William 193
Finch, David S. 82
  Sally, Mrs. 82
Fincklay, Thomas G. 67
Finklea, Mary Mrs. 183
  Thomas G. 111, 165
  Thomas W. 166
Finson, William 80
  William Alexander 88
Fishburne, William, Maj. Gen. 68
Fitzgerald, Henry T., Rev. 65
Fitzwilliam, Vincent Lord 33
Flagg, Arthur B., Dr. 190
  Ebenezer 45
  Ebin Belin 196
  Henry Collins, Dr. 17
Flagler, Margaret G. 184
Fletcher, Betty, Mrs. 50
Fleming, Benjamin Huger 84
  Hariot, Mrs. 24
  Mathew, Capt. 24(2)
  W. H., Dr. 84
  W. H., Rev. 139, 150, 153, 156,
          158(2)
Flicx, Theresa E. 37
Flowers, Igantius 24
  Rachel, Mrs. 84
Floyd, Benjamin R. 134
  James L. C. 134
  Lewis 134
  Lewis H. 134
  Sarah A., Mrs. 134
Fluitt, Mary S. 131
Folk, Martha, Mrs. 116
Forbes, William 168, 189
Ford, Anna 98
  Archibald T. 106
  Caroline 131
  Charles 2
  Esther B. 97
  F. W. 196
  Frederick 152, 190
  George 9
  George, Dr. 84
  George G. 196
  George T. 79, 97
  Hess B. 182
  Jane C., Mrs. 168
  John H. 171
  John P. 114, 116, 138, 195
  John Richard, A. M. 192
  M. Helen 194
  Margaret, Mrs. 100, 101
  Mary, Mrs. 98
  Mary Allston, Mrs. 165
  Mary H. 108
  Robert T. 190
  Robert Thurston 189
  S. 101
  Sarah 27
  Sarah, Mrs. 79
  Sarah E. 199
  Sarah Helen, Mrs. 9, 79
  Stephen 33, 100, 108, 114, 119,
          131, 168, 177, 181

Ford (contd.)
  Stephen Jr. 2
  Stephen Charles 49, 193, 194
  Stephen E. 79
  Thomas 27, 98, 114(2)
  Thomas Jr. 101
  William 25
  William H. 84
Forde, Peter 35
Fore, Daniel 132
  James 132
  Joel 132
  John 132
  Mary 132
  William 132
Forrest, John Rev. 196
Forster, Rev. Mr. 112, 118
  A., Rev. 109(3)
  A. M. Rev. 139, 144
  Alexius, Mr. Dr. 139
Forsyth, Eleanor 120
  W. S. 113
  William S. 119, 120
Fort, Allen 52
  Daniel D. 52
  Fred Rogers 37
  M. 46, 76
  Moses 37
  Sarah Scott, Mrs. 52
Forte, Josephine 128
Foster, Rev. Mr. 109(2)
Fountain, Jacob 149
Fowler, Enos 207
  Mathias 45, 71
  Rev. 75
Foxsworth, Mary, Mrs. 159, 165
Fraser, Agnes 116
  Alonzo J. B. 179
  B. P., Dr. 53(2)
  Benjamin P. 62, 91, 116
  Francis Buford 108
  Hugh 25
  Hugh, Rev. 58, 91, 108, 109
  Jane Rose 177
  John 159
  M. L. L., Jr. 179
  Peter W. 50, 109
  Peter W., Col. 158, 162, 165, 177
  R. E. 129, 206
  Rev. Dr. 10
  Rev. Mr. 18, 62, 67(2)
  Robert 8
  Robert E. 181
  Robert L. 150
  Samuel 113, 129, 158
  Samuel W. 206
  Sarah G., Mrs. 169
  Thomas Lauren 158
  William 8
Freear, Esther 28
Freeman, Benjamin 86
Freer, Esther 28
  Zacharias, Capt. 28
Freligh, Peter D., Rev. 28
Frink, Samuel 49, 78
  Sarah B. 78
Frisbe, Samuel 123
  John R. 107
Fuller (infant) 29
  C., Dr. 29
  Thomas 21
Furman, C. M. 107
  Rev. Dr. 75
Fusteney, Jacob Sr. 36
Futhey, Jane, Mrs. 9
  John 9
  John, Dr. 39, 41, 57

Gadsden, Rev. 69 Christopher 177
Gaillard, D. A. 191
  S. T. 94, 191
  Theodora C. 191
  William S. 137
Gainey, Henry L. 173
Gallagher, S. F., Rev. 48
  Rev. Mr. 116
Gallaher, Rev. Dr. 22
Gallavant, M. P. 108
Galliard, _____ 109
Gallivant, Susan 87
Galuchat, Rev. 57
Gamble, Elizabeth 81
  James 183, 184
  Sarah E., Mrs. 194
  Susan 50
Gamewell, John Rev. 83
Gano, Rev.Dr. 82
Gardiner, Julia 134
Gardner, George 22
  Mary, Mrs. 32
  Samuel 22
  Weld 22
  William 22
Garfield, Rev. 53
Garnie, Ann, Mrs. 77
Garnier, Ann, Mrs. 47
Garrell, James 9
  Samuel 9
Garvin, Catharine Mrs. 23
Gasden, Rev. Mr. 196
Gaskins, Julian O. 183
Gasque, Esther Charlotte 177
  Harris Simons 189
  James O. 71, 72
  Jehu 184, 191
  John 146, 192
  John Wragg 89
  Mary 35
  Mary E. 192
  Mary E., Mrs. 191, 192
  Nathan 41
  S. S. 48, 87
  S. S., Dr. 89, 104, 105, 177
  Sumpter S. 185
Gaston, William 38
Gause, Anne 79
  B. 165
  Benjamin 74, 78, 79, 83, 95, 113, 163
  Elizabeth, Mrs. 163, 164
  Elizabeth B., Mrs. 49
  John J. 49(2)
  Lucy, Mrs. 146
  Samuel 146
  Sarah B. 165
  Sarah Emily 151
  William Drayton 171
  William J. 104
Geanerett, Elias M. 168
Gellaspie, Daniel H. 32
George, Hannah 60
  Kelly 10
George, Prince Regent 36
Gerard, P. G. 197
Gerganus, Jas. 186
Gerson, George 41
Gibbes, Benjamin 69
  Henry, Rev. 72
  Mary 69
  Mary, Mrs. 11
  Rev. Mr. 62
  Stafford 11
Gibbs, Ann, Mrs. 107
  Cannon, Capt. 179
  George 95, 156
  Henry 61
  Henrietta 179
  M. G. 107
Gibson, D. 99
  George 95
  John 114
  Jordan 16
  Nathaniel 16
  Samuel Ferdinand 94
  Stephen, Capt. 186
  William 13
Gilbert, Cephas, Capt. 205
  Cleland J. 159
  Elizabeth, Mrs. 29
  Joseph R. 59
  Mary Elizabeth, Mrs. 31
  Wiley 31
Giles, Hugh 54
Gilleland, John 57
Gilman, Samuel Manual 137
Girard, Harriet 57
  Stephen 57(2)
Gist, Mordecai, Brig. Gen. 2
Gladinning, William, Rev. 36
Glanis, Rev. Mr. 108
Glascow, Martha, Mrs. 88
Glass, Joseph A. 147
  Joseph Alexander 21
  Mary, Mrs. 21
Glenmore, Ann C. 156
Glennie, A. Rev. 178, 190
  Alex. 190
  Alex, Dr. 177
  Rev. Mr. 98, 139
Glidden, M. M. 204
Glover, Moses 10
Godbold, Charles F., Dr. 79
  Mary 86
  Thomas, Gen. 74, 86
Goddard, Elizabeth C., Mrs. 98
  Mary E. 166
  P. C., Dr. 155
  Thomas F. 98(2), 166
  William H. 160
Godfrey, Benjamin H. 8
  Elizabeth, Mrs. 51
  Harrington 8(2)
  Mary Rachael 94
  William 51
  William Wilson 78
Goldfinch, D. 192
  Daniel 183, 200
  Mary C., Mrs. 200
  William 192
Gomez, Isaac 176
Good, John, Rev. 31
Goode, Catharine Ann, Mrs. 161
Goodlett, James 170
  Nancy 170
Goodrich, Chauncey 28
Goodwin, Abel 10, 11, 12, 15
  Ann(e), Mrs. 12, 15(2), 25
  Patsey, 11
Gordon, Elizabeth S. 186
  Jane M., Mrs. 112
  John 112, 193
Gorman, Ann 54
  John Alexander 188
  John B. 143, 148
  Magdeline A. 188
Gota, John Sr. 51
Gotea, George C. 136(2)
Goud, L. S. S. 198
Goude, Elizabeth A. L. K. 183
Gould, Patrick 64(2)
Gourdin, Elizabeth Frances
  Allston, Mrs. 101
  Theodore, Dr. 101
  Theodore Sr. 49
Gourdine, Theodore 43
Gourly, Ann J. 102
Graham, Ann 68
  Archibald 68
  Elizabeth 29
  James 11
  John 11, 90
  John, Jr. 59
  John S. 153, 156
  Samuel E. 92
  Sarah M., Mrs. 198
  William B. 137
  William J. 185
  William J. H. 200
Granger, J. C. 90

Grant, Benjamin Wallace 203
  Dr. 203
  Emma 155
  J. A., Dr. 194
  M. A. (Tucker) 203
  Samuel D. 88
  William 14, 16
Grason, John R., Capt. 39
Graves, Elizabeth, Mrs. 130
Gray, Catharine Dangerfield, Mrs. 77
  Jacob 126
  Jane M. 126
Greaves, Francis 107
  Joseph, Capt. 90
Freder, Aphia 42
Greeman, O. C. 200
Green, Ann, Mrs. 148
  B. 78
  Benjamin 44, 52, 77
  Clementine, Mrs. 107
  E. W., Dr. 142, 143
  Ezra 107
  Francis 18, 73, 138, 181
  Hannah 10
  Hannah, Mrs. 63
  J. R. 161
  James 6, 44, 146
  John 20, 110
  John Coachman 65
  John F. 44, 73, 80
  John J. 75, 107, 168
  Margaret Ann 182
  Martha Rebecca, Mrs. 64
  Mary 142, 143
  Mary Agnes 75
  Rev. Mr. 27
  R. G., Capt. 135
  Richard 82, 83, 191
  Richard, Capt. 190
  Richard G. 77
  Samuel 88, 97, 142
  Samuel, Rev. 146
  Sarah E. 43
  William 63
  William Glenn 72
Gregg, Eliza Jane 79
  James 1
  Polly 1
  Robert J. 79, 131
  Thomas 131
  William 127
  Zilpha, Mrs. 79
Greggs, Harry 32
Gregorie, John W. 181
Gregory, Capt. 79
Grice, Mary, Mrs. 65
  William H. 65
Gridlis, Lydia, Mrs. 50
Grier, B. M. 140
  Benjamin 58
  Eliza W., Mrs. 70
  James M. 27, 70, 81
  John 20
  Judith 6
  L. A. 202
  L. A., Rev. 194, 202
  Lemuel A. 165, 190, 198
  L. S., Rev. 169(2)
  Martha, Mrs. 187
  Martha Gamble 70
  Mary E. 202
  Mary Jane 104
  P. M. 170
  Rev. Mr. 183, 184
  Samuel 104, 107
  Samuel Cogdell 29
  William G. 95
  William Kennedy 184
Griffin, George 48
Griggs, Henry 184
Grimke, John F., Judge 64
Grimsey, William Pinckney 195
Grissette, Charrity Ann 206
  G. W. 206

Groce, Patsey 34
Grosvenor, A. S. 108
  Ellen E., Mrs. 108
  Rev. Mr. 73
  Silena Caroline 108
Grouter, Robert B. 136
Groves, Richard 16
Guerard, Edw. P. 191
Guerry, Catherine, Mrs. 15
  David A. 146
  Mary Martha 146
  Peter 15
  Sarah E., Mrs. 146
Guess, Mary 1
Guild, Ann D. M., Mrs. 194
  Samuel T. 194
Gulliver, Henry S. P. 140
Gulton, John, Capt. 65
Gun, Rhode 19
Gurganus (see also Gerganus)
  Elizabeth S., Mrs. 186, 193
  John E. 193

Hadly, Sallie J. 175
  T. 175
Hahm, Barbara 83
Haile, John 36
Hails, Robert, Capt. 32
Hale, Elizabeth R. 68
  William, Dr. 68
Hales, Alexander 55
  Edward, Capt. 86
  Eliza, Mrs. 86
  Howell G. 151
  Margaret, Mrs. 55
  Thomas 150, 151
Hall, Ann 124
  John 89(2), 92
  Margaret, Mrs. 92
  Thomas 100
  William 54
  William H. 89
Ham, Cyrus 141
  Elizabeth 129
  Henry B. 190
  James D. 113
  Oscar Eugene 184
  Sarah E., Mrs. 184
  Thomas A. 184
Hamckle, Rev. Dr. 205
Hamer, L. M., Rev. 202
Hamilton, Alexander 25
  Dowager Lady 33
  Jas, Gen. 124
  Jefferson, Rev. 114, 115
  John 96, 125
  Mary 96
  Paul (Sec. of Navy) 37
Hamlin, Irvinia 141
  J. J. 183
  Jos. J. 157
  T. B. 191
  Thomas B. 141
Hammond, Samuel, Col. 126
Hampton, Frank, Capt. 36
  Ma--- A. 170
  Wade, Gen. 36
Hanckel, ___ D. D. 204
  C., Rev. 187
  Rev. Dr. 176, 177
Hancock, Thomas 22
Hanion, Ann Catharine 73
  Elizabeth, Mrs. 104
Hankins, Dennis 137(2)
  Hannah 59
  Nancy 137
Hanks, Thomson Hargroves 57
Hanna, Hugh 126
  J. D. B. 184
Hanson, Alexander C. 61
Hardwick, Ann 2
  James 57
  John 2, 119, 151

Hardwick (contd.)
  John (Jr.) 119
Hardy, Chas. Rev. 76
  Rev. 73(2), 74
Hargate, John 8
Harllee, Robt. Dr. 102
Harper, John D. 204
  Robert G. 18
  William 152
Harrell, Francis Marion 134
  J. B. 172, 192
  J. L. 184, 186
  Josiah R. 202
  Major 55
  Martha 169
  Mary Eliza 172
  S. J., Mrs. 172
  Sarah Jane, Mrs. 206
  Sarah R. 185
Harrelson, Catharine G., Mrs. 136
  Jesse 128
  John 102, 109
  Moses 90
  Sarah, Mrs. 135
Harrington, John C. 103
  Martha A., Mrs. 119
  Rev. Mr. 78
  William 119
Harris, Mary Elizabeth 157
Harrison, E. F. 159
  Elizabeth H. 63
  Pres. 117
Harriss, James F. W. 28
Harrman, M. 148
Hart, Benjamin, Capt. 57
  Benjamin S. 75
  James A. 120
  John 28
  Mary Ann, Mrs. 57
Hartley, Amos 55, 78
  Isaac, Rev. 78
  Joseph 52
  Mary Jane, Mrs. 52
  Thomas 55, 78
Harvey, Benjamin Boneau 2
  Frances Ann 39
  G. V. 78
  Isabel 28
  Jacob William 2
  John, Capt. 3
  John B., Capt. 16
  Mary, Mrs. 73
  Samuel, Capt. 78
  Thomas Herbert 2
  W. S. 99
Haseldon, Ann, Mrs. 106
  Esther Elvira 160
  Jane 153
  John Capers 193
  Mary 127
  S. M. B. 160, 163
  Stephen M. B. 173
Hasell, Christopher Gadsden 40
  Lewis C., Dr. 205
  William S. 30
Hasford, Sam'l 18
Hasvin, A. N. 143
Haswell, Anthony 35
Hautreux, Peter 6
  Sarah, Mrs. 6
Hawes, Oliver, Dr. 12
Hawkins, Alafair D. 179
  Amanda M. 150
  Benjamin, Col. 36
  Elizabeth Mrs. 149
  John 81, 95, 129
  John Jr. 56
  Margaret Ann Desdamona 112
  Mary, Mrs. 112
  Mary N., Mrs. 129(2)
  S. A. 102
  Sarah E. 97
  Susan A., Mrs. 134

Hawkins (contd.)
    Thomas, Rev. 37
    Wm. Gov. (N. C.) 62
Haws, Mary Ann Elizabeth 39
    Oliver, Dr. 39
Hayle, William 183
Haynes, J. E. 186
Haywood, Eliza R. C. 30
Hazelton, James 86
Hazerentine, John 39
Hearl, Joseph E. 189
Heaseldon, Stephen C. 144
Heath, J. M. L. 199
Helen, Sarah 9
Hellen, Jane S. 151
Hemingway, Edward 126
    Eliza Jane, Mrs. 126(2)
    Hariet Malvina 126
    Jas. A. 126
    Joseph A. 126
    Martha A. R. 171
    Mary Ann, Mrs. 146
    Thomas 40, 79, 149
    Thomas, Mrs. 40
Henderson, Elizabeth Mrs. 183
    George 49
    Rebecca Mrs. 51
Hendricks, Benjamin 38
Henesy, Allen 138
Hennesy, A. L. 194
Henning, Anna B., Mrs. 52, 64, 118, 121
    E., Mrs. 165
    Elizabeth Mrs. 6
    Emma A., Mrs. 128
    J. G. 180
    James G. 112, 121, 128, 131, 161, 165
    James Green 165
    Martha Emma 128
    Thomas 51, 52, 64, 77, 78, 118, 135
    Thomas W. 135
    Thomas William 64
Henry, Isaac 130
    Meriam, Mrs. 67
    M. L. & Co. 66
    Morris L. 66, 67
    Patrick 9
    Thomas Carlton, Rev. 83
Hepburn, James 10
    Mrs. 10
Herbert, Nancy, Mrs. 68
Hereford, Wm., Dr. 31
Heriot, Robert 91
    Sarah Caroline 91
Heriot, A. Glennie 207
    Ann, Mrs. 97
    Daniel T. 81
    Edward T. 87, 120
    Edward T., Dr. 139
    Eliza J. 190
    Emily 21
    E. T. 154
    E. T., Dr. 190
    F. W. 190
    F. W., Col. 199
    George 21, 128
    George, Dr. 122, 136
    George Washington 30, 140, 144
    Henry F. 145
    John O. 83, 97
    Maria E., Mrs. 136
    Martha Ann, Mrs. 97
    Mary 139
    Mary Ouldfield 34
    Robert 5, 9, 21, 26, 136
    R. S. 190
    -- R. Starr, M. D. 194
    Susanna 8
    Thomas 111, 119
    William 21, 26
    William F. 120
    Wm(?) 117

Heron, Samuel Dr. 5, 9
Herrington, James 47
    Mary, Mrs. 47, 81
Herschel, Dr. 17
Hewet, Ann 53
Hewit, Mary A. 190
Hext, L. P. 196
    Mary Brisbane 196
Hickey, Priscilla 36
Hickman, Josephine 183
    L. Mrs. 183
    N. C. 183
    Sarah E.192
Hicks, Elijah Rev. 179
Hickson, Thomas W. 189
Hiddleston, E. Lucille, Mrs. 192
    Henry Mansfield 192
    H. M. 170, 192
    Laura 172
    Mary P. 199
    Rev. 19(2)
Hill, Rev. Mr. 63(2), 67
    William, Col. 42
Hillen, Dudley, Lt. 155
    Mary Mrs. 155, 156
Hilson, Thomas 75
Hinds, Hannah J. 185
    James 98
Hines, Isaac 165
    Mr. 164
    Robert 165
    Solomon 148
Hoddy, Lucretia Mrs. 54
    Sarah T. 54
Hodge, David 208
Hodges, John J. 40
    Robert 40
    Samuel, Dr. 119
Holes, Thomas 30
Holliday, Henry 199
Hollinshed, Rev. Dr. 11
Holmes, Ann Mrs. 54
    Elizabeth Mrs. 49
    John Jr. 19
    Joseph 49, 84
    M. 28
    Mary 154
    Maybery 19
    Rachael, Mrs. 118
    Sampson (coloured) 79
    Thomas H. 135
Holroyd, Mathew 40
    Susannah, Mrs. 40
Holt, Benj. Rev. 95
    Charles, Rev. 101
    Mrs. 82
    Rev. 18
Honeywell, Gilbert 83
Hook, Susannah 50
Hoole, Mary Mrs. 24
    William 24
Hopkins, Charles, Capt. 72, 73
    George 128
    Hary [Mary?] Mrs. 128
    Lucretia, Mrs. 72
    Mary Matilda 128
    Stephen A., Gen. 31
    T. T., Rev. 170
Hopkinson, Francis 1
Horne, James 23
Horry, Hugh 1(2)
Horton, J. W. 93
    Martha L. P. 93
    Mary E. C. 91
Howard, Elizabeth Sarah 85
    H. M., Mrs. 202
    Jacob J. 121
    John 37
    John, Rev. 85
    Mary 120
    Mary B. 40
    R. T. 134, 202

Howard (contd.)
    Rev. Mr. 122, 131, 133
    Robert Lee 202
    Robert T., Rev. 134, 150, 151, 154, 161(2), 165, 171, 175, 179, 182, 187(2), 192(2), 194(2), 197, 199, 204, 207
    William J. 132(2), 138, 152, 166
Howe, Cornelius 53
Howell, Elizabeth Anderson 118
    James 118
    John Rev. 54
    Rebekah 138
Howren, Ann J. 178
    David W. 38
    James 64
    James Rev. 38
    James C. 64
    James C., Capt. 52
    James C. Rev. 87
    John M. 142
    John S. 89
    Martha Mrs. 73, 89
    Mary, Mrs. 52
    Nimrod 91
    Robert 41, 73, 89
    Robert M., Capt. 161
    Sarah 73
Hubbard, F. M. Rev. 124
Hucks, David Porter Calhoun 198
    J. S. B. 105, 111
    James S. B. 132
    Joseph 198
    Martha W. 193
    Mary A., Mrs. 198
    Mrs. 105
    Sarah, Mrs. 163
Hudson, Sarah Q. 190
Huger, Ann 3
    Cleland K. 123
    Elizabeth Mrs. 9
    F. K., Col. 71
    Francis 3, 22
    Harriet Lucas, Mrs. 71
    Isaac, Gen. 9, 22
    Mary, Mrs. 3, 107
    Thomas P. 123
Huggins, Ann 18
    Charles, Col. 133, 162
    George S. B. 181
    Maria, Mrs. 176
    Nathan 133
    Nathan, Col. 176
    Rev. Mr. 131, 133, 135(2) 136
    Robert Capt. 176
    T., Rev. 128, 129, 134
    Theopilus, Rev. 134
Hughes, Cader 155
    Israel Rev. 170
    John 129, 203
    Martha L. 199
    Sarah A., Mrs. 199
Hughs, David 127
    Franklin 206
    Neill 57
Hume, Alexander Dr. 196
    John 117, 162
    Mary M. 196
    Mary M., Mrs. 162
Hunt, Col. 179
Hunter, Ann Eliza 175
    Benjamin Allston 152
    J. M. 152(2), 175
    James M. 123, 159
    James Madison 152
    John, Rev. 191
    Joseph Ross 203
    Joseph, Rev. 203
    Rev. Mr. 184
    S. W., Mrs. 175
    Sarah, Mrs. 152(2), 159

Hunter (contd.)
   Thomas W. 159
Hurlbut, Aaron 64
Hutchinson, Mary 20
   Mary Mrs. 21
   Thomas (V. M.) 5, 9, 17, 20(2),
      21
Hux, Francis 192
Hyams, Hannah D. 158
   Moses D. 158
Hyde, Louise Mrs. 166
   M. H. 166
Hymen, Elizabeth Mrs. 142(2),
      178
   L. 142
   Larry 177
   Mary Jane, Mrs. 177
   William 142, 178
   William Benjamin 177
   William (Jr.) 142, 178

Inglesby, Edward 193
Inglis, Charles, Rev. D. D. 32
Ingraham, James 49
I'on, Mary Ashby 16
Irvin, David 74
Irvine, Matthew 1
   Mathew Dr. 82
   William 156
Irving, George Dr. 46
Izard, Adela D. Lancey 104
   Georgiana 104
   Ralph 104
   R. S. 163

Jacks, Elizabeth 162
   John S. 48, 162, 188(2)
   John W. 138
   Lydia, Mrs. 188
   Sarah, Mrs. 138
Jackson, Andrew Gen. 140
Jacquith, Abraham 23
   Abraham (jr.) 23
   Adford 23
   Benjamin 23
   Ebenezer 23
   Elizabeth 23
   Hannah 23
   John 23
   Mary 23
   Sarah 23
   Sarah Mrs. 23
James, Francis Marion Dr. 76
   Rev. Mr. 52
   S. C., Rev. 199
   W. 25
   W. D. 76
   William H., Col. 75
Jaudon, Ann 28
   Isaac 60
   Martha Mrs. 60
   Paul 28, 102
Jayroe, Agnes S. 207
   Andrew B. 52, 138(2)
   Francis 161
   J. B. 162
   Mary H. 205
   M. G. 205
Jeanerett, see also Geanerett
   John W. 66, 134
Jefferson, Euphemia 28
   Joseph 28
   Thomas 53
Jenkins, Edward H. 64
   Elizabeth, Mrs. 125
   James Rev. 125, 150
   Rev. Dr. 24
   Rev. Mr. 10
Jervey, James 139
Jinkins, Thomas 113
Joachim, King of Naples 77
Johnson, Andrew 155
   Charles 119
   D. Mrs. 72

Johnson (contd.)
   Eleanor Augusta 75
   Frances P. 194
   Gilbert 51, 90
   Hannah 36
   J. B. 202
   J. L. 150
   Jacob 121
   John Dr. 67
   Joseph 1, 80
   Joseph Ben. 191, 198
   Mary 75, 160
   Mary, Mrs. 9, 10
   Mary A. Fearwell, Mrs. 152
   Mary Hannah 202
   Nicholas F. 144
   Prudence A. 173
   Sarah C. 186
   Rev. Dr. 69
   Thomas 68, 90
   William 160
   William B., Rev. 75
   William Samuel LL. D. 69
Johnston, Anna Maria 60
   Mary Farewell, Mrs. 162
Joiner, John W. 187
Jones, Ann 67
   Calvin Gen. 61
   Edward 46
   Elizabeth 46
   Jesse 156
   John 207
   Mary 46, 69
   Milly 169
   Joseph, C. Mrs. 146
   Henry, Mrs. 84
   Joseph 44
   Lizar, Mr. 15, 16, 59
   Molsey 59
   Sarah 45
   Thomas 155
Joy, W. F. 204
Judon, A. M. 188
Jumel, Eliza Mrs. 99
June, Peter 1(2)
   Sarah 1
   William 1

Kade, Samuel 187
Kahn, Lt. 42
Kalb, Tilman 71
Kales, Harriet Mrs. 139
Kedney, Edward 120
Keeffe, D. J. 158
   Daniel J. 162
Keele, John 92
Keiffe, D. J. 160
   Gabrella M. 160
   R. S., Mrs. 160
Keith, Alexander 1
   Benjamin 156
   Eliza L., Mrs. 102
   Elizabeth L., Mrs. 102
   J. 143
   John 1, 10, 13, 26
   John, Maj. 70, 78, 129, 175
   Magdalen E., Mrs. 175
   Major 61
   Mariah L., Mrs. 111, 113
   Mary L. 143
   Matthew Irvine, Col. 202
   Paul Trapier, Rev. 49, 78, 79,
      80, 84(2), 85, 86, 87,
      90, 91, 96, 105(2), 108(3),
      109,112
   Rev. Dr. 23
   Rev. Mr. 23
   Sarah B., Mrs. 129
   Thomas J. 102, 111, 113
Kennedy, Owen G. 107, 140(2)
   William M., Rev. 66, 67
Kerton, Rev. Mr. 49
Key, Philip Burton, Col. 28

Keyes, Isaac L. 52
   M., Mrs. 108
   Margaret Mrs. 52
Keys, Jane 68
   Pebody 85
   Stephen P. 85
Kidd, David 148
Kieth, Rev. Dr. 23
Kimberly, Geo. Capt. 80
Kimbrough, John, Maj. 15
Kind, Abraham 82
King, Amelia 151
   Benjamin 104, 122, 130, 186
   Eli 94
   E. M. Mrs. 136
   John 34
   John R. 156, 157, 167
   Lucy 28
   Martha C., Mrs. 200
   Mary E. 94
   Salomon 110, 136
   Samuel V. 130
   Samuel Vinson 92
   Sarah Mrs. 70
   Thomas Rev. 86
   T. S., Rev. 90
Kinloch, Cleland 58
   Francis 31, 49, 117
   _____ Miss 58
   _____ Francis, Mrs. 31
   Frederick 32
Kinloch's plantation 75
Kirkpatrick, Agnes 62
   Agnes, Mrs. 83
   Robert 7
Kirtion, Philip, Rev. 196
Kirton see also Kerton
   Ann 93
   Elizabeth 80
   Daniel 93
   Jane, Mrs. 93
   Philip, Rev. 71, 196
   S. 140
Kittera, John Wilkes 19
Knox, James 54
   John 54, 62, 139
   Mary, Mrs. 139
   Mary E. 179
   Rev. 18, 23, 34
   Rev. Mr. 9
Kokon, Dr. 117
Krauss, Michael 40

LaBruce, Catherine (Ward) 79
   Joseph P. 61, 79
LaFayette, Marquis 69
Lafrage, Isaac Sidney 195
Laing, Elizabeth 162
Laird, James Rev. 32
Laileland, Charles Sr. 57
Lallemand, Henry, Gen. 57
Lamar, John 127
Lamb, Rebecca 43
Lambert, John K. 196
Lance, Francis 69
   Maurice Harvey, Rev. 40, 50,
      68, 73, 184, 187
   Rev. Mr. 33, 58, 59, 61, 69,
      70
Lane, James 24
   M. H. Rev. 58
Laney, Noah Rev. 94
Langdon, John, Gov. 66
Langton, John 16
LaRebour, John B. 70
   John M., Capt. 197
   Martha Agnes 197
Larebour, John M. 70
Last, William 126
Lathrop, George T. 144
Laval, Mary E. 139
Law, Elizabeth 73
Lawrance, Isaiah 118

Lawrence, A. 118
Lawson, Esther 62
   Francis S. 66
   John 32, 66
Lear, Tobias Col. 39
Leard, Rev. Mr. 116, 119, 120, 123, 127
   Samuel Rev. 141
   Susan M., Mrs. 141
Lebour, Elizabeth Eveline 207
Ledbetter, Thomas Rev. 96
Ledington, Eliza A. 206
Lee, Jesse Rev. 39
   Thomas Jefferson 73
   William L. 174
Leeper, Robert 107, 113
Legen, Mary F. 206
Leger, James 93
   Moses S. 81
   William 44
Leggett, Ann 52
   David, Rev. 113, 163
   Elizabeth Ann 129
   Jesse, Rev. 52
Lehue, Charles Capt. 97
   Mary Anna 97
Leigh, John 12
   Mary Bonneau 12
   Thomas 5
Lenerieux, William G. 179
Leneriux, William G. 179, 181
Lenud, C., Mrs. 124
   Caleb C. 49, 124
Lenuel, Caleb C. 72 [Lenud?]
   Charlotte, Mrs. 72
Leonard, Joshua Capt. 41
Leopold of Belgium 36
LeRebour, Adaline Forrester 156
   Benjamin Franklin 172
   E. F. W., Mrs. 172, 192
   Elizabeth, Mrs. 156
   Elizabeth Eveline, Mrs. 207
   J. B. 172, 192
   J. M. 156
   John B. Capt.160
   John M. 207
LeResour[LeRebour?], John B., Capt. 160
Leseinger, P. 61
Lesesne, Ann, Mrs. 168
   Buleh 8
   Charles 24
   Edward Matthews 176
   H. E., Mrs. 176
   J. F. 176
   John F., Dr. 134, 136, 168
   Joseph 107, 168
   Peter 7
   Peter Jr. 8
Lessesne, Mary Mrs. 7
Lester, Bannester 88, 89, 134
   B. S. 198
   John C. 119
   Margaret 4, 6
   Margaret Mrs. 89
   Mary D., Mrs. 207
   Mary M. 134
   Robert 19, 181
   William 19, 70, 122, 145, 176
   William H. 175, 194
Lewis, Caroline E. J. 183
   James Rev. 109
   Josiah Rev. 87
   P. Charleston 194
   Theophelus 173
Lide, T. P. 149
   William Henry 24
Liggett, Archibald 145, 146
Lilley, Samuel Rev. 25, 26(2)
Linerieux, Louise E. 84
   Jane C., Mrs. 115, 116
   Joseph C. 115, 116
   Mary 44
   Mary S., Mrs. 72

Linerieux(contd.)
   William G. 50, 51, 56, 84, 125
Ling, Mary Elizabeth 160
   Mr. 160
Litchfield, W. 99
Little, Rev. Mr. 162
Littlefield, Abbey 165
   Emmer, Mrs. 165
   Jonathan Greenleaf 155, 165
Livingston, Thomas 95
Lloyd, Elizabeth Josephine Mrs. 134
Lock, Edward 19
Lockey, Cain 117
Lockhart, Rachel Mrs. 88
Lockwood, Jacob A. 182
   Nathan 48
Logan, Catharine 161(2)
Lohse, Frederick 202
   H. G. 202
London,John 32
Long, John 155
   L.G. 207
Lopez, A., Dr. 88
   Aaron 88, 176
Lord, Susan Anna Mrs. 141
Losee, Elizabeth 169
Lovell, Daniel 60
Lowndes, Mary P. 32
   Thomas 32
Lowry, Louisa 69
Ludlow, Peter 81
   P., Rev. 52(2), 81, 84(2)
   Rev. Mr. 78
   William Jackson 81
Lynch, Thomas 123
   William 10
   William (Jr.) 10
Lyon, Stephen 43

N. B. for Mc's see also M' and Mac
Mc---anan, Catharine Mrs. 186
   James Logan 186
   J. N. 186
McCauquedale, Rev. Mr. 161
McClary, Samuel G. 121
   Selina 208
McCleary, David 76
   Jane Louisa 76
McClellan, Archabald 131
   Archibald J. 144, 153
   Mary Mrs. 131
   Wm. H. 153
McClenaghan, John 133
   M., Mrs. 133
McClennan, Archibald 128
McClennon, A. J. 145
McCloud, Rev. Mr. 110
McColl, Solomon 70
McCollough, Celia Mrs. 71
   J. A. 131
   Mary Celia 71
   Sarah G. 150
   William 71, 72
McCollum, Jane Mrs. 169
   Mary Ann 151
   John 151,169
McConnell, J. H. 184
   J. Henry 198
   J. T. 196
   James Zuill 39
   Mary L., Mrs. 198
   Mary Martha 198
   Sarah E.139
   Thomas 32, 39, 92, 96, 183, 184
McCormick, W. B. 200
McCracken, Ann Mrs. 93
McCrea, Alexander J. 184
   R. W. Capt. 181
   S. T., Mrs. 147

McCrea (contd.)
   T. Armstrong 147
McCright, Emily 195
McCutchen, Wm. 140
McDaniel, Elizabeth 182
   John 138
   John B. 126(2), 135, 136, 174
   Priscilla, Mrs. 126(2)
   Randle 182
   Robert C. 67
   Sarah Rebekah, Mrs. 147
   Sarah Tabithey 147
   Solomon King 126
   William S. 147
McDonal, Edwin 206
McDonald, Adam 58
   Catharine Mrs. 58
   D., Rev. 181
   Edward 185
   Eleanor 30
   Elizabeth Mrs. 130
   Enos 121, 130(3)
   H. T. 206
   James 130
   Mary H., Mrs. 121
   Rebecca Ann 174
   Samuel N. 58
   W. S. 174, 203
   William S. 175
McDowell, Catharine 129
   Davidson 125, 129
   Davidson (Jr.) 129
   Davison 122, 126
   Thomas 125
McFaddin, James 185
McFarlane, Daniel 172
   Duncan 36, 38
   John 55
   Mary, Mrs. 36
McGehze, John 208
McGill, John 208
McGinney, Albert A. 187
   Charles 101
   Martha Mrs. 132
   Samuel 189, 200
McGrath, Michael 32
McGregory, Harriet Roach 100
McIntosh, William 39
McKay, D. L. 131, 144, 153(2)
   George 113
   Hugh 169
McKenzie, William 76(2)
McKnight, Jane 55
   John G. 55
McKune, Patrick 516
McLellan, Archibald 149
McMillan, John 165
McNamee, J. M. 198
McNeel, Samuel 76
McNight, Jane Mrs. 158
McNulty, Eliza M. 198
   William 163
McPherson, J. P., Rev. 151, 153, 173, 174
   M., Rev. 167
   Rev. Mr. 139, 149
McQueen, D., Rev 179
   Donald, Rev. 186
McQuorquodale, Rev. 165
McRae, James 70
McSwane, W. A., Rev. 119
McWhite, Alexander 130, 161
McWilliam, Daniel 95

M'Bride, James Archibald 10
M'Call-see also M'Coll, McColl
   Ann B. 94
   Hext 94
M'Cleary, David 47
   Jane Louisa 47
   William 49
M'Clinchy, Alexander 45, 71, 78

M'Clinchy (contd.)
  Elizabeth Mrs. 45, 71,78
M'Coll, J. W., Rev. 106, 107
M'Collough, Sam'l 73
  William 113
M'Conlag, Mary 32
M'Connell, E. M. O. 92
  Thomas 92
  Matt. 40
M'Cracken, Charlotte A. 154
  Robert 86
  Samuel 91
  Sarah 86
M'Crea, Alexander Jr. 2
  Alexander Sr. 2
  Charles Dr. 2
  Margaret, Mrs.2
M'Cullock, John 24(2)
M'Daniel, John B. 69
  Robert R. 69
M'Donald, Archibald 18
  Christiana Coachman 122
  Daniel P. 122
  James 33
  Margaret A., Mrs 122
  Sarah, Mrs. 33
M'Duel, Maria 30
M'Faddin, Agnes Eliza 67
  John 67
M'Farlan,Andrew 25
  Mary Mrs. 25
M'Gill, Elizabeth A. 52
  Samuel 52
  Susan 40
M'Ginney, Mary 38
  Sarah 114
M'Henry, James 34
M'Intosh, Alexander Capt. 40
  Louisa 39
  Mary 40
  William E. 39
M'Intyre, Archibald 68
  John, Rev. 68
M'Iver, John 18
  John K. Dr. 149
M'Kab, Alexander 44, 85(2)
  Alexander Mrs. 85
M'Kenzie, Wm. 46
M'Kinne, Col. 55
M'Knight, Alexander Capt. 53
  I. G. 52
M'Lean, Daniel 89
M'Lennan, Murdock 44
M'Lorinan, John 64
M'Millan, Rev. Mr. 87
M'Neall, Mary C. 36
M'Neill, A. F. Col. 36
  D. Dr. 36
  M. 36
M'Netle, Isabella K. 36
M'Night, Alex. Capt. 55
M'Pherson, Ann 20
  Isaac 17
  Sarah 17
M'Rae, Agnes 32
M'Ree, Jane 4
  John 4

MacDonald, John 36
Macfarlan, Allan 160
  John 160
Machin, Thomas Capt. 33
Macrae, John 49
Madison, Andrew Lewis, Capt. 35
  George W. Gov. 40
Magee, Arther, Capt. 170
  John, Capt. 197
Magell, William 22
Magill, Ann Mrs. 13
  Ann Rebecca 176
  Ella M. 183
  Henry Mattie 183
  James 13
  James S. 183

Magill(contd.)
  John 13
  John D., Dr. 72, 176
  Mary E. 106
  R. N., Maj. 202(2)
  William, Dr. 106, 139
  William Joseph 158
  W. J. 202
Magille, Agness Ann 139
Magnien, Bernald, Col. 69
Magrath, Patrick 101, 102
Mahoney, James Rev. 199
Malcomson, Rev. Dr. 6
  Samuel,Capt. 55
Malden, Wm. J. 84
Malet, Wyndham, Rev. 152
Malone,George 31
Mammy Lucy (woman of colour) 40
Mann, Rev. Mr. 155
Manning, Gov. 75
  Joseph, Dr. 132
Mansfield,Richard 23
Mariano, A. L. 194
  Ann Catharine Mrs. 84
  Anthony 85
  Anthony L. 204
  Anthony Lewis 73, 84
  E. Lucille 170
  Maria, Mrs. 194
Marlow, Elizabeth 96
  Elizabeth R. Mrs. 128
  Vardaman 128
Marra, Casper 121
Marrh, Robert Capt. 141
Marrott, Simon 36
Marsh, Emma Anna 108
  Frances Mrs. 108
  Frances S. Mrs. 168
  Mary Maria 1-9
  Mary Mrs. 90
  Nimrod Howren 168
  Robert 131(2)
  Robert,Capt. 87, 90
  Samuel 168
  Samuel N. 108, 131
  Susan A. 109
Marshall, Adam 1
  Ann 90
  Elizabeth A. 204
  Jane, Mrs. 6
  J. J. 204
  William 35
Martin, Isaac 149
  James 45
  John 1
  Mrs. 35
  Thomas 192
  W. D., Rev. 194
Marvin, A. 27, 86
  Ann Murray 89
  Azor S. 42
  A. & A. S.,House, of 42
Mason, A. T. Gen. 59
  John 3,22, 39
Mastin, Ann Mrs. 61
  Richard 61
Mathews, John 126
  Louisa Mrs. 126
Matthews, Ann Mrs. 95
  Charles P. 109, 138
  Francis S. 106
  John 48, 88, 95, 100, 138
  Joseph Raven 2
  Mary Esther 148
  Mary Louise, Mrs.88,100
  Rev. Mr. 3
  Samuel M. 131
  Samuel P., Capt. 105
  Susan Ann 100
  William 158
Matoon, Elizabeth 60
Maxwell, Anna Mrs. 139
  Emma Georgianna 139
  Wm. R. 60, 139

Mayer, Rev. Dr. 199
Mayrant, S. H. Mrs. 133
  Sarah Ann 133
  Wm. 133, 175
Mazeen, Ezekial 52
Mears, Wm. B.36
Megargee, Charles S. 121
Meier, Joseph 183
Mellishamp, T. W. Rev. 146
Mendenhall, John David B. 111
Merceir, John 44
  Margaret Mrs. 44
Mercer, Gen. 57
  John Col. 57
Merriman, John N. M. 161
Michael, Elias 149
Michau, Manasseh 90
  Mary C. 80
  Noah 31
  Paul 31
  Paul Jr. 3, 15
  Peter 166
  Peter Jr. 77
Mickel, Rev. Mr. 196
Middleton, Alvira 124
  Annie 192
  Henry 146
  Henry A. 58, 117
  John 124
  John Izard Jr. 95, 138
  L. G. S. 108, 192
  Ralph Izard 104
Miller, Abner 68
  Catherine 149
  Caroline V. 201
  E. H. 139
  Jane M., Mrs. 131
  John 60, 167
  John B. 139
  John C. 201, 203, 205
  John, Capt. 111
  John H. A. 141
  J. W. Rev. 197, 201, 206
  Margaret 131
  Mary F. K. 113
  Mary Mrs 135(2)
  Morrison & Co. 28
  Moses 59, 135
  M. S. 141
  Sarah Ann 167
  S. G., Mrs. 141
  Stephen D. 149
  Thomas 68
  W. C. 195, 205
  William C. Dr. 150
  William Capers Dr. 205(2)
  William Edwin 117
  William G. 191
Milliken, Elizabeth Mrs. 104
Millikin, Frances Ann Mrs. 201
  William 187, 188
  William Minnick 203
Mills, E. I. Rev. 81
  E. J. Rev. 47, 48(2), 76
  Elam J., Rev. 89
  Mary Jane 198
  Sarah, Mrs. 89
Minick, J. A. Rev. 156
Minnick, John A. Rev. 183, 194 205
Minis, Miss 62
  Mrs. 62
Minott, Wm. Butler 23
Mintzing, Jacob F. 123
Mishaw, J. M. 192
  Susan R. 192
Mitchell, A. R. 176
  Ann 69
  Ann Mrs. 7(2)
  Edward 7, 65
  George 46, 47(2), 150
  John 35, 37
  John, Capt. 69

Mitchell (contd.)
  Margaret 134
  N. 105
  Sarah, Mrs. 170
  Rev. Mr. 195, 197
  Thomas 7, 94, 105
  Thomas Rev. 199(2), 202
  Thomas R. 179
  Virginia Ann 69
  Wade 193
  William Nesbitt 49
Moid, Ezekiel P. 159
Mollendorff, Field Marshall 33
Momer, Count 33
Monroe, Pres. [James] 139
Montgomery, William 60
Moody, T. Rev. 86
  William 112, 149
Moore, Alfred 35
  Drucilla, Mrs. 135
  Francis A. Mrs. 203
  John Elias 7
  Nicholas R. col. 39
  Percy Keyes 138
  Rebecca C. 35
  Sarah 60
  William R. 201
Morgan, Abigail Mrs. 36
  N. Rev. 79
Morison, John 25
  Keneth 25
Morrall, John, Capt. 6
Morriss, Benj. 126, 174
  Elizabeth, Mrs.126, 127, 189
  Governor 41
  Hannah 134(2)
  Hannah, Mrs. 194
  Hansford Jennings 119, 194
  Harriet 174
  H. J. 134, 171
  Isaac 104
  James K. 176
  James M. 127
  Mary Green 189
  William 189
  W. P. 158
Morrison, Allan 32
  John 28
Morrow, Ann M. 94
  James 94
Mortimer, Elizabeth 176
  S. H. Col. 176
Moses, S. Gratz, M. D. 108
Motte, A. 1
  F. 1
Mounger, Edwin Maj. 35
Mouzon, Henry Capt. 194
  Leonard W. 132
  Peter 18
Moyd, Mary Jane Mrs. 157
  Joseph W. 186
  Robert 157
Moye, L. H. 175
Mulliken, Samuel 25
Mullins, Thomas Rev. 42
Muldrow, Robert Dr. 182
Munds, Rev. Mr. 6
Munnerlyn, Amelia Mrs. 141
  A. J. Mrs. 182
  Charles 61, 67, 89
  Charles Sr. 204
  C. J. 193
  Emma A. 187
  Francis W. 130, 141, 183
  Frances Waterman 145, 154
  Frances Waterman Jr. 154
  F. W. 109
  Gurdon Wright 183
  Hannah C. Mrs. 89
  Hannah Josephine 130
  J. K. 182
  James K. 141, 185, 187
  Julia Shaffer 176
  Marietta 106

Munnerlyn (contd)
  Mary Ann Elizabeth 89
  Mary Rebecca 145
  Rebecca W., Mrs. 176,179
  Robert 67
  Robert Gibson 182
  Samuel G.143
  Sarah 163
  Sarah A., Mrs. 130, 145, 154
  Sarah H. K. 183
  Thomas Rev 130
  William C. 106, 152, 176
Munro, Archibald 145
  E. A. Mrs. 184
  Elizabeth THurston Mrs.145
  George C. 145
  W. J. 184
  William J. 184
Munroe, Annie Throop 189
  Goerge C. 189
Murray, Achille 77
Murdock, D. A., Rev. 206
  James 29
  John 134
  Samuel 17
  William 17
Murphy, James 119
Murray, Ann D., Mrs. 27, 129(2)
  James 13
  William, Major 27, 129
Murrell, Ann 135
  Charles 135
  John R., Capt. 53
Murrow, James 122
Myers, Abraham 171
  Abram 77
  A. C. 133
  George W. 173(2)
  Jacob 15, 24, 53, 77
  Levi Mrs. 62
  Lewis, Rev. 72
  Moses 4,15
  Solomon Etting, Dr. 133(2)

Nagot, Francis Charles, Rev. 33
Napier, Rev. Mr. 151
Nappier, R. Rev. 185
Neals, R. H. Rev. 90
Neilson, Eliza 28
Nelson, George 151
  Jane M. 151
Nesbit, Mary Mrs. 202
  Robert 96, 125, 202
  Robert, Dr. 159
  Robert Major 159(3), 165
Nesmith, Benjamin Moses 138
  John F. 156, 184
  Joseph 151
  Nathan 96
  Samuel 11
  Samuel (Jr.) 11
Nettles, Augustus H. 141
  Caleb H. 103, 141, 149
  John Joseph 149
  Mary E. Mrs. 141, 149
Newcomb, Mary Mrs. 50
  Richard E. 50
Newton, James 38
  James Dr. 206
  John T. Capt. 104
  Sarah Ann 187
  William W. 187
Niblet, Solomon 30
Nicholson, Peter 6
Nipper, Jacob Rev. 133
Nones, Leon A. 162
Norman, James H. 199
  Joseph 127
  Joshua L. 157
  Mary Mrs. 132
Norris, John B. 114
  Mary W. 114
North, John G. 81, 91

Norris (contd.)
  William 19
Norton, Allen 44
  James Rev. 75
  Josephine Haseltine 123
Norum, John 3
Nottage, Nathaniel 60

Ogle, Chaloner Adm. 41
Ogburn, H. R. Rev. 186
"Old Deborah" (black woman) 35
Oliver, Agnes 176
  Ann R. Mrs. 200, 201
  David P. 66
  E. Rev. 87
  Elijah 108
  Ezekiel 170
  Jesse 108
  John 44
  Martha 87
  Robert 37
  Samuel L. 99, 176, 200(2), 201
  Solomon 149
  Thomas, Lt. Gov. 32
  Wm. C. 202
  W. S. 199
Ones, Temperance, Mrs. 61
Orr, John 8
Oultcalt, William 28
Owens, Ezekiel 183
  James 185

Paccarotti, Rackeline 62
Paesiello 39
Paine, William Col. 83
Paisley, Ann 130
  Ann Mrs. 75
  Robert. 18
  Robert A. 57
  Thomas Jefferson 75 Wm. 18
Palmer, A. 63
  Allston Mrs. 106
  Asa 48, 102(2)
  B. M., Rev. 152
  David 51, 71, 106(2), 124, 125, 126
  Eleanor Caroline 63
  Elizabeth, Mrs. 51, 71
  Elizabeth Ann 71
  Jesse 52, 54, 113(2), 199
  Jesse, Mrs. 54
  Laommi 95
  Loame 51
  Rachael, Mrs. 48
  Rebekah Ann Mrs. 113
  William, Rev. 48, 125
  William G. 95(2)
  William Manley 199
Park, Susan S. 40
  Thomas 13
Parker, George 31
  Iorona 205
  Isaac 120
  James 91
  Mary J. Mrs. 205
  Rev. Mr. 167, 198
  Simon 98
  W. A. 205
  William A. 165
Partridge, Harriet B. 36
Pasiley, William 18
Patch, Eleanor 107
  Mary, Mrs. 107
  N., Capt. 156
  Nathaniel 107
  Theodore 156
Petterson,Catharine C. Mrs. 74
  Daniel 37
  David 6
  John 64
  John C. 74
  William Rev. 147

Pauls, William F. 99
Pawley, Anthony 34
  Elizabeth Mrs. 67
  George 27, 59
  George, Col. 10
  George H. 133
  John W. 67, 68, 81
  Mary A. 50
  Perceval 27
  Sarah 109
  Sarah, Mrs. 10
  Susan, Mrs. 68
Paxton, Henry W. 23
  Samuel 2
Peacock, Sally Mrs. 54
Peadon, A. G. Rev. 131(2)
Pearce, Jas. 47
Pearson, John 69
  Tabitha, Mrs. 36
Peart, Francis 29
Pedreaux, Samuel 62
Peedreau, Samuel 28(2)
Peavy, Delia Maria 42
  Samuel 42
  Walter K. 58
Percival, J. Chapman 158
  Mary E. 158
Perdriau, Dupuy Miss 25
  John 124
Perrett, Elizabeth G. Mrs. 200
  John 132
Perritt, Sarah 132
Perry, Major 101
  Mary M. Mrs. 127
  Oliver Hazard 66
Pestch, Julius D. 144
Peterson, Andrew 92
Petigru, Adeline 96
  James 81
  Jane G. 81
Petigrue, Capt. 142
Pettigrew, Alexander 8
Peyong, Rosena 99
Phillips, Anna Maria 203
  David 91
  J. A., Mrs. 189
  James 48, 85, 86
  James Henry 189
  L., Mrs. 203
  L. R. 189
  Mary Eliza Mrs. 85, 86
  Rev. Mr. 78, 114
  R. J. A. 203
  Wm. L. 91, 182
Pickett, John W. 137(2)
  J. W. Rev. 148
Pierfon, Phineas 23
Pierce, Ann 184
Pierson, P. Rev. 153
Pigott, Elizabeth 123
  Jane 137
  Joseph 82
  Rachel 82
  Sophia 122
Pinckney, Thomas, Gen. 71
Pinnell, Reubin Rev. 69
Pinner, John 191
Pipkin, Ann 202
  Catherine E. 143
  Daniel 95
  D. J. 202
  Levi 143
  Levin 141
Pitcock, Lewis 17
  Mary Mrs. 17
Poellnitz, C. H. B. 15
  Frederick Charles Hans Bruno 18
Polk, President 164
Pollock, Robert 52
Pomp, Rev. Mr. 82
Pope, Richard B. 138
  Richard Jr. 127
  Samuel, Capt. 170
Porcher, Richard S. 177

Porter, A. Toomer 179
  Caroline Lawrence 160
  Eliza, Mrs. 11
  Elizabeth, Mrs. 7
  Esther Ann, Mrs. 84
  Frances, Mrs. 139
  Francis 139
  Francis Asbury 172
  H.C., Mrs. 185
  H. H. Rev., 193
  Hannah E. 134
  J. C. 186
  John 7, 84, 119
  John C. 130, 157, 172
  John C., Mrs. 172
  John, Col. 134
  John Jr., Col. 70, 84, 119
  J. R. 123
  W. 160
  W., Mrs. 160
  William 80
Porter and Waterman, House of 138
Poss, Patty 19
Post, D., Rev. 160
Postell, Anna Maria 53
  James C. 72
  James C. Rev. 53, 91, 92, 96, 97
  James Coachman, Rev. 185
  John, Col. 42, 60
  John G., Rev. 117
  Major 185
Poston, Hannah Mrs. 42
Potter, Amey Ann 66
  Eugenia E. 119
  George 92
  James 159, 163, 165, 196, 197, 199, 200, 201
  John 79, 90
  John Obadiah 163
  Mary McMillan, Mrs. 163, 165
  Obadiah 92, 119
  Pleg A. 164, 165
  Rev. 109
  S. E. E. 199
  Wm. Henry 79
Potts, Anthony 10, 34, 71
  Hannah 134
  Hannah, Mrs. 81
  Thomas 3
Powell, Jacob S. P. Rev. 88, 91
  James 149
  John Dr. 55
Powers, Gideon 132
Poyas, Susan M. 60
Pratt, Leonard B. Capt. 156
Prescott, Benjamin 62
Pressley, William James 81
Prezbyrowski, Susan D., Mrs. 182
Price, Elizabeth A. 144
  Isham 144
  Joseph B. 199
Prichard, C. H. Rev. 185
Primer, Elizabeth 28
Prince, Ann, Mrs. 57
  Lawrence 58
Pringle, J. J. 17
  Robert 198
  W. B. 195
  William B., Major 135, 136
Prior, David 25, 58(2), 65
  Elizabeth, Mrs. 106
  Emma Margaret 189
  Margaret 58
  Martha, Mrs. 142, 189
  M. J. 197
  Thomasine Maria 142
  William R. T., Dr. 142, 189
Pris---, Miss 69
Pritchard, C. H., Rev. 188, 189, 190(2), 198(2)
  Rev. Mr. 192, 193
Provaux, Mary 67(2)
  Mary Mrs. 40

Przyborowskie, Mary Frances 177
  Susannah Mrs. 177
Puche, Harriet, Mrs. 162
  Joseph M. 90
Punch, Eliza Wilds 59
  John 59
Purcell, Rev. Dr. 20
Purifoy, Archibald, Rev. 73, 78, 83, 87
  Mrs. 83
  Rev. Mr. 80, 83
Push-Ma-Ta-Ha (Choctaw) 45
Pyatt, John 12
  John F. 128, 204
  Jos., Capt. 64
  Mary 12
  Mrs. 153
Pzuill, Jane 84

Queer, Susan 82
Quimby, Jos. 147
  Susan 147

Rafferty, Jas. 63
  Phillip 65
Ragan, John Col. 34
Ralston, John 108, 123
Rambert, Esther 19
  Gabriel 25
  Raphael 171
  Sarah E. Mrs. 171
Ramsay, Elenor 5
  Ephraim Judge 22
Rantin, William 76
Raphill, Charlotte Elizabeth 55
  John J. 55, 95
  Sarah Mrs. 55
Ravenell, James 201
Raymond, H. K. Rev. 195
Read, Anna Maria 188
  Col. 130
  Frances H. 205
  Jas. B. 13
  J. H. Jr. 119
  J. H. Sr. 154
  John H. 139, 145
  John Harleston Jr. 188
  Rev. Mr. 81
  Wm., Dr. 139
  Wm. Bond 145
Reaves, Edward C. 137
  George 137(2)
  R. H. 119
  Solomon 137
Rebb, Lewis 135
Rembert, Raphael 79, 171
  Stephen J. 172
Remley, William 78
Remoussin, Daniel 22
Renolds, Edward 186
  Mrs. 186
Theuark, Jane M. 169
Rhodes, John 1
  Martin 166
  William 17
Rhodus, Nancy, Mrs. 25
  Solomon 25
Rhuark, William J. 162
Rice, Daniel 52
  David 48
  Esther Ann 151
  Esther Ann, Mrs. 90
  Joel 86
  John Benjamin 90
  John P. 45, 55, 86
  Mary Ann 55
  Rachel, Mrs. 55
  Rhoda 73
  Shadrach 84
  Thomas G. 78, 90
  William D. 171
Rich, Mary Mrs. 48
  N. Gustavus 109

Richardson, Elizabeth 99
  Francis Deliesseline 116
  G. W. 198
  J. 99
  J. J. 202, 204
  John David 176
  Judge 133
  Robert 158
  Sarah Mrs. 178(2)
  V. 178(2)
  William 128
  William E., Major 133
  William F. 126
  William Walter 178
Richmond, Jos. J. 207
Richwood, Sarah 170
Rickard, Jos. 53, 77
Riggins, ___ Mrs. 43
Riley, John Sr. 23
  Jonathan J. 138
Ritchie, James W. Rev. 198
Robbit, John B. 36
Roberts, August Anna Rosabelle 198
  E. D. Mrs. 198
  Elizabeth 12(2)
  I. M. Rev. 22
  James 185
  John 5
  M. 129
  O. M. 129
  O. M., Dr. 112
  Wilhelmina 129
  William 135
Robertson, A. 154, 165
  Alex. 126, 180
  Betsey 29
  J. H. Rev. 79
Robertson & Thurston,House of 118
Robinson, George W. 197, 198
  G. W. 197
  Sarah L. 199
Rodgers, Ann 105
  Mary Jane Susan Elizabeth Clementine 134
  W. Rev. 134
Rogers, Edward T. 199
  Elizabeth, Mrs. 121
  E. P. Rev. 117
  Francis 142
  John Sr. 154
  Jonah C. 87
  Joseph 72
  Joseph D. 142
  Joseph R. 47, 98
  Margeret R. Mrs. 81
  Martha 80
  Mary Green 72
  Sarah P. 117
  S. M., Mrs. 142
  Thomas G., Rev. 134
  William Windham Trapier 121(2)
Rolando, Francis G. 67(2)
Rolling, Rev. Mr. 143
Rollins, J. L., Rev. 202
Rolster, Isaac, Gen. 42
Roney, Andrew 120
Roque, Stephen 51
Roquie, Hannah, Mrs. 97
  Stephen 97
Rosa, Charles D. 206
  D. D. 206
  H. T., Mrs. 206
Rose, James 95
Rosenfeldt, J. Rev. 162
Ross, A. W.,Rev. 52
Rothmahler, E. B. 48, 105(2), 133, 144, 216
  Elizabeth 50
  Erasmus 3, 15
  Esther, Mrs. 10
  Henrietta, Mrs. 48, 74
  Job 10,11

Rothmahler(contd.)
  Mary Wragg 84
Rotureau, Peter 194
  Rosalie Alice 194
Rouquie, Gabriel 77
  Hannah, Mrs. 77
  Stephen 77
  Stephen W. 173
Rouse, Robert N. 184
Rowe, Stephen 194
  Thomas Nelson 182
Rowell, Ann Maria 194
  D. C. 72
  Eliza 71
  Olive 194
  Rachael 45
  Robert W. 194
  R. W. 199
  Valentine 71
  William B.80, 92
Rowland, John 42
  Martha, Mrs. 42
  Mary 29
Rozier, Celia 109
Rumney, Benj. 140
Runtlett, Ebenezer 39
Rush, Frederick, Rev. 184
Russ, Harriet 163
  William, Dr. 163
Russell, Jeremiah 85
  Jeremiah, Rev. 59, 69
Rutledge, F. 164
  John 31
  John, Gen. 65
Ryan,D. T., Capt. 189
  Elizabeth H., Mrs. 189
Rynolds, Richard 40

Salomon, Benjamin 67, 82
  Jos. 96
  Levi 82
  Levy, 67, 82
  Martin 168
Salomon & Joseph 16
Salomons, Israel Mrs. 195
  Jos. 96
Salters, Sarah Mrs. 101
  William, Col. 101
Sampson, Joseph 169
  Samuel, Capt. 146
Sanderlin, ___ Mrs. 72
Sanders, Sophronia 141
  William 130
Sands, Robert A. 77
Santee, ___ Baily Miss 101
  John 101
Sarvis, C. B. 120, 120, 138, 149, 162, 170, 182, 184, 186
  Cornelia Mary 184
  Cornelius 187
  D. B. 132
  Elizabeth L. 117
  M. H., Mrs. 184
  Margaret L., Mrs. 202
Saultus, Henry 15
Saunders, Eleanor 38
Sawyer, J. H. 205
  Ruth 60
Sawyers, Lewis Sr. 42
Say, Will Worthy 132
Schroder, M. Rev. 46
Scott, Jannet E. 173
  John T. 52, 173
  Joseph 2
  Samuel 36
  Sandy 51
  Thomas 36
  Thomas G. 35
Screven, Benjamin 7
  Jane M. 85
  John 9, 85
  John, Capt. 41
  John M. 86

Scriven, B. Rev. 37
  John M. 155, 161
Seale, David R. Rev. 156
Segeant, Eliza Ann 24
Seitz, D. A. 120
Sellers,Julia Ann, Mrs. 107
  Samuel S. 107
  Solomon 148
Service, Louisa Pawley 86
  John 86
Session, Sarah Mrs. 170, 171
Sessions, B. E. 182
  David Davies 147
  I. M. Dr. 148
  Isaac C. 178
  Jane F., Mrs. 147
  Jane T. Mrs. 148
  J. E. Mrs. 168
  Julia Anna 37
  Margaret H. 149
  Mary Anna 168
  Ramsom 37, 99
  Samuel T. 141
  Solomon 86
  Thomas R. 112, 147, 171
  T. J. 199
  T. R. 168
  William 70, 124
  William W. 125
Sessons, S. C. 118
Seward, Amos 150
Sewell, Parker D. 168
Shackelford-Shackleford
  Ann B. 12
  Anthony Bonneau 73, 86
  Clara Elizabeth Mrs. 56, 80
  Clara Withers 56
  Elizabeth S. Mrs. 63
  Elizabeth F. W. 160
  Esther 73
  Francis 11, 25, 73, 80
  Francis R. 56, 80(2), 115
  Hannah 61
  Hanna Martha 63
  J. 3
  J. W. 44, 47
  James 1
  Jane P. 115
  John 2, 8(2), 21, 49, 8, 44, 73
  John W. 63, 164, 33, 71
  John & Son, House of 33
  Mary, Mrs. 73, 147
  Mary Ann 49
  R. W. 130
  Richard Jr. 67
  Richard Sr. 67, 68
  Richard W. 143, 144
  S. W. 130
  Sarah Mrs. 143, 144
  Sarah Jane 164
  Susan E. F.113
  W. W. 182
  William Archibald 130
  William C. 160, 82
  William Cartwright 143, 145
Shaffer, Rebecca W. 152
Shaler, Asa D. 110
Shand, Rev. Mr. 149
Shaw, Annette Mrs. 112
  Archibald J. 192, 197
  Archibald Jas. 197
  Benjamin F. 78, 104
  Eliza M'Clinchy, Mrs. 104
  Hasford Walker 157
  Magdalen W. 112
  Mary E. Mrs. 197
  Nannette Mrs. 110, 157
  Thomas L. 110, 112, 157, 169, 192
  Thomas Lynch 84
  William Peter 110
Shell, James E. Dr. 34

Shelter, Catharine Mrs. 40
Shepherd, Margaret 23
Sheridan, Richard B. 38
Sherrell, Mary W., Mrs. 83
  William 76, 83, 87, 89
Shields, Ann 31
Shinner, Elizabeth Mrs. 22
  George 22
Short, Sarah Mrs. 60
Shuford, J. L., Rev. 183, 184, 193
  L. Rev. 190
Shum, Ann Mrs. 5
  Conrad 5
  Susan E. 113
  William B. 100
Shumake, Hugh 132
  Mary 132
Shute, Michael 60
Siau, A. A. W. 170
  A. L. 136
  Alexander 173
  Anna R. 171
  Augustua 88
  Augustus L. 178, 181
  Caroline M., Mrs. 173
  F. L. 120
  Francis 74
  Francis James Sparkman 120
  Hannah M., Mrs. 190
  Hannah Maria, Mrs. 183
  Louis 167
  Mary A., Mrs. 167
  Sarah, Mrs. 120
  Sarah Ann, Mrs. 136
  Sarah Eliza 183(2)
Siddons, Jane S. Mrs. 156
  John 137
Simmons, Ann Mrs. 106
  Anne Elizabeth 111
  Eliza A. Mrs. 111
  Joseph M., Dr. 106, 111, 162
  Jane 106
  Martha 41
Simons, Eleanor Mrs. 53
  Keating Lewis, Col. 64
  James, Major 75
  John A. 53
  S., Capt. 17
  Sarah Tucker, Mrs. 75
  Shadrack 18
Sims, A. D. 135
  Margaret A. P., Mrs. 135
Sinclair, Cecilia, Mrs. 148
  Elijah Rev. 145, 148
Sinclaire, Jas. Rev. 72
Singellton, Dorothy Mrs. 14
  John, Major 13, 14
Singleton, Benjamin 148
  Bushrod M. 147, 149
  Catherine Mrs. 141
  Elizabeth Mrs. 44
  Emily H. 129
  Isaac 104, 156 (2), 157
  James Rev. 86, 116, 138
  John 25, 44, 161
  Magdalen M. 109
  Mary Elizabeth 111
  Richard 25, 74, 109, 141
  Richard Jr. 141
  Samuel 159
  Samuel G. 148, 149
  Sarah 162
  Sarah Angelica 109
  T. D. Dr. 101
  Thos. D. 101
  Thomas D. Col. 109
Singletary, Agnes Mrs. 158
  Isaac J. 80
  Samuel J. 147
Sith, Henry 41
Skinner, Ann 189
  Christiana, Mrs. 150(2)
  Elizabeth, Mrs. 21

Skinner (contd.)
  George 17, 21
  James W. 178, 182
  Margaret 81
  Mary E. 142
  Sa--- Mrs. 178
  William 142
  William, Rev. 87, 150
Skipper, Haveliah Irenah Adaline 189
  Joel B. 189
Skrine, Mary Susan Malvina 57
  Thomas 40
  W. H. 108
Slate, A. 147, 161
  Asahel 146
Slewson, Rufus 30
Small, Christopher 31
  Francis 31, 86, 97
  Margaret Mrs. 86
  John S. 53
  Mary Mrs. 72(2), 104
  S. A. 159
  Samuel 200
  Sarah Elizabeth 188
  Sophrona Mrs. 188
  Susannah Mrs. 103
  William 72, 97, 103, 141
  William F. 188
Smalley, H. Rev. 75
Smart, Jennet Mrs. 32
Smith, Adam 59
  A. J. 197
  Andrew 3, 6
  Ann Mrs. 82
  Archar B., Rev. 90
  Archer, Rev. 150
  Benjamin 52
  Bishop 16
  C. F. 105
  D. H. 161, 191, 195
  David H. 182
  Edward D., M. D., 65
  Ellen, Mrs. 182
  Elizabeth 59
  Elizabeth Mrs. 84, 99
  Francis Ann 188
  George 58
  George Savage 191
  George W. 157
  Gorman, Capt. 29
  G. S. 191
  Henry 100
  Henry, Capt. 89
  Henry C. 113(2)
  Henry I. 82
  James 81, 82, 85, 99, 114, 116, 171
  James, Capt. 28
  James M. 197
  Jane Ellen 168
  Jane Field 23
  Jesse 124
  John 6, 33, 42, 57, 99, 139
  John, Capt. 14
  John (Jr.) 6
  Laura L., Mrs. 64
  Margaret Mrs. 3
  Marilda Mrs. 122
  Martha 146
  Martha Elizabeth 89
  Martha L., Mrs. 124
  Mary 76
  Mary E. 83
  Mary Rutledge 146
  Peling 65
  Ralph 6
  Rebekah Mrs. 114, 116
  Samuel 26, 57, 59, 85, 187
  Samuel Stanhope, D. D., 64
  Samuel W. 100
  Sarah, Mrs. 38
  Sarah Ann 206
  Sarah Edith 183, 188

Smith (contd.)
  Sarah Laura 187
  Sarah N. 52
  Savage 1, 17, 22, 58, 83, 84
  S. S. 58
  Susan Antenia 172
  Thomas A. 117
  Thomas J. 102, 105
  Thomas J., Capt. 79
  W. C. 52
  Whiteford, Rev. 156, 178
  William, Lt. 20
  W. T. 172
  W. T., Mrs. 172
Smyth, Thos. Rev. D. D. 160
Snow, James 124, 125
  Mary Port Mrs. 34
  Susan 124
  William 11
Snowden, Samuel J., Capt. 132
Snipes, Mary Mrs. 22
  Sarah 5
  William 5
Snyder, Simon Gov. 69
Solomon, ___ Dr. 64
  Moses 55(2)
  Sampson 55
Solomons, Eleanor Mrs. 73
  Eleanor J. Mrs. 93
  Henry 73
  Isabella 88
  Israel 73, 92, 93
  Lizzie 197
  M. J. 199
  Molsey Mrs. 88
  Moses 77
  Sampson 59, 77, 88, 100
Sowerby, Samuel 60
Spann, Henry 50
Sparkman, Elizabeth Mrs. 145
  James 59
  James R., M. D. 139
  J. R. 135, 190
  William E. 109, 145
  William F. 145
Sparks, Alex. 137, 164
  David G. 137
  Wm., Dr. 164
  Wm. Alex., Dr. 124
Speery, D. A. 205
  David Anson 205
  S. E., Mrs. 205
Speight, Hobhead 54
Speirin, Rev. 9
Spencer, Charlotte 46
Sperry, Bacot Allston 205
  D. A. 205(2)
  David A., Capt. 134, 168
  David A., Mrs. 168
  David Anson 205
  Frances M. 176
  Mary Martha 168
  S. E. Mrs. 205(2)
Spicer, John E. 39
Spierin, Rev. Mr. 5, 8, 9, 12(2)
  Rev. G. H. 9, 10, 12
  George H. 112, 12(2), 18
  Margaret Mrs. 10
Spiller, Henry 42
  Mrs. 42
Spindler, Harriet Miss 66
Spooner, Eliza I. 82
Springs, Lemuel S. 201
Squires, Emily 187
Stacy, James Rev. 170(2), 171(3), 173, 174, 175, 179
Staggers, William 50
Stalvey, C. E. 198
  Elizabeth E. 187
Standley, Mary Mrs. 200
Stanford, Richard, Col. 33
Stanley, Sarah 200
Stanners, Walter 203

Stanton, Ed. 46
Stark, Robert 93
Steadman, W. B. 166
Stebbins, Elijah Rev. 60
Steel, David, Capt. 106
  Georgiana L. 153
Steele, James 55
  John 54
  John Gen. 28
  John J. 174
  John J., M. D. 167
  Sarah Mrs. 55
  Sarah Ann 144
  Sarah Ann, Mrs. 174, 197
  Sarah E. 145
  William 53
Stell, John 142
Sterrett, James Capt. 74
Stewart, Donald 189
Stevens, Andrew 149
Stevenson, Ann R. 99
Stewart, Alexander 5
  James 8
  Tabitha Ann 67
Stiles, Rebecca Mrs. 42
Stillman, William S. 155
Stocking, D. L. 187
Stokes, G. W., Rev. 198
Stone, Austire 127
  James Rev. 169
  James H., Rev. 181, 183, 184,
    185(4), 186(4), 187
  J. H. Rev. 159, 182
  Leonard 176
  Rev. Mr. 127, 160
Storrow, Samuel Appleton 62
Story, Joseph 141
Strong, Caleb Gov. 69
Strong, John, Gen. 36
  Nathan, Rev. D. D. 42
Strother, Charles 24
  Lucy, Mrs. 24
  Obedience 41
  William 24
Stubbs, Wiley W., Dr. 137
Sturges, Ann J., Mrs. 148
  Henry A. C. 71
  James T. 165
  John W. 156, 166
  William Sr. 148
Suggs, Elizabeth Massey 117
  Jonas 117
Sullard, Eunice Mrs. 35
Sullivan, Elizabeth Ann 137
  Esther Ann 109
  Mary H., Mrs. 112, 137, 154
  R. M. 158
  R. W. 112
  Richard W. 137, 154, 167
  Robert Atkinson 112
Summerfield, John, Rev. 73
Sumter, Thomas, Gen. 96
Sunkan, Chancellor 123
  Mary A. 123
Sutton, Robert Capt. 50
Swaley, Joseph Maj. 33
Swanson, Ann Mrs. 96
  David 15
Swanston, Ann 43
  D. 25
  David 91
  Mrs. 90
  Margaret 91
Sweet, Anthony 163(2)
  William 163(2)
Swinton, DeKalb 175
  John 94
  John W. 163

Tait, Elizabeth S. 33
  Hannah Mrs. 7, 100
  Henry 7
  James 7

Talley, George R., Rev. 149,
    153, 154, 160
  Nicholas Rev. 66
Tallmadge, Matthias B. 69
Tallman, John 147(2)
Tally, G. K. Rev. 146
Tampler, A. G., Mrs. 183
  Charles Walter 183
  J. J. 183
Tamplet, C. D. 196
  Hannah E., Mrs. 191
  Henry 14
  John 14
  John J. 160
  Paul 169,191
  Willie N. 191
Tarbell, Joseph Capt. 31
Tarbox, David 27
  Esther Jane Mrs. 170
  Francis Green, Capt. 175, 191
  George W. 138, 157
  John 64
  John P. 189
  John W. 190
  Lucy S. Mrs. 174
  Maria Margaret 91
  Paul 30
  Richard David 138
  Sarah, Mrs. 138
  Sarah F. 189
  Sarah P., Mrs. 46
  Thomas 38
  William 76
  William, Capt. 46
Tart, Enos 20
  John 20
Taylor, Alexander Capt. 106
  Ann 113
  Ann, Mrs. 9
  Archibald 12, 20, 22
  Benjamin 101
  Caroline 190
  Christopher 11
  David J. 113, 119, 126
  E., Mrs. 130
  E. A. 128
  Edward R. 45, 130
  Elizabeth Mrs. 172
  E. O. 117
  George Keith 30
  George S. 88, 109, 111
  Isaac 131
  John 160
  John Sr. 25(2), 86
  John M. 26
  John N. 11, 36
  Joseph 100
  Joseph G. 100
  Mary, Mrs. 20
  Mary Frances 143
  Robert Andrew, Col. 55
  Samuel 25
  Samuel A. 142
  Sarah Elizabeth 88
  S. P., Rev. 128
  S. Procter, Rev. 134, 137,
    141(2), 142(2),
    143(2), 171, 174
Stafford 142
Thomas, Col. 101
  Thomas H., Rev. 76
  William J. 124
  William W. 155
Thomas, Alexander 73
  Alexander, Rev. 193
  David 3
  Edward 33, 96, 121, 122, 136,
    181
  Edward G. 133
  Edward G., Dr. 112, 120
  Edward Gibbes 26, 171
  Emily, Mrs. 120, 121, 122
  Emma 112

Thomas (contd.)
  Eugenia Withers 171
  J. B. 201
  John S. 200
  Rebecca, Mrs. 199
  Samuel 26, 178
  Sarah 36
  Sarah, Mrs. 193
  T. Burrington 85
  Thomas B. 87
  Washington 122
  William F., Capt. 193
  William L., Capt. 144
Thompson, Andrew P. 129, 147
  Ann, Mrs. 5
  Anna 160
  B. A. 171
  Benjamin S. 170
  C. P. 195, 207
  Edward 96
  Elias 161
  Elizabeth 83, 98
  Elizabeth, Mrs. 96, 147
  Hugh S. 160
  James W. Rev. 32
  John 83
  John, Capt. 5
  John P. 143
  Margaret E. W. 173
  Mary A., Mrs. 207
  Samuel D. 197
  Sarah, Mrs. 52
  Trisvan Ferrel 147
  W. 3
  William 26, 52
  William S. 96, 98
  William T. 44, 111
Thorp, Otho 88
  Susan L. 185
Threadcraft, Bethel 24
Thurston, Elisha 42
  Jane, Mrs. 118, 119
  Robert 118
  Samuel I. 118
  Samuel Isaac 9, 41, 57
Thyne, Wm. Capt. 139
Tidyman, Dr. 31
Tields, Elias 97
Tilley, Ann E. Mrs. 205
  George Henry 205
  Thomas S. 205
Tillman, B. Allston 162
  Paul W. 102
  Sarah A. D. Mrs. 162
Tilton, William 184
Timmons, Elizabeth 181
  John M. 118
  Rev. Mr. 173
  Simeon, Capt. 67
  William Col. 118(2)
Timothy, Ann Mrs. 2
Titus (an African) 57
Tobey, Henry 157, 198
  Herriot Francis Foster 157
  Limir, Capt. 191
  Nancy, Mrs. 191
  N. D., Mrs. 157
Todd, Ann 86
  Mary 31
Toler, Benj. H. 94
  Matt. M. 94
Tommy, Polly 34
Tompkins, Daniel D. 74
Tomson, Jane Mrs. 14
  William 14(2)
Toomer, Anthony 12, 26, 70, 79
  Esther Ann 70
  Mary Warham 79
Trapier, Benjain Foissin 107
  B. F. 70, 98, 109
  P. 12
  Paul 70, 71, 105
  W. H. 109

Trapier (contd.)
　W. W. 42, 71, 77, 78, 85, 98(2)
Tripp, Peleg 61
Tucker, Benjamin W. 105
　Daniel 203
　Daniel Mrs. 203
　Edmund H., Dr. 30
　Elizabeth Blyth 98
　Harriet, Mrs. 99
　Herior, Mrs. 105
　John H. 98, 99
　Joseph R. 201
　Martha A., 194
　Mary, Mrs. 18, 24
　Matilda 105
　Sarah Heriot Mrs. 201
Turbeville, Frances 173
　William 173
Turnage, George Augustus 193
　S. B. 193
　Virginia Mrs. 193
Turner, John Sidney, Sir 83
　Miss 83
　Rev. 36
Turnbull, Robert J. 94
Turrentine, M. C., Rev. 188
Tuttle, Moses 78, 134
Twentyman, Sarah Mrs. 41
Twiggs, John, Maj. Gen. 33
Tyler, Benjamin 203
　Jane Mrs. 203
　John, Pres. 134

Uptigrove, Ann H., Mrs. 177
　Georgianna Virginia 177
　William C., Capt. 177

Vail, Capt. 20
　Nathaniel 20(2)
Vailey, Elizabeth 208
Valk, Harriet 20
Valli, Dr. 41
VanBuren, Abraham Maj. 109
Vance, W. R. 186
Vandamme, Gen. 57
Vanderhorst, Arthur 113
　R. Gen. 94
　Susan E. T. 140
Van Rensselar, K. Gen. 38
Vanzilver, Robert Dr. 16(2)
Vaughan, Jas. Col. 34
Vaux, Catherine Ann Mrs. 166
　Percival E. 114, 116, 138
　R. W. Dr. 164(2), 166
　W. P. 114, 116, 138
Vener, John 23
Vereen, C. W., Capt. 85
　Ebenezer 11
　Eliza P., Mrs. 24
　Jane, Mrs. 11
　Jeremiah 155
　John E. 80
　Mary 131
　Mary Ann, Mrs. 80
　Mary E. 72
　William Sr. 14
Verner, Benjamin T. 175
　Esterh Ann 78
　John 78
　Mary E. 198
　S. A. Mrs. 200
Vernon, Francis A. 135
　Henry 111, 122, 135
　Mary, Mrs. 111, 122
　M.H. 201
Vernor, Benjamin T. 176
Villepontoux, Benjamin M. 182
　Charlotte 3
　Paul 3, 147
Vines, Sarah Mrs. 202
Vinson, James 7, 11, 13
　Samuel 13
Vreeland, Peter 63

Wadsworth, Jeremiah 44
Wakefield, E. G. 83
　Sarah Cannon 135, 136
　William 83
　William, Mrs. 83
Waldo, Catharine Mrs. 116
　Hannah Mrs. 57
　John 55, 57, 72, 116
　Samuel, Rev. 57
Walker, A. W. Rev. 151
　Archibald Rev. 30
　Ary Ann 188
　Benjamin 69, 87, 91, 129
　Charles A. Rev. 160
　Elenor S. 18
　H. A. C. Rev. 183
　Hannah Mrs. 57
　Hasford 172(2)
　James 27, 30, 84, 99, 188
　Jane Mrs. 128
　Julius H. 36
　Le Grand C. 87
　Le Grand G. 72, 79(3), 84
　Le Grand G. (infant) 72
　L. G. 60, 78, 84
　Lydia, E. Mrs. 99
　Mary Mrs. 30, 64(2), 69, 188
　Mary A.E. Mrs. 172
　Mary E. Mrs. 87, 192
　Mary Elizabeth, Mrs. 96
　Nanette 84
　Peter 72, 77, 87, 100
　Richard 57
　Robert D. 155
　Sarah 53
　William 6
　William Archibald 100
Wall, Margaret 110
　Washington B. 197
　William 137(2)
Wallace, Ann E., Mrs. 189
　John Dallam 189
　R. 205
　Ruben 189
　R. W. 205
　Stephen Samuel 89
Walsh, F. R. Rev. 117
　Rev. Mr. 153
　T. R. Rev. 116
Walter, Hellin 33
Ward, Catharine 61, 205
　Elizabeth 5
　Elizabeth, Mrs. 87, 203
　Georgeanna 190
　J. J. 190
　J. J., Col. 205
　John D., Capt. 146
　Joshua 87, 176, 203
　Joshua, Col. 137
　Joshua Jr. 203
　Joshua, Major 56
　Joshua John 56, 146, 165, 181(2)
　Joshua John, Col. 98
　Major 61(2)
　Mary 196
　M. C. 99
　William N. 156
　William W. 174
Warden, Sarah A., Mrs. 174
Ware, Harriette Julia Lavinia 160
　James M'Call, Major 160
　Rev. Mr. 102
Warham, Elizabeth 139
　Mary Mrs. 96
Waring, Emma 59
　Sarah M. 107
　Thomas 26
Warren, Gen. 50
Wasdin, Harriet M. Mrs. 204
　Harriet Mariah 206
　Sarah A. 175
　Thomas W. 175, 188
　T. W. 204, 206

Washington, George Gen. 11
Wates, John, Major 3
Water, E. 121
Waterman, Anna 70
　Anna Mrs. 70
　Ann Eliza 107
　Asaph 145
　Benjamin 113
　David 39
　E. 44, 47, 58, 71, 78, 81,
　　100, 107, 118, 119, 130,
　　136, 137, 146, 151, 154,
　　162, 166(2)
　E. G. Mrs. 113
　Eleazer 70, 107(2),113
　Eliza Grant, Mrs. 107(2), 151
　Ellen 107
　Hannah Catharine 100
　John 107
　Mary E. Mrs. 205
　Sarah 123
　Thomas Hardwick 138
　W. C. 175
　William 39
　William Capers 142
Waterman & McGinney 187
Waters, Esther 132
　John 132
　Kiddy 132
　Moses 132
　William 132
Waties, John, Maj. 3
Watson, Amanda F., Mrs. 195
　John Alexander, Capt. 33
　John Rt. Rev. D. D. 38
　Julia A. 195
　Mr. 39
Watts, Absalom D. 186(2)
　A. D. 174
　Chris. 86, 186
　George 86
　Joannah 80
　John D 94, 166, 174, 201
　M. B. 154
　Rebecca 156
　Rebecca, Mrs. 147
　Sarah S., Mrs. 166
　Stephen 192
　William 106
　William Christopher 201
　William D. 147, 157
Wayne, Augustus Britton 62
　Daniel Gabriel 160
　Eleanor 127
　Elizabeth, Mrs. 65, 131
　Eliza Charlotte 65
　E. M., Mrs. 148
　Esther Trezerant 65
　F. A. 148
　Francis A. 65(2)
　Gabriel W. 62
　Gabriel W., Rev. 85, 89, 92
　Jacob 28, 100, 127, 131, 154
　Mary 65
　Mary, Mrs. 62
　Marinda R., Mrs. 92
　Miranda, Mrs. 98
　Mowren 28
　Nannette 100
　Rev. Mr. 23, 37
　William 24
　William, Rev. 154
Weaver, Elizabeth 3
Webster, Noah 128
Weems, Mason L. Rev. 74
Weightman, Richard 63
Wells, Avey 159
　Catharine Mrs. 130
Wesberey, Mr. 134
West, George 32
Westberry, Ann, Mrs. 127
　Benjamin 81, 92
　Benjamin F. 115

Westberry (contd.)
  Martha A. 92
Westbury, A. N. 175
  Andrew 75
  Ann, Mrs. 75
  John G. 164
  Martha Susanah Mrs. 195
  Thomas 75
  William J. 195, 205
Western, Francis 98
Weston, Charles 196
  Charles, Capt. 5
  Francis 121
  Francis Marion 190(2), 196
  Mary, Mrs. 196
  Mr. 148
  P. C. J. 190
  Plowden C. J. 148
  Plowden 152
Wethers, John 8
Weymour, John Wesly, Capt. 188
Wheeler, E. B. 132
  Elizabeth Mrs. 127
  William 127
Whitby, Rev. Mr. 104
  W. 108
White, A. Jr. 186
  Anthony 14, 49
  Anthony, Sr., Capt. 11, 14(2)
  C. F. 184
  Charles C., Capt. 156
  Deborah 19
  Elizabeth B. 202
  Isabella J. 1b5
  J. 143
  James 97
  James H. 46, 73, 75, 123
  J. B. 27
  J. B., prof. 197
  John 43, 155, 160, 188(2), 189
  John C. 155
  John, Capt. 68
  Joseph 6, 14
  Leonard 27
  Leonard, Capt. 66, 182
  Mary Ann, Mrs. 11
  Mary, Mrs. 75
  Mary Eliza, Mrs. 46
  M. Euphemia 160
  R. G. 189
  Samuel Anthony 29
  Susan Elizabeth 46
  Thomas B. 195
  Thomas W. 20, 29
  W. C. 189
  William 27, 68
Whitehurst, J. 33
  James 33
Whitman, J. R. 136
  Samuel 136
Whitney, Eli 71
Whitworth, Isaac D. 137
Wiggins, Baker 87
  C. E. Rev. 202
  Frances 142
  J. W. 142
  Jesse 50
  Jesse Mrs. 50
  Jesse W. 206
Wightman, J. W. Rev. 194
Wilcox, Aaron 84
  Enoch, Capt. 85
  John 3
  Moses 84
Wilkins, S. B. 94
Wilkinson, Anna 105
  Jemima 63
  Virginia 124
  W., Dr. 105
  Willis, Dr. 124
Wilks, Eliza P. 14
  Lemuel 15
Will, Charlotte J. 57

Willard, George D. 201
  Mary Mrs. 164
  Walter 204
  William 205
William [of Würtemberg] 36
Williams, A. E. Mrs. 142, 166
  A. W. 150
  Allard Belin 157
  Ann Elizabeth 142
  Ann Rebecca 138
  Bedford, Dr. 1
  B. M. 193
  C. Dr. 157, 189
  Catherine Mrs. 200
  Charles, Dr. 139
  Daniel G. 56
  David R., Col. 149
  David R., Gen. 114
  Elizabeth, Mrs. 114, 178
  Elveny E., Mrs. 201
  G. Rev. 91, 92
  G. W. 178
  H. C. 155
  Henry 138
  Henry F. 201, 205
  Jane, Mrs. 150
  John A.,Gov. 163
  Malsheek S. 115
  Malachi S. 178
  Mary E. Mrs. 157, 189
  Mary Jane 189
  Moreland 117
  Paul A., Rev. 113(2), 114
  Rev. Mr. 120, 131
  Richard G. 105
  Sarah 21
  Thirza 91
  William 4, 114
  William Jr. 4
  William A. 135, 136, 137, 142
  William Thomas 189
Williamson, Benjamin 19, 20
  Sarah, Mrs. 20
Willis, Byrd C., Maj. 77
Willington, A. S. 110
  Harriet Elizabeth 110
Willson, Elizabeth M. Mrs. 88(2)
  William M. 88(2)
Willton, Susana 72
Wilmot, Mary Mrs. 145
  Minerva 178
  Samuel 166, 178
  Samuel Jr. 145
  Samuel Sr. 145
  Thomas Townsend 145
Wilson, _____ 35
  Abigail G. 80
  Alfred 119, 131, 132
  Benjamin H. 137
  Benjamin T. 179
  Charles Rev. 99
  D. D., Col. 182
  David E. 181
  David J. 193
  Dr. 14
  Elizabeth, Mrs. 157
  Hannah 49, 169
  Helen Augusta 157
  Jante T. Mrs. 173
  J. L. 32
  John 18, 174
  John G. 82, 150, 151
  John L. 46, 76
  Louisa 119
  M., Mrs. 14
  Margaret E. Mrs. 204
  Margaret J., Mrs. 140
  Martha 27
  Robert 121
  Robert (Jr.) 121
  Robert F. 140
  Robert G. 206
  Samuel 93

Wilson (contd.)
  Sarah M. 171
  Thomas 26, 83, 157, 167(2)
    171
  William 173(3)
  William M. 56, 80
Windham, Jesse 57
Wingate, William 140
Winn, Thomas Lawson Rev. 80(3),
  81(2), 82, 83
Wish, C. A. G. 158
Witherbe, Harriet Mrs. 60
Withers, Caroline Mrs. 79
  Elizabeth Mrs. 44, 80
  Francis 23, 26, 27, 33, 44,
    70(2), 139, 153, 154
  John 11, 27, 58, 59, 67, 76
  John Jr. 68, 70
  John Francis Robert 68
  Richard 143
  Robert 46, 70
  Robert F. 79
  Sarah Ann 9
  Sarah P., Mrs. 154
Witherspoon, J. D. Col. 124
  James, Capt. 2
  Jane 124
  John M. 36
  R. Sidney 67
  S. W., Dr. 182
  Sarah E., Mrs. 182
  William 12
Wolfe, George 83
Wood, Alfred H. Capt. 46
  Anson 45
  Eliza 94
  Lucy 94
  William, Rev. 94(4)
Woodberry, Evander M. 186
  Joseph A. W. 173
  Richard 49, 116, 198
  W. Gen. 116
Woodbury, Collin, Rev. 45
  Collins, Rev. 45
  Martha 95
Wooddy, John 122
Wooden, Elizabeth 39
Woodville, Rev. Mr. 62
Woodward, John Rev. 109(3),
  139, 149
  Rev. Mr. 118, 119, 171, 192
Woody, John 104, 122
Woolf, Robert 166(2)
Worthington, Eliza 38
Wragg, A. L. 101
  Augustus L. 100
  Eleanor Mrs. 90, 91
  John 84
  John Dr. 87(2), 105
  Joseph 18(2)
  Joseph, Lt. 73
  Samuel 16
Wright, Elizabeth Mrs. 22
  Griffith 58
  Martha 123
  Mrs. 6
  Sarah A. 109
Wylie, Alexander Dr. 35

Yancey, Benjamin C. 57
Yeadon, Eliza Ann 23
Young, Hannah 117
  Henry G. 101
  Michael 117
  Mary Mrs. 23
  Mary E. 169
  Thomas 12, 23
  William, 110
  Rear Admiral 110

Zimmerman, C. Dr. 118
Zuill, James 3
  James Capt. 66

Zuill (contd.)
  [Pzuill], Jane 84
  John Jr. 66

———— John p. 169

www.ingramcontent.com/pod-product-compliance
Lightning Source LLC
Chambersburg PA
CBHW050631300426
44112CB00012B/1755